To Leslye, Mike, Keane & Ryan —
Thanks for your support over the years and wish you all the best!

Bryan Michnowski
2011

BAY AREA LEGENDS

Bay Area Legends

BAY AREA LEGENDS

THE GREATEST ATHLETES

FROM THE

SAN FRANCISCO BAY AREA

Brian Michnowski

BAY AREA LEGENDS

Copyright © 2011 by Brian Michnowski

ALL RIGHTS RESERVED

No part of the contents of this book may be reproduced or transmitted in any form or by any means without the written permission of the author other than brief excerpts for review purposes.

Printed by CreateSpace, a DBA of On-Demand Publishing, LLC

www.createspace.com

Library of Congress Cataloging-in-Publication Data

Michnowski, Brian; 2011

Bay Area Legends/Brian Michnowski 1964 -

p. cm.

ISBN-13: 978-1466314689
ISBN-10: 1466314680

1. Sports. 2. San Francisco 3. Baseball players – United States – Biography. 4. Football players – United States – Biography. 5. Basketball players – United States – Biography.

Cover Design by Brian Michnowski

Printed and bound in the United States of America

DEDICATION

For Gloria and Adam, my very own Bay Area heroes.

TABLE OF CONTENTS

5	Joe DiMaggio	1
5	Jason Kidd	25
6	Bill Russell	47
8	Willie Stargell	65
8	Joe Morgan	75
11	Lefty Gomez	93
11	Norm Van Brocklin	101
12	Tom Brady	111
14	Dan Fouts	123
16	Jim Plunkett	133
20	Frank Robinson	147
20	Gary Payton	157
24	Rickey Henderson	171
24	Jeff Gordon	189
25	Barry Bonds	207
31	Helen Wills	223
32	O.J. Simpson	235
33	Ollie Matson	255
34	Max Baer	269
34	Dave Stewart	281
43	Dennis Eckersley	295
51	Randy Johnson	303
52	CC Sabathia	319
73	Johnny Miller	341
88	Lynn Swann	351

Bay Area Legends

PREFACE

Many of the greatest champions in professional sports history grew up in the San Francisco Bay Area. The "Bay Area," defined here as a 70-mile by 70-mile square that begins at Pt. Reyes Seashore and connects east to Pittsburg, down to southern San Jose and west back to the Pacific Ocean, has watched its native sons and daughters win enough hardware to fill Oracle Arena. The athletes profiled in this book alone have collectively captured 48 NFL, MLB, and NBA championship trophies, 23 Hall of Fame plaques, and an astounding 30 season MVP awards. Add to the mix seven Cy Young awards, four Rookie of the Year trophies, a pair of Heismans, some U.S. Opens, Wimbledons, and nearly 200 All-Star selections, and it is clear that the cities by the bay produce the kids that come to play.

Bay Area athletes have also enjoyed immense success in Olympic competition, bringing home hundreds of medals in a wide variety of sports. Such spectacular accomplishments clearly deserve their own publication. The professional athletes described on these pages were selected based on their Hall of Fame playing careers, with emphasis on playoff productivity. Those who played for Bay Area professional or college teams were given slightly more consideration, even if not elected to their sport's Hall of Fame. Conversely, some of the region's Hall of Famers from the early 20th century were not selected due to their relatively unknown careers.

They came from the peninsula, the city, the east shore, the tri-valley and the south bay. From inner cities and from quiet suburbs, from both public schools and private. Together, these 25 legendary players regularly made national headlines on and off the field. Most of them positive, but some of them not. Like any other group of people, they were and are human, with strengths and weaknesses, with confidence and with insecurities. But it was their amazing athletic gifts that enabled them to outshine thousands of competitors as they grew from high school prospects to the pros. These young homegrown stars took their talents across America to places like Los Angeles and Dallas, New York and Boston. They took on the fiercest competition and came home winners. These are the Bay Area's very own hometown heroes — their stories, their lives, their legacies.

5

JOE DIMAGGIO

An American sports icon, Joe DiMaggio is remembered as one of baseball's most graceful and natural stars. Experts say his 56-game hitting streak in 1941 is one of the most unattainable sports records of all time. Known as "Joltin' Joe," his powerful bat, superb defense and baserunning helped bring nine World Series titles in 13 years to New York and immeasurable pride to Italian-American communities on both coasts. His fabled marriage to Marilyn Monroe and the quirks of his reclusive senior years further added to the DiMaggio mystique.

Giuseppe DiMaggio was an Italian fisherman off the coast of Palermo on Isola delle Femmine, as were generations of DiMaggios before him. Giuseppe married Rosalia Mercurio shortly before the turn of the century. Rosalia's father, also a fisherman, ventured to America to explore new opportunities. He wrote to them that Giuseppe could earn a better living in America, specifically near San Francisco Bay. In 1898, Giuseppe left expectant Rosalia in Italy to explore this new fishing haven in California.

Giuseppe set sail for America, eventually settling near Rosalia's father in Pittsburg, California. Mr. Mercurio's advice panned out as Giuseppe netted barrels of fish in and around San Pablo Bay. After four years, he earned enough money to send for Rosalie and daughter Nellie, who was born after he had left for the United States.

Joseph Paul DiMaggio, officially named Giuseppe Paolo DiMaggio, Jr., was born on November 25, 1914 in a small wooden house on Berrellesa Street near the Martinez waterfront. Joe was the eighth of nine children born to Giuseppe and Rosalia. According to his birth certificate, he was delivered by a midwife named Mrs. J. Pico. Joe was named after his father: "Giuseppe" was Joseph in Italian and "Paolo" was from Saint Paul, a favorite saint of his parents.

In 1915, the DiMaggios moved to the North Beach section of San Francisco when Joe was a year old and just before youngest brother Dominic was born. The neighborhood was an Italian enclave during an influx of European immigrants. The DiMaggios – all 11 of them -- lived in an apartment at 2047 Taylor Street near the Wharf. The children were Nellie, Mamie, Tom, Marie, Mike, Frances, Vince, Joe, and Dominic. Italian was the predominant language of the household. Rosalia spoke very little English and Giuseppe or "Zio Pepe" as he was known, spoke some English, but with a heavy accent.

In the 1920s, Giuseppe was disappointed that only two of his five sons joined him in his San Francisco fishing business. Giuseppe had his boat docked at Fisherman's Wharf and had their mother's name *Rosalie D* painted across the stern. He wanted his five sons to become fishermen, just like generations of DiMaggio men. Two of Joe's three older brothers followed suit, but Joe was not of the same mind… or stomach. When Joe was old enough, he joined Tom and Michael on the bay but hated cleaning his father's boat, and the smell of dead fish made him feel seasick. As a result, his father called him "good for nothing" and "lazy." Giuseppe did not have an understanding of how his interest in baseball could ever help him earn a living and make something of himself.

"Baseball didn't have much appeal to me as a kid, but it was better than helping Pop when he was fishing, or helping clean the boat," said DiMaggio. "I was always giving him excuses, principally that I had a weak stomach, but he insisted I was 'lagnuso' (lazy) and to tell you the truth, I don't know which he thought was the greater disgrace to the family, that a DiMaggio should be lazy or that a DiMaggio should have a weak stomach."

Giuseppe may have successfully convinced the older brothers to join him on the bay, but Joe and brothers Vince and Dominic couldn't stay away from baseball. The San Francisco sandlots and the North Beach Playground were the places they learned the game. DiMaggio boys were always the first chosen in pickup games. Joe went to the Catholic elementary school, taking advantage of the Salesian Boys Club programs offered, and was soon recognized as a great athlete.

"I believe I was 10 years old when first played baseball," said DiMaggio. "As I got older we'd buy individual shoe spikes and have a cobbler attach them to ordinary shoes."

Giuseppe was not very thrilled with his sons' attraction to baseball over good honest work. Yet all three of these DiMaggio boys actually went on to play center field in Major League Baseball. Vince played professionally for 11 seasons, while his brother Dominic played 10 years in the majors. Joe had the edge when it came to natural talent, however. He was the star of the sandlots, and at 12 years old he was already slugging home runs out of the park.

DiMaggio enrolled at Galileo High School, but was a truant. He also tried to attend classes at Continuation High School. Schoolwork was always difficult for Joe, and he dropped out in 1930 at age 16, leaving fishing and education behind in order to earn a little money playing baseball, as did Vince. He spent much of his time practicing baseball at the dairy-wagon parking lot, an open space in the city where milk drivers parked their horses and wagons, near the Wharf. They used dried horse manure, covered with a sack, for bases. Despite his protests, he occasionally helped his father on the boat and he took numerous odd jobs including selling newspapers – *The Call* – on Sansome and Sutter. His neighbors and friends of his parents were always looking for work -- trying to make a buck, pay the bills and survive the Depression era.

As a teenager, DiMaggio played for the Rossi Olive Oil sandlot team, a semi-pro team sponsored by a local olive-oil distributor. "There was an olive oil dealer in our neighborhood, named Rossi, who took our club out of the Boys Club League and outfitted us with better uniforms and equipment than we ever had before," said DiMaggio. "He was a real fan and took great pride in having a ball club of his own. We won the championship in a playoff, in which I hit two home runs. As a reward for this, I received two gold baseballs and two orders for merchandise worth about $8 each. It was my first financial return from baseball."

DiMaggio was playing for Rossi when 20-year-old Vince was playing for the San Francisco Seals in the Pacific Coast League and talked his manager Lefty O'Doul into allowing 17-year-old Joe to fill in at shortstop. The PCL was a highly respected independent league that produced scores of big leaguers. Joe made his professional debut on October 1, 1932 and smashed a triple his first PCL at-bat for the Seals. He played the final three games at shortstop, hitting .222. He was signed by Spike Hennessey and Charley Graham to a Seals contract of $225 a month for the 1933 season.

The lanky 6-foot-2 DiMaggio became a Bay Area celebrity for the Seals in 1933, hitting safely in 61 consecutive games. From May 27 to July 25, he set the all-time professional baseball record, while hitting .340 and driving in 169 runs. "Baseball didn't really get into my blood until I knocked off that hitting streak," DiMaggio said. "Getting a daily hit became more important to me than eating, drinking or sleeping. Overnight I became a personality." Joe's streak was finally stopped by pitcher Ed Walsh Jr., who threw a no-hitter for the cross-bay Oakland Oaks.

"When I broke the record, my whole family was on hand and my mother hugged me for joy. She didn't understand much about baseball but she realized I was being honored and that was enough for her."

O'Doul was an outstanding ex-major league player that took DiMaggio under his wing. Lefty would often take Joe to lunch and told him stories of his playing days. O'Doul was a popular hero to San Francisco locals – everyone knew him, waved to him, and asked him for autographs. He was always well-dressed and was polite, especially to women and children. DiMaggio, who said very little as a youth, had instant admiration for Lefty's magnetism and classy reputation.

In 1934, DiMaggio's baseball career almost ended at 19 years old. One of the most graceful athletes in sports tripped over his own two feet. Arriving at his sister's house for dinner, he tore the ligaments in his left knee while stepping out of a taxi. The Seals were hoping to sell Joe's contract for $100,000, but were now unable to get anything close to that. Even the Chicago Cubs would not allow him a tryout.

The New York Yankees were the only ones still interested. Yankee scout Bill Essick was convinced that DiMaggio would fully recover from his knee injury and pestered the club to give him another look. After Joe passed a physical on his knee, Seals owner Charlie Graham sold the rights to DiMaggio to the Yankees for $25,000 and five players on November 21, 1934. The Seals would keep him for the 1935 season. Joe had consulted Lefty about his first big league contract and he even called Hall of Famer Ty Cobb to act as DiMaggio's negotiator.

"I had the good luck to spend my minor league career in the PCL in which the travel and accommodations were first class, and with my hometown team, the San Francisco Seals at that," said DiMaggio of his three minor-league seasons. "I could live with my parents, and eat meals at the family table. Most players were on the road for the entire seven months of the season."

In 1935, DiMaggio totaled a ridiculous 270 hits, hit for an average of .398, belted 34 home runs, and drove in 154 runs. He led the Seals to the PCL title in 1935 and was named the league's Most Valuable Player.

Invited to Yankee spring training in 1936, rookie DiMaggio was billed as the next Babe Ruth. But Joe was very different than the former Yankee slugger. The legendary Ruth was gregarious, boisterous, crude, and lovable. Fellow Hall of Famer Lou Gehrig, still with the Yankees, was known as a steady, quiet captain. DiMaggio simply went about his business without bragging, joking, or shouting. His newcomer attitude was "play well and look classy," although inside his will to win burned hotter than anyone.

After Ruth left, Gehrig could not carry the team and the Depression slowed ticket sales considerably. The Yankees needed a spark to return to their wining ways and sellout crowds. When spring training rolled around, DiMaggio was to take his first trip east of the Rockies. Teammates Tony Lazzari and Frankie Crosetti, also Northern California natives, were instructed to pick up DiMaggio from North Beach and drive him to Florida in Lazzari's new Ford. When it was Joe's turn to take the wheel, he surprised his new teammates by saying "I don't drive." DiMaggio, who had been taken care of by his mother and sisters, was now in the care of the Yankees, which included hotel living and an accommodating staff.

Meanwhile, thousands moved into the Bay Area seeking work on the Golden Gate Bridge construction project that lasted from 1933 to 1937 and lived in shanty towns awaiting work for $55 per week. Giuseppe still didn't really understand Joe. He sent his son a letter during that first spring training with the Yankees, in 1936. "Come home, Joe," the letter said. "The fish are running. Give up this game of baseball. It is for loafers."

But Joe was already a young master of the baseball diamond. DiMaggio was the full package. He could hit for average, hit for power, fly around the bases and track down every fly ball in centerfield. He glided to balls with the grace of a gazelle. Not only could he field like no one else, he had an excellent throwing arm. He played a level above the others at his position in his era. At the plate, his wide legged stance produced a quick but smooth swing with a long, photogenic follow-through. And he was driven by the promise of baseball success, not a life of fishing or school work. "A ball player has to be kept hungry to become a big leaguer," he said. "That's why no boy from a rich family has ever made the big leagues."

With an $8,500 contract in hand, DiMaggio made his major league debut on May 3, 1936, batting ahead of Yankee legend Gehrig and wearing uniform number 9. In his first at-bat he hit into a fielder's choice, wound up on second and later scored. Joe was the lead in New York newspapers – all two dozen of them -- for every game as the Yankees started 6-1. New York had not been to the World Series since 1932, but DiMaggio burst on to the major league landscape and helped the Yankees begin another dynasty. After winning only one World Series in the previous seven years, they celebrated four straight world championships in Joe's first four years.

The 21-year-old rookie outfielder became an instant star. He was named to the American League All-Star team as a rookie, and all 13 years of his career. While Gehrig's production slowed due to a burned leg, DiMaggio contributed mightily by hitting .323 with 29 homers, scored 132 runs and drove in 125 runs. He also led AL outfielders with 22 assists.

In the 1936 World Series, DiMaggio batted .346 with three doubles as the Yankees defeated the Giants in six games. Gehrig homered twice as New York averaged seven runs per game. Despite DiMaggio's spectacular debut, the MLB Rookie of the Year award did exist for another few years. "I'm just a ballplayer with one ambition, and that is to give all I've got to help my ball club win," he said. "I've never played any other way."

After the Yankees clinched the 1936 title in October, Joe collected his $6,431 World Series bonus and hopped a train back to the west coast to digest his awesome rookie season. When he arrived home, San Francisco held a ticker tape parade for DiMaggio and he was presented a key to the city by the Honorable Angelo Rossi. He had gone from having lunch with Lefty to a celebrity himself in less than two years time.

Meanwhile, fishing brothers Tom and Mike had saved enough to buy their own boat and Tom even became vice-president of the California Fishing Association. Vince and Dom were progressing towards major league dreams of their own. Yankee owner Colonel Jacob Ruppert mailed DiMaggio a contract for the 1937 season and Joe promptly sent it back – unsigned. He wanted double what he got paid as a rookie, $17,000. They settled at $15,000, making DiMaggio the highest paid second-year player in baseball.

San Francisco wasn't the only city that experienced immigration as Italians were now the largest ethnic group among New York's massive population of five million. They helped build New York's churches, schools, and city infrastructure when they could find work. A superstar like DiMaggio made Italian immigrants feel less alienated and was an inspiration for them to excel. He was a powerful figure at a time when discrimination was still part of life for Italians. With his smashing success on the baseball field and in the classy way he carried himself, he became a shining example of hope for them. For Italian-Americans of a certain generation, meeting Joe DiMaggio meant more than meeting the Pope or the President. If you asked any New York Italian who's the greatest they might have said "Dante, Verdi, and DiMaggio."

"DiMaggio had a connection to Italian-American families in the 1940's, as Italy was at war with the nation of their choice and their home, America," said former New York mayor Rudy Giuliani. "Americans of Italian origin during that difficult time had Joe DiMaggio to look up to, to give them pride and to reaffirm through his actions and theirs, their allegiance to this great nation, America, which after all, gave him the opportunity for such great success and could give them the same thing."

An arm injury sidelined DiMaggio to start the 1937 season, but he bounced back quickly by blasting 35 home runs by August 8. He finished with 46 homers to lead the American League, a .346 batting average, scored 151 runs and drove in an amazing 167 runs. The Yankees again beat the Giants in the Series, this time in five games as Joe homered in the clincher.

No one in big league history had ever broken in the way he did those first two years. DiMaggio is still tied for 3rd place all-time with Mark McGwire in home runs in his first two years in the majors with 77. Only four players in history totaled 200 hits in each of their first two years, at the time Joe did it. During his first two seasons, DiMaggio was pictured on the cover of *Time*, hit two home runs in an inning, set a record with four extra-base hits in a game, hit three homers in a game, hit for the cycle, and had three triples in a game.

Unlike the Ruth era, the Yankees no longer had a power advantage over teams and determined that playing harder and smarter was the only way to win consistently. DiMaggio fit the mold perfectly with total focus and maximum effort. If the team lost, Joe was as bitter as anyone. If they lost on his account, he was miserable. Cobb continued to advise DiMaggio in his early years on topics such as lighter bats and how to stay healthy.

After the 1937 season, Joe bought his family a new house just a mile away at 2150 Beach Street in the Marina, and helped move them out of the overcrowded apartment. The new house had a living room, garage, washing machine, electric icebox, and a backyard. The DiMaggios left all their old furniture, drapes, and rugs – and their early struggles -- on Taylor Street.

The family also opened Joe DiMaggio's Grotto restaurant on the Wharf. Giuseppe took great pride in preparing meals for baseball players who visited the Grotto during the off season. He often cooked them *cioppino*, a dish invented by Italian fisherman in San Francisco. He gave them towels for bibs and urged them to dig in with their hands.

In 1938, DiMaggio hit .324, and the Yankees won their third consecutive World Series title. In November, Joe joined brothers Vince and Dom as the three DiMaggio brothers played together for the first time, making up an outfield for an all-star team in a West Coast charity game. "If anyone wants to know why three kids in one family made it to the big leagues," said Joe. "They just had to know how we helped each other and how much we practiced back then. We did it every minute we could."

DiMaggio was nicknamed the "Yankee Clipper" by Yankee Stadium announcer Arch McDonald in 1939, when he compared DiMaggio's outfield speed to the new Pan American airliner. But 'Clipper' is also the name of a beautiful sailing ship and to the people that watched him play, DiMaggio looked smooth and graceful, like a ship. He looked just as smooth off the field, typically arriving to games in expensive dark suits and cashmere overcoats.

DiMaggio earned his first American League Most Valuable Player award and his first batting championship in 1939 with a .381 average as New York won its fourth straight title. Flirting with .400 late in the season, Joe was also on the cover of *Life*. Vision problems, and possibly the pressure, kept him from staying above the .400 mark. DiMaggio again homered in the World Series as the Yankees swept the Cubs.

That was also the year that Gehrig announced he was stricken with a deadly illness. "It was sad to see," DiMaggio said of ALS victim Gehrig. "At Spring Training, suddenly he couldn't hit anymore or he'd hit a hump line drive. He had no power. One time he went to sit down and missed the bench."

"He is the only player I ever went overboard on," said Gehrig of DiMaggio's future. "You mark my words; he is going to be the greatest right-handed hitter in baseball."

DiMaggio met singer and actress Dorothy Arnoldine Olson of Minnesota on the movie set of 1937's *Manhattan Merry-Go-Round*, in which he had a minor role and she was an extra. The couple dated and eventually married on November 19, 1939 as 20,000 well-wishers jammed the streets around Sts. Peter and Paul's Church at Washington Square, the cathedral whose steeples tower over North Beach and that serves San Francisco's Italian-American community. Some of the old Martinez neighborhood also attended the fanfare to celebrate DiMaggio's marriage and the end of his bachelor days.

During the 1940 season, DiMaggio captured his second consecutive AL batting title at .352, but for the first time in five years with the Yankees, something very strange happened. They did not win a World Series championship, finishing just two games behind Detroit.

In 1941, DiMaggio was mired in a 7-for-52 hitting slump in early May. But on May 15, he launched a magical 56-game hitting streak that captivated the nation. His consistency led to one of the most remarkable records of major league baseball, one that still stands today. The prior record for the longest hitting streak of 44 games was set in 1897 by Wee Willie Keeler, at a time when foul balls did not count as strikes.

In June, he was credited by the official scorer with a hit in his 30th consecutive game when an easy grounder to shortstop took a bad bounce. While DiMaggio admitted only to feeling "a bit of a strain," it was clear that pressure was building. He already had the professional record of 61 straight and now wanted the major league record. He consumed more coffee and cigarettes than usual and developed stomach pains. Joe kept to his hotel room, so as to avoid the crowds that followed him. He had teammate and fellow Bay Area native Lefty Gomez talk to the press for him. He kept going, getting his hit day after day -- sometimes two or three.

"A long hitting streak is sustained by control," said Yankee manager Joe McCarthy. "And Joe had that. You go up there knowing what you have to do and then wait patiently to do it. That was Joe. That's what made him the perfect player."

The streak packed ballparks. Since very few people owned televisions in those days, radio programs were disrupted for "Joe D" updates. The U.S. Congress designated a page to run bulletins and newspaper switchboards lit up every afternoon with fans asking "Did Joe get his hit?" DiMaggio's streak was at the center of the nation's focus, a story that spread to off the field coverage. The press, as the media was known, conspired to scrutinize DiMaggio's every move. America needed a hero, or at least a distraction during the Great Depression, followed closely by World War II. Men were being drafted by the hundreds of thousands, and in late May President Roosevelt, responding to Germany's attacks on England, declared that the U.S. was in a state of "unlimited National emergency." Despite the threat to national security, radio bulletins still interrupted reports of the Nazis with news that DiMaggio had again extended his streak.

On July 1, he hit safely in both games of a doubleheader sweep of the Boston Red Sox to extend the streak to 44 games, tying Keeler. The next day, he homered off Boston's Dick Newsome to break Keeler's record. Finally, on July 17, the streak came to a halt in Cleveland as Indians pitchers Al Smith and Jim Bagby held DiMaggio hitless before a crowd of 67,468. Two outstanding plays by third baseman Ken Keltner and a good one by shortstop Lou Boudreau took away two, maybe three hits. DiMaggio immediately began a 16-game hitting streak, hitting safely in 72 of 73 games, another record. The streaks vaulted DiMaggio from baseball star to American icon. Late that summer, the Les Brown Orchestra's "Joltin' Joe DiMaggio" became a staple on radios and diner jukeboxes with lyrics like "*He started baseball's famous streak that's got us all aglow...*"

Baseball analysts agree that only players that average more than one hit per game could ever challenge DiMaggio's feat. Since the record was set in 1941, only one player has hit in even 40 consecutive games -- Pete Rose had a 44-game run in 1978. Determining the odds of a player hitting in 56 straight games has proved difficult. Scores of probability theorists and math professionals have tried, and conclusions have ranged from saying a streak like DiMaggio's should occur once every 794 years to once every 18,519 years, with numerous estimates in between. And none of the analyses reflect the internal and external pressures.

At the end of the '41 season, the Yankees beat the Brooklyn Dodgers in five games for their fifth championship in six years. DiMaggio was named AL MVP for the second time as his streak edged out Ted Williams and his .406 batting average by a margin of 291-254 in the voting.

"Joe DiMaggio was the greatest all-around player I ever saw," said Ted Williams. "His career cannot be summed up in numbers and awards. It might sound corny, but he had a profound and lasting impact on the country."

DiMaggio had another reason to celebrate in the 1941 off-season. Dorothy gave birth to Joe's namesake and only child, Joseph Paul DiMaggio Jr. at Doctors Hospital in Staten Island on October 23. DiMaggio, usually unemotional, spoke with joy at the arrival of his son. "You ought to see the little fellow, he has the most perfect nose," Joe said. "And I never saw such a pair of hands on a baby."

Even after Joe Jr. was born, DiMaggio continued to spend many nights at his New York City hangout, Toots Shor's restaurant. He enjoyed a celebrity's life while his midwestern wife Dorothy wanted a husband for her and a father for Joe Jr. The result was conflict. Arnold said that she had hoped their child's birth would have made her husband "realize his responsibilities as a married man" but that "even the baby's arrival did not change him."

During the spring of 1942, much publicity surrounded DiMaggio's holdout for a pay raise. A group of soldiers from Camp Blanding, Florida, sent him a telegram that read: "In event the Yankees don't kick in with more than $37,000, we cordially invite you to a tryout with the 143rd Infantry."

During the 1942 season, DiMaggio batted .305, and scored 123 runs. He was drafted by the armed forces along with thousands of other young men. He was opposed to enlisting as other MLB stars had done, but Joe was finally talked into it in 1943. Apparently Dorothy wanted him in the Army and she threatened divorce if he didn't serve. On February 17th, 1943, DiMaggio traded his $43,750 a year job playing centerfield for the Yankees for $600 per year as an army enlisted man. He served his country mostly by playing Air Force exhibition baseball in California and Hawaii.

He was assigned to Special Services with the Army Air Force and reported for duty at Santa Ana Air Base in Southern California. DiMaggio was a big boost to the team. The lineup featured a mix of majors, minors, and college players. Santa Ana compiled an impressive record including a winning streak of 20 straight games, and DiMaggio strung together a 27-game hitting streak. In addition to the Santa Ana team, DiMaggio played for a team of Armed Forces all-stars managed by Babe Ruth on July 12, 1943, against the Boston Braves.

Sergeant DiMaggio was transferred to Honolulu, Hawaii in June 1944. He served and played with the Seventh Air Force with Red Ruffing, Johnny Beazley, and Joe Gordon. The Navy was also bringing many of their top players to the island including Phil Rizzuto, Pee Wee Reese, Johnny Mize, and Joe's brother Dom. But a stomach ailment sidelined DiMaggio and he was hospitalized in August. He transferred to the Army Air Force Station in Atlantic City and eventually to St Petersburg, Florida, again suffering from stomach ulcers. He was granted his discharge on September 14, 1945.

"Though he never came within a thousand miles of actual combat," wrote David Jones in *Joe DiMaggio: A Biography*, "DiMaggio resented the war with intensity equal to the most battle-scarred private. It had robbed him of the best years of his career."

DiMaggio's military service further split Joe and Dorothy, and led to their divorce in 1944 after five years of marriage. A judge ordered the settlement: $14,000 in a lump sum to Dorothy, $150 a month to care for Little Joe. Joe Jr., three years old at the time of the divorce, never had a close father-son relationship with DiMaggio. The elder DiMaggio wouldn't talk about him to reporters. Dorothy wanted full custody of Joe Jr. "He's a little young for the smart set," Arnold said of Joe's New York lifestyle.

Prior to his Army service, DiMaggio had been a 28-year-old superstar, still at the height of his athletic powers. By the time he was released, he was nearly 31, divorced, underweight, and bitter. Those three years would carve a hole in DiMaggio's career totals, creating a statistical gap between him and stars with 20-year careers. Back with the Yankees in 1946, Joe batted a career-low .290 after having been a .300-plus hitter every season before military service. But he quickly bounced back and helped guide New York to four more World Championships in 1947, 1949, 1950, and 1951.

He was an uncompromising perfectionist who drove himself and his teammates. No one hated to lose more than DiMaggio. "I came up twice in the game with the bases loaded and both times I hit balls into the alley, four-hundred and fifty feet away. Home runs in any other park," he once described. "Well, each time my own brother robbed me by making catches on the warning track. Instead of a possible eight RBI, or at least five or six, I got nothing. That night, Dom came over to my place for dinner. I remember letting him in the door and then not speaking to him until we were almost done eating. I was that mad."

The greats often make things look easy. But DiMaggio, especially in his later career, often played through great pain. A friend once asked him why he continued to play so hard, and Joe replied, "There is always some kid who may be seeing me for the first or last time, I owe him my best."

By 1947 he was fully back in form, hitting .315 to lead New York to another title. He again started the season injured, this time on crutches with foot pain. He was named the AL MVP for a third time, setting off a controversy. He edged Williams, the Triple Crown winner, by a single point. In addition to his renewed hitting,

DiMaggio also fine-tuned his defense, tying the AL fielding record of only one error in 141 games. He was an uncanny judge of fly balls; no matter where ball was hit he was waiting. Joe played his position in center field with such precision that some uneducated fans thought he was lazy. He rarely had to crash into outfield walls or dive for balls, he was simply there to catch them.

Detroit Hall of Famer Hank Greenberg said that the fleet DiMaggio covered so much territory that the only way to get a hit against the Yankees was "to hit 'em where Joe wasn't." This was no small feat for Joe, considering Yankee Stadium had the largest centerfield in the majors. DiMaggio also stole home five times in his career.

"Sometimes a fellow gets tired of writing about DiMaggio -- there must be some other ballplayer in the world worth mentioning. But there isn't really, none worth mentioning in the same breath as DiMaggio," wrote *New York Times* columnist Red Smith.

On February 7, 1949, DiMaggio set another record – he signed a $100,000 contract, more than anyone had earned for one season in baseball history. But the injuries kept coming, and he left spring training to have his right heel examined at Johns Hopkins hospital. He missed the first 69 games but made a legendary return on the weekend of June 28, hitting four homers and knocking in nine runs as the Yankees swept in Boston. DiMaggio said of his heels, "it felt as if a nail was stuck into them - only 20 times worse." An operation in November 1948 failed to correct the problem, and he wasn't able to play again until June 28, 1949. DiMaggio hit .346 in 76 games, and the Yankees won the pennant on the season's final day by beating the Red Sox.

The Yankees gave DiMaggio a 22-foot speedboat on Joe DiMaggio Day, a celebration attended by 69,551 fans at Yankee Stadium on the last day of the 1949 season. The boat was called the "Joltin' Joe" and he promptly donated it to the city of Martinez. "I'd like to thank the good Lord for making me a Yankee," he announced to fans during the ceremony.

By August of 1950, DiMaggio found himself stuck in a 4-for-38 slump. He was hitting just .279 on the year, and was benched for the first time in his career. He responded with a .373 explosion for the final six weeks of 1950 -- raising his average to .301 -- and driving home 122 runs. His furious finish looked like the DiMaggio of old and probably convinced him he had one more year left despite nagging injuries. He didn't, and sunk to career-lows of .263 and 12 homers in 1951.

In 1951, DiMaggio was replaced in centerfield for the first time in his career by fellow Bay Area outfielder Jackie Jensen in the second inning after Joe's misplay in the first. The incident aggravated a growing rift between DiMaggio and manager Casey Stengel, which ultimately influenced his retirement decision. There is speculation that Joe's treatment of star rookie Mickey Mantle ranged from indifferent to critical. DiMaggio said on several occasions that there was no one that could replace him. Not in centerfield or in the hearts of the fans, certainly not some "Oklahoma rube." While many players in Joe's situation would have tutored Mantle for the good of the team's future, DiMaggio did not assume a mentor role. In the end Joe was moved to right field, so that Mantle could cover more territory including part of DiMaggio's.

DiMaggio announced his retirement on December 11, 1951. The Yankees offered him his full $100,000 to play only home games in 1952 but Joe declined. "I feel like I have reached the stage where I can no longer produce for my club, my manager, and my teammates," he said. "I had a poor year, but even if I had hit .350, this would have been my last year. I was full of aches and pains and it had become a chore for me to play. When baseball is no longer fun, it's no longer a game, and so I've played my last game."

DiMaggio earned three American League MVP (1939, 1941 and 1947) awards and became the only major leaguer to play in the All-Star Game every season of his career. He won two batting championships: in 1939 he hit an amazing .381, then "slipped" to .352 a year later. He hit over .300 11 times and totaled 100+ RBI nine times, including 167 in 1937.

He ranked in the Top 10 in AL batting average, on-base percentage, slugging percentage, runs scored, hits, triples, home runs and RBI nearly every season. When DiMaggio retired, he was sixth on the career home run list (361), and sixth in slugging. His 369 career strikeouts (in 6,821 at bats) is a stunningly low total for a power hitter – he had almost as many homers as strikeouts. In 1969, baseball fans voted him the sport's greatest living player. His rival, Red Sox legend Williams, called him "the greatest baseball player of our time."

DiMaggio earned $704,769 in his New York Yankees career. He became the hero who replaced Babe Ruth while he and his teammates won nine World Championships. Statistically, Joe was handicapped by playing at Yankee Stadium with its cavernous outfield. Left-center field went as far back as 457 feet, compared to ballparks today where left-center rarely reaches 380. He hit 148 home runs in 3,360 at-bats at home, and in contrast, he hit 213 home runs in 3,461 at-bats on the road. His slugging percentage at home was .546, and .610 on the road. He never hit a single home run over the fence at Yankee Stadium in left center's "Death Valley." It was just too far. Like Ruth, he benefited from a few easy homers each season due to the short foul pole distances. But he lost many more than he gained with center field flyouts. Statistician Bill James calculated that DiMaggio lost more home runs due to his home park than any other player in history. If he had hit the same exact pattern of batted balls with a typical modern stadium as his home, he would have belted about 80 more career homers.

After he retired in 1951, Joe returned to the family home in the Marina. His older brother Tom said, "He quit because he couldn't be Joe DiMaggio anymore." The skinny kid from the family of a poor fisherman with a ninth-grade education was now a worldly man. In New York, he had met celebrities, presidents, and dined with Manhattan socialites. DiMaggio's private life was always an enigma. To the world he portrayed utter class and near perfection on the baseball field. His personal life, however, was very different. Those who served him said DiMaggio was a troubled, cold, often angry and impatient man. But his friends said he was warm, if a bit reclusive. Quiet and shy, he kept to a small circle of friends including old baseball buddies Dante Benedetti and O'Doul, and also saloon keepers such as Reno Barsocchini and Don Russo.

According to Ben Cramer's biography *DiMaggio: A Hero's Life*, DiMaggio had mafia connections. His alleged relationship with the Mob started in the 1930s, when his appearances at various clubs run by racket guys were rewarded by cash deposits in a secret DiMaggio trust account. By 1951, the hidden money reportedly totaled about a million untaxed dollars. Joe would bring dates to clubs like El Morocco, Copacabana, the Stork Club, or the Cotton Club. He dined for free and eventually all the club managers knew, if the Clipper made an appearance, they were expected to contribute $100-$200 to Joe's Bowery Bank account by the following day.

In 1952, New York retired DiMaggio's uniform number 5 in a ceremony at Yankee Stadium. Later that year, author Ernest Hemingway saw in DiMaggio the perfection of grace under pressure. Hemingway befriended him and had Santiago, the Old Man in "Old Man and the Sea" refer to Joe as "the great DiMaggio." DiMaggio told *Baseball Digest* that the Brooklyn Dodgers had offered him their managerial job in 1953, but he turned it down.

It was in 1953 that he started dating internationally-known actress Marilyn Monroe. According to her autobiography, Marilyn originally did not want to meet DiMaggio, fearing he was a typical arrogant athlete. "I was surprised to be so crazy about Joe. I expected a flashy New York sports type, and instead I met this reserved guy who didn't make a pass at me right away," said Monroe. "I had dinner with him almost every night for two weeks. He treated me like something special. Joe is a very decent man, and he makes other people feel decent, too."

They were unexpectedly married in San Francisco at City Hall on January 14, 1954 and this only added to DiMaggio's iconic status in American culture. He was 39, she 27 when they wed. He and Monroe posed for photos on the steps of Sts. Peter and Paul's -- they couldn't be married in the church because of his divorce. Catapulted by his marriage to one of Hollywood's most glamorous and mystifying silver-screen divas, a legion of new DiMaggio fans made him one of the 20th century's most recognized personalities.

Though they made a handsome couple, their marriage lasted only nine months. Joe Jr. even lived with his father and Monroe after the two were married. She ended up being connected to her stepson for the rest of her life. The marriage seemed doomed almost immediately as neither seemed willing to share the spotlight nor realizing how popular the other was. According to Gay Talese in *Esquire*, "disharmony in temperament and time: he was tired of publicity, she was thriving on it; he was intolerant of tardiness, she was always late."

After just a few months as husband and wife, Joe and Marilyn were experiencing problems. She had collapsed several times during the filming of *Show Business*, supposedly because of the tension and stress at home. Most accounts of her life reveal that the marital problems resulted from Marilyn's career. DiMaggio became increasingly annoyed with the shadiness of the movie industry and the studio's repeated efforts to cast Marilyn in "dumb blonde" roles.

In September, DiMaggio left their Beverly Hills residence and joined his bride in New York on the set of *The Seven Year Itch*. Their relationship moved from shaky to disaster after the shooting of one of Marilyn's most legendary scenes: the moment Marilyn's white dress billows up as she stands above a subway grate to feel the rush of air whenever a train passes beneath her. The famous shot is still identified with her image today. The scene was shot at 52nd Street and Lexington in front of New York's Trans-Lux Theater in the middle of the night. Despite the late hour, thousands of fans showed up to catch a glimpse of Monroe. It was director Billy Wilder's idea to turn the shoot into a media circus. So much camera flash showered the area that Wilder made a deal with the amateur photographers and the press: If they would allow him to shoot the scene first, he would ask Marilyn to pose for pictures.

During the proceedings, DiMaggio walked onto the set, dismayed at the sight of his wife on exhibit for more than 2,000 strangers. Joe bulled his way through the crowd and his shouted, "What the hell's going on here?" Angry at Marilyn and her profession, Wilder recalled "the look of death" on DiMaggio's face. That night, the couple had a "yelling battle" in the theater lobby, then a famous fight on the seventh floor of the St. Regis hotel. Shortly after this highly publicized event, she filed for divorce on grounds of mental cruelty 274 days after the wedding. Their divorce was granted in November 1954.

According to Monroe, "Joe wanted me to be the beautiful ex-actress, just like he was the great former ballplayer. We were to ride into some sunset together. But I wasn't ready for that kind of journey yet. I wasn't even 30, for heaven's sake."

Meanwhile, DiMaggio still wasn't very interested in parenthood. Close by in New York in the 1950s, DiMaggio never attended his boy's football games while Joe Jr. was at New Jersey's prestigious Lawrenceville School. For Joe Jr., it was a life brought up in hotels, camps, military school and boarding school – but with little quality time with his famous father. After high school, he attended Yale University for one year but dropped out to enlist in the Marines.

The baseball writers elected DiMaggio to the Hall of Fame in 1955. In the largest induction ceremony since 1939, DiMaggio was easily the Cooperstown, New York crowd favorite according to the *New York Times*. Hall of Famers who returned for the ceremony included Cobb, Bill Terry, Mel Ott, Frankie Frisch and 87-year-old Cy Young. "Now I've had everything except for the thrill of watching Babe Ruth play," he said during his enshrinement speech.

In his retirement he acted as a spokesman for commercial concerns and worked for charitable causes. Though known to be short-tempered in private, DiMaggio refrained from showing such behavior in public. A painfully private person, he always was careful and protective of his image, understanding that it was his legacy.

"It is not for DiMaggio's records that we remember him," wrote Ira Berkow of the *New York Times*. "He is best remembered for the persona of Joe DiMaggio. He remains a symbol of excellence, elegance, power and, to be sure, gentleness."

DiMaggio often visited Martinez for long afternoons of fishing with cousins and old friends. He avoided crowds, skipping funerals and showing up unexpectedly at the mortuary to pay his last respects. He would then slip over to a local restaurant for a meal. He'd sit in the back room, away from oglers and autograph seekers.

"His head was always down, he wouldn't look around. No eye contact," said Ernie Lasell, who owned a Martinez hardware store and used to sell DiMaggio his fishing licenses. "He was just a naturally shy guy, very modest."

On the waterfront in Martinez, the "Joltin' Joe" is still berthed quietly. When city leaders proposed building a Joe DiMaggio Museum, DiMaggio didn't offer assistance or promise any memorabilia, and the idea faded. One resident remembers staring out his window in awe as newlyweds Joe and Marilyn strolled from a limousine into a neighbor's house in Martinez in 1954. "Joe just slipped into town and he slipped out," Lopas said. "The city wanted to claim him, but he didn't claim it."

DiMaggio re-entered Monroe's life as her marriage to playwright Arthur Miller crumbled. On February 10, 1961, he obtained her release from Payne Whitney Psychiatric Clinic. Marilyn had been locked away like her mother, a prisoner in a padded cell. After three days, she was finally permitted one call and phoned DiMaggio. He was at the Payne Whitney reception desk the next day. "I want my wife," DiMaggio said, although he and Marilyn had not been married for six years. "And if you do not release her to me, I will take this place apart, piece of wood by piece of wood." Monroe was released within a few minutes. Joe had Marilyn transferred to Columbia Presbyterian, where she could rest in a private room which he visited daily and which he filled with flowers.

She joined him in Florida where he was a spring training batting coach for the Yankees. Their "just friends" comments did not stop re-marriage rumors from flying. Joe allegedly had a change of heart about his role as a controlling husband. He had been to therapy regarding anger management. He supposedly told her she could do whatever she wanted, including decisions about the movies, where they lived, or the therapist, or the medications, or the money. He wanted her back—and he would stay with her. The years matured Marilyn as well, and as she approached her 35th birthday, she was ready to settle down. In Florida, Joe and Marilyn took care of each other like an old married couple. Fearful of losing her again to show business people, he quit his job with a military post-exchange supplier on August 1, 1962 to ask her to marry him, again.

Marilyn accepted Joe's proposal and the couple selected August 8, 1962 as their second wedding day. But on August 5, the stunning news spread that Marilyn was found dead. DiMaggio's son, Joe Jr., had spoken to Monroe on the phone the night of her death and had claimed she seemed fine. Her death was deemed a "probable suicide" but has been the subject of endless conspiracy theories.

Devastated, Joe claimed her body and took charge of the funeral arrangements, barring Hollywood's elite. In DiMaggio's anguish, he ranted about the Kennedys, and Frank Sinatra, and J. Edgar Hoover and spent all night beside her casket. She was buried on August 8, the day they were to be re-married. He had a half-dozen red roses delivered three times a week to her crypt for 20 years. Unlike her other two husbands or others who knew her, he refused to talk about her publicly or otherwise exploit their relationship. Her suicide turned the ex-ballplayer toward reclusion. He never married again.

He re-emerged in later years as a popular spokesman for and the TV face of "Mr. Coffee" coffee makers. He also became a spokesman for several other companies including Bowery Savings Bank, Louisville Slugger, Wheaties cereal, and Chesterfield Cigarettes. But he carried himself with grace even when he appeared in ads or on TV. There was never a sense he had cheapened himself.

When DiMaggio visited Martinez in March of 1964, he went to a local park and signed baseballs for scores of thrilled children. Paul Simon of Simon and Garfunkel fame helped keep Joe's name alive a few years later when he wrote the song "Mrs. Robinson," which included the lines *"Where have you gone, Joe DiMaggio? A nation turns its lonely eyes to you,"* hoping to recapture a touch of the lost innocence of Joe's era. It worked - the song became a hit and a classic.

DiMaggio's legend grew so large during his career that he has been referenced in dozens of films, television shows (including I Love Lucy, Everybody Loves Raymond, The Simpsons, and Seinfeld), literature, comic books, paintings, sculpture, drawings, and 16 pop music songs. When ESPN's Chris Berman says "back, back, back" on highlights, he's referring to a long fly ball Joe hit in the 1947 Series.

"Cab drivers yelled to him and almost drove into store windows because they couldn't take their eyes off of him," said Red Smith. "People stopped dead in their tracks and stared at him. It was a modest whiff of what the second coming might be like. I never felt more invisible when I was in Joe's company."

DiMaggio was a man of extremes, superbly talented on the field but privately insecure, passive, and even dysfunctional. In his later years, he allowed himself to be turned into a sports memorabilia money machine to finally earn the millions he never did as a player. Near the end, DiMaggio insisted that at all events he was to be introduced last and always announced as "the greatest living baseball player." He also instructed stadium announcers to always pause for applause at least 30 seconds longer than any other player at the event. Few of DiMaggio's teammates remained friendly with him or even tried to maintain a relationship with the legend after their playing days ended.

In 1968, Joe took a position in the Bay Area as a coach and front office executive for Charles O. Finley, owner of the Oakland A's. He returned for the 1969 season, also the year that a plaque was dedicated in his honor in Yankee Stadium's Monument Park, alongside Ruth and Gehrig.

DiMaggio received the Presidential Medal of Freedom in 1977 from President Carter. For Game 1 of the 1977 World Series at Yankee Stadium, DiMaggio was tabbed to throw out the first pitch, a service for which he charged. He became angered over a mix-up concerning extra tickets he requested (later revealed he had no use for) and refused to throw out the first pitch only minutes before gametime.

When the Loma Prieta earthquake rocked San Francisco in October 1989, Joe moved through police lines to the family house in the Marina, entered his private quarters and left with a trash bag of items. In 1992, the Joe DiMaggio Children's Hospital opened in Hollywood, Florida, for which he raised over $4,000,000.

DiMaggio hired attorney Morris Engelberg in 1983 to protect himself against California's tax laws. New laws required athletes with large revenues for autographs and memorabilia to pay back taxes and penalties. No one took home more cash from autograph sales than Joe. Engelberg helped DiMaggio escape taxes and establish residency in Hollywood, Florida, where no state income tax exists. Engelberg's marketing efforts enabled DiMaggio to increase his net worth from $300,000 to nearly $15 million at the time of his death. They sold autographed balls, bats, photos, hats, and anything Joe could get a pen on. On September 27, 1998, DiMaggio appeared at Yankee Stadium on "Joe DiMaggio Day," his last trip ever to the park. The special tribute was supposedly orchestrated by Engelberg and netted DiMaggio – with a percentage to Engelberg – more than $5 million in special edition memorabilia sales. Engelberg certainly profited from Joe and whether he stole from the elderly DiMaggio in his final days is unclear.

Meanwhile, Joe Jr. seemed to live more and more simply as the years passed. Divorced from his wife Susan after six tumultuous and violent years of marriage, Joe Jr., was separated from adopted daughters Paula and Katherine in the 1960s. Sometimes Joe Sr. would cruise the streets of Martinez, looking for his son, as Joe Jr.'s address changed often. He battled drug and alcohol problems, and ran with a motorcycle gang between Martinez and Antioch. Joe Jr. often lived alone on the streets, and took shelter at one point in a trucking container. At one time, he was the manager of a trucking company in Oakland. DiMaggio Sr. funded several failed business ventures for Joe Jr., including long-haul trucking and a foam insulation company. Sometimes Junior would take cash from his father; other times he would ignore him. When his father was gravely ill, Joe Jr. was asked why he didn't visit. "You know, I never got the words, 'Come now,' or I would've been there in a flash. When he wants me there, I'll be there."

DiMaggio, a heavy smoker nearly all his life, was admitted to Memorial Regional Hospital in Hollywood, Florida, on October 12, 1998 for lung cancer surgery and remained there for 99 days. He returned to his Florida home on January 19, 1999 and was scheduled to throw out the first pitch to Yogi Berra in April. But he died at his home on March 8, at 84 years old. America could no longer turn its lonely eyes to Joe.

DiMaggio's funeral was held on March 11, 1999 at Sts. Peter and Paul's Roman Catholic Church in San Francisco. The hearse made its way from the cathedral to Beach Street, where it drove past the DiMaggio home. Mayor Willie Brown ordered city flags lowered to half-staff in memory of the baseball player who began his career with the San Francisco Seals. "Joe DiMaggio was one of San Francisco's finest. A man of integrity and class, a superb ballplayer, a man both inspiring and inspired," said the mayor.

DiMaggio was interred at Holy Cross Cemetery in Colma. His funeral was very private, with fewer than 75 people attending. New York's West Side Highway was officially renamed Joe DiMaggio Drive in his honor and the Yankees wore DiMaggio's number 5 on the left sleeves of their uniforms for the entire 1999 season. DiMaggio's son was a pall-bearer that day, his face anonymous to the national audience. When his father died, Joe Jr. was living in a trailer and working in a junkyard. DiMaggio left him only a $20,000 per year trust fund, but Joe Jr. passed away five months later at age 57 due to respiratory and gastrointestinal problems. A large part of DiMaggio's estate was reportedly left to Paula, Katherine, and their children.

After DiMaggio's death, some biographers portrayed him as indifferent, a jealous brother; a dreadful father, and a wretched husband. They say he used friends as gophers and flunkies, and dropped them abruptly when it suited his purposes. He lived as if he expected someone else to pick up the tab: for food, lodging, clothes and personal services. He took home leftovers of free meals and filled his pockets with anything free. He did his own laundry and housekeeping before he was elderly and rarely took his car to get washed.

In 2000, the city of San Francisco proposed to honor DiMaggio by naming the North Beach Playground – the place where it all started for Joe – after the late slugger. But Engelberg charged that San Francisco's plan was not a suitable honor for someone of DiMaggio's stature. In addition to forcing the city not to rename the playground where DiMaggio and his brothers played ball as kids, Engelberg sought unspecified damages. When Supervisor Gavin Newsom, who worked to find a suitable honor for the longtime Marina district resident, sent Engelberg a long list of possible honors for DiMaggio, the attorney instead suggested either the Bay Bridge or San Francisco International Airport. But Mayor Brown and Newsom later said those were unworkable ideas.

An auction of DiMaggio's personal items was held in 2006 by the adopted daughters of Joe Jr. Highlights included the ball hit to break Keeler's hitting-streak record ($63,250); 2,000th career hit ball ($29,900); 1947 Most Valuable Player Award ($281,750); uniform worn in the 1951 World Series ($195,500); Hall of Fame ring ($69,000); Marilyn-autographed photograph "I love you Joe" ($80,500); her passport ($115,000); and their marriage certificate ($23,000). The event netted a total of $4.1 million. In 2009, 200 Martinez locals filled the Shell Clubhouse for a Sons of Italy benefit dinner to raise money for the restoration of DiMaggio's boat, the "Joltin' Joe."

The words "grace" and "class" are difficult to define and mean different things to different people. But DiMaggio fans insist he possessed both qualities. Often, they cited the things that Joe would not do. In an era of endless celebrity overexposure, DiMaggio never sat with Barbara Walters to weep about Marilyn. He never published a tell-all autobiography, retailing his sexual exploits or his loneliness. He was never vulgar or critical of contemporary players.

DiMaggio ranked #11 on *The Sporting News'* list of the 100 Greatest Baseball Players, and was elected by fans to the MLB All-Century Team. There are few people left alive who ever saw him play. His time as a ballplayer (1936-1951) preceded the age of television and was witnessed only by paying fans in an era when there were no major league teams west of the Mississippi. DiMaggio was hailed as the prototypical "five tool" player of his generation with his outstanding offensive and defensive skills. He was a player for the ages, for the flagship franchise at a time when baseball was a far larger part of our national culture than today.

"The man who was called the greatest living ballplayer will live forever in the hearts and minds of all New Yorkers," said Giuliani at his funeral. "He graced our city with nine World Championships, but more important than that, he graced our city with a style and a dignity and a class that made New York City better than it actually is. He helped to create and build the pride of the Yankees and he helped to create and build the unique spirit of New York City. "

Joe DiMaggio was born in Martinez, achieved his greatest fame in New York, lived in Beverley Hills and died in Florida. But San Francisco was his home, the city he loved more than any other. "He became New York City's face," old neighborhood pal Don Russo said. "But I don't think there was ever any doubt. He never thought of himself as anything but pure San Francisco.

5

JASON KIDD

Ranked by many NBA experts as one of Top 10 greatest point guards, Jason Kidd beat opponents in a variety of ways. Superior ball-handling, precision passing, tenacious rebounding and lockdown defense were his specialties, but he could also nail a game-changing shot in the final seconds. His end-to-end speed, strength and durability rewarded him with a 20-year career that included 11,000 assists, two Olympic gold medals and one shining NBA championship.

Jason Frederick Kidd was born in San Francisco on March 23, 1973 and raised in an upper middle-class section of Oakland. His father Steve was an African-American supervisor for Trans World Airlines and his Irish Catholic mother Anne was a programmer for Bank of America. The oldest of three children, Jason's been stared at and talked about since birth.

"I was different from the day I was born," Kidd says. "Dad is black. Mom is white. I had two different cultures and two different backgrounds to learn from. I think that helped me to be special."

Anne Kidd was a San Francisco native while Steve was a Baptist from Missouri. They married in San Francisco in 1971 when he was 33, and she 22. Steve began as a baggage handler for TWA and eventually rose to a highly paid supervisor position. Anne started her career as a bookkeeper. The Kidds taught their children to respect others and other cultures and how to set and exceed goals. The lessons Jason learned from his parents helped him become a better player and teammate throughout his career.

Kidd attended St. Paschal Baylon elementary school in the Oakland Hills. In third grade, nine-year-old Jason played soccer at St. Paschal. When teachers and coaches were short a few players for a fourth-grade team, he gave basketball a try. Because he was one of the youngest and smallest, Kidd learned the value of passing the ball at an early age. "I was always one of the young ones, and for a long time I would be one of the last ones chosen," he said. "So I learned to pass."

Kidd broke his first record in a fourth-grade CYO game. He scored 21 of the team's 30 points. He added further intensity and power by the sixth grade. "During a Thanksgiving street football game, I caught a pass, knocked over a mailbox and just kept going," Kidd said. "Didn't feel a thing until I got home."

The incident ended any hope Jason had for a football career. "I felt Jason would hurt himself because he's so aggressive," said Steve, who prohibited his son from playing football. "In basketball, everybody started saying how great Jason was. We were flattered, but afraid to accept it. I guess by high school we started believing he might be something special."

The Kidds lived a comfortable suburban life and even owned three horses. Every summer, the family took vacations, including trips to visit Steve's relatives in Plattsburg, Missouri. Meanwhile, Jason was heavily influenced by Magic Johnson. He watched the Los Angeles Lakers whenever they were on television. Jason loved the way Magic passed the ball and orchestrated the team's 1980s Showtime attack.

During his youth, Kidd excelled at soccer, basketball, baseball and other sports. He continued to develop court skills at school and sometimes with neighborhood kids at Grass Valley Elementary, because they had nine-foot rims. Jason soon became a regular player on the Oakland playground scene. Though he came from a different side of town than those he competed against, he earned respect with his unselfish play. Kidd sometimes found himself pitted against future Oregon State guard Gary Payton, who graduated from nearby Skyline High School in 1986. Already a notorious trash-talker, Payton was headed for NBA stardom, and everyone knew it. Payton was the older and better player, but the experience was great for Jason. They never faced each other in a high school or college game but they did hang out in the summer, whether on a local playground or in a gym. They played baseball and basketball.

"It was never a thing where we hung out all the time," Payton said, "but we played together and against each other. We weren't like, tight, but we were friends."

"We'd go to a playground and play Strikeout," Kidd said, describing a pickup baseball game. "I was the better hitter, but he was a better fielder. You almost couldn't hit the ball past him. I remember we'd play for hours, and even if he was losing, he could still talk you into an out when he wanted to."

Payton was also Kidd's mentor by example. "I remember one time in the summer, we were playing at Harmon," Kidd said. "We were just shooting around, doing nothing, when all of a sudden he just started playing defense, the way he does in games. I couldn't get off a shot, I could barely get around him, and he was dogging me like it was a real game. He was showing me without telling me that this is what happens in the NBA, and how I have to step up my game that much to survive."

Payton provided Kidd many more lessons, many of them at the San Francisco Pro-Am League, a summer staple for 25 years. Payton began playing in the league in 1986 and when Kidd signed on in 1992, he joined Payton's Bay Pride team. Kidd was highly scouted for AAU teams and tourneys, garnering various all-star and MVP awards.

"Gary took control," said summer league official Jon Greenburg. "That was from the get-go. They had good eye contact almost from the first time they went on the floor together. But when Gary wanted the ball, they looked at each other, and Gary got the ball. They would spread, and Gary loved to go one-on-one. But you could tell they respected each other."

The two still reminisce about the playing days of their youth. Kidd has often paid homage to Payton. The two are examples of how the Oakland style of play is passed on, and Oakland matters to both of them. From hard-nosed defense to cross-over dribbles, Oakland is both Kidd's town *and* Payton's Place. They are both beneficiaries and financial supporters of the East Oakland Youth Development Center at East 14th and International, and they come home every off-season to visit friends.

Kidd began to draw national attention while he was barely a freshman at St. Joseph's of Notre Dame High School in Alameda. Jason teamed with senior Calvin Byrd to lead St. Joe's to an East Shore Athletic League championship under the guidance of coach Frank LaPorte. Kidd, who wore number 32 in honor of Magic Johnson, was named the California High School Freshman of the Year.

In high school, Kidd mesmerized fans with spectacular ball-handling moves and no look passing while leaping and twisting at full speed. He fooled defenders with embarrassing ease. It took a couple of years, but Jason led St. Joseph to consecutive Division I state championships in 1991 and '92. During Kidd's four years, the Pilots were 122-14. He was repeatedly picked as America's top high school player. The *Oakland Tribune* wrote in March 1992 that Kidd "is probably the most canonized, publicized and analyzed prep basketball player in state history."

Fans mobbed Kidd for autographs before and after high school games. St. Joseph sold Jason Kidd T-shirts by the thousands. St. Joe's coach Frank LaPorte recalled "Our 800-seat gym couldn't handle the crowds, so we eventually had to play in the Oakland Coliseum." LaPorte said that when he took Kidd out during a blowout win in front of 5,000 fans, "I'll bet 4,900 walked out."

When Kidd's senior season began, he focused on capturing another state championship. Jason averaged 25 points, 10 assists, seven rebounds and seven steals. The teenager claimed the Naismith Award as the nation's top high school player and was named Player of the Year by *Parade Magazine* and *USA Today*. The all-time prep leader in assists (1,155) and California's sixth all-time career scorer (2,661 points), he was also voted California Player of the Year for the second straight season. Jason was a McDonald's All-American, sharing MVP honors in the 1992 All-American Game with Georgetown-bound forward Othella Harrington.

Off the court, Kidd tried to sort through the dozens of college scholarship offers he received. But it wasn't only colleges showing interest in Jason -- there was also talk of him leaping directly to the pros. Some coaches and scouts thought that Kidd could have gone straight from high school to the National Basketball Association upon graduation in 1992. Golden State Warriors coach Don Nelson and UCLA coach Jim Harrick both went on record saying Jason had the talent to bypass college. East Coast NBA executives also became familiar with Jason—most notably Willis Reed, who received video from a pro scout and friend of Steve Kidd's.

Kidd had originally declared he was going out of state, far from home. But family and friends were worried that he might lose focus from his studies and basketball. Jason made national headlines when he announced his college choice: the University of California at Berkeley. It was assumed that Arizona, Kentucky, Kansas, and Ohio State were at the top of his list. In fact, Cal didn't even appear to be in the running — somewhat because of his mediocre SAT scores but mostly because he never made an official visit. Suddenly, Kidd announced that he was staying home. He would play basketball at Cal in nearby Berkeley despite the fact that the Bears were 23-33 in their last two seasons and hadn't won a Pac 10 title since 1960.

"I want to be near my family and friends," Kidd said. His parents felt comfortable turning him over to coach Lou Campanelli, known for making players maintain good grades and graduate. Jason was also friendly with many of the Bears, having met them in pick-up games at Harmon Arena. Campanelli met with Kidd and his parents. "We went over basic things like academics, not basketball," Kidd said. "My parents wanted to know if Coach Campanelli would help me."

"It was a life decision. It came down to staying home and letting my parents see me play like they did in high school." There was a question of Jason's SAT scores not being acceptable for admission to Cal. But he retook the test and satisfied all scholarship requirements. Although SAT scores are supposed to be confidential, Kidd learned that only applies to folks who aren't famous. Jason could take media criticism about his on-court game, but not headlines in his hometown *Oakland Tribune* such as: "Kidd Fails SAT Again." Frustrated and still immature publicly, Kidd lashed back: "I know there are people out there who want to see me fail. ... They laugh, but when I pass, I'll be the one laughing in their faces. I just tell myself they would love to be in my shoes. ... I am 16 or 17 years old, and I am getting drilled in the papers."

Jason arrived in Berkeley in September of 1992 under the pressure of great expectations. The Bears, coming off a 10-18 season, hadn't won a Pac 10 title since Pete Newell guided them to an NCAA national championship 32 years before. In addition to Jason and fellow freshman recruit Jerrod Hasse, sophomores Lamond Murray, Al Grigsby, K.J. Roberts, and Monty Buckley had all logged major minutes the year before. If senior forward Brian Hendrick could successfully return from knee surgery, the Golden Bears had plenty of firepower.

During his freshman season at Cal, Kidd averaged 13 points, 7.7 assists, 4.9 rebounds, and 3.8 steals per game which earned him 1992-93 NCAA Freshman of the Year honors. Jason and fellow freshman Danny Anderson were selected to the All Pac-10 team, something only four rookies in conference history had accomplished. His 110 steals broke both the NCAA record for most steals by a freshman and set a Cal record for most steals in a season. His 220 assists shattered another school record.

Kidd's play was the engine that drove the resurgence of Cal basketball and helped the 19-8 Bears earn an NCAA Tournament bid. In the first round, Jason sparked an upset over LSU. With the score tied, Kidd converted a twisting lay-up in the final seconds. Tigers coach Dale Brown called the basket the "pretzel shot." Cal then shocked all of college basketball when they upset two-time defending national champion Duke before losing to Kansas in the Sweet 16.

Halfway through Kidd's freshman season, Campanelli was suddenly fired after eight years in Berkeley. Campanelli was accused by Cal officials of demoralizing the team. He filed a $5-million lawsuit in 1993 claiming unjust dismissal. He cited a February 1993 article quoting a Cal official who claimed Steve Kidd said: "Campanelli was putting so much pressure on his son he was making him physically ill."

Steve denied ever saying those words. "My wife and I thought Campanelli was the greatest guy in the world," he told *The Sporting News*. "Jason never said anything like that to me." Todd Bozeman, an assistant coach who helped recruit Kidd, was promoted to head coach. Under Bozeman, Jason continued his phenomenal play.

Kidd's first participation in USA basketball came after his first season at Berkeley. He was the only freshman chosen to take part in Team USA's 10-member team, which played five games in Europe and finished 3–2. Jason scored 20 points in an 85-83 overtime loss to Spain. He posted final averages of 8.4 points, 4.2 rebounds, 4.0 assists and 1.4 steals per game.

In May 1993, United Airlines clerk Alexandria Brown filed a paternity suit in San Francisco, claiming she was pregnant and Kidd was the father. Jason Alexsander Kidd was born November 16, 1993. Kidd's paternity was confirmed with a blood test. Jason and his mother, Anne, say Brown and Kidd had "a one-night stand." Anne adds, "I never even met her. She had a plan. She follows Jason around."

As a sophomore, 20-year-old Kidd continued his intense physical play. He led the nation with 9.1 assists per game and also added 16.7 points, 6.9 rebounds, and 3.1 steals per game. Jason was selected first-team All-America by the *The Sporting News*, the Associated Press and U.S. Basketball Writers. Kidd set a new Pac-10 season assists record with 272 and single-game record with 18, smashing Cal records set by Kevin Johnson. Jason also made 51 three-pointers, more than double that of his freshman year. He became the first Cal player and first sophomore to win the Pac-10 Player of the Year award.

"Jason's fans, the crowds, got so large before and after games, we had to have security guards get us to the locker room," Bozeman said. "Once, in Washington, two fans slipped through security, hid themselves inside two lockers and jumped out when we got inside. Another time, a fan walked right onto the court by the referees while Jason was shooting a free throw. At Berkeley, we had to move him off campus, out of the dorm, because they were chasing him day and night. It was crazy."

Cal was ranked in the Top 20 in 1993-94 and the Bears returned the heart of their roster. Jason, who had packed on 10 pounds of muscle, was focused on improving his outside shooting, the only glaring weakness in his game. His other goal was to lead Cal to the Final Four. Things didn't exactly go as planned. Injuries to Grigsby and Roberts left Kidd and Murray as the team's only reliable scorers. The fifth-seeded Golden Bears made the NCAA Tournament again, but were upset in the first round by Wisconsin–Green Bay. Kidd was named a finalist for both the Naismith and Wooden Awards. Despite his disappointing showing in the tournament, Jason felt he had proven everything in college and declared himself eligible for the 1994 NBA draft.

On May 24, 1994 -- 39 days before the NBA draft -- Kidd again showed that he was still a kid. Jason was arrested for a hit-and-run collision and speeding after leaving the scene at 2:30 am. According to the California Highway Patrol interview with Kidd, he was cruising around Oakland in a 1994 Toyota Landcruiser he had bought for his dad. He spotted two men he knew, both of whom had histories of crack cocaine arrests, violating probation and drunken driving. Jason gave them a ride to the OT Club, a dance hall in neighboring Emeryville.

On the freeway at 2 am, Kidd said he was driving about 65 mph when something hit his car "that caused me to go out of control.... I really didn't see any cars that would possibly hit me. I was trying to think of what could have happened."

Officers got a different version from others. Jonathan Cook of San Francisco said Kidd passed his motorcycle "at the very least 110 mph.... He then saw (Kidd's car) start to lift in the front end as if it was taking off." The car skidded for about 100 yards, hit a wall, flipped and slid 150 yards. Cook and another man heard Kidd's passengers yell: "Get the kid! Get the kid!" Cook thought they meant a child. Kidd crawled from the wreckage and sat on a curb.

Brown, the mother of Kidd's son, drove up. Jason got in and they sped away, leaving the others. One struggled with officers, was handcuffed, and then kicked out the rear window of a patrol car. Another driver said he saw the other companion or maybe Jason flashing a gun. Kidd denied being drunk or having a gun. He was later charged with speeding and misdemeanor hit and run. He entered a plea of no-contest. Jason was immediately convicted and sentenced to two years' probation, 100 hours of community service and the maximum fine of $1,000.

Speaking of Brown, Kidd was now under court order. The judge directed him to pay $1,500 a month child support beginning June 1, 1994. But when Jason declared for the NBA draft, Brown's lawyer drafted a new paternity suit two days before the draft. This time, she increased demands from $1,500 a month to $10,000 per month child support, $25,000 for a new car and $10,000 for the household.

Brown claimed she needed more money because she had to quit her $1,200 per month job when Kidd refused to pay daycare costs. She and Jason Jr. allegedly lived on welfare while Jason drove a $100,000 Mercedes. Brown and Jason Jr. share a yardless, one-bedroom apartment that is "sparsely furnished" and equipped with "only the bare rudiments," while Dad lives in a "reportedly luxurious home."

Brown asked the judge to set up a trust fund for Jason Jr. because of his father's risky career. Her attorney fought to get a percentage of Kidd's endorsement deals. The court ruled in August that Kidd pay $4,000 a month child support, health insurance, plus $15,000 for Brown's legal fees. Jason must also inform Brown of future contracts.

Longtime college scout Don Leventhal, publisher and editor of "The Don Leventhal NBA Draft Report," submitted this analysis on Kidd:

- Is extremely fundamentally sound, has superior court awareness and is one of the rare players who truly has the ability to make his teammates better. Tremendous passer and defender who plays the game with intensity. Good speed, great quickness, and moves well without ball.

- Improved from his freshman to sophomore season in every offensive category. His 3-point shooting percentage went up from 29 percent to 36 percent. Has really gotten better at shooting off the dribble. His range now extends to 20 feet.

- Inconsistent as a catch-and-shooter. Needs to improve his free throw shooting Superb playmaker. He passes quickly and decisively when he spots the open man. Seems to have the sixth sense and anticipation that only the truly great players possess. Excellent passer off the dribble. Runs the fastbreak extremely well and makes very good decisions.

- Very good ballhandler with a quick first step who can blow by defenders. Has a good crossover dribble. Is a fine penetrator who often drives to the hoop, draws defenders and hits the open man. He can score on his drives to the basket, has great agility when he gets into the air and is a wonderful finisher. Dunks with ease, but is more efficient than flashy.

- He is 6 feet 4, 205 pounds. Is built very well, possesses strength and is a good rebounder for his size. Shows stamina. Uses his size and strength to post up smaller defenders. Can play physically and works hard at both ends.

In the 1994 NBA draft, the Milwaukee Bucks selected Glenn "Big Dog" Robinson of Purdue No. 1 overall while the Dallas Mavericks chose Kidd with the second pick, just ahead of Duke swingman Grant Hill. Jason soon signed a nine-year, $54 million contract. Before he had ever played an NBA game, Nike, Classic Cards, and Sega Genesis also inked him to lucrative deals.

The Mavericks ended the previous season with the worst record in the NBA at 13–69. Many believed that "J-Kidd" was headed for lots of losing in Dallas. Head coach Dick Motta welcomed the return of center Roy Tarpley, who had missed three straight seasons because of a drug suspension. Jimmy Jackson and Jamal Mashburn were also returning and Jason, Dallas's "Third J," was assigned to keep everyone happy by distributing the ball. The new chemistry worked immediately. In his very first game as a pro, Kidd made only three baskets but piled up 11 assists and nine rebounds to lead the Mavericks to a win over New Jersey. The Mavs went 9-7 in their first 16 games, and Jackson and Mashburn each topped 50 points in a game. By New Year's Day, Dallas had more wins than the entire previous season.

After Kidd's debut season, the Mavericks improved their record to 36–46, the best turnaround of the 1994-95 NBA season. Only 21, Kidd had a huge rookie impact. Jason excelled after Jackson went down with a season-ending ankle injury, averaging 15 points and eight assists in his absence. Kidd averaged 11.7 points, 5.4 rebounds, 7.7 assists, and led the NBA in triple-doubles. He became the only rookie to finish in the league's Top 10 in two categories (assists and steals). Jason shared 1995 NBA Rookie of the Year honors with Hill.

After the paternity settlement, Kidd and his parents also had to defend claims by Tameka Tate. She accused Jason of assault, stemming from a drunken outburst in March of 1994. She sued Kidd in June for $250,000. Tate was a high school senior living with her mother in Oakland. Her best friend dated Kidd while Tate dated one of his friends. "I became part of that crowd," Tate said. "To me, Jason was human. He treated me very respectfully. But when he drinks, I think he has a major problem."

The incident leading to Tate's lawsuit began at a party Kidd threw at his house while still at Cal. Jason was turning 21 and had recently announced he was going pro. According to Tate, she and her best friend went into Kidd's bedroom at 2:30 am. Tate said that "Jason goes down the hallway flinging doors open, screaming obscenities and, 'Who's in these rooms?'" Tate "tapped" Kidd and said "Good night and bye. Then he hit me in the chest real hard. It was a shock. Then he poured a 22-ounce bottle of Mickey's Big Mouth over my head. I said, 'Why did you pour beer on me?' He punched me in the jaw and started swinging wildly. I tried to defend myself. He kept saying, 'You hit me first.' Like a little kid on the playground." Tate says Kidd threw her from the house and chased her, screaming, 'Get off my property!'

The Alameda County District Attorney's office dismissed criminal charges due to lack of evidence. Kidd told *The Sporting News* that Tate was "being used by outside influences" to extort money. The Mavericks publicly supported Kidd but were starting to get concerned over his trend of trouble. "Jason has a lot of energy," said Anne Kidd. "A lot. You've got to keep Jason busy and occupied. You must, or he gets himself in trouble."

The Mavericks headed into the 1995-96 season with big expectations. Though Motta made no public predictions, playoffs were the goal. But by mid-December, Dallas was 6-12, Tarpley and center Donald Hodge were both facing drug suspensions, and Mashburn was lost for the year to a knee injury. The club never recovered and finished a frustrating 26-56.

Kidd, upset with Jackson for his selfishness, barely spoke to him the rest of the year. Fans in Dallas appeared to side with their sophomore point guard. In a *Fort Worth Star-Telegram* poll, Jason was voted the city's second most popular athlete, finishing behind Troy Aikman and ahead of Emmitt Smith. Despite a disappointing year, Kidd posted impressive numbers. He raised his scoring average to 16.6 points, ranked second in the NBA in assists, and led all NBA guards in rebounding. With 783 assists and 553 boards, Jason became the sixth player in league history to record at least 700 assists and 500 rebounds in a season. The last to accomplish the feat was hero Magic Johnson in 1990-91.

During a 1996 Nike-sponsored trip to Japan, Michael Jordan lectured Kidd and accused him of not maximizing his awesome potential. Meanwhile, Dallas fired Motta and hired disciplinarian Jim Cleamons, formerly an assistant in Chicago. Cleamons and Kidd met and seemed to be on the same page. Days later, Jason said publicly he might not be able to play with Jackson much longer.

Friction resurfaced when Kidd couldn't get along with Cleamons. By December, Dallas actively shopped their point guard, no longer sold on his leadership skills and work habits. To minimize public criticism from Kidd fans over a mid-season deal, the team leaked its private concerns about Jason to a handful of media, who printed them as news. Another off-court incident occurred but this time he was a passenger in a car accident. On the day after Christmas in 1996, Kidd was traded to the Phoenix Suns with Tony Dumas and Loren Meyer for Michael Finley, A.C. Green, and Sam Cassell.

Phoenix fans were elated and Kidd was looking forward to a fresh start after 2.5 years in Dallas. In his first game in a Suns uniform, Jason collected nine assists and seven rebounds in 20 minutes. Coach Danny Ainge paired him in the backcourt with fellow Cal alumnus Kevin Johnson, both of whom finished in the league's Top 5 in assists. Jason's scoring touch also improved. Against Golden State, he set season highs with 33 points and eight three-pointers. The Suns surged into the playoffs, giving Kidd his first postseason appearance. Payton and Seattle, however, eliminated Phoenix in the first round.

Despite the Suns' early exit from the playoffs, Kidd was building a life outside of basketball after the 1996-97 season. After dating for more than a year, he married girlfriend Joumana Samaha and they became the unofficial first couple of Phoenix. When they first met, Joumana was not interested in Jason. A career-oriented television reporter, she felt Kidd was a typical athlete. Kidd began to win her over but what really sold Joumana was Jason's family. After spending time with the Kidds, she was convinced he knew what family meant.

Kidd continued to work hard in the extended NBA lockout off-season in 1997. Joumana helped him in practice by running sprints and feeding him pass after pass as he worked on his shooting. She accomplished this within a month of giving birth to their first child, Trey Jason Kidd.

Kidd arrived for training camp in 1997 looking forward to his first full year with Phoenix. Joumana had worked with him to improve his image, coaching him to become better with the media. With proven scorers like Cedric Ceballos, Rex Chapman, Danny Manning and Cliff Robinson, the run-and-gun Suns expected to challenge for the Pacific Division title. The acquisition of Antonio McDyess from Denver deepened the roster.

Despite an assortment of injuries, Phoenix stayed close to first place in the division. Every night a different scorer stepped up. Thanks to a 10-game April win streak, the Suns posted a 56-26 record, third in the division. In the playoffs, they were again ousted, this time by the San Antonio Spurs and their stars Tim Duncan and David Robinson. Now ranked among the elite NBA players, Jason was named All-NBA First Team and All-Defensive First Team.

Kidd's parents regularly attended games in Oakland when Jason played against the Warriors. Anne also traveled on occasion to Phoenix to see him play, as Steve did until his death from a heart attack in 1998. At that point, Jason faced the most difficult period of his life. The reality of it stunned him, but his dad's passing helped him put things in perspective. "It feels funny sometimes to play back home and him not be there," Kidd said. "But you know how some fathers are. They never tell you when they don't feel right. He was stubborn. He'd always say, 'Just give me a couple of aspirin, and I'll be fine.' It's taken time to get over it."

That summer, Jason traveled to Puerto Rico with Dream Team III for the Pre-Olympic qualifying tournament. Kidd and Duncan kept the Americans focused on the court. The team won all 10 of its games, took the gold medal and earned a spot in the 2000 Olympics. Jason led the squad in assists and steals. Kidd's impressive showing in Puerto Rico improved his maturing national image within the league and the Phoenix organization. The NBA began promoting him as one of the sport's top attractions.

In 1999, Suns management worked with Kidd on how to improve the club. Jason successfully recruited free agents Penny Hardaway and Oliver Miller. These acquisitions appeared to give the Suns the size Phoenix needed to compete in the tough Western Conference. But Ainge shocked everyone by quitting two months into the season. His replacement was 36-year-old Scott Skiles, the youngest head coach in the NBA. Skiles stepped in and guided the Suns to a 40-22 finish.

Jason continued his All-Star play until a broken right ankle seemingly ended his season in March. For the second year in a row, he earned All-NBA First Team honors and led the NBA in assists. He also set a new career-high by pulling down just over seven rebounds per game, an average better than 17 of the league's 29 centers. Hardaway, Chapman, and Gugliotta also spent significant time on the injured list. But thanks to improved play by Shawn Marion, Johnson's comeback from retirement, and the energy of Skiles, Phoenix made the playoffs with a record of 53-29.

Once in the postseason, there was speculation that Kidd might make an appearance in the first round against the Spurs. Suprisingly, the Suns took a 2-1 lead without Jason. He returned for Game 4 and helped Phoenix eliminate San Antonio. In 31 minutes, Kidd contributed nine points, 10 rebounds and three steals. The underdog Suns were outmatched by the Lakers in the next round. One of Jason's brightest moments came in Game 4 when he recorded the first playoff triple-double (22 points, 16 assists and 10 rebounds) of his career. Once again, Phoenix fell to the eventual NBA champions, as LA took the title.

Soon after the playoffs ended, Kidd was off to the Olympics in the summer of 2000. Named a tri-captain of Dream Team III, he led the U.S. squad to a gold medal in Sydney. Though the Americans went 8-0, they survived some close battles. Jason got all of his All-Star teammates involved, and averaged six points, five rebounds and four assists per game.

In 2000-01, the Suns got off to a hot start, winning seven of their first eight games. But the season quickly became a soap opera of off-court drama. Hardaway was accused of waving a gun in a woman's face. Robinson, the team's top scorer, was convicted of a DUI. Even bigger headlines focused on Kidd. In January of 2001, police arrested Jason for assaulting his wife Joumana in anger during a domestic dispute. The story was covered by the national media, including regular updates on ESPN. Kidd quickly issued a public apology at a press conference with his wife at his side. Jason told the media that they planned to stay together and work out their problems.

Kidd pleaded guilty to a domestic abuse charge and was ordered to attend anger management classes for six months. He completed the mandatory counseling and continued to attend on his own, and it was rumored that Kidd had given up alcohol. He and his wife were both active in their church and were thought to have completely reconciled. Jason left the team for several days but when he returned, Phoenix experienced a resurgence. With the Suns encouraging him to shoot more, Kidd became a dangerous scorer. He scored 30 or more points six times during the year, including a career-high 43 at Houston.

Phoenix responded to their floor leader's inspiring play and ended the year at 51-31. Jason pushed his scoring average to 16.9 points per game and still led the NBA in assists. In the process, he joined John Stockton, Oscar Robertson and Bob Cousy as the only players to lead the NBA in assists for three consecutive seasons.

In the 2001 playoffs, the Suns faced the powerful Sacramento Kings. After winning the first game on the road, the Kings won three straight to take the series. Another early playoff exit gave team executives an excuse to trade Kidd. The Suns and owner Jerry Colangelo had grown very protective of the team image and even though Jason had made great strides in rebuilding his public relations, management wanted him out of town. Never mind that Phoenix had made the playoffs in each of Kidd's five seasons.

In June, Phoenix dealt Jason and Chris Dudley to New Jersey for Stephon Marbury, Johnny Newman, and Soumaila Samake. Kidd answered plenty of questions about his desire to join the Nets. Why would a veteran from California who played in Dallas and Phoenix want to play in New Jersey? The Nets, similar to the Mavericks in 1994, were a losing team before Kidd's arrival.

Kidd led the 2001–02 Nets to an impressive 52–30 record, and assembled perhaps his best all-around season ever as he finished second to Duncan in the NBA Most Valuable Player voting. Many in the media argued that Jason deserved the MVP because of his impact in New Jersey. He helped transform the Nets from perennial last-place finishers into championship contenders virtually overnight. His contributions resulted in one of the greatest team turnarounds in NBA history. Under Kidd's leadership, the young Nets team rolled through the Eastern Conference playoffs and reached the NBA Finals, a career first for Kidd. New Jersey's Cinderella season ended without a title, as Jason and the Nets were swept in four games by the Lakers, who won their third consecutive NBA championship.

In November, Kidd was selected to participate in the 2002 USA Basketball Men's World Championship Team. However, he had to withdraw from the team due to an injury. Jason entered the 2002-03 NBA season in charge of a winning team. A free agent at the end of the season, he specified to the Nets how he wanted the team built, including trading away Keith Van Horn and Todd MacCulloch for Dikembe Mutumbo. Despite an injury to Mutumbo, the Nets re-established themselves as one of the East's top teams. Richard Jefferson and Kenyon Martin were maturing into stars, and the bench players took turns providing sparks. Kidd put together another MVP-type season including 12 double-doubles and 18.7 points, 8.9 assists, and 6.3 rebounds per game.

At 49-33, New Jersey was the second seed in the 2003 Eastern Conference playoffs, losing the top spot to Detroit. New Jersey faced Milwaukee in the opening round. Before the trade deadline, the Bucks had acquired Payton and paired him in the backcourt with Cassell. Behind Jason's 14-point, 14-assist performance in Game 1, the Nets made a statement with a 109-96 victory. Though the Bucks won Game 2, the New Jersey dismantled Milwaukee in five games.

Facing the Celtics next, New Jersey cruised to an impressive four-game sweep. The rested Nets entered the Eastern Finals with NBA title hopes. Against the Pistons—a low-scoring team with a suffocating defense—the Nets prepared for a physical series. New Jersey won the first two games in Detroit with a pair of two-point victories. Martin starred, opening eyes with his scoring ability. Sensing Detroit's despair, Jason seized complete control of the series. In Game 3, he burned the Pistons with 34 points, spearheading a 97-85 victory. Two days later he put Detroit out of their misery and the Nets back in the NBA Finals.

The national media gave the Nets no chance of beating San Antonio in the 2003 NBA Finals. Duncan was the NBA's best player, and when he teamed up with Robinson, the Spurs held a clear advantage in the paint. With point guard Tony Parker and swingman Manu Ginobili, San Antonio had a talented starting five.

Duncan and Parker were the stars of Game 1, as San Antonio posted a 101-89 victory. Kidd answered in Game 2, hitting two difficult bank shots in the fourth quarter to seal an 87-85 upset win. With the series shifting to New Jersey, the Nets had an opportunity to capture the title on their home floor. But Duncan scored whenever the Spurs needed a bucket, spotted the open man every time he was double-teamed, and dominated the boards at both ends.

New Jersey scratched out a 77-76 victory in Game 4 to even the series at 2-2. San Antonio, however, shut down Martin and Jefferson and dared Kidd to shoot more. Less effective when thinking shot first, Jason and the Nets sputtered on offense. When the Spurs won Game 5, the series appeared all but over. New Jersey tried to send the series back to Texas, but a 19-0 third-quarter run by the Spurs buried the Nets. San Antonio claimed the title and Duncan was named the MVP.

Kidd came back the next year and participated at the 2003 FIBA Americas Olympic qualifying tournament in Puerto Rico. Jason again led the team to a record of 10–0, bringing home the gold medal and a berth at the 2004 Olympics. Later in 2004, 10 years after Jason's departure, Cal retired Kidd's No. 5 jersey.

Meanwhile, Kidd's contract was up and he had the option of signing with another team. Jason thought about what was best for Joumana and the kids, too. After the 2001 birth of his twins, Miah and Jazelle, family became even more important to him. Ultimately, Jason had to decide between the defending champion Spurs and the Nets. When New Jersey offered a six-year, $99 million deal, Kidd began preparing to take another shot at a NBA title.

In 2003-04, New Jersey wound up 47-35, capturing the Atlantic Division title and the second seed in the playoffs. Jason finished the season averaging 15.5 points, 9.2 assists (tops in the NBA), and 6.2 rebounds. The Nets faced the cross-river Knicks in the first round and swept them in four games. That set up a showdown with Detroit, who attacked with a swarming defense to grab a 2-0 series lead. The Nets stormed back and won the next two to even the series. Kidd was sensational in Game 4, dropping a triple-double on the Pistons with 22 points, 11 assists and 10 rebounds. When the Nets took Game 5, they were one win from a third Finals appearance. But Detroit bounced back in Game 6, and then edged New Jersey in Game 7. Kidd was awful in the final game, shut out on 0-for-11 shooting.

Kidd wasn't pleased after the Nets let Martin walk to Denver as a free agent. In his place, they signed a collection of NBA retreads, none of whom were expected to have much of an impact. Kidd had to withdraw from the 2004 Olympic team due to another injury. On July 1, he underwent microfracture surgery to repair a damaged knee. When the 2004-05 season opened, New Jersey looked like it had nothing left in the tank. Jason was clearly unhappy and when Jefferson went down with a wrist injury, things looked bleak.

But Kidd made a full recovery and returned to action in December, when New Jersey acquired star swingman Vince Carter from the Toronto Raptors. Revitalized by his exit from Toronto, Carter regained his All-Star form. With the injured Nets facing the prospect of missing the playoffs for the first time since 2001, Carter and Kidd sparked the team to a late-season surge that earned them the eighth and final 2005 playoff berth in the East. Their season ended quickly as they fell in four games to the Miami Heat in the first round.

The Nets opened the 2005-06 season with the trio of Kidd, Carter and Jefferson intact. That gave New Jersey a great chance to contend in the NBA's ever-weakening Atlantic Division. Jason received much of the blame for a .500 start, but he ended up leading the Nets to wins in 17 of its last 22 games to end the season. He averaged 13.3 points, 8.4 assists and a team-high 7.3 rebounds. Carter, meanwhile, broke the team scoring record with 1,911 points and scored 20 or more

23 times in a row during one stretch. The Nets disposed of the Pacers in five games in the opening round of the 2006 playoffs. In the second round, the eventual champion Heat again eliminated the Nets.

In the off-season, Kidd again was the subject of criticism. Although he was still a solid defender and a superb floor general, there were questions about his motivation and his age. Jason hoped to answer them in the 2006-07 season. The development of Nenad Krstic as a fourth scoring option led some to predict the Nets would make another run at the NBA Finals. But New Jersey was quickly overwhelmed by injuries. Krstic suffered a season-ending knee injury, and Jefferson missed two months with a bad ankle. Jason was a key contributor in a another playoff push. He enjoyed an excellent year, averaging 13.0 points, 9.2 assists, and 8.2 rebounds. He was named to the All-Star team and the NBA's All-Defensive Second Team.

On January 9, 2007, Kidd filed for divorce against Joumana, citing "extreme cruelty" during their relationship. Jason contended intense jealousy, paranoia, and the threat of "false domestic abuse claims" to the police as reasons for the divorce. In February, Joumana filed a counterclaim for divorce, claiming that Jason—among countless instances of abuse—"broke her rib and damaged her hearing by smashing her head into the console of a car."

On April 7, 2007, Kidd and Carter became the first teammates to record triple-doubles in the same game since Michael Jordan and Scottie Pippen did it in 1989 for the Chicago Bulls. In the 2006-07 postseason, Jason notched his 10th postseason career triple-double against the Toronto Raptors. He tied Larry Bird for second all-time in career postseason triple-doubles as the Nets defeated the Raptors in six games.

Against LeBron James and the Cleveland Cavaliers, Kidd recorded his 11th postseason triple-double with 23 points, 14 assists and 13 rebounds, breaking the tie with Bird for second place on the all-time career list. He became the second player in NBA history to average a triple-double for an entire postseason, but Cleveland won the series and advanced to the Eastern Conference Finals.

In 2007, Kidd participated in the FIBA Americas Championship 2007. He helped the team to a 10–0 record where he brought home another gold medal and a berth at the 2008 Olympics in Beijing, China. With Kidd's help, Team USA averaged 116.7 points per game, and defeated their opponents by an average margin of 39.5 points. In Beijing, the team went undefeated in winning their first gold medal since 2000. The team, given the "Redeem Team" nickname because of failures in the 2002

FIBA World Championship and 2004 Summer Olympics, were once again crowned the best team in world basketball.

Kidd's USA basketball totals include an undefeated record of 56–0 including exhibition games. He has brought home two gold medals: one from the 2000 Sydney Olympics, and one from the 2008 Beijing Olympics.

After two trips to the NBA Finals, it seemed clear that the 35-year-old Kidd no longer felt the supporting cast in New Jersey was strong enough to contend for a championship, his ultimate career goal. He eventually told the team he wanted out. A deal with the Lakers seemed apparent, but LA refused to part with young center Andrew Bynum, a New Jersey native. On February 19, 2008, Jason was traded to Dallas, the team that originally drafted him. The Nets sent Kidd, Malik Allen and Antoine Wright to the Mavericks for Keith Van Horn, Trenton Hassell, Devin Harris, DeSagana Diop, Maurice Ager, two first-round picks, and $3 million in cash.

Kidd was voted by the fans to start in the 2008 All-Star game in New Orleans as a guard along with Dwyane Wade. On April 16, 2008, Kidd reached a new career milestone, achieving his 100th career triple-double in the final regular-season game against the New Orleans Hornets.

The Mavericks had gambled Harris and two first-rounders that Jason would be the player to get them back to the NBA Finals. That would be no easy task, as the Western Conference competition was fierce. The Lakers added Pau Gasol while Dallas failed to find front-court help for star Dirk Nowitzki. Kidd would have to find a way to win playoff games and learned this lesson when Dallas was blown out of the 2008 playoffs in the first round. A few days later, coach Avery Johnson was fired and replaced by Rick Carlisle.

In the 2008–2009 season, Kidd became just the fourth player in NBA history to reach the 10,000 assist milestone and is now the only player in NBA history with 15,000 points, 10,000 assists and 7,000 rebounds. Kidd passed Magic Johnson at third on the all-time assist list in a convincing 140–116 victory over the Suns. Kidd scored 19 points on 6–8 shooting with a season-high 20 assists, giving him a total of 10,142 career assists.

Jason led the Mavs to their ninth straight 50-win season but it was barely enough to secure a playoff berth. Dallas squeaked into the postseason by going undefeated at home late in the season. They defeated the Spurs in the opening round of the playoffs, but fell to the Denver Nuggets in the conference semifinals.

Kidd's contract with Dallas was up for extension after 2009. Were the Mavs all in to become a championship contender? Should they re-sign aging Jason to be their court leader for several more years? Owner Mark Cuban committed to doing everything it took to be a champion. Dallas signed the 36-year-old Kidd to another three-year deal worth $25 million. Cuban knew that Jason could help Nowitzki in ways he never had before. Even at Kidd's age, he could still quarterback a game as well as anyone in the league.

Midway through the 2009–10 season, Dallas dealt Josh Howard for three quality players—Brendan Haywood, Caron Butler, and Deshawn Stevenson. Along with Jason Terry, this gave Kidd and Nowitzki a real supporting cast. In November, Kidd moved into 2nd place on the all-time assists list in a win against the Houston Rockets, surpassing Mark Jackson on the list. Once again, Dallas stumbled in the playoffs. After beating San Antonio in Game 1, the Mavs lost the series in six games.

During the offseason, Dallas declared interest in LeBron James but failed to sign him. Instead, they traded for Tyson Chandler, a seven-foot center who would relieve congestion for Nowitzki. Along with Marion and Terry, Dallas headed into 2010–11 with an excellent lineup. In November, Kidd dished out his 11,000th assist, an alley-oop dunk to Chandler. Jason had rarely played for a team with all the pieces in place such as Dallas. He'd had his two cracks at a championship and missed. But Kidd never stopped grinding, no matter how older, injured, or tired he was. Fundamentally sound, he's continually pushing the ball up the court, searching for the next victory. Early in the season, Kidd spoke to his teammates -- not a single title among them -- and simply stated that "This team could be special."

The Mavs played consistently well all year and were among three teams (including the Thunder and Spurs) considered strong enough topple the two-time defending champion Lakers. With 57 wins and the third seed, Dallas anticipated a chance at #2 LA in the second round. After beating Portland in the opening round, Kidd and Dallas squared off against the Lakers as expected.

In Game 1, Kidd was energetic, focused, and intense. He was everywhere and in the fourth quarter he played brilliant defense on Kobe Bryant. Nowitzki made shot after tough shot, and Dallas squeaked out a 96–94 win. Among Jason's 11 assists was an alley-oop to Chandler that shook LA and changed the feel of the series. Two nights later, the Mavericks won Game 2 on LA's home floor. Dallas finished off the sweep at home, winning Game 4 in a blowout.

The 2011 Western Conference Finals matched Dallas against Oklahoma City. The Mavericks took the series in five games thanks to a 15-point fourth-quarter comeback to force overtime in Game 4. Dallas outscored the Thunder 11–4 in OT to take a 3-1 lead in the series. Back in Dallas, Jason had seven rebounds, 10 assists and just one turnover as the Mavs won the West with a 100–96 win.

The Mavericks earned a rematch of the 2006 NBA Finals and faced the Heat. Instead of Shaq and Payton, Wade's Miami teammates were James and Chris Bosh. Miami took Game 1 at home, but Dallas rebounded from a double-digit deficit in the final quarter to win Game 2, 96–94. Wade had a huge game but his premature celebration in front of the Dallas bench riled up the Mavs and sparked their spirited comeback.

When the series moved to Dallas, the Heat won Game 3 behind another superb effort from Wade. Worse yet, Nowitzki was suffering from flu-like symptoms as the Mavs got behind in Game 4. But Kidd and Dallas launched another fourth quarter rally. Working with Terry and Jose Barea, he helped five different Mavs score 10 or more points in a thrilling 86–83 win. Dallas went on to win Game 5 and Game 6 to win what eluded Kidd his entire career -- the NBA championship. Jason had 13 points, six assists and three steals in Game 5 and nine points and eight assists in the clincher. After 17 years in the NBA, the oldest guard ever to start in the NBA Finals finally had his ring.

"It's not real right now,' Kidd said after winning the crown he doubted he would ever see. Not at age 38, when the NBA had been passed on to jackrabbits Chris Paul, Deron Williams, Derrick Rose and Russell Westbrook. In the process, Jason validated his Hall of Fame career, the Mavericks, and his owner. "Do you think we won that trade yet?" Cuban said soon after the victory parade, citing the criticism he absorbed for giving up so much – twice – to get his point guard.

Looking back over his still-active career, Kidd does not need to score to dominate a game. He is a hustling, gritty and respected leader but his greatest asset is his floor vision. Like an NFL quarterback, he anticipates mismatches on a wide peripheral. Jason loves to push the tempo with speed and teammates are eager to run with him because they know they'll get many chances to score. Combined with his 6-4 size, amazing hands, defense and precision passing, he was a matchup nightmare for opponents.

Kidd is not a trash talker like Payton, nor does not have Payton's assortment of expressions and gestures. His language is cool and calm but he explodes to get a step on you. He does not show you up as he blows past you, and he doesn't have any kind of "gotcha" stare. In fact, he is more likely to be looking away from you after he beats you. You look away from him at your own risk.

Kidd owns a condo in Dallas on the 21st floor of the Azure, which he bought in 2008. In 2001, Jason bought an 11,952 square foot New Jersey home on the same street as his friend Vince Carter. Kidd has a good relationship with his oldest son, even though they live on opposite sides of the country. Jason Jr. is a high school basketball player in Southern California but also keeps in touch with half-siblings T.J. and the twins.

Jason is putting the finishing touches on a career that has spanned three decades—with two Olympic gold medals, 10 All-Star game appearances, 11,000+ assists, and 2,400+ steals. A triple-double machine, Kidd is among the all-time leaders for point guards in every significant statistical category. In his prime, J-Kidd was arguably the NBA's fastest end-to-end performer and was at his best in an up-tempo game. At 38, Jason has aged gracefully into a senior Maverick facilitator, who runs half-court offenses and occasionally makes a big three-pointer.

Kidd became the only player in NBA history to record at least 15,000 points, 7,000 rebounds, and 10,000 assists in his playing career. He is often ranked in Top 10 lists of the Greatest Point Guards of All Time and is a first-ballot Hall of Famer when eligible. In 2006, sixteen NBA analysts selected Kidd and nine other new additions to the NBA's 50 all-time greatest players list to honor the league's 60th birthday.

6

BILL RUSSELL

Legend. Leader. Ultimate teammate. Game-changer. Winner. Those are the words that begin to describe the unimaginable basketball career of Bill Russell. A Hall of Famer and considered one of the greatest players of all-time, Russell propelled his teammates to championships at Oakland's McClymonds High School, the University of San Francisco, the Olympics, and an incredible 11 times in the NBA.

William Felton Russell was born to Katie King and Charles Russell on February 12, 1934, in Monroe, Louisiana. At the time, racism was pervasive in Louisiana and blacks were not allowed many of the rights and opportunities whites took for granted. After his mother was confronted by police and threatened with arrest for looking too well-dressed, "as if she thought she was white," Russell's father decided to pack up and move his family north.

They sped off across the country and as the train left the South, Russell recalls a stunning experience. Further along the journey, the train stations stopped separating drinking fountains and restrooms for blacks and whites. After a brief stop in Detroit, the Russell family moved to the San Francisco Bay Area and settled in Oakland. Nine-year-old Bill, his parents and his older brother Charlie, started their new life. Charles set up his own trucking business, and Bill and his brother entered Oakland's public schools. The Russell boys attended integrated schools, made friends white and black, and enjoyed freedoms that surely would have been off-limits in the segregated South.

When he was 12, disaster struck as Russell's mother passed away quickly after an illness. Charles sold his business to be with his children while Russell escaped into books at the public library. A biography of Henri Christophe, a slave who led an insurrection and became emperor of Haiti in the early 1800s, made a life-long impression with Bill.

Russell first tried playing basketball on Oakland's playgrounds. An uncoordinated schoolboy, he showed no signs of becoming an elite athlete. His brother Charlie was becoming a star player at Oakland Tech, a mostly white high school. Bill was scrawny and awkward compared to Charlie. By 14, he grew to 6-foot-2 but only weighed 128 pounds of skin and bones.

When his grades suffered after the death of his mother, Bill was denied admission to Oakland Tech and instead enrolled in a neighborhood school, McClymonds High School in Oakland's flatlands. When he walked into the McClymonds gym during his sophomore year he looked like a one-iron, with rail-thin legs sticking out from his shorts, and skinny arms and hands dangling all over. "I was so skinny I had to keep moving in the shower to get wet," he would later say.

Bill tried out for the football, baseball, and basketball teams and even the cheerleading squad. None of those teams wanted him. A famous picture shows him adorning an Indian clothing and headdress to depict the McClymonds mascot, the Warrior. A natural right-hander, he switched to a lefty at the urging of an uncle, who felt the advantage lefties had in baseball might also work in basketball.

Although he was again cut from the junior varsity basketball team the following season, the frustrated Russell finally drew some attention from a coach. Despite his rawness, coach George Powles saw potential in Bill and kept him as the 16th man of a 15-man roster. Russell would wear the last jersey every other game, sharing it with a player named Roland Campbell.

In his book *Go Up For Glory*, Russell emphasized the significance of Powles and that event. "I believe that man saved me from becoming a juvenile delinquent. If I hadn't had basketball, all my energies and frustrations would surely have been carried in some other direction."

"For the first time in my life I came in contact with a white person who brought things down front, who talked to us realistically," Russell recalled. He would say repeatedly through the years that "I have never met a finer person. I owe so much to him it's impossible to express. This is a compassionate man, honest in the truest sense of the word."

Powles was a respected baseball coach who had coached high school players that later excelled in the pros. But Powles did not exactly have a high basketball IQ. He took over the JV team only after the principal demanded it. He was not really a fan of basketball but he did know how to mentor athletes and how to get the best out of them. On the first day of practice Powles brought the game rule-book with him. "Our very first practice there was no running, no jumping, no shooting," Russell said. "We were going to learn the rules." That rulebook came in handy when Russell started to perfect the art of shot-blocking.

Powles called benchwarmer Russell into occasional action, mostly during one-sided games. McClymonds spectators would chant, "We want Russell," and he would play his heart out only to hear laughter from the crowd. Bill wanted to quit, but Powles wouldn't hear of it. "[Allowing me to share the sixteenth uniform] was an act of kindness on Powles's part," Russell said. "He used to tell the guys I'd be a pretty good basketball player. But George was the only guy on the planet who thought that."

Powles instead gave Russell two dollars so he could join the Boys Club and play every day. Russell also practiced at Oakland's DeFremery Park. "What really attracted me to Bill was his smarts," said former playground director Bill Patterson. "He not only had the gift of gab, he liked to investigate. He was inquisitive about everything and anything. He was very outgoing, very outspoken." Russell also participated in teen meetings at the park that tackled topics such as drugs, alcohol, police, and race relations. Patterson believed Russell's strong social views grew from his attending those workshops.

By Bill's senior year Powles had moved up to coach varsity basketball -- another break for Russell. The team lost its other two centers to graduation so Russell won the job by default. "[Powles] may not have known too much about basketball, but he taught me a lot of other things, how important your heart and your attitude [are]," Russell later said while in college.

Now a varsity starter but clearly not a standout player, Russell immersed himself with love for basketball. He read every article about the game he could find, a habit he continued during college years. Russell continued to improve and he helped McClymonds win the 1952 Oakland Athletic League championship. Having never scored more than 14 points in a game in his Warrior career, Russell did not make the all-league team. Or the second team. Or even the third team, in a conference of only six teams.

One of Russell's teammates at McClymonds was Frank Robinson, who went on to Major League Baseball fame as a rookie of the year, an MVP in both leagues and a rare Triple Crown winner. Other famous McClymonds alumni include NBA players Antonio Davis and Paul Silas, Olympic gold medalist Jim Hines, Grammy-winning rapper MC Hammer, and MLB players Vada Pinson and Curt Flood.

In an era filled with racial tension, Powles also taught Russell and his teammates clean play and good sportsmanship, specifically because they were African-American and game officials might be watching them extra closely.

"No matter how unfair a call may be, keep your temper. Anyone who gets mad gets pulled out of the game," Powles explained to the team. "In order to be good at anything, you have to be a gentleman at it. If you play like the rest of the teams, you're going to be called roughnecks, dirty, and worse. If you get into a fight, it's a riot. So we're not going to get into any fights. We're going to play good, clean basketball. You are a Negro team, and the second there's any trouble everyone is going to blame you, whether it's your fault or not."

USF forward Dick Lawless had played three-on-three pickup against Russell at the Boys Club in Oakland before Russell's last year at McClymonds. Lawless gave USF coach Phil Woolpert rave reviews about the "string bean" who jumped and towered over the six-foot-four Lawless. Bill had blocked almost every shot the Oakland All-City player had taken. "I couldn't believe it," Lawless said.

Woolpert sent scout and former USF player Hal DeJulio, who also recruited Lawless, to evaluate Russell. Bill sparkled with a very strong performance at a game attended by DeJulio. It was Russell's last game at McClymonds -- vs. Oakland High -- and he played the game of his life, scoring 14 points. It was Bill's only career game in which he scored more than 10 points. What impressed DeJulio was that Russell scored eight consecutive points just before halftime and six in row at the end of the game as McClymonds won. Russell had a habit of being around the ball even though he frequently got tangled in his own legs and arms. DeJulio saw Russell as a game changer and liked his defense, jumping ability, and hustle.

Powles admitted to DeJulio after the game that no college showed any interest in Russell. "But I wanted him," DeJulio said. "I could feel the magnetism of the kid.

He was raw—couldn't shoot—but he was all over the court, tenacious, tough in the clutch. He had great timing. The tighter the game, the tougher Bill got. I could feel the electricity." DeJulio was so taken that he offered Russell a USF scholarship instead of another player he had come to scout. It was the only college scholarship offer Russell received and he accepted it gratefully.

Russell graduated from McClymonds in midyear 1952, and toured the Pacific Northwest with a group of California high school all-stars. Towering in height at 6-10, he became a more refined and accomplished player after returning to Oakland.

At USF, Russell developed into a dominant defensive force. He and his roommate K.C. Jones—who would also play with Bill on the great Celtics teams of the 1950s and 1960s—discussed basketball constantly. He made the varsity team in his sophomore year, and in his junior (1955) and senior year (1956), USF won two consecutive NCAA championships. The Dons first caught fire in Game #3 of Russell's junior year, running off a streak of 55 consecutive victories that extended well into his unbeaten senior year.

Russell literally changed the way college basketball was played when, after the 1955 NCAA tournament, collegiate coaches enacted two key rule changes in direct response to Bill's dominance. The free throw lane or "key" where defensive players were not allowed to linger was widened from ten feet to twelve, and "goaltending" (touching the ball on its downward arc toward the basket) was banned.

"I was an innovator," Russell said. "I started blocking shots although I had never seen a shot blocked before that. The first time I did that in a game, my coach called timeout and said, 'No good defensive player ever leaves his feet.' "

Russell was named the Most Valuable Player of the NCAA tournament in 1955, and was named an All-American in both 1955 and 1956. He was also a world-class high-jumper in college and came within centimeters of shattering the world record. Bill's 27 rebounds in USF's 83-71 victory over Iowa in the 1956 championship game remains a Final Four record, as does his 50 rebounds in the two games. Russell was a 20-20 man at USF, averaging 20.6 points and 20.3 rebounds in his 79 games.

Russell had come a long way from the days when he wasn't even wanted as cheerleader. As a graduating senior he was one of the players most coveted by NBA teams. Even the Harlem Globetrotters—who he considered more of a frivolous sideshow than basketball—offered him a $32,000 contract.

After graduation, Russell wasn't the first selection in the 1956 NBA draft. The Rochester Royals chose Sihugo Green, a guard from Duquesne with the No. 1 overall pick. At No. 2, Russell was drafted by the St. Louis Hawks, but he was immediately traded to the Boston Celtics. Boston coach Red Auerbach wanted Bill badly enough to trade two of his star players -- Ed Macauley and Cliff Hagen -- to St. Louis for their pick. The Celtics drafted Russell for his defensive abilities, rebounding and shot-blocking. The Hawks won the NBA championship in 1958 and Hagan had a standout career but in the long run, the Celtics got the better of the trade -- by far.

Russell did not accept the Celtics $19,500 rookie offer right away. He wanted to maintain his amateur status to compete in the 1956 Olympics in Melbourne, Australia. Bill missed the first month of his rookie season, serving as captain on the gold medal-winning Olympic team. The Russell-led U.S. team went 8-0 and its average margin of victory of 53.5 points is still an Olympic record.

Days after his return from Australia in December 1956, Russell married his girlfriend, Rose Swisher. They would have three children together, William Jr., Karen, and Jacob, before divorcing in 1973. On December 22, 1956, three weeks after the gold-medal game in Melbourne, Bill made his Celtic debut - he scored six points and grabbed 16 rebounds in 21 minutes. Most impressive was his blocking of three straight Bob Pettit shots in the second half. When Russell joined the Celtics, he was the only African-American on the team.

With the 6-foot-10 Russell at center, Boston became a nearly unstoppable force, winning 11 championships in 13 years during his reign, including the last two seasons with Bill as player and coach. The first title came in 1957, Russell's rookie season. The Celtics lost to the Hawks in 1958 -- primarily because Russell suffered an ankle injury in Game 3 of the Finals – and then won eight championships in succession.

In an era where scoring points was a major focus for many teams, Russell honed his abilities on defense and changed team strategies. He helped the Celtics win nine championships in his first 10 seasons and continually led the league in rebounding. Russell won MVP awards in 1958, 1961, 1962, 1963, and 1965. He also changed the way basketball was played and coached, with opposing players copying his techniques.

With the added defensive presence of Russell, the Celtics had laid the foundation for a dynasty. The team utilized a strong defensive approach to the game, forcing opposing teams to commit many turnovers which led to easy fast break points. Russell was an elite help defender who allowed the Celtics to play the so-called "Hey, Bill" defense. Whenever a teammate needed defensive help, he would shout "Hey, Bill!" Russell was so quick that he could run over for a quick double team and get back in time if opponents tried to find his man. He also became famous for his shot-blocking skills. The media called his blocks "Wilsonburgers," referring to the Wilson brand basketballs he rejected back into the faces of opposing shooters. Bill's shot-blocking also allowed the other Celtics to gamble on defense. If they were beaten, they knew that Russell was collapsing toward the basket. This approach allowed the 1957 Celtics to finish with a 44–28 season and a playoff berth during Bill's rookie year, the team's second-best record since the 1946–47 season.

Russell also received some negative press. Provoked unfairly by New York Knicks center Ray Felix during a game, he complained to coach Auerbach. Auerbach told him to take matters into his own hands, so after the next incident, Russell threw a punch that knocked Felix unconscious. Bill paid a $25 fine and was no longer the target of cheap shots. Russell had a good working relationship with all of his teammates, the notable exception being fellow rookie and old rival Tommy Heinsohn. Heinsohn felt that Russell resented him because Heinsohn was named the 1957 NBA Rookie of the Year. Many thought that Russell was more important to the Celtics, but Bill had also missed a chunk of the season.

In Game 1 of the 1957 Eastern Conference Finals, the Celtics met the Syracuse Nationals, led by Dolph Schayes. In Russell's first NBA playoff game, he finished with 16 points and 31 rebounds, along with an estimated 7 blocks (blocks were not yet an officially registered statistic). After the Celtics' 108–89 victory, Schayes quipped, "How much does that guy make a year? It would be to our advantage if we paid him off for five years to get away from us in the rest of this series." The Celtics swept the Nationals in three games to earn Boston's first appearance in the NBA Finals.

In the 1957 Finals, the Celtics opposed the St. Louis Hawks, led by Pettit and former Celtic Macauley. The teams split the first six games. In Game 7, Russell tried his best to slow down Pettit, but it was Heinsohn who netted 37 points and kept the Celtics alive. Bill's block preserved Boston's slim 103–102 lead with less than 45 seconds left in regulation, preventing elimination for the Celtics. In the second overtime, the Celtics won, earning their first NBA Championship in franchise history.

Russell was revolutionizing the game in ways that were clearly understood, even if they weren't always quantified through statistics. He was unrivaled at swooping across the lane like a huge bird to block or change shots by opponents.

In the 1957–58 season, Russell averaged 16.6 points per game and a league-record average of 22.7 rebounds per game. He was voted the NBA's Most Valuable Player, but curiously he was only named to the All-NBA Second Team. This would occur repeatedly throughout his career. The NBA reasoned that other centers were better all-round players than Russell, but no player was more valuable to his team. Bill also set the record for most rebounds in a half with 32, set against Philadelphia on November 16. The Celtics won 49 games and captured the top seed in the 1958 NBA Playoffs, and advanced to the NBA Finals against their familiar foe, the Hawks. The teams split the first two games, but Russell suffered a season-ending foot injury in Game 3. The Celtics surprisingly won Game 4, but the Hawks prevailed in Games 5 and 6, with Pettit scoring 50 points in the clincher.

His foot injury healed by the 1958–59 season, Russell continued his excellence, averaging 16.7 points and 23.0 rebounds per game in the regular season. The Celtics eclipsed last year's record by winning 52 games, and Bill's strong play again helped lead the Boston to the NBA Finals. In the Finals, the Celtics recaptured the title by sweeping the Minneapolis Lakers in four games. "We don't fear the Celtics without Bill Russell," said Lakers coach John Kundla. "Take him out and we can beat them... He's the guy who whipped us psychologically."

In 1959 Russell went to Africa on a tour with the State Department. The tour had such an impact upon him that he bought part ownership of a rubber farm in Liberia and named his baby daughter Karen Kenyatta after Jomo Kenyatta, the prime minister-designate of Kenya and former Mau Mau leader.

For the 1959–60 season, the Philadelphia Warriors drafted the era's other dominant center, 7-foot-1 Wilt Chamberlain. Chamberlain, who grew up in Philadelphia, made his NBA debut after an All-American career at the University of Kansas. Duels between Russell and Chamberlain quickly became one of the NBA's greatest on-court rivalries of all time. Chamberlain averaged a record-breaking 37.6 points per game in his rookie year. On November 7, 1959, the Celtics hosted the Warriors, and media called the faceoff between the best offensive and best defensive center the "Battle of the Titans." While Chamberlain outscored Russell 30-22, the Celtics won by nine points, and the game was hailed a "new beginning of basketball."

Chamberlain typically led the NBA in scoring and won two championships, but when it came to crucial playoff games, Russell's teams usually won. Their teams squared off against each other eight times in the playoffs, and seven times Bill's team walked off victorious. Chamberlain often scored 30 points or more in a game, but Russell would collect 20+ rebounds, block 6-10 shots, and dish out another half-dozen assists. Bitter rivals on the court but in reality, they were friends. The Celtics and Warriors traditionally played each other in Philadelphia on Thanksgiving Day, and Russell and some of the Boston players ate turkey dinner at Chamberlain's house cooked by Wilt's mother.

Russell's legendary battles with Chamberlain lasted for over a decade. They met 142 times, with Bill scoring 23.7 points and grabbing 14.5 rebounds per game, compared with 28.7 points and 28.7 rebounds for Chamberlain.

In 1960, Russell's Celtics again broke their regular season wins record with 59 and met the Warriors in the Eastern Conference Finals. Chamberlain outscored him by 81 points in the series, but Boston won the series 4–2. In the Finals, the Celtics again took on the Hawks, winning 4–3 for their third championship in four years. Bill grabbed 40 rebounds in Game 2 -- an NBA Finals record -- and added 22 points and 35 rebounds (more than all Hawks starters combined) in the deciding Game 7, a 122–103 victory for Boston.

In the 1960–61 season, Russell totaled 16.9 points and 23.9 rebounds per game and the Celtics finished the regular season at 57–22. Boston defeated the Syracuse Nationals 4–1 in the Eastern Finals. The Lakers had worn out the Hawks in a seven-game Western Conference Final, and the Celtics easily won another championship, in five games. As Bob Cousy, Bill Sharman, Tom Sanders, Sam Jones and Frank Ramsey shot a horrid 23-68 from the field, Russell scored 30 points on 17 shots and grabbed 38 rebounds in the Game 5 clincher.

In 1961-62, and now in his fifth year as a pro, Russell scored a career-high 18.9 points per game to go with 23.6 rebounds. Meanwhile, Chamberlain set new records with 50.4 points per game and 100 points in a game. But the Celtics became the first NBA team to record 60 wins in a season, and Russell was again voted the NBA's Most Valuable Player.

The Celtics matched up with the Warriors in the East playoffs and the teams split the first six games. In Game 7, Sam Jones sank the winning shot with two seconds left that won the series for Boston. In the Finals, the Celtics again opposed the Lakers with star forward Elgin Baylor and star guard Jerry West. Again the series went seven games and again Game 7 was tied in the final seconds when the Lakers missed an open shot that would have won L.A. the title. Russell had the unenviable assignment of defending Baylor with little front court help, as three Celtic forwards - Loscutoff, Heinsohn and Tom Sanders - had fouled out. In overtime, another Boston forward, Frank Ramsey, fouled out and Russell was essentially playing with reserves. But Bill and fifth forward Gene Guarilia effectively pressured Baylor into missing his shots. Russell scored 30 points and tied his own Finals record with 40 rebounds in a 110–107 overtime win that gave the Celtics another championship.

After the 1962–63 season, the Celtics lost point guard and leader Cousy to retirement. They drafted John Havlicek for his similar skill set. Russell, who averaged 16.8 points and 23.6 rebounds per game, won his fourth MVP award, and also earned MVP honors at the 1963 NBA All-Star Game with his 19-point, 24-rebound performance for the East. Bill led the Celtics to the 1963 Finals where they again defeated the Lakers, this time in six games.

In 1963–64, the Celtics finished with a league-best 58–22 record. Russell scored 15 points and grabbed a career-high 24.7 rebounds per game to win the rebounding title for the first time since Chamberlain entered the NBA. Boston disposed of the Cincinnati Royals 4–1 to advance to the NBA Finals, and then beat Chamberlain's recently relocated San Francisco Warriors 4–1. It was the Celtics' sixth consecutive title, a streak unmatched in U.S. professional sports. Bill called the Celtics' 1964 defense "the best of all time."

Russell continued to sparkle during the 1964–65 season. The Celtics again broke their own record with 62 wins, and Russell averaged 14.1 points and 24.1 rebounds per game, another rebounding title and his fifth MVP award. In the playoffs, Boston faced Philadelphia in the Eastern Finals. The 76ers had recently traded for Chamberlain, bringing him home to Philadelphia. In Game 5, Russell racked up 28 rebounds, 10 blocks, seven assists and six steals. In another dramatic Game 7, the Sixers were down 110–109, and Russell turned the ball over. Philadelphia's Hall of Fame guard Hal Greer inbounded, John Havlicek stole the ball, and Boston broadcaster Johnny Most screamed "Havlicek stole the ball! It's all over! Johnny Havlicek stole the ball! The Celtics had an easier time in the NBA Finals, winning 4–1 against the Lakers. In Game 2, Russell was 10-11 from the field with 25 rebounds and 10 assists as the Celtics won 129-123.

After Chamberlain signed a $100,000 a year contract for three seasons in 1965, Russell said he would retire unless he got paid at least one dollar more. The Celtics eventually increased their contract offer from $75,000 to $100,001, and Russell signed.

"It wasn't a matter of Wilt versus Russell with Bill. He would let Wilt score 50, if we won. The thing that was most important to him was championships, rings and winning," said Havlicek on ESPN's SportsCentury.

In 1965–66, the Celtics won an incredible eighth consecutive NBA championship. Boston again beat Chamberlain's 76ers 4-1 in the East Finals, and went on to win the NBA Finals in yet another pressure-packed seven-game showdown with the Lakers. During the season, Russell averaged 12.9 points and 22.8 rebounds per game, the first time in seven years he totaled less than 23 rebounds a game.

Following NBA Championship No. 8, Auerbach retired as head coach of the Celtics. Still acting as general manager, Red wanted former Celtic Ramsey as coach, but Ramsey was busy running three nursing homes. Cousy was his second choice but he refused, saying he had no interest in coaching his former teammates. Auerbach's third choice Heinsohn also said no, because he did not think he had Russell's respect but Heinsohn proposed Bill as a player-coach. When Auerbach asked his 32-year-old center, Russell said yes. He became the first African-American head coach in NBA history, and said to the media "I wasn't offered the job because I am a Negro, I was offered it because Red figured I could do it." The Celtics' championship streak ended that season at eight, however, as Chamberlain's 76ers won a record-breaking 68 regular season games and overpowered the Celtics 4–1 in the 1967 Eastern Finals.

The Sixers played run-and-gun versus the Celtics, shocking the vaunted Boston defense by scoring 140 points in the Game 5 clincher. For Russell, it was the first "real" loss in his career (he had been injured in 1958 when the Celtics lost the NBA Finals). He visited Chamberlain in the locker room, shaking his hand and congratulated him. That game still had a positive for Bill. After the loss, he accompanied his grandfather through the Celtics locker room, and the two saw white Boston player John Havlicek taking a shower next to his African-American teammate Sam Jones while discussing the game. Russell Sr. broke down and cried and said how proud he was of Bill, being coach of an organization in which blacks and whites coexisted peacefully.

When the Celtics failed to win the 1967 championship, many in the basketball world questioned the concept of player-coach and whether Russell was a good enough bench coach to win a title. He remained with the team, contributed 12.5

points and 18.6 rebounds per game, and in the 1967-68 season Coach Russell and the Celtics regained their dominance with another NBA championship, Bill's first coaching championship.

In the 1968 Eastern Finals, the top-seeded 76ers had the home court advantage over the Celtics and were slight favorites. National tragedy struck as Martin Luther King was assassinated on April 4, 1968, the day before the series. With eight of the ten starting players being African American, both teams were stunned and expected the series to be postponed. The Celtics won 127–118 on April 5. In Game 2, the 76ers tied the series with a 115–106 win. In Games 3 and 4, Philadelphia won, with Chamberlain often defended by backup center Wayne Embry, causing the media to conclude Russell was exhausted.

No NBA team – even the Celtics -- had ever come back from a 3–1 deficit. But the Celtics rallied back, winning Games 5 and 6 fueled by Havlicek's intensity and assisted by terrible 76er shooting. In Game 7, Boston stunned Philadelphia and its fans with a history-making 100–96 defeat, making it the first time in NBA history a team lost a series after leading 3–1. The Celtics then beat the Lakers 4–2 in the Finals, giving Russell his 10th world championship in 12 years. Russell was named *Sports Illustrated's* Sportsman of the Year. After losing for the fifth consecutive time against Russell and his Celtics, West said, "If I had a choice of any basketball player in the league, my No. 1 choice has to be Bill Russell. Bill Russell never ceases to amaze me."

In 1968, Russell felt the cumulative stress of being a star player, NBA coach, a Civil Rights advocate, husband, and father. He began to suffer the emotional effects of widely reported violence occurring during the late 1960s. His 35-year-old body had become vulnerable to injuries. His marriage soured. He questioned his purpose in his life.

Russell pulled himself together to score 9.9 points and grab 19.3 rebounds per game, but the "old" Celtics slipped to 48–34, the team's worst since 1956. Finishing fourth in the Eastern Conference, it appeared the Boston dynasty was crumbling. In the playoffs, however, Bill and his Celtics found a way to do what they do best: win championships. The Celtics scored upsets over the 76ers and Knicks to again battle the Lakers in the 1969 Finals.

Determined to finally beat Boston, the Lakers added Chamberlain to established stars Baylor and West. In Games 1 and 2, Russell ordered single coverage on West, who burned the Celtics for 53 and 41 points, both Laker wins. Bill then called to double-team West, and Boston won Game 3. In Game 4, the Lakers were looking to go up 3-1 and were leading by one with seven seconds left. On the last play, Sam Jones's buzzer beater equaled the series. As in so many Celtics playoffs in the 1960s, it all came down to Game 7. Lakers owner Jack Kent Cooke wrankled the Celtics by printing game leaflets including "proceedings of Lakers victory ceremony." Russell used a copy as extra motivation to fire up his crew.

In the first half, Russell was shut out by Chamberlain, 15-0, but the Celtics still led, 59-56. Taking control in the third quarter, they extended their lead to 100-85 with nine minutes left. With under six minutes remaining, Chamberlain suffered a knee injury and was replaced by Mel Counts.

Russell didn't think Wilt was seriously injured and that he should not have left the court. "Wilt's leaving was like a misspelled word at the end of a cherished book," Russell wrote later. "My anger at him that night caused great friction between us later."

West was also limping heavily after a Game 5 thigh injury. The Lakers launched a desperate rally but coach Butch van Breda Kolff kept Chamberlain on the bench until the end of the game. After the Lakers closed to 103-102, the Celtics' Don Nelson got a lucky bounce off the rim, Bill grabbed a key rebound, and made a block in the final seconds. The Celtics and Russell won their 11th title, 108-106, and the thousands of balloons that Cooke stored in the Forum rafters were never released in victory. Chamberlain finished with 18 points and 27 rebounds, compared to Russell's six and 21.

The 35-year-old Russell had played and coached all 48 minutes. The "King of the Rings" claimed his 11th championship in 13 years. It was his last game, a walkoff Finals upset against maybe the greatest scorer ever and one of the great teams of all time. His knees stricken with arthritis, the game turned out to be Russell's last hurrah. With nothing left to accomplish and nothing left to prove, he announced his retirement later that summer. The Celtics fell to sixth place the following year, 26 games behind New York.

Days later, 30,000 Boston fans cheered their returning heroes, but Russell was not there. He said he owed the public nothing and cut all ties to the Celtics. Russell left Boston without a coach and a center and sold his retirement story for $10,000 to *Sports Illustrated*.

NBA fans could not believe Russell was gone. He changed the game by jumping to block shots, and playing dominating defense with a technique and intelligence unheard of in his era. Shot-blocking, rebounding, and overall defense were Bill's specialties. He had springy legs -- he high jumped 6'10" in college -- and pursued the ball relentlessly, five times leading the NBA in rebounds per game. He was a player who could dominate a game without scoring. Russell proved that offense really is only half the game. With Bill clogging the middle, opposing teams were forced to shoot from outside, unable to find an easy lay-up.

Russell became synonymous with winning: 11 championships in 13 years, unmatched by anyone in sports. His USF, Olympic and Celtics teams were an astounding 28-2 in games when a loss meant elimination. USF was 9-0 in two NCAA tournaments, the U.S. was 2-0 in Olympic elimination games and the Celtics were 17-2, including 10-0 in Game 7's.

Russell averaged 15.1 points over 13 NBA seasons. His career high was 18.9 points during the 1961-1962 season, the year Chamberlain averaged 50.4. It was consistent winning and making teammates better that distinguished Bill from the other greats and made him the NBA's MVP five times. Russell's Celtics won seven of their eight playoff series against Chamberlain's teams. They were 4-0 in Game 7's against him.

A 12-time All-Star, the angular center amassed 21,620 career rebounds, an average of 22.5 per game, second in NBA history to Chamberlain's 23,924. In a game against Syracuse in 1960, he grabbed 51 boards in one game, 49 in two others, and had a dozen consecutive seasons of 1,000 or more rebounds. Records of blocked shots weren't kept until the 1970s, but officials estimated that Russell blocked 8-10 shots a game for most of his career. He fouled out just 24 times in 963 regular-season games.

"The idea is not to block every shot," said Bill. "The idea is to make your opponent believe that you might block every shot."

In 1970, Russell was named to the NBA's 25th Anniversary All-Time Team. In 1974, he was elected to the Basketball Hall of Fame. In 1980, Bill was named to the NBA 35th Anniversary All-Time Team and the Pro Basketball Writers Association of America ranked him "the Greatest Player in the History of the NBA," higher than Chamberlain, Baylor, Oscar Robertson, or Cousy. He was voted No. 18 among great athletes of the 20th century by ESPN SportsCentury's distinguished 48-person panel. Frank Deford, the renowned sportswriter, called Russell "the very epitome of ability and victory in sport."

Russell once said the athletes he admired were Ted Williams, Jackie Robinson and Sonny Liston. In 1999, he said Jim Brown was the athlete of the 20th century.

As gifted as the former McClymonds teammates Russell and Frank Robinson were, their accomplishments were as much sociological as they were athletic. It was Russell who took over as player-coach, thus becoming the first African-American coach in any major U.S. pro sport. Nine years later, Robinson debuted as Major League Baseball's first African-American manager with the Cleveland Indians. In 1968, Russell became the first African-American coach to win an NBA championship. Bill was a pallbearer at Jackie Robinson's funeral in 1972 and spoke at Chamberlain's funeral in 1999.

"What's more important than who's going to be the first black manager," said Russell. "Is who's going to be the first black sports editor of the New York Times?"

An outspoken advocate for civil rights, Russell was one of the first celebrities to openly wear his black pride, when "Negro" was still the socially accepted term of the era. At least twice, he refused to play a scheduled game when his black teammates were given inferior hotels or restaurants, and since Bill's play increased ticket sales, problems with accommodations were quickly fixed. He spoke at the 1963 March on Washington, and established an off-season sports training camp open to kids of any color.

Upon retirement, Russell worked as a coach and sports commentator. "I wasn't doing anything on weekends anyway," he quipped. Russell also coached the Seattle SuperSonics for four seasons and the Sacramento Kings for one, making the playoffs twice. He wrote two autobiographies -- *Second Wind* and *Go Up For Glory* -- as well as *The Memoirs of an Opinionated Man* and *Nothing But A Man*.

His brother Charlie became a playwright whose most famous work, *Five on the Black Hand Side*, was produced in New York and made into a movie featuring Godfrey Cambridge. His daughter Karen is a TV reporter and commentator with the *Huffington Post*. His second wife, 1968 Miss USA Dorothy Anstett, was white, which made their marriage controversial at the time. They married in 1977 and divorced in 1980. His third wife, Marilyn, died in 2009.

In 1972, Russell's No. 6 Celtics jersey was raised to the famous rafters of Boston Garden. At Bill's urging, it was a private ceremony, and no fans were invited. On

May 26, 1999, Russell allowed his No. 6 to be re-raised to the top of the Fleet Center with an estimated 12,000 fans attending the ceremony. In 1992, 28 years after signing his last autograph, Russell began signing again - reportedly for $2 million over seven years.

"Young man, you have the question backwards," Russell said when asked how he would have fared against Kareem Abdul-Jabbar.

In 2010, President Barack Obama awarded Russell the Presidential Medal of Freedom, the nation's highest civilian honor. The medal is presented to people who have made notable contributions to U.S. interests, from cultural achievements to security matters. President George H.W. Bush, poet Maya Angelou and investor Warren Buffett, and 11 others also received the honor.

"These outstanding honorees come from a broad range of backgrounds and they've excelled in a broad range of fields, but all of them have lived extraordinary lives that have inspired us, enriched our culture, and made our country and our world a better place," Obama said. "I look forward to awarding them this honor."

Russell, giving back to those where it all started for him, made a rare appearance at his alma mater McClymonds High School to greet and congratulate members of the Warriors state champion basketball team. Currently living in Seattle, he also appeared at the Oakland Museum to preview the opening of "Sports: Breaking Records, Breaking Barriers," a Smithsonian Institution traveling exhibition.

During the 2009 NBA All-Star Weekend in Phoenix, NBA Commissioner David Stern announced that the NBA Finals MVP Award would be named after Bill Russell.

The debate of who is the greatest player will rage on forever. Some point to the fact that Russell might be overrated because he played with Hall of Famers such as Sam and KC Jones, Heinsohn, Cousy and Havlicek. But those players will tell you they are in the Hall of Fame because of Russell. As for Boston before and after Bill, they didn't win before him and stopped winning when Russell left. After 11 titles in 13 years, the Celtics missed the playoffs two years in a row.

What made Russell special is that his game was designed to help teammates excel. He'd adjust how he played based on the opponent and who was in the game. He expected nothing different from what they were used to. Russell used unique skills to cover up many of his teammates' mistakes, making them more effective players within their role.

From an embarrassingly awkward teen to NCAA champion to leading the Boston Celtics to 11 championships in an NBA career that included five MVP awards, Bill Russell's life has been an incredible journey. Decades after his retirement, his name is synonymous with teamwork, defense, and most of all – winning. Throughout his brilliant career on and off the court, Russell has been a shining example for people all over the world, leaving behind a legacy of improving the game of basketball -- and society -- for many generations to follow.

8

WILLIE STARGELL

Popular and powerful, Willie Stargell crushed 475 Major League home runs for the Pittsburgh Pirates. Stargell was a hulking Hall of Fame slugger and his titanic blasts helped popularize the term "tape-measure home run" during the 1960s and 1970s. His leadership helped the Pirates win two world championships and earn him a National League MVP award.

Wilver Dornell Stargell was born on March 6, 1940, in Earlsboro, Oklahoma. His first name combined elements of his parents' names -- William Stargell and Gladys Vernell Russell. At the age of six, Stargell's parents divorced and upon their separation, Willie was passed about the United States between relatives. One of his longer stays landed him in Orlando, Florida with an aunt. Unable to bear her own children, his aunt withheld Stargell from contact with his mother and assigned him daily household chores.

Stargell and his aunt moved to Oakland and later to nearby Alameda. In his autobiography *Willie Stargell*, he described his aunt as cruel and harsh but nevertheless credited her with creating a sense of discipline within himself. Meanwhile, Stargell's mother was persistent in regaining custody and, at the age of 12, Willie was reunited with Gladys and her new husband in Alameda.

For the majority of his youth, Stargell lived in governmental project housing in Alameda. His family struggled with poverty but the area was safe. Willie's humble upbringing in the projects also brought the experience of working hard to survive. Having to contribute money for his family's expenses, he labored at several jobs, gaining a strong work ethic and leadership skills. There were also social aspects of the projects, including Willie's passion – baseball.

"In my heart I knew I wanted to play baseball and my mom would be the first to tell you," said Stargell at his Hall of Fame induction speech in 1988. "She probably thought something was wrong with her son when I used to tell her that all I wanted to do was play baseball and she knew that playing baseball was fine but the percentages of anybody getting to the big leagues were far fetched and the numbers were very small."

Pickup games in the Alameda streets eventually sharpened Stargell's skills and he made his Encinal High School team. Two other major leaguers -- Tommy Harper and Curt Motton -- were Willie's high school teammates. Stargell and Motton, who played for the Baltimore Orioles, would later be on opposing teams during the 1971 World Series.

"You always talked about Stargell. He was the highlight of the city," said Alameda native Nick Cabral, an Encinal classmate of Stargell in the 1950s. "You can talk to many, many people in Alameda about Willie."

Stargell's powerful bat and productive high school baseball career for the Jets did not go unnoticed. Neither did he. A giant of a man who stood 6-foot-4 and weighed well over 200 pounds in his prime, Willie was a natural home run hitter. He attended Santa Rosa Junior College for a year, but dropped out in 1959 to sign with the Pittsburgh Pirates as an amateur free agent for a bonus of $1,500. He had attracted the attention of Pirate scouts while at Encinal and they placed Stargell into their Class D minor league farm team.

Oakland athletes of the 1950s and 1960s such as Frank Robinson, Joe Morgan and Bill Russell experienced very few examples of racism growing up in the multicultural Bay Area and were stunned by their early experiences of playing professionally in the south and mid-west. Stargell's experience was no different. He reported to the Pirates' minor league affiliate in the Class D Sophomore League. There he discovered a different world, which included angry and hateful attitudes toward African-Americans.

Baseball slowly began to integrate after Jackie Robinson's 1948 colorline breakthrough, but the small Southwestern cities where Stargell played in the minor leagues were well behind the times. Since many hotels in these areas did not allow black guests, Willie often slept on small cots and even on outdoor areas of private homes owned by other blacks. Restaurants also discriminated and he often had to wait in kitchens, where he was given small scraps. At other times, Stargell had to wait on the bus while the white players visibly ate in roadside diners. Examples of segregation were infuriating to Willie. The severe racial hostilities that Stargell and other black players experienced left the slugger feeling understandably bitter. "We had to drink from different fountains," he recalled. "There was always a constant reminder that we were less superior."

On one occasion, Stargell was threatened by a Ku Klux Klan member who placed a shotgun against his head and threatened to blow his brains out if he took the field in Plainview, Texas that night. "I couldn't understand how the color of my skin could make people hate me for something I had never done," Stargell said about the incident. "But I played an outstanding game," he told the *Montreal Gazette*. "I had made up my mind that if I was going to die, I was going to die doing what I really wanted to do. I didn't want to go back to the projects in California. I wanted to play baseball, in the worst way."

Stargell played for minor league teams in New Mexico, Iowa, and Texas. Willie first arrived in the major leagues as a 22-year-old call-up on September 16, 1962. A massive but fleet outfielder with a surprisingly strong arm, Stargell showed flashes of thunder at the plate. He would remain in Pittsburgh for 21 seasons and never played for any other team.

"Coming out of Oakland, California and Alameda, California, little did I know that once given the opportunity to do something that I had dreamed of for many years of putting on a uniform," he said in Cooperstown. "Something unique happened after spending four years in the minor leagues honing my skills so that I could get to the big leagues and perform such as so many of these great men behind me who have made such a tremendous impact on the game."

In the late 1960s and 1970s, the talented Pirates were perennial National League contenders. At the heart of their lineup was the dynamic duo of Stargell in left field and the pioneering Latin American superstar Roberto Clemente in right field. Willie soon became known not for just smashing home runs over the fence, but hitting it out of stadiums. His mastery of the longball paid off in 1964 with his first of seven All-Star selections.

When the New York Mets unveiled their brand new Shea Stadium in 1964, Stargell christened the stadium with its first home run on April 17. His power production rose steadily over the 1960s, and he grabbed the spotlight with towering long balls. Willie still holds the record for the longest home run ever hit in several different National League parks, the longest the game had seen since Mickey Mantle's slams of the 1950s. His resume of tape-measure blasts included two launched completely out of Dodger Stadium, one of the toughest parks for hitters. Only four home runs have ever been hit out of Dodger Stadium, and Stargell hit two of them. The first came on August 5, 1969 off Alan Foster (506 feet) the longest ball ever hit at Chavez Ravine. The second left on May 8, 1973 against Andy Messersmith (493 feet). Said Dodger starter Don Sutton: "I never saw anything like it. He doesn't just hit pitchers, he takes away their dignity."

Stargell's career was off to a solid start based on his natural abilities. He really didn't fully commit himself to disciplined practice and preparation after he suffered a poor 1968 season, batting only .237. "I wondered if all I wanted to be was a player who stayed around for 10 years and didn't really accomplish anything," Stargell told *Baseball Digest*, "Or did I want to make myself a real good ballplayer, an outstanding ballplayer?" He realized that he had been cheating himself. "Once I used to think that all there was to this game was to show up at the ballpark a couple of hours before gametime, go through the usual routine, play nine innings, and go home."

Stargell's batting stance became famous with fans for the way that he "windmilled" his bat in a rhythmic circle. As he awaited a pitch, Stargell rocked in the batter's box, pointing and motioning his bat for a moment toward center field, and then repeat the process. The windmilling ritual seemed to calm Willie and help his timing. The constant motioning of the bat must have inspired fear in opposing pitchers, as they envisioned the behemoth ready to unleash his ferocious knockout swing. Stargell used an unorthodox grip of holding only the knob of the bat with his lower hand. This provded extra bat extension. When most players would use a simple weighted bat or two in the on-deck circle, Stargell swung a sledgehammer, adding another level of intimidation.

Soaring home runs defined Stargell the player, but they only scratched the surface of portraying his overall contributions to the game, including his role of teammate and public citizen. Willie had a gift for connecting with fans. After he purchased a restaurant in The Hill section of Pittsburgh in 1970, he created a special promotion. The restaurant would give free chicken to anyone placing an order at the time he hit a home run. The promotion prompted legendary Pirates announcer Bob Prince to proclaim, "Spread some chicken on the hill!" when Stargell homered. Willie reached out to all Pirate fans by regularly talking baseball with them prior to games and happily signing autographs.

"I have to say my greatest honor was the moment that I arrived in Pittsburgh for what I thought was the most grandest exhibition of how a city can open its arms to any one individual," said Stargell of the Iron City. "I came in through the Fort Pitt tunnels and it was most beautiful thing that I had ever observed. Pittsburgh didn't know an awful lot about me but I certainly knew an awful lot about Pittsburgh. I knew there was a tradition, a very proud tradition. It wasn't a fancy place because the people are real. If you went out and did what was expected of you, you could win the admiration of that city."

Stargell impressed the baseball world with his home run power and ability to drive in runners. People within the game also took notice of Willie's willingness to devote time to humanitarian causes as did teammate Clemente. During the 1970-71 off-season, he took part in a USO tour for American soldiers in Vietnam. Locally, he performed volunteer work for the Job Corps and the Neighborhood Youth Corps in Pittsburgh, working in the ghettoes as part of the "War on Poverty." He became president of the Black Athletes Foundation, an organization dedicated to helping African-American athletes negotiate better contracts and endorsement opportunities. Willie also served as chief spokesman for the Sickle Cell Anemia Foundation, successfully raising public awareness of a disease that had little publicity in the 1960s. "So many people know so little about this disease," Stargell said to the *New York Times*. "These people live a short, miserable life. We need the help of everyone."

Stargell's production at the plate grew more consistent in 1969 and in 1970, when he homered in all 13 NL stadiums. But it was in 1971 that his strength, experience and talents came together to make him a star. He reported to spring training in the best physical condition of his career and blasted his way through a record-breaking April. He enjoyed the best season of his career with 48 home runs and 125 runs batted in, and became a key player in the Pirates quest to win a World Series title.

On June 25, 1971, Stargell hit the longest home run in Veterans Stadium history off Jim Bunning as the Pirates won 14-4 over the Philadelphia Phillies. The spot where the ball landed was eventually marked with a yellow star with a black "S" inside a white circle until Stargell's 2001 death, when the white circle was painted black. The star remained in place until the stadium's 2004 demolition.

At the 1971 All-Star Game in Detroit, NL manager Sparky Anderson of the Reds was discussing his lineup with the media. When he came to Stargell, he said that "He's got enough power to hit home runs in any park -- including Yellowstone."

The Pirates advanced to the 1971 World Series against the Baltimore Orioles, but Stargell struggled mightily. He batted only .208 for the series with no home runs. Never giving up and trying to contribute in any way possible, Stargell reached base in Game 7 and scored the winning run that finally gave the Pirates their world championship.

Stargell emerged as the Pirates' new team captain after the plane crash in 1972 that killed Clemente as he delivered relief supplies to Central American earthquake victims. Willie's leadership could be felt throughout the clubhouse, and was given the nickname "Pops." Father figure to "The Family," as the Pirates of that era were called, he helped boost team morale which further added to his likeability. Noted far and wide for his sense of humor—he once flashed a time-out sign at the umpire on finding himself well short of second base—Stargell developed an easy rapport with the Pirate squad at a time when American baseball clubhouses were not always peaceful places. "To keep factions from developing," Pirates player Phil Garner was quoted as saying in the *New York Times*, "you have to have someone that the blacks respect and the whites respect, and the guy that puts that all together for us is Stargell." According to Newsday, Willie told the team that "you can't play piano with just white keys or black keys."

One of the elite sluggers in the major leagues, Stargell's personal life included many challenges. His first of three marriages ended in divorce, his second wife suffered a paralyzing stroke. Willie had four daughters -- Wendy, Precious, Dawn, and Kelli -- and he also had a son named Wilver, Jr. One of his daughters was stricken with sickle-cell anemia. Stargell himself frequently suffered from poor health even during his years on the field.

He won his second National League home run title in 1973. Stargell achieved the rare feat of leading the league in both doubles and homers with more than 40 of each. He was the first 40-40 player since Hank Greenberg in 1940 although other players have done so since, including Albert Belle, the only 50-50 player.

Until 1974, Stargell shuttled between the outfield and first base and took over at first base full-time in 1975. From 1964 through 1979, Willie hit at least 20 homers every season but one. Stargell would uncork a powerful swing that would almost take the air out of the ballpark but on 1,936 of those at-bats, Stargell failed to make contact, the fifth most strikeouts in baseball history. Willie always had fun playing the game. "They say *play* ball not *work* ball," was a favorite quote of his. Another was "Sometimes I hit him (Steve Carlton) like I used to hit (Sandy) Koufax, and that's like drinking coffee with a fork. Did you every try that?"

As team captain, Stargell originated the practice of giving his teammates "stars" for their caps for an exceptionally good play or game. These stars became known as "Stargell Stars." The practice began during the turbulent 1978 season, as the Pirates stormed back from 11.5 games back in August to challenge the first-place Phillies for the division title. Against Wayne Twitchell of the Montreal Expos, Willie hit the only fair ball ever to reach the upper deck of Olympic Stadium. The seat where the ball landed (measured at 535 feet) was painted yellow, while the other seats of the upper deck remained red.

The 1978 season was scheduled to end in a dramatic four-game showdown against the rival Phillies. The Pirates had to win all four games to claim the title. Following a Pittsburgh sweep of the Friday night double-header, Stargell belted a grand slam in the bottom of the first inning of Game 3 to give the Pirates an early 4-1 lead. Pittsburgh, however, relinquished that lead and eliminated themselves from contention for the pennant. Stargell called that team his favorite ever, and declared that Pittsburgh would win the World Series the following year.

Pirates manager Chuck Tanner said of Stargell, "Having him on your ball club is like having a diamond ring on your finger." Teammate Al Oliver once said, "If he asked us to jump off the Fort Pitt Bridge, we would ask him what kind of dive he wanted. That's how much respect we have for the man."

"I had two very special managers, Danny Murtaugh, and Chuck Tanner," said Stargell. "I learned an awful lot from both of these men. Not to say that the other managers that I played for were not equally important but there was just something very special about both of them."

Everything once again clicked for the Pirates in 1979. When most players his age had already retired, Stargell hit 32 home runs. At his urging as captain, the team adopted the Sister Sledge song "We Are Family" as the team anthem, a choice so successful that the team became known as "The Family."

Similar to the 1978 season, the Pirates once again came back from the dead in 1979. They were in last place in the division at the end of April, and clawed their way into a first-place battle with the Montreal Expos during the latter half of the season.

Pittsburgh thrilled fans with many come-from-behind victories along the way to clinch the division pennant on the last day of the season. In the World Series, the Orioles took a 3-1 lead, but Stargell capped the season by hitting a dramatic home run in Baltimore during the late innings of Game 7 to seal another Pirates championship. The home run credited Stargell with the winning runs in Game 7's of both Pirate titles. In addition to his NLCS and World Series MVP awards, Willie was named the co-MVP of the 1979 season (with St. Louis' Keith Hernandez). He is the only player to have won all three trophies in a single year. At 39, he was the oldest MVP ever. He shared the *Sports Illustrated* "Sportsmen of the Year" award with Pittsburgh Steelers quarterback Terry Bradshaw.

"Now when they walk down the street, the people of Pittsburgh can say that we come from a city that has nothing but champions!" said Stargell during the celebratory parade in the city after the 1979 World Series. That was the year that Pittsburgh won both their third Super Bowl and second World Series of the 1970s.

By the start of the 1980 Pirates season, Willie Stargell was 40 years old; he played a part-time role over the next three seasons and retired at 42 in 1982. The man who once described hitting as "they give you a round bat and a round ball and tell you to hit it square" hung up his cleats for the last time.

When Stargell ended his career in 1982 with 475 home runs and 1,540 runs batted in, the Pirates permanently retired his uniform No. 8. By the end of his career he had successfully won two World Series, six division titles, and was the most prolific home run hitter of the 1970s. On 11 occasions, Willie had 90+ RBI seasons. His 475 home runs in a Pirate uniform are 174 more than the next highest total in team history, Ralph Kiner's 301. Observers believe his home run total was depressed by playing in Forbes Field, whose deep left-center field distance was 457 feet. Clemente estimated that Stargell hit 400 fly balls to the warning track during his eight seasons in the park. In addition, the short fence in right field was capped by a screen more than 20 feet high. The Pirates moved into Three Rivers in mid-1970, and it boosted Willie's power numbers. He hit 310 of his 475 career home runs from 1970 (at age 30) until his retirement.

Stargell served as a coach and as the general manager's assistant in the Pirate organization in the 1980s and 1990s, and also coached in Atlanta for former Pittsburgh manager Chuck Tanner. After retirement, Stargell spent several years as a coach for the Atlanta Braves. While working for the Braves, he heavily influenced future Hall of Famer Chipper Jones.

Stargell was inducted into the Baseball Hall of Fame in 1988, only the 17th player to be elected in his first year of eligibility. He was selected on 82.4 percent of the ballots returned to the Baseball Writers Association of America. In order to be elected, a player must be named on at least 75 percent of the ballots.

"All that hard work and sacrifice. I never thought it would feel like this," said Stargell, on hearing the Hall of Fame news in 1988. "I never thought I would have a day like this. I'm overwhelmed."

A seven-time All-Star, Stargell ranked 81st on *The Sporting News* list of the 100 Greatest Baseball Players, and was also nominated as a finalist for the Major League Baseball All-Century Team. Stargell was the last person to throw out the first pitch at Pittsburgh's Three Rivers Stadium before its demolition.

Plagued by high blood pressure and kidney disease, Willie Stargell died on April 9, 2001 in Wilmington, North Carolina. After a long bout with illness, Stargell passed away on the same day he was supposed to attend opening ceremonies of Pittsburgh's PNC Park and the unveiling of a 12-foot bronze statue of himself outside its left-field entrance. Meanwhile, it was a sad day at Encinal High School where the school's football and baseball facilities are called Willie Stargell Field. Television cameras were set up at different spots around the school's campus. The flag in the front of the school stood at half-staff. The baseball team said a prayer before practice. The city of Alameda lost its hero.

Few players retired from pro baseball as highly respected as Willie Stargell. "Pops" was known to be as good of a person as he was a player, and he was the personification of class. One of the great sluggers in baseball history, Willie ranks among the Top 20 home run hitters ever to play the game. Over the course of a two-decade career with the Pittsburgh Pirates, Stargell set numerous team records and led the Pirates to two World Series championships. Yet, as important as his exploits on the field were, the role Willie played in the clubhouse, as comedian, friend, inspirational figure, diplomat, and eventually team captain was immensely valuable to the club. Noted baseball historian Roger Angell called Stargell "the most admirable player of his time."

BAY AREA LEGENDS

8

JOE MORGAN

Joe Morgan was the little engine that powered the "Big Red Machine," the 1970s Cincinnati Reds that some experts consider the greatest team of all time. Morgan was that rarest of all-around talents: a Gold Glove infielder who could hit for All-Star average and power, not to mention elite speed on the basepaths. Praised for his baseball intelligence throughout his 22-year career, "Little Joe" has proven successful off the field as well, building profitable businesses and an Emmy-winning broadcast career.

Joseph Leonard Morgan was born on September 19, 1943, in Bonham, Texas. The first of six children born to Leonard and Ollie Morgan, he would later call his family the main source of his strength. While Joe was still a child of 10 in 1953, the Morgans left Texas, headed west and settled in an Oakland neighborhood.

Morgan attended Brookfield Elementary School and although he grew up in an African-American Oakland neighborhood, he said in his 1993 autobiography that he never really experienced any childhood incidents of segregation or racism. His was a tight-knit family, and all of its members -- especially the children -- received much support from each other. Morgan led a typical childhood filled with school studies and sports. Joe, his sister Linda, and their father Leonard regularly attended Oakland Oaks minor league games. The Oaks, a charter member of the Pacific

Coast League, played at Oaks Park at San Pablo and Park Avenues, just a few blocks from the Morgan residence. Joe was an active participant in sports and social programs at the Brookfield Community Center.

Morgan was an avid player of "Army Ball," a three player variant of stickball. He participated in many sports pickup games, but did not play on an organized team of any kind until he was 13 years old. "I always wanted to be a big-league ballplayer," Morgan said. "We lived on 61st Street, not far from the old Oakland Oaks Park, and my father took me to five games a week when the Oaks were home. When I was 12, Jackie Robinson was the only thing in my mind. I had a Jackie Robinson glove and a Jackie Robinson bat. Then when I was 14, I became a Nellie Fox fan. He was a little guy, and I figured that if he could make it to the big leagues, I could, too. Nellie and I later became good friends."

Leonard Morgan, a tire and rubber worker, was a former semi-pro baseball player and he told his son that the secret to success was the ability to do everything well. Leonard would express his dislike for those players who hit home runs but were not concerned about their defense or those who could run fast but did not seem to take pride in their hitting. "Be everything," Leonard would say. Joe took his father's advice and learned to beat teams in more ways than anyone else.

"Joe has always been 'Little Joe' around Oakland," recalled childhood friend Ron Trentler. "We played baseball together as kids down at Elmhurst Park on 98th Avenue in East Oakland. I still remember our first meeting. I was captain of the Dukes in the Young American League, and I had first choice when we selected players for the teams. I didn't know Joe Morgan from a hole in the ground, but I had heard a lot of the other captains say they were going to pick Joe Morgan first. So I beat them to it and picked Joe for the Dukes. Then this little kid popped out of the crowd, the smallest kid around, and I thought I had been taken. After I picked my team, I asked each kid where he wanted to play. Joe said, 'I play second base,' not 'I want to play second base.' He batted .900-something for the Dukes every year, and he always led the league in home runs. There were no fences at Elmhurst Park, and Joe hit line drives over the first baseman's head that didn't stop rolling until he had raced around the bases."

"Joe was overly aggressive on the field in those days. One day he wanted to pitch, so I said, 'OK, I'll play second base.' Well, the first two batters hit balls that went right through my legs for errors, and Joe was hopping mad. He walked out to second base and glared at me. 'They weren't even bad hops, Ronnie,' he said.

'Here. You take the ball and go back to pitching, and I'll show you how to play second base.'"

As a teenager, Morgan played in the local Babe Ruth League and was a standout at Castlemont High School. He tried out for semi-pro teams while in high school, but was never offered a contract. Oakland was a hotbed of young baseball talent in the middle 1950s and Morgan, a leading hitter and base stealer on his teams, should have quickly attracted major league attention. But Joe had a major handicap in the eyes of most scouts—Morgan was barely five feet, seven inches in height. Little Joe was always an afterthought when scouts came to town. "I was a star," he wrote in his autobiography. "I played second, short, hit for average and power, stole bases, but I might as well have been playing in Little League." Even later, he never looked the part of a star. "Whenever someone had something kind to say, there was nearly always a double edge to it: I was known as a good, little player with emphasis on the second of the two adjectives."

After his senior year at Castlemont, Morgan enrolled in Oakland City College in 1961 intending to study business and played on the baseball team. He also attended classes at Merritt College and California State University at Hayward from 1961 to 1963. Joe was already showing a knack for playing on successful teams. His high school team won the Oakland Athletic League championship and his college team won its divisional title. Morgan earned both academic and athletic honors. Developing into an outstanding player in college, rumors surfaced about him playing professional ball.

Nothing serious happened until a scout from the expansion Houston Colt .45s -- later to become the Houston Astros -- saw something in Joe despite his small stature. In 1963, Houston offered amateur free agent Morgan a $500-a-month minor league contract along with an unspectacular signing bonus of $3,000. He was nonetheless delighted by the chance to play big league ball. His father was excited for his son, but Morgan's mother took a more practical view. She was concerned that once Joe left college to play pro ball he would never return and would never earn a college degree. Morgan promised her he would re-enroll and bring home a diploma.

In 1963, 19-year-old Morgan began his minor league instruction in Moultrie, Georgia, in the Georgia-Florida Class A league with the Colt .22s. Within a month he was sent to the California League's Modesto Reds, and then to the Durham (South Carolina) Bulls in the Carolina League. In his first at-bat with Durham, he hit a game-winning home run. He batted a sizzling .332 with 107 hits in 95 games for the Bulls.

For the first time in his life, Morgan experienced the ugliness of racism while playing in Georgia and South Carolina. The hotels, restaurants, and drinking fountains were segregated, and he endured obscene racist insults. He was the only black player on the team, had to endure verbal taunts from fans, and was prohibited from staying in all-white motels on the road. It shook him so much that he briefly considered leaving baseball. He thought of quitting, wanting no part of a team or league that would tolerate prejudice, but his coaches and teammates rallied behind him, saying that they did not agree with the segregationists. Morgan vowed to maintain his focus, to seek refuge in teamwork, and to work harder than ever. Through his dedication to perfecting his baseball skills and the fear that he would be letting down his parents, Joe found the strength to continue.

Morgan was 20 years old when he briefly broke into the big leagues on September 21, 1963, with the Houston Colt .45s against the Philadelphia Phillies. He delivered an important hit in the late-season game. "Have you no shame?" said Phillies manager Gene Mauch to his team. "You just got beat by a guy who looks like a Little Leaguer!"

Morgan appeared in only eight games that season with Houston, collecting six hits in 25 at-bats for a .240 batting average. The left-handed hitting second baseman made another brief appearance with the Colt .45s in 1964, struggling terribly at the plate with a .189 batting average in 37 plate appearances. For most of the season, Joe was assigned to Class AA ball in the Texas League with the San Antonio Bullets and had a spectacular year, batting .323 with 12 home runs, 42 doubles, 90 RBI and 47 stolen bases. He was named the Texas League Most Valuable Player.

In 1965, Morgan skipped AAA minor league ball and reached the big leagues for good with the recently renamed Astros in their modern new stadium, the Houston Astrodome. Although the dome was a difficult place to play due to bad lighting, poor field, and cavernous dimensions, Joe studied it from every angle. "I was a player of the future, ideally suited to these new [larger] parks," he wrote in his book. He worked on his running, base stealing and defense on baseball's newest surface, Astroturf.

Early in his career, Morgan had trouble with his swing because he kept his back elbow down too low. Houston teammate and former childhood idol Nellie Fox suggested to Joe that while at the plate he should flap his back arm like a chicken as a reminder to keep his elbow up. Morgan followed the advice, and his flapping arm became a familiar sight to baseball fans. He hit .271 in 1965 with 14 home runs, 100 runs scored, and a National League-leading 97 walks. He finished second in Rookie of the Year voting to Los Angeles Dodgers second baseman Jim Lefebvre.

"I owe Foxie a lot," said Morgan. "His attitude was the main thing. I was where he would be if he was four or five years younger. Whenever I did anything wrong, Foxie came over and talked to me about it. And when I did something good, he was there to pat me on the back."

Morgan was off to a hot start in his first full major-league season, but he also had to face the indignities all rookie ballplayers must endure: pitchers threw at his head, older teammates kept him in his place, and he had to battle his own mood swings. Joe knew that he was still up against another barrier -- his race. Even though he started playing ball 20 years after Jackie Robinson broke the big league color barrier, Morgan and other African-American players were still targets of racism.

Morgan wrote in his autobiography that "You could not help being aware that no matter how fairly others tried to treat you, it was always a struggle to go from town to town, hotel to hotel, restaurant to restaurant. Even in those places where black people were allowed, there was still an underlying sense of being out of place. It was as though, without anyone ever saying it, a black player could just feel the silent judgments and objections to his presence. When you stayed in the same hotel with your teammates, when you went to a bar or a restaurant, there was always that unvoiced question, 'Why is he here?'"

In 1966, Morgan collected 89 walks and hit .285 with a 41% on-base percentage despite missing 40 games with a fractured knee cap. He was selected to the NL all-star team but did not play due to injury. Wedding bells rang the following season for Morgan. "I met Gloria when I was in the 11th grade and she was in the ninth," said Joe. The Castlemont High sweethearts wed in 1967 and were married for 21 years.

After missing virtually all of the 1968 season with a new knee injury, Morgan struggled somewhat when he returned to the Astros in 1969. Although he smashed 15 home runs, scored 94 runs, stole 49 bases, and walked 110 times, he batted only .236 and saw his strikeout total increase rise to 74, the second highest total of his career. Joe was more effective in 1970, raising his batting average more than 30 points to .268, and finished among the NL leaders with 102 runs scored, 102 walks, and 42 stolen bases. Finally healthy, he helped the National League win the '70 All-Star game by singling, scoring, and turning a double play in a tight 5-4 game.

Although Morgan produced another solid season in 1971, the Astros wanted more power in their lineup. Additionally, manager Harry Walker considered Joe a troublemaker. After seasons of tension between Walker and the players of color on the Houston team, Morgan was at his boiling point. He had endured much prejudice but had no tolerance for bigotry when it extended to his own manager.

On November 29, 1971, Morgan was traded to the Cincinnati Reds as part of an eight-player blockbuster deal, a trade that at first made him upset, but that later would prove to be a huge boost to his career. Morgan was traded to the fourth-place Reds in exchange for Lee May, Tommy Helms, and Jimmy Stewart. Along with Morgan, the Reds also received pitcher Jack Billingham, outfielders Cesar Geronimo and Ed Armbrister, and infielder Dennis Menke.

After the deal was done, Reds manager Sparky Anderson told General Manager Bob Howsam, "You just won the pennant for the Cincinnati Reds." Sparky was right. While the Astros got power-hitting Lee May, the deal is now considered one of the most one-sided trades in baseball history. To this day it is considered an epoch-making deal for Cincinnati and one of the worst trades in Astros history. Geronimo became their regular center fielder and Jack Billingham soon joined the top of the Reds pitching rotation.

The trade with division foe Houston facilitated a shift in Reds team identity to "small ball" over home run hitting. The team's offense had been predicated largely on the slugging abilities of May, Johnny Bench, and Tony Perez. Cincinnati management felt a need to complement its long ball threats with a smart and aggressive baserunner such as Morgan. With Joe and outfielder Pete Rose – both among the best at getting on base –now batting 1-2 in the lineup, the trade turned out to be one of the shrewdest moves the organization ever made. Morgan added unusual power for a second baseman as well as speed on the basepaths and excellent defense. He gave the Reds leadership in the infield and an outstanding glove up the middle. Furthermore, Geronimo gave them a very solid defensive centerfielder, and Menke enabled them to shift third baseman Perez back to his more natural position of first base. With all the pieces in place, Cincinnati became the National League's dominant team for the next several seasons.

When Morgan left the Astrodome for Cincinnati's Riverfront Stadium, his production increased significantly. Morgan had his first truly great season in 1972, batting .292, stealing 58 bases, and leading the league with 122 runs scored, 115 bases on balls, and a .419 on-base percentage. Morgan was an All-Star and team MVP for the NL Champion Reds, leading the league in runs scored, walks, and on-base percentage. Cincinnati battled the Oakland A's in the 1972 World Series but lost in seven games. Joe followed that up by batting .290 and scoring 116 runs in 1973, while also establishing new career highs with 26 home runs, 82 runs batted in and 67 stolen bases.

Despite the presence of several other All-Star players in the Reds lineup, Morgan was arguably the key to the Big Red Machine. In 1972, Anderson recognized the many unique talents his new second baseman possessed. Morgan was not only a fine fielder and an exceptional baserunner, but he was also an extremely patient hitter and a very intelligent and instinctive player. Anderson gave Morgan a green light, giving him total decision-making freedom both at the plate and on the basepaths.

"People don't realize it, but it's harder to be a good base stealer than it is to be a good hitter," said Morgan. "Everyone loves to hit. The first thing every kid does is reach for a bat. Same thing in the big leagues. Hitting is fun. When you're a base stealer, you've got to do more things than a hitter. A base stealer has to go back to the bench, take a seat and study the people directly involved with his base stealing. The rhythm of the pitcher, the habits of the catcher, the motions of the first baseman. By doing this, when the base stealer finally does get on base, he will not have to waste two or three pitches figuring out what's going on. I almost always steal on pitchers, not catchers, and there's a good reason for that. If I get my jump against the pitcher, the catcher has very little chance of throwing me out. Sometimes he will make a great throw and nail me, but there's never a time when I'm counting on a catcher to make a really poor throw, a throw so bad that I'll be able to get in there safely."

Anderson says that there was no divine intervention. He did not have a brilliant dream or an epiphany while lying around at the pool. He had simply tried so many lineup combinations, it was inevitable that he'd come across an effective one. On Independence Day, 1975 he unveiled what would become one of the most famous lineups in baseball history.

1. **Pete Rose**, 3B
2. **Ken Griffey**, RF
3. **Joe Morgan**, 2B
4. **Johnny Bench**, C

5. **Tony Perez**, 1B
6. **George Foster**, LF
7. **Davey Concepcion**, SS
8. **Cesar Geronimo**, CF

The Reds rarely lost when Sparky ordered that lineup. They went 57-25 the rest of the season to win the NL West title by 20 games. The lineup had all the elements of greatness: Rose's hustle and spark, Griffey's speed, and Morgan's blend of everything. Bench provided power, Perez RBIs, Foster home runs, Concepcion great plays at shortstop, and Geronimo defensive grace in centerfield. During the '75 season, the Reds produced two notable streaks: they won 41 out of 50 games in one stretch, and once went a month without committing an error.

The famed 1927 New York Yankees had four Hall of Famers in their Murderers' Row lineup — including Babe Ruth and Lou Gehrig — and averaged more than six runs per game. The Brooklyn Dodgers of the 1950s had the balance of Jackie Robinson, Duke Snider, Pee Wee Reese and Roy Campanella. But the lineup Anderson put on the field had something more. The Reds had three African-Americans in the lineup, three Latin Americans, two Caucasian Americans and Bench had Native American blood. They truly were the Great American Ballclub.

"We made fun of each other," recalled Bench. "We made fun of the way players talked. We made fun of the way players looked. But when it came down to it, we were the Cincinnati Reds. We were…the Big Red Machine."

Morgan powered the Reds to the 1975 World Series championship, erasing Cincinnati's playoff disappointments of 1972 and '73. He capped the season by driving in the winning run in Game 7 against the Boston Red Sox in one of the most exciting World Series of all time. Joe came to bat in the bottom of the ninth, with the score tied, two outs, and with the potential winning run on third base. In that clutch situation, with a 2-2 count, he singled to drive in the run that gave the Reds the World Series championship.

Morgan won his third straight Gold Glove award for fielding excellence, led the league with 132 walks, finished second in stolen bases with 67, was fourth in hitting with a .327 average, was fourth in runs scored with 107, drilled 17 home runs, drove in 94 runs and grounded into only three double plays, a league low. Joe also tied Perez as the Reds leader in game-winning hits with 15 as the club won 108 games. For his brilliant season, Joe earned the NL's Most Valuable Player Award, which he won 321-154 over Philadelphia's Greg Luzinski in the most lopsided

MVP balloting in league history. The Reds rewarded him by increasing his salary to $200,000 for the 1976 season.

Morgan was even better in 1976, establishing career highs with 27 homers and 111 RBIs, batting .320, scoring 113 runs, stealing 60 bases, walking 114 times, and leading the league with a .453 on-base percentage and a .576 slugging percentage. He became the first second baseman in the history of the National League to win back-to-back MVP awards.

In the 1976 postseason, the Reds ran the table with an undefeated 7-0 record. In the World Series, Cincy crushed the Yankees in four games, having already swept the Phillies in the NLCS in three games. The Reds won 102 games and were at the height of their power, one of the most impressive teams in baseball history. When the Reds swept the Yankees, Morgan hit .333 and slugged .733 as Cincinnati proved to everyone once again that they were undoubtedly MLB's superior team.

Morgan had his last big year in 1977, hitting 22 home runs, knocking in 78 runs, batting .288, and finishing among the league leaders with 113 runs, 49 stolen bases, 117 walks, and a .420 on-base percentage. By the time the dust had settled, he finished among the league leaders in runs scored, stolen bases, walks, and on-base percentage each season from 1972 to 1977. Joe also placed near the top of the league rankings in batting average twice and finished in the Top 5 in MVP voting four times. Morgan and Concepción both won four straight Gold Gloves, joining a select list of eight shortstop-second baseman combinations to have won the honor in the same season.

When baseball fans think of Morgan, who played with five different teams over the course of his career, they inevitably picture him in a Reds uniform. That is the team where he became nationally famous, playing in eight consecutive All-Star games, winning two World Series rings, four pennants and six division titles. Morgan calls the Reds of the 1970s the "best defensive team ever," with Bench, Morgan, Concepción and Geronimo all winning Gold Glove awards *five years straight* beginning in 1973. Joe used the smallest glove in the majors. It fit easily inside a standard infielder's model. "I got the idea from Nellie Fox," he said. Lacking an exceptionally strong arm, Morgan knew he needed to get rid of the ball quickly. "With a small glove, you know where the ball is all the time. The glove is the pocket."

Morgan also demonstrated leadership and enjoyed great chemistry with his Big Red Machine teammates. His definition of leadership is simple, and it doesn't involve loud histrionics. As he said in his book, "The only criterion for team leadership is the sense of absolute trust others have in a teammate that he will *always* put the team before himself, that everything he does on the field will clearly have the objective of winning in mind."

"People don't know Joe Morgan the baseball player," he said. "They don't know about Joe Morgan's dedication. There were times last year when I was hitting .330 and still went to the batting cage and hit for an hour or more because my swing was not where I wanted it. Ted Kluszewski is our hitting coach, and he stays on my case, which is cool. When he sees that I'm beginning to uppercut the ball, he tells me, 'Joe, you're hitting funky,' and off we go to the cage. I have a batting tee in my garage, too, and I hit tennis balls off it in an attempt to keep my swing level. I also watch films for hours on my video machine, studying my swing to pick out little things that might keep me from falling into a slump. In fact, I've even got a little poem that I like to recite to myself when I'm slumping. It goes like this:

> *See the ball before you stride,*
> *Let it go if it's outside.*
> *If it's a curve, it should break down,*
> *So jack up and hit it downtown.*

"Believe me, Ted and I have worked long, long hours to get all the fly balls out of my swing. You know what they say: 'When a little guy hits the ball in the air, it comes down and he's out, but when a big guy hits the ball in the air, he trots around the bases.' What power I have comes from my bat speed; in fact, my bat is probably as fast as anyone's in baseball. The quickness in my bat actually makes the ball jump off it. This quickness also allows me to have a fraction more discipline at the plate than other guys, because I know I can wait longer to see the ball. And the longer I wait, the better I am able to determine whether the pitch is going to be in or out of the strike zone."

In the late 1970s, the Dodgers won back-to-back NL West titles and the Reds began to dissolve. Perez was the first to go, followed by the firing of Anderson. Morgan's offensive productivity began to decline in 1978. He led Cincinnati to one last playoff berth in 1979, losing in the NLCS to the Pittsburgh Pirates. It was Joe's turn to leave in 1980 when he became a free agent.

"I cherish the fact that I'm considered the most complete player in the game," Morgan said. "I'm not saying the 'best' but the 'most complete.' The 'best' is always a matter of opinion, but the 'most complete' is right there on paper. I'm blessed with the ability to do more things than other people can. I'm not the best power hitter in baseball, not the best hitter for average, not the best fielder, not the best base stealer. But when you put all those things together, no player in baseball can do any two of them better than Joe Morgan. Take stealing. Forget how many bases people steal. No one in the world can steal a single base better than I can. If there's one base to be stolen with two out in the bottom of the ninth inning, I can steal it."

In 1980, Morgan returned to Houston to help turn the attitudes and performance of the young Astros around. He hit only .243 and failed to make the NL All-Star team for the first time in nine years. Joe's tough talk to his teammates worked as they won the NL West title, but it drove a wedge between him and manager Bill Virdon, who thought Morgan was usurping his role. Later, in the final game of the 1980 NLCS, Virdon took Joe out of the lineup, a move that angered the proud veteran and which might have cost Houston a chance to go to the World Series. Philadelphia advanced, and Morgan vowed never to play for Virdon again.

In 1981, Morgan signed with the San Francisco Giants for two seasons, earning Comeback Player of the Year honors in '82 by hitting .289 with 14 home runs and a .400 on-base percentage at age 38. He grew up a Mays, McCovey, and Marichal era Giants fan. This made it particularly appropriate that Morgan's 1982 home run in the final game of the season knocked the rival Dodgers out of the pennant race and sent Tommy Lasorda into tears. He won the 1982 Willie Mac Award for his spirit and leadership. At the end of '82, several teams approached Morgan with manager opportunities but Joe instead opted to continue his playing career.

Morgan signed with the Phillies in 1983, where he rejoined ex-teammates Rose and Pérez. During the September stretch run, the Phillies' second baseman had a week where he batted .484 with 15 hits, six doubles, scored seven runs and drove in eight. He also had two home runs, both on his 40th birthday on September 19. Joe finished the season with 16 home runs and scored 72 runs. He appeared in his fourth and final World Series as Philadelphia lost to the Baltimore Orioles in five games.

In 1984, Morgan completed his career with his hometown Oakland Athletics. His 30 years as an amateur and pro baseball player ended almost exactly where it began — at the Oakland Coliseum, about a half-mile from Elmhurst Park. Joe played his final major league game on September 30, 1984 against the Kansas City Royals, doubling in his only at-bat against Mark Gubicza. He hit second in the A's lineup that day behind a rising young hometown star named Rickey Henderson.

During his career, Morgan played on no less than eight divisional champs, five NLCS winners, and two World Series champions. When he quit baseball, his 268 career home runs were a record for a second baseman and is currently second on that list. "Pitchers don't mind me stealing a base or driving in a run with a single or double. But I see it in their eyes when I'm circling the bases on a home run. They don't like a little man taking them downtown."

He also hit 449 doubles and 96 triples, excellent power for a middle infielder of his era, and was one of the finest base stealers of his generation. Morgan finished his career with 1,650 runs scored, 2,517 hits, 1,133 runs batted in, 689 stolen bases, 1,865 walks, a .271 batting average and a superb .395 on-base percentage. In addition to his prowess at the plate and on the bases, Morgan was an exceptional infielder, and locked up the Gold Glove Award from 1972 to 1976. He once played in a record 92 consecutive games without an error. He played in 10 All-Star games and established a record by getting at least one hit in seven consecutive All-Star contests.

Morgan had eight seasons with 100 or more runs scored, eight seasons with 100 or more walks, four seasons with at least 20 home runs and twice hit over .300. Additionally, he had 14 seasons with at least 20 stolen bases, nine seasons with at least 40 steals and five seasons with over 50 stolen bases. Joe rarely struck out (just 1,015 times, or about one every nine at-bats). He won two MVP awards, was in the running for six and was described by analysts as "the perfect second baseman" and "one of the most underrated and unappreciated players in baseball history."

Morgan began his television broadcast career in 1985, calling Reds games for Cincinnati's WLWT. On September 11, 1985, he and broadcasting partner Ken Wilson were on hand to call Rose's record-breaking 4,192nd career hit. In 1986, Joe became an announcer for the Giants and added another local gig when he joined the Athletics' broadcast team for the 1995 season.

The Reds inducted Morgan into the team Hall of Fame in 1987 and retired his No. 8 uniform. As a player, he had spent some of his off-seasons learning the ropes of the beverage distribution business. Joe was eventually granted a distributorship for Coors beer in Northern California known as Joe Morgan Beverage Company in 1987. He also established three Wendy's Restaurant franchises in Oakland between 1985 and 1988.

Success did not shield Morgan from adversity, however. While walking through Los Angeles International Airport in 1988, he was accosted by two undercover police officers, held in detention and accused of dealing drugs. Joe was not permitted to file a complaint until after the LAPD realized their mistake and let him go. He also contended he was roughed up by officers. In 1993, the Los Angeles City Council agreed to pay Morgan $796,000 to settle the suit.

After Joe and Gloria divorced in 1988, Morgan married Theresa in 1990 and they are still married today. The Morgan daughters are Angela, Lisa (first marriage), Ashley and Kelly (second marriage).

In 1988, Morgan became a national announcer for ABC, where he helped announce *Monday Night* and *Thursday Night Baseball*, the 1988 American League Championship Series, and served as a field reporter for the 1989 World Series between the Giants and A's. Morgan was on the field at San Francisco's Candlestick Park alongside Hall of Famer Willie Mays the moment the Loma Prieta earthquake struck at 5:04 p.m.

"The memory I have is that we're on the field. I'm with Willie Mays. We're doing the World Series and I'm getting ready to interview Willie before the first pitch and I remember Al Michaels is talking and they're saying, 'Joe, to you in five, four, three, two …' I think it got to two and then the earthquake hit, so it starts shaking. Willie Mays says in his high-pitched voice, 'Hey, man, let's get out of here.' I said, 'Willie, come on.' So we ran to the mound because I thought that would be away from everything, the center of the field. So we stood out there and obviously it calmed down. Again, I had been in earthquakes before, because I lived there, so I said, 'Willie, OK, let's get ready.' Willie said, 'I'm leaving.'"

"The truck had video of fires down by Fisherman's Wharf, the collapse of the Bay Bridge, the collapse over in Oakland. I could see all this stuff on individual monitors. Obviously now I'm in a panic. My family is over there, so it was just a devastating thing, and I remember driving home. I had a car taking me home and I remember driving through San Francisco, and it looked like a futuristic movie because the lights were all out, the street lights and the lights in the homes, and people were standing outside big old barrels with fire for light. The car that was driving me had a television in there, and I was watching. We didn't have cell phones and all that stuff at your disposal, so I wasn't sure about houses, family and all that stuff until I got across the bridge."

By 1990, Morgan became ESPN's top analyst and teamed with Hall of Fame broadcaster Jon Miller for *Sunday Night Baseball*. The two made a great pairing — Morgan brought an intelligent view of the game from the player's prospective while the gregarious Miller delivered smooth play-by-play mixed with quick wit.

In August, Morgan became the first second baseman to be elected to the National Baseball Hall of Fame since Jackie Robinson entered in 1962. Joe was inducted after receiving votes on 81.76% of the ballots. Only six other second basemen in history have been enshrined in the Hall of Fame. Morgan was inducted in his first year of eligibility along with Orioles pitcher Jim Palmer. The two players were only the 20th and 21st players ever inducted in their first year of eligibility.

"I take my induction ... as a vote for the little guy in the middle of the diamond, who doesn't hit 500 home runs," Morgan was quoted as saying in the *New York Times*. "I accumulated my stats for the team, not for myself. Although Willie Stargell was my hero and the reason I wore number 8, there are a lot of things more important than a home run. I like to think that's what made me a little special." Clearly the concept of "the team" meant everything to Morgan. He informed the *Boston Globe:* "I think the thing I'm most proud of -- I want to make this clear -- all those numbers you see, the good ones, the in-between ones, were achieved with the team coming first and me coming second. I never stole a base without the team needing it."

Morgan spoke of another source of pride during the Cooperstown, New York Hall of Fame ceremony. The *New York Times* quoted Joe as telling press conference attendees: "Last month ... I received my bachelor's degree. It took me 22 years in the major leagues to get a plaque in the Hall of Fame, and it took me 27 years to get my degree, but I'm thrilled to have both. The reason the college took so long was that when I graduated from high school, I was offered a pro contract. My father wanted me to take it. My mother wanted me to get an education. I said to her, 'If you let me sign, I promise I'll get the degree.'" More than 25 years later, Joe kept the promise. He graduated from Cal State Hayward on June 16, 1990, the same year he was elected to the Hall of Fame, fulfilling a long-term promise to his mom Ollie.

From 1994 to 2000, Morgan teamed with Bob Costas to broadcast games on NBC. Joe helped call three World Series (1995, 1997, and 1999) and four All-Star Games. He had spent a previous (1986–1987) stint with NBC calling regional *Game of the Week* telecasts and was also a broadcaster in the *MLB 2K* video game series.

Morgan has co-authored a number of books on baseball, including *Baseball for Dummies* and *Joe Morgan: A Life in Baseball*. In 2006, he called the Little League World Series Championship with Brent Musburger and Orel Hershiser on ABC. During the 2006 MLB playoffs, the network assigned lead baseball analyst Morgan to cover playoff games at different stadiums by calling the first half of the Mets–Dodgers game at Shea Stadium before traveling across town for the Yankees–Tigers night game at Yankee Stadium.

In 1998, Morgan returned to his Oakland alma mater -- Brookfield Elementary -- to help with a new mentoring program in the city's public schools. He is one of the sponsors of Project COOL, or Controlling Our Own Lives. Project COOL matched 100 students from Brookfield in East Oakland and Cole Performing Arts Magnet School in West Oakland with adults who work with them one-on-one as tutors and role models. The program will be a partnership between the school district and the Joe Morgan Youth Foundation, which is providing more than $100,000 in financial support.

"I want to make it possible for other youth to have the kind of support I had from people like (Oakland community leader) Bill Patterson and Harrison Flowers, who was my head coach when I attended Castlemont High School," Morgan said. "One of the most difficult things to do is to be a kid."

In 1999, Morgan ranked number 60 on *The Sporting News* list of the 100 Greatest Baseball Players, and was nominated as a finalist for the Major League Baseball All-Century Team. In 2008, Cal State East Bay awarded alumnus Morgan an Honorary Doctorate of Humane Letters degree during the June graduation ceremony for the university's College of Business and Economics.

"This degree is awarded to one who has demonstrated intellectual and humane values that are consistent with the aims of higher education, and with the highest ideals of a person's chosen field," Mohammad H. Qayoumi, Cal State East Bay president, said in a statement. "This award is reserved for individuals who demonstrate excellence and extraordinary achievement and embody the objectives and ideals of the California State University."

Morgan told graduates that he values the importance of education. "I've always felt that the quality of your life is directly related to the quality of your education," said Morgan in his speech. "If you continue your education, I believe you'll continue to improve the quality of your life."

"Getting a college education helped me after baseball," he said. "I think it gives me credibility when I tell a kid in high school to consider college. That's important when talking with my own kids about education. The things I learned through my education helped me to play the game better and helped me carry myself better so I could get to the Hall of Fame. All the things I've done education-wise contributed to who I am today."

In his time at ESPN, Morgan had been a vocal critic of statistics-based analysis of baseball, sometimes called sabermetrics. Michael Lewis's book *Moneyball*, which describes Billy Beane's sabermetric-influenced approach to running the Oakland Athletics, is a particular target of Morgan's criticism. Ironically, Joe's stance has caused him to refute the opinion expressed by noted sabermetrican Bill James that Morgan himself was the best second baseman in history. Joe has often expressed the belief that statistical analysis—often using complex calculus equations—to evaluate player performance and value is not more effective than observation when analyzing players. Morgan considered the notion ridiculous, arguing that Roger Hornsby batted .358 over the course of his career, while Joe never came close to batting that high even once in his 22 seasons.

"He was the perfect Billy Beane player," said ESPN.com writer Rob Neyer, co-author of *The Neyer/James Guide to Pitchers*. In fact, Morgan's career has gotten nothing if not a boost from the statistics folks, which makes his crusade even more puzzling. "A lot of people, myself included, think Joe Morgan was the greatest second baseman of all time," Neyer says. "I suspect that if you had done a poll 25 years ago, you would've seen a lot of names like Rogers Hornsby, Nap Lajoie, Frankie Frisch. But if you did one now, Joe Morgan would pop up a lot, in part because we have a greater respect for the things he did so well."

"I've read excerpts of things from Bill James," Morgan says. "I've read excerpts of *Moneyball*. But I don't read either one of those books, because I don't think statistics are what the game is about, and so I'm never going to agree with it, and I don't care — I'm not saying it's wrong. You can look at it that way. I don't look at the game that way."

In 2010, Morgan was honored by the Reds by throwing out spring training's first pitch at Goodyear Ballpark in Arizona. Joe was also featured at a special Oakland Hilton dinner for his charitable contributions to the city of Oakland. NBA Hall of Famer Bill Russell was master of ceremonies and was joined by greats such as Rose and Tony LaRussa. Proceeds from the event benefited the youth and family programs offered by the George P. Scotlan Youth and Family Center. Morgan, who now lives in Danville, was further honored when the city renamed a portion of 66th Avenue in Oakland "Joe Morgan Way."

On April 21, 2010 it was announced that Morgan was returning to the Reds in the role of "special advisor to baseball operations." Joe will work in both the baseball side and community outreach side for the club. In November, ESPN announced that Morgan would not be returning for the 2011 season as an announcer on *Sunday Night Baseball*. His former broadcast partner Jon Miller's contract expired in 2010 and ESPN chose not to renew his contract. Miller was asked to stay on as the radio voice for the network's coverage of *Sunday Night Baseball*. Dan Shulman replaced Miller's play-by-play while Orel Hershiser, who joined Miller and Morgan in the booth last season, remained on the broadcast team.

ESPN Vice President Norby Williamson said that "Jon and Joe have contributed greatly to the success of *Sunday Night Baseball* for the past 21 seasons. Over the last two decades, Joe went from Hall of Fame player to one of his sport's top analysts and Jon's Hall of Fame voice and tremendous knowledge of the game have connected with baseball fans everywhere. We owe them our deepest thanks for an outstanding body of work."

"I will miss the broadcasting," Morgan said. "But I won't miss the travel, all that getting on airplanes. It will be great to get away from so much travel." In his broadcasting career, Morgan won a CableACE award in 1990 and Emmy awards for sports analysis in 1998 and 2005.

In 2011, Morgan entered a new phase of his life. He is a highly-paid corporate and motivational event speaker. He also focuses on his new role with the Reds as a front office adviser and cherishes the long-term friendships he made in Cincinnati. Joe has had a locker with the Reds well after his retirement. He served as Grand Marshal and Honorary Captain for the Reds Opening Day game.

Morgan's name often comes up when the discussion turns to the greatest second baseman in history. In the *New Bill James Historical Baseball Abstract*, James named Joe the best second baseman in baseball history, ahead of No. 2 Eddie Collins and No. 3 Rogers Hornsby. He also ranked Morgan as the "greatest percentages player in baseball history," due to his strong fielding percentage, stolen base percentage, walk-to-strikeout ratio, and walks per plate appearance.

At 5-foot-7, Morgan stood out as a star among stars - a player that had mastered every single aspect of the game and excelled in each. He brought a rare combination of power, speed and an instinct for victory that cannot be denied. Morgan was what is described today as a five-tool player long before the term was ever in use, and could help his team win in a variety of ways - with his bat, glove, throwing arm or with his speed on the bases. He also played more games at second base than anyone but Eddie Collins, proof of his fitness and durability.

At his peak, he was able to carry a team. He won back-to-back MVP honors in 1975 and 1976, and his Cincinnati squad won the World Series both seasons as well. James even once determined that Morgan had the highest baseball I.Q. in history, measured in terms of on-field decision making when it comes to situations that require thought and strategy as opposed to pure athleticism.

Joe Morgan and his legacy of success is an inspiration to all who know him. His Hall of Fame baseball career, community interest, patience and love for children, and family example make him an exceptional individual. He contributes personally and financially to the Young America baseball program and the Oakland Unified School District Sports Program, and many other charities as he has throughout his career. A huge jazz fan, the charity Morgan has supported the longest is AIM, or Adventures in Movement. AIM uses music to help handicapped children experience movement in an enjoyable way. That is classic Joe Morgan – a great teammate always ready to help others achieve their dreams.

11

LEFTY GOMEZ

Lefty Gomez was a fire-balling Portuguese-American pitcher who won 189 games in the American League between 1930 and 1942. He was a seven-time All-Star and helped the New York Yankees win five championships with his career World Series record of 6-0 in seven starts. In addition to his Hall of Fame accomplishments, Lefty was beloved for his colorful, warm personality and humor throughout his career and life.

Vernon Louis Gomez was born November 26, 1908, the youngest of seven children. Lefty's father, Manuel Gomes Jr., was born in 1870 in Pinole to dairy farmers Manuel Sr. and Annie Gomes, both natives of the Azorean Islands of Portugal. In 1892, Lefty's father married Elizabeth Herring, who gave birth to Earl, Milfred, Lloyd, Irene, Cecil and Gladys. Just before Lefty was finally born in 1908, the family moved from Pinole to Rodeo – a very small town of a few thousand people on the San Pablo Bay about 20 miles north of Oakland.

Manual Jr. was a teamster for years, but by 1920 he was working as a farmhand and by 1930, he was a construction worker. While Lefty used the surname Gomez most of his life, his parents and siblings used Gomes (the correct Portuguese spelling) and Gomez interchangeably. His brother Lloyd, in fact, is buried in Golden Gate National Cemetery under the name Gomes.

Gomez honed his southpaw pitching skills at Richmond High School and also played sandlot ball in Oakland. He was signed by the San Francisco Seals for a $100 signing bonus by manager Nick Williams, who also signed Hall of Famer Paul Waner.

"I was the first one to hear of Gomez," said Denny Carroll, a former Seals trainer. "I had a kid catcher on a semipro Oil Company team who had sore arm. He used to come and see me once a week. I asked him if he knew anyone good and he mentioned Gomez, who was 16 at the time. So a couple of years later Nick went down to a beer joint and sat around until Lefty pitched. He met a guy who knew Gomez and the more the guy talked the more beer Nick drank and the better Gomez sounded. Nick went around and signed Gomez sight unseen that afternoon."

After high school, the Seals assigned the 19-year-old Gomez to the Class C Salt Lake City Bees of the Utah-Idaho League in 1928. Lefty went 12-14 with the Bees, posting a 3.48 ERA in 28 starts. He then reported to the hometown Seals of the Pacific Coast League in 1929. His Seals pitching debut was a sparkling three-hitter against the Pittsburgh Pirates. Major League scouts were well aware of the PCL talent and frequently made long trips to evaluate west coast prospects. Lefty finished the '29 season 18-11 with a 3.44 ERA in 267 innings for San Francisco.

Following an eight-game winning streak, Gomez was signed by the New York Yankees, where his career was about to accelerate with the same speed of his famous fastball. The Yankees purchased Gomez from the Seals late in 1929 for $35,000.

Gomez told zany stories about the days he spent pitching in the minor leagues. One season, Lefty was living in a boarding house and somehow got way behind in his rent. When the landlady demanded cash, "Goofy" as he was known, tried to talk his way out of tight spot. "Just think," he said to her, "Someday you'll be able to say Lefty Gomez the great pitcher once lived here." The landlady wasn't impressed. According to Lefty, she answered "I know...and if you don't pay me, I'll be able to say it tomorrow."

After appearing in 17 games with the Class AA St. Paul Saints in 1930, 21-year-old Gomez arrived in New York and broke into the big leagues. His smoking fastball was fired from a deceptive slender frame. He was a 6-foot-2 stick, with a whiplike arm and a high leg kick. Along with right-hander Red Ruffing, this lefty-righty combination was the core of a dominant New York pitching staff in the 1930s. The

Yankee offense was loaded, featuring Hall of Famers Babe Ruth, Lou Gehrig, Bill Dickey and fellow Bay Area native Tony Lazzari.

Lefty won only two games while losing five in his rookie season. New York general manager Ed Barrow strongly suggested that Gomez gain some weight, and after he put on 20 pounds in the off-season there was a marked change in his effectiveness. In 1931, Gomez elevated to a 21-9 record, with a 2.67 earned run average. Lefty was even better the next year, posting a mark of 24-7 in 1932. He received major run support to work with that year, as evidenced by his 4.21 ERA. In the '32 World Series against the Cubs, Gomez nailed down a complete game win, allowing just one run as the Yankees, led by Ruth and Gehrig, swept Chicago in four games. The series is remembered today for Ruth famously "calling his shot" at Wrigley Field.

"No one hit home runs the way Babe did," said Gomez of playing with Ruth. "They were something special. They were like homing pigeons. The ball would leave the bat, pause briefly, suddenly gain its bearings, then take off for the stands."

Gomez's unique and eccentric attitude towards life made him a breath of fresh air and an instant media favorite. Reporters loved interviewing him because of his frequent oddball quotes. A reporter discussing Lefty's tight brushback pitches once asked Lefty if he would throw at his own mother. Gomez replied, "Yes, she's a darn good hitter."

On February 26, 1933, Lefty married June O'Dea (born Eilean Frances Schwarz) of Revere, Massachusetts. A Broadway comedic headliner who starred in *Of Thee I Sing*, O'Dea gave up her performing career in 1936. By 1937, the marriage was on shaky ground. In an effort to rekindle their marriage, they romantically sailed the Atlantic Ocean to Bermuda and returned to New York. But the cruise didn't appear to help much, as Lefty traveled to Hollywood soon after and June returned to Massachusetts to stay with family.

Through the press, June learned in December that Lefty was filing for divorce in Mexico, charging incompatibility. A devout Catholic, she refused a divorce but agreed to a formal separation, citing "abandonment and cruel and inhuman treatment." Publicly, Lefty said the whole idea of divorce was ridiculous, but by early 1938 he moved to Reno to get a six-week divorce to be finalized by the start of spring training in Florida. Separation proceedings continued for months, but were canceled in May 1938. Although they experienced difficult times and teetered on the edge of divorce, Lefty and June stayed together for 55 years and went on to have two daughters, Vernona and Sharon, and two sons, Gary and Duane. The Gomezes had seven grandchildren.

In the first-ever Major League Baseball All-Star Game of 1933, Gomez was not only was the starting -- and winning pitcher -- for the American League, but also drove in the first run of the game. This was unthinkable for him, as he was one of the worst hitters in the majors. "I never broke a bat until I was 73 years old," Lefty said. "And that was from backing the car out of the garage."

Gomez had the distinction of starting five of the first six All-Star games for the AL in the 1930s, and while he was later known for his hilarious storytelling, he was a four-time 20-game winner with the 1930s Yankees. New York rarely lost when Lefty took the ball. After a 16-10 record in 1933, Gomez posted his best season in 1934 with a sizzling 26-5 record in 1934. He led the league in seven major categories, including wins (26), ERA (2.33), and strikeouts (158), an achievement known as the Pitching Triple Crown. He certainly would have won the Cy Young award for outstanding pitching but the award did not yet exist.

One of baseball's most dominant pitchers of the '30s, Gomez was also known as a clubhouse joker who constantly tried to keep the team loose. He also entertained many Depression era fans who needed a good laugh at the ballpark. Earning the nicknames "Gay Caballero" and "El Goofy," Lefty's wackiness set him apart from the conservative Yankees. "I talked to the ball a lot of times in my career," he said, "I yelled, 'Go foul! Go foul!'" He even stopped a World Series game once to watch an airplane pass by, exasperating manager Joe McCarthy.

Gomez slumped in 1935 and '36, winning only 25 games in 60 starts in those seasons. But Lefty again overpowered hitters in the 1936 postseason, leading the Yankees to another World Series title by winning Game 2 and the clinching Game 6 against the New York Giants.

Lefty again swept all major pitching honors in 1937 with a 21-11 record, and won another Pitching Triple Crown by leading the league in wins (21), ERA (2.33) and strikeouts (194). He again led the AL in shutouts. In the World Series rematch versus the Giants, Lefty went 2-0, pitching the opener and the clincher.

Fellow Bay Area native Joe DiMaggio broke in with the Yankees in 1936 and McCarthy decided that Gomez -- six years older -- would be Joe's big brother. He would help lead him through the hazards of adjusting to life in New York City and the major leagues. DiMaggio, however was an shy, quiet, withdrawn, insecure person – and also a superstar that constantly drew attention from the extensive New York media.

They became great friends and Lefty was with Joe at almost all times. He also got away with needling DiMaggio because like everyone else, he enjoyed the Gomez wit. On the road or in New York, Joe would sulk about an occasional bad day and he thought an 0-for-4 was the end of the world. Gomez understood that the season was 154 games long and even Ruth had bad days. Even Gehrig, their teammate, had bad days. So he helped DiMaggio through those bad stretches and especially during Joe's historic 56-game hitting streak in 1941.

Always humble, Gomez often deflected praise and compliments with self-deprecating humor, saying things such as "I want to thank all my teammates who scored so many runs and Joe DiMaggio, who ran down so many of my mistakes" and "The secret of my success was clean living and a fast outfield."

In 1938, Gomez won his final World Series game, as he went seven innings versus the Cubs, who were swept in four games. Lefty also set a World Series record: six consecutive wins without a loss. In 1939, he earned his fifth World Series ring with New York. He started Game 3 but did not get the win as the Yankees swept the Cincinnati Reds.

Yankee captain Gehrig announced he was stricken with ALS in 1939. When a despondent Lou finally took himself out of the lineup after his record 2,130 consecutive games streak, Gomez tried to cheer him up by saying "Hell, Lou it took fifteen years to get you out of a game. Sometimes I'm out in fifteen minutes."

In 1940, Lefty suffered an arm injury and went 3-3, causing Gomez to transition from a power pitcher to a finesse pitcher with a slow curve. "I'm throwing as hard as I ever did," he quipped, "the ball's just not getting there as fast." In 1941, Gomez fooled hitters with the newly perfected off-speed pitches and made a tremendous comeback in 1941 with a record of 15-5, leading the American League in winning percentage at .750.

Arm problems resurfaced in 1942 and Lefty appeared in just 13 games. Gomez won his last game for the Yankees on August 14, 1942 against the Philadelphia A's. After the '42 season ended, the Yankees were close to releasing Lefty and he took a job as a dispatcher with the General Electric River Works, a defense plant in Lynn, Massachusetts, which paid $40 a week. Then on January 27, 1943, the Yankees sold Lefty to the Boston Braves for $10,000, but Gomez instead signed with the Washington Senators and appeared in only one game.

After the 1943 season, Gomez retired from baseball. He compiled a 189-102 career won-loss record with 1,468 strikeouts and a 3.34 ERA in 2,503 innings pitched. The 189 wins are still fourth all-time in Yankee history after he was recently passed by Andy Pettitte. Known for his great wit, Lefty often remarked, "I'd rather be lucky than good." He was both.

Though he was fortunate to be on powerhouse Yankee teams, his dominant 6-0 World Series performance in seven starts gave him the most wins without a loss in World Series history. His three victories in All-Star Game competition is also a record and includes a win in the first All-Star game ever. Gomez also holds the record for the most innings pitched in a single All-Star game (six). And though a notoriously poor hitter, he produced the first RBI in All-Star history and singled home the series-winning run in the 1937 World Series.

A 20-game winner four times and an All-Star every year from 1933 to 1939, Gomez twice led the league in wins, winning percentage and ERA, and three times in shutouts and strikeouts. At career's end, he had a winning record against every American League rival. His .649 career winning percentage ranks 15th in major league history among pitchers with 200 or more decisions, and among pitchers who made their debut from 1900-1950, only Lefty Grove, Christy Mathewson and Whitey Ford have more victories and a higher winning percentage than Gomez.

Lefty was surprisingly drafted into the U.S. Armed Forces in 1944 at the age of 36. After his discharge, Wilson Sporting Goods hired Gomez as a goodwill ambassador. He also became a sought-after dinner speaker known for his humorous anecdotes about his playing days and the personalities he knew. He recalled being a bit of a screwball nicknamed "Goofy Gomez," and told stories of playing practical jokes on everyone from teammates to umpires.

Though he took his pitching talents to New York City, Gomez's heart stayed in the Bay Area and he returned to Novato for his senior years. During the 1960s, he often coached children at the Carquinez Grammar School in Crockett, just east of hometown Rodeo. At the time, Rodeo didn't have a school but he wanted to help kids. Nearing 60, he had not lost his sense of humor and entertained the children as much with his anecdotes as his coaching and lectures on sportsmanship. "One rule I had was make your best pitch and back up third base," he said in 1961. "That relay might get away and you've got another shot at him."

On February 2, 1972, the Veterans Committee unanimously inducted Lefty Gomez into the National Baseball Hall of Fame, along with Giants outfielder Ross Youngs and former AL President Will Haridge. The Committee noted that Lefty pitched in seven World Series games and never lost one. In 1981, Gomez was inducted into the Bay Area Sports Hall of Fame and his plaque resides at AT&T Park.

In 1987, Lefty and Ford were honored with plaques placed in Monument Park at Yankee Stadium. His plaque says he was "Noted for his wit and his fastball, as he was fast with a quip and a pitch." Despite his advancing age, Gomez attended the ceremony.

Lefty spent the last years of his life in Novato, and passed away of congestive heart failure on February 17, 1989, in Marin General Hospital in Larkspur. He was 80 years old. A decade later, he was ranked #73 on *The Sporting News*' list of the 100 Greatest Baseball Players, and was a nominee for the Major League Baseball All-Century Team. Gomez's memory and history is kept alive today by his daughter Vernona.

After Gomez's death, Yankee catcher Bill Dickey recalled that all pitchers feared slugger Jimmie Foxx. Gomez once said about Foxx, "He's got muscles in his hair." One time, with Foxx at bat, Dickey gave one signal after another and Lefty shook them all off. Finally Dickey ran out to the mound and asked what Lefty wanted to throw him. "I don't wanna throw him nothing" said Gomez. "Maybe he'll just get tired of waitin' and leave."

Today, the Lefty Gomez Recreation Building and Ballfield Complex at 470 Parker Avenue in Rodeo is designated as a "Point of Historical Interest" by the State of California Historical Resources Commission. The Rodeo Ballfield Complex is the actual location where Gomez spent his youth honing his pitching arm.

In 2010, former University of Connecticut head coach Andy Baylock received the 50th annual Lefty Gomez Award, one of the most prestigious awards in amateur baseball. Named after the All-Star southpaw hurler, the award is presented by the American Baseball Coaches Association to the individual who has distinguished himself amongst his peers and contributed significantly to baseball locally, nationally, and internationally. The presentation was made at the annual ABCA Hall of Fame Banquet.

"I was surprised and deeply honored to receive the Lefty Gomez award," said Baylock. "I actually got to meet Lefty several times and it was a great experience."

Previous Gomez Award recipients include Jack Kaiser, St. John's; Rod Dedeaux, USC; Peter Ueberroth, MLB Commissioner; Ron Polk, Mississippi State; Ron Fraser, Miami; Archie Allen, Springfield, and Dennis Poppe, NCAA.

According to his friends and teammates, Vernon "Lefty" Gomez was a wonderfully warm, funny, and genuine human being who just happened to be a dominant pitcher. He understood that baseball was a joyous way to make a living and sometimes questioned why he actually got paid money for doing it. Lefty was known for his quick wit and quirky ways, and he played with the likes of Ruth, Gehrig, and DiMaggio, entertaining them all. But make no mistake. When Lefty took the sign from his catcher, he and his Hall of Fame fastball were all business.

11

NORM VAN BROCKLIN

Nicknamed "The Flying Dutchman," fiery Norm Van Brocklin was one of the smartest and most fearless quarterbacks of the 1950s. He played in five NFL Championship Games (later renamed the Super Bowl) and in the final game of his career, Van Brocklin led his team to a league title and retired on top. A member of the Pro Football Hall of Fame, he is remembered for one of the greatest touchdown passes of all time and also the greatest passing game in NFL history.

Norman Mack Van Brocklin was born in Eagle Butte, South Dakota on March 15, 1926, the eighth of nine children born to farmers Mack and Ethel Van Brocklin. Soon after Norm was born, the family moved to California and settled in Walnut Creek. He attended Acalanes High School in Lafayette, and was a three-sport varsity star in baseball, basketball, and football. In 1941, Mt. Diablo High School played its first game with its new "offspring" school Acalanes. The game nearly ended in a scoreless tie before Norm place-kicked a 35-yard field goal in the closing minutes to give the Dons a 3-0 victory.

After graduation from Acalanes, Van Brocklin served in the United States Navy from 1943 until the end of World War II in 1945. He was overlooked by California colleges after his high school career and decided to follow his classmate and friend George Bell to the University of Oregon. Once at Eugene, Norm was almost lost among hundreds of training camp players until coaches noticed his passing, running, and kicking skills. When Jim Aiken became head coach in 1947, he brought in the T-formation and built the entire offense around Van Brocklin's ability to run and throw. Navy veteran Norm had tremendous field leadership and was highly respected by his teammates. Meanwhile, coaches gave him complete freedom to run the attack while on the field.

An intelligent play-caller, Van Brocklin led the Ducks to outstanding seasons in 1947 and 1948. He was one of the first collegiate quarterbacks to call audibles, a play change at the line of scrimmage based on the defensive formation. Norm utilized his ability to read opposing defenses and led Oregon to a 16-5 record as a two-year starter. Aiken stressed fundamentals and for the combat vets that made up most of the '47 and '48 teams, the approach was effective.

In 1948, the Ducks finished tied with California in the Pacific Coast Conference standings, forerunner of the Pac-12. Oregon did not go to the Rose Bowl because Cal was voted by the other schools to represent the PCC in the New Year's Day game. Among the Cal voters was the University of Washington, which elevated the intensity of the Oregon-Husky rivalry.

Oregon instead received an invitation to face Southern Methodist University with stars Doak Walker and Kyle Rote in the 1949 Cotton Bowl. It was the first time that a Pacific Coast team played in a major bowl game other than the Rose Bowl. In Van Brocklin's final college game, SMU won 20–13 as both Walker and Van Brocklin received Outstanding Player recognition for their performance in a Cotton Bowl classic.

Van Brocklin's 1948 All-American season raised his two-year career totals to 1,949 passing yards and 18 touchdowns, outrageous numbers for his era. He holds the distinction as being Oregon's first quarterback to earn All-American honors and finished sixth in the Heisman Trophy voting, won by Walker.

Van Brocklin completed his required four years of study in three, and left Oregon for the NFL with one remaining year of college eligibility. At that time, a player wasn't allowed to sign with an NFL team until four years after high school graduation. Though he had only been in Eugene for three years, he became eligible due to his time Navy service. Having recently married Gloria, his biology professor, Norm declared himself eligible for the 1949 NFL draft.

Van Brocklin was drafted in the fourth round -- 37th overall -- of the '49 draft by the Los Angeles Rams. Although he joined a team that already had future Hall of Fame quarterback Bob Waterfield, Norm quickly established himself as one of the best deep passers in football. In his rookie season with the Rams, he backed up Waterfield and appeared in eight games. The Dutchman saw only brief action until the final game against Washington, which LA needed to win for the divisional title. Norm responded with a four-touchdown performance for coach Clark Shaughnessy. Los Angeles advanced to the NFL Championship Game, but lost to the Philadelphia Eagles, 14-0. Because of his impressive rookie season, he and Waterfield created the NFL's first version of the Quarterback Controversy for several seasons, a situation the Dutchman deeply disliked.

New Rams coach Joe Stydahar solved the QB problem in 1950 by platooning Waterfield and Van Brocklin. Waterfield played in the first and third quarters, Van Brocklin in the second and fourth, or vice versa. The Flying Dutchman threw for more yards than any other NFL quarterback and the Rams won the West for a second straight year. In his six starts, he had his team at 5-1. He had a QB rating of 85 in 1950, more than double the league average, 14 points better than runner-up Waterfield and 20 points better than third-place Otto Graham.

Stydahar's early 1950s Rams were the greatest show on grass 50 years before Kurt Warner's St. Louis team. They ranked first in points in 1950, '51, and '52, scoring in every way possible from anywhere on the field. The 6-foot-1, 190-pound Van Brocklin was also an outstanding punter over the course of his career, twice leading the NFL in that category with the Rams. His longest career punt covered 70 yards.

The 1950 Rams scored a then-NFL record 466 points with a high octane passing attack that featured Hall of Famers Tom Fears and Elroy "Crazy Legs" Hirsch. Their 38.8 points per game is still a record. Fears led the league and set a new NFL record with 84 receptions. Los Angeles again fell short of their goal, defeated by the Cleveland Browns in the 1950 title game, 30-28.

The dominant passing offense of their era, the Rams also ran the ball with authority. Two LA running backs made the Pro Bowl each season, with "Mr. Outside" Glenn Davis and Dick Hoerner selected in 1950, and then Dan Towler and Tank Younger earning those honors in each of the next three seasons. Towler, Younger and Hoerner were nicknamed the "Bull Elephant Backfield."

In 1950, Van Brocklin threw for over 2,000 yards and 18 touchdowns in only six games of playing time. He was the only QB in the NFL that season to throw more

TDs than interceptions. Norm led the league in passer rating and finished second in completion percentage. He topped Graham in every category, and was second to Bobby Layne in interception percentage. The Flying Dutchman was on pace for over 4,000 yards and 36 TDs if he had seen the full complement of playing time in 1950. Many Rams fans believe LA would have won the NFL championship if Van Brocklin had played instead of the older, more experienced Waterfield.

In 1951, Van Brocklin and Waterfield again split quarterbacking duties and the Rams again won the West. On the final day of the season, Waterfield edged out Van Brocklin for the passing title by less than .010 in average yards per attempt, the key statistic for determining passing leaders during that era.

On September 28, 1951, Van Brocklin threw for an amazing 554 yards, shattering Johnny Lujack's single-game record of 468 by 86 yards. Sixty years later, it's still an NFL record. That was in 1951, when teams typically threw for about 165 yards per game. Norm received the start that day when Waterfield was injured. The two quarterbacks were constantly entrenched in a fierce battle for the starting role and Dutch made the most of his opportunity. He completed 27 of 41 passes and tossed five touchdowns - four to Hirsch - en route to a 54-14 blowout win over the New York Yanks.

Van Brocklin nearly made it six touchdown passes in the closing moments but Tommy Kalmanir was pulled down a yard short and Towler punched it across the goal line. The Rams set a league record when they piled up 34 first downs and 735 total yards, topping the old mark of 682 set by the Chicago Bears in 1943.

Hirsch set an NFL record that season with 1,495 receiving yards and tied Don Hutson's record of 17 touchdown catches. In the 1951 NFL Championship Game, the Rams won the rematch against Cleveland, 24-17. Waterfield (9-24, 125 yards) took most of the snaps and Van Brocklin sat on the bench for three and a half quarters while the Rams and the Browns fought to a 17-17 stalemate. Called into action late in the game, Dutch connected with Fears on an historic 73-yard pass play that finally ended the Browns' long NFL domination.

In 1952, Van Brocklin won the second of his three NFL passing titles. Waterfield ended the Rams quarterback "problem" by retiring after the 1952 season. Norm thrived after Waterfield's retirement, but had his differences with Sid Gillman, who took over as head coach in 1955. Gillman expected to call the plays and emphasized sideline passing versus vertical, not exactly Van Brocklin's style.

Van Brocklin continued to quarterback the Rams, leading them to the championship game again in 1955. The Browns won 38-14 while Norm threw a horrid six interceptions. After missing games with an injury in 1956, he returned to split time with Billy Wade at QB, a tenuous situation. The Rams slumped badly in '56 and '57 and Dutch hinted of retirement. Increasingly at odds with Gillman, Van Brocklin finally told the front office to trade him or he would quit football.

Van Brocklin's exit from Los Angeles was created by a coach-player dispute that few fans would ever understand. As he himself wrote in 1961's *Norm Van Brocklin's Football Book*, co-authored with Hugh Brown: "My nine years with the Rams were happy and prosperous. I probably would still be serving out my time with them, except for a delicate situation that arose in 1957 involving coach Sid Gillman and myself. It has been publicized extensively, and needs no retelling here. Suffice it to say that we both wanted to call the signals; Gillman from the sidelines, the way Paul Brown does. I thought I could call the plays better from my position back of the center. The Rams felt they had to back their coach, so we parted company."

He specified that Philadelphia and Pittsburgh were places to avoid, but he was traded to the Eagles anyway for guard Buck Lansford, defensive back Jimmy Harris, and a first-round draft pick. His record with Los Angeles was an impressive one: he led the NFL in passing and yards per attempt on three occasions, in yardage once, and set the single-game passing record.

Although the Rams ignored Van Brocklin's desire to call the plays and be a "coach on the field," this was not the case in Philadelphia. New Eagles head coach Buck Shaw gave Van Brocklin complete freedom with the offense, and he was virtually an offensive coordinator in the huddle during his time in Philadelphia. He didn't just call plays, but took on a teaching role with his teammates which he performed very effectively. "If it's the game plan you want, see Dutch," an Eagle player once told a writer looking for Shaw.

The deal that brought Van Brocklin to Philadelphia was easily one of the best in Eagles history. At first, he was upset about having to relocate his family to the East Coast from California to play for a team that hadn't won more than four games in the last three seasons. Success didn't come instantly – in fact, the 1958 Eagles finished even worse than a year before – 2-9-1. For the season, the Dutchman led the NFL in both attempts (374) and completions (198), and ranked third in passing yards (2,409) and TD passes (15).

With Van Brocklin's supporting cast continuing to improve, the Eagles jumped to 7-5 in 1959. Dutch threw TD passes of 33 and 55 yards to Tommy McDonald in a 49-21 thrashing of the Giants, threw two more to McDonald in a 28-24 win over the Cardinals, and hit McDonald for three TDs, including a 50-yarder, in a 34-14 win at Washington. Van Brocklin completed a career-high 56.2 percent of his passes and ranked second in the NFL in passing yards (2,617), third with 16 TD passes, and fourth in passer rating (79.5).

In 1960, Van Brocklin showed football fans nationwide why he is considered a true NFL legend. Temperamental, demanding, and stubborn, he was also an outstanding leader, teammate and tactician who could carry a team with his arm and iron will. The season started poorly with a 41-24 loss to the Browns at home, but the Eagles reeled off nine consecutive wins, and 10 of 11, to win the Eastern Conference title with a 10-2 record.

With his fiery personality and outstanding precision, Van Brocklin became the key offensive weapon in the Eagles' success. During the 1960 season, the Dutchman fired three scoring passes in a 31-27 win over the Cardinal, threw three more in a 31-29 win at Cleveland, tossed three to McDonald in beating the Steelers, 34-7, completed a crucial sweep of the Giants with three TDs in a 31-23 win at Franklin Field, and wrapped up the regular season with a 38-28 win at Washington in which he connected with scoring passes of 52 and 64 yards.

In the 1960 NFL Championship Game against the Green Bay Packers at Franklin Field, Van Brocklin completed 9-of-20 passes for 204 yards, including a 41-yarder to end Pete Retzlaff. Dutch fired a 35-yard scoring pass to McDonald in the second quarter and led the Eagles on a 39-yard game-winning drive in the fourth quarter as the Birds upset the favored Packers, 17-13. Van Brocklin became the only man to defeat Vince Lombardi in a championship game during his years at Green Bay. On that frigid Monday afternoon, on the hard bleachers of Franklin Field, along with 60,000 others, sat Van Brocklin's wife, three daughters, and mother bundled up in 28-degree weather. They were there to watch Norm play his last game as an Eagle, his last game in the NFL, and ride off into the sunset a Philadelphia hero.

Van Brocklin's 1960 performance earned him unanimous all-NFL honors and several Most Valuable Player trophies, including the Maxwell Club's Bert Bell award, the Jim Thorpe trophy, the UPI MVP, and the Associated Press MVP. He was also named the *Sporting News* Marlboro Pro Player of the Year and was on the cover of *Sports Illustrated* in December. For the season, Dutch ranked second in the

NFL in passing (86.5 rating), passing yards (2,471), yards per attempt (8.70), and TD passes (24).

Van Brocklin was selected to the Pro Bowl after all three of his seasons in Philadelphia. For his career with the Eagles, Dutch completed 542 of 998 passes (54.3%) for 7,497 yards, 55 touchdowns and 51 interceptions. He averaged 7.51 yards per attempt and a passer rating of 75.7 (5th all-time for Eagles with 500 attempts). He also punted 167 times for a 42.4-yard average, which is still tied for third in team history. He started all 36 games in Philly, compiling a 19-16-1 record. Norm is a member of the Eagles Honor Roll and was selected as quarterback on the All-Time Eagles team in 1965. The Dutchman was a standout passer for more than a decade in the NFL but his field general leadership in 1960 was his most prized accomplishment. It was the last time Philadelphia won a championship

In 2010, daughter Karen Van Brocklin-Vanderyt returned to Philadelphia with her family at an Eagles-Vikings game at Lincoln Financial Field to commemorate the 50th anniversary of the 1960 title game. Norm's family cheered wildly for the Eagles, wearing No. 11 in honor of her father, and waved a large banner with a photo of the "ol' Dutchman."

"Instead of having presents under a tree, this is what we decided to do," Vanderyt said. "Life is not about what you accumulate. It's about making memories. It's about what you do, not what you have. We're here to pay homage to ol' No. 11. I've been thinking about this for a long time, and we're all very excited. We just hope people remember."

During his 12-year career, Van Brocklin played on two NFL championship teams, led the NFL in passing three times and in punting twice, averaging 42.9 yards over his career. In his ninth and final Pro Bowl appearance, he threw for touchdowns of 46, 43 and 36 yards and then completed six straight passes in the game's final drive.

Van Brocklin's career highlights also include four NFL All-Pro selections (1952, 1954, 1955, 1960). In 140 career regular season NFL games, he passed for 23,611 yards (second all-time when he retired), completing 1,553 of 2,895 passes (53.6%) with 173 touchdowns and a passer rating of 75.1 when the league average was in the 50s. He averaged more than eight yards per attempt, productive even by today's passing standards.

The Dutchman believed he had a commitment from the Eagles front office to succeed Shaw as head coach upon Shaw's retirement. The team changed their tune after 1960, reportedly offering Van Brocklin the opportunity to be a player/coach if he played another season. Assistant coach Nick Skorich got the job instead. Norm cut his ties with the Eagles claiming that the team had misled him, and that he'd been enticed to move east with the promise that he would eventually succeed Shaw. Instead, he was hired by the Minnesota Vikings.

In 1961, Van Brocklin accepted the head coaching position for the expansion Vikings. General Manager Bert Rose knew that a new club would struggle but that Norm had faced much adversity and had always prevailed. He stayed in Minnesota thru 1966, using the same challenging and competitive style he demonstrated as a player. The Vikings won only three games in 1961, but played exciting football, mainly because of the way he used scrambling quarterback Fran Tarkenton. That was ironic, considering that Van Brocklin was essentially an "immobile passer." In his 12-year pro career, he ran only 102 times, for a grand total of 40 yards. In Tarkenton's first season with the Vikings, he rushed 56 times for 308 yards.

An opposing coach once said "He runs like a woman trying to get out of her girdle." The Dutchman didn't run well, preferred not to, and the stats show it – his best season rushing total was 13 yards in 11 attempts in 1959. In spite of his immobility, he had a reputation as a difficult quarterback to sack due to his quick release.

Van Brocklin got Minnesota as far as a second-place conference finish by 1964, but the Vikings failed to improve in 1966 and he was fired. The tenure was highlighted by his contentious relationship with Tarkenton, a feud that culminated with Norm's resignation on February 11, 1967. Tarkenton, a Hall of Famer, was traded to the Giants shortly after Dutch's departure, but reacquired by coach Bud Grant in 1972.

Van Brocklin was inducted into the NCAA College Football Hall of Fame in 1966 and was named to the University of Oregon Athletics Hall of Fame in 1992. During his first year off the field in over two decades, he served as a commentator on 1967 NFL broadcasts for CBS. After a year out of coaching, Norm took over as the Atlanta Falcons head coach on October 1, 1968, replacing Norb Hecker. Atlanta had started the season with three defeats, extending its losing streak to 10 games. Over the next seven seasons, Van Brocklin managed only a 37-49-3 mark. He led the Falcons to their first winning season in 1971 with a 7-6-1 record, then challenged for a playoff spot two years later with a 9-5 mark.

Van Brocklin was inducted into the Pro Football Hall of Fame in 1971, while he was still actively coaching. To those who knew anything of his career, the only surprise connected with his election was that it took so long for the Hall's Board of Selectors to recognize him.

Atlanta's 1972 and 1973 teams both finished second in their division. On paper, the 1974 Falcons started the season with talent to challenge the division powerhouse Rams. The *Sporting News* picked Atlanta to compete for the NFC West title. But the '74 off-season was a tumultuous one for the NFL. The rival World Football League signed several star players. The Players Association called a July strike. A Falcons employee was called off the picket line after one week and told by Van Brocklin: "You and your sign have been traded to New Orleans."

When the team reunited in August, Van Brocklin had lost his Falcons. They were beaten 24-0 by the Cowboys in the season opener. After a 16-10 loss to the 49ers the following week, team owner Rankin Smith suggested that Dutch's job was in jeopardy. The Falcons suffered an embarrassing sweep at the hands of the Saints. "All the trouble started with the strike," Norm said after losing to New Orleans at home. "It was an all-time low."

Two weeks later, Van Brocklin shoved a cameraman out of a hotel elevator. With the team stuck at 2-6, he was dismissed after a hostile meeting with Smith with six games left in the season. Following his dismissal, Norm returned to his pecan farm in Social Circle, Georgia. His only connections to football during this era were as a running backs coach for Georgia Tech in 1979, and as a college football broadcaster. Dutch compiled a 66-100-7 career NFL coaching record.

Extremely bright and quotable, one of Van Brocklin's more oft-repeated quips was "If I ever needed a brain transplant, I'd choose a sportswriter's because I'd want a brain that had never been used." Norm was one of the greats who literally changed the entire nature of how games are planned and adjusted. In retirement, Van Brocklin suffered a number of illnesses, including a brain tumor. He died at 57 on May 3, 1983, one day after suffering a stroke.

He was noted for his angry play and his sarcasm. Former coach Pool once predicted Van Brocklin would break every NFL passing record "if somebody doesn't break his neck first." He was known to whip a football at any teammate who wasn't paying attention. He spotted an LA reporter at practice who wrote something unfair, he called a sweep to be run in the reporter's direction. As a coach, he didn't have patience for amateur advice or second-guessing and made his share of enemies among the news media.

He was one of the pioneers of the NFL Players Association. When his attempts to organize players were ostracized by the Redskins anti-union (and notoriously stingy) owner George Preston Marshall, Van Brocklin said "The best thing that could happen to Marshall's players and the National Football League would be for him to step in front of a moving cab."

Norm Van Brocklin was cool under the pressures of hard-charging defenses. The quarterback and Navy veteran from the East Bay was calm and quick-thinking, a master at calling audibles when his brain detected an opponent's weakness. He understood that a great passer watched the defense, not the receivers. Norm was gifted with a wide field of vision that allowed him to view the entire panorama of play. This gift, along with a strong passing arm, made Van Brocklin college football's premier quarterback in the 1940s, a nine-time All-Pro in the NFL with the Los Angeles Rams and Philadelphia Eagles, and a permanent fixture in the Pro Football Hall of Fame.

12

TOM BRADY

He quarterbacked the New England Patriots to four Super Bowls, winning three of them. A two-time NFL MVP, he won two Super Bowl MVP awards, has been selected to seven Pro Bowls, and holds the NFL record for most touchdown passes in a season. But before Tom Brady starred in Super Bowls, before he dated international supermodels and before he was stalked by paparazzi, he was "Tommy," just a regular kid from San Mateo.

Thomas Edward Patrick Brady, Jr. was born on August 3, 1977 in the San Francisco bedroom community of San Mateo, California. He grew up on quiet Portola Drive, the youngest of four children of Tom Sr. and Galynn. His three older sisters were also standout athletes and introduced sports to their baby brother. "Tommy" was raised around baseball and football. His Irish-American parents were passionate San Francisco 49ers and Giants fans and regularly took him and his sisters to games that included tailgating at Candlestick Park.

"The Niners were my team," said Brady in a CBS *Under the Helmet* interview. Tom was a particular fan of 49er Super Bowl quarterbacks Joe Montana and Steve Young. When not going to football games or watching football on television, Tom was cheering on his sisters at their games. An altar boy while attending St.

Gregory's elementary school in San Mateo, he played touch football at recess and after school.

Brady was a Little League baseball standout, often associated with his sister Maureen, an All-American softball pitcher for Hillsdale High in San Mateo and later at Fresno State. His two other sisters also played college sports, Julie at St. Mary's College (soccer) and Nancy at Cal-Berkeley (softball). Even Mom Galynn was a nationally ranked amateur tennis player.

"From what I recall, a driving force for Tom was to not be known simply as Maureen's little brother," said Dean Ayoob, a former classmate of Brady's.

"I can't tell you how many golf clubs I broke as a 10-year-old. Every time I hit a bad shot, I'd try to break my club. I once busted our TV with a video game," says Brady. "I threw the remote through the screen. Every time I'd lose, I'd just throw a fit. That was me growing up. I guess it's still the same." At 14 and having never played organized football, Brady's family, friends and Tom himself fully expected a career in baseball.

He attended high school at Junipero Serra High School, an all-boys Catholic school in San Mateo and also the alma mater of Barry Bonds and Lynn Swann. Serra has produced 22 professional athletes and its famous alumni often make headlines. In a six-month period in 2001, Brady (Class of '95) quarterbacked the Patriots to an upset Super Bowl championship, Bonds (1982) smashed Mark McGwire's season home-run record with 73, and Swann (1970), the former Pittsburgh Steelers wide receiver and a Super Bowl MVP, was inducted into the Pro Football Hall of Fame.

"I think that it would be safe to say that (Serra) has had the most prolific year for alumni ever," said Serra football coach Patrick Walsh in a letter to *Sports Illustrated*. "Not bad for a little school in a sleepy suburb like San Mateo."

At Serra, Brady campaigned for freshman class president "not to be cool, but because he thought that would look good on a possible application to the Naval Academy." He was a two-sport varsity letterman, earning two letters in both football and baseball as a catcher.

In freshmen football, Brady sat on the bench and watched the Padres' Kevin Krystofiak handle the starting quarterback spot. The team struggled to score and went 0-8-1 that season, getting shut out in three league games. "Tom was a linebacker, and also our third-string quarterback," freshman teammate Bill Harke said. "Our first-string QB was pretty fast and athletic. It was the fourth game of the season before Tom ever got to play quarterback."

"I think he got into a play or two as an outside linebacker," former Serra varsity coach Tom MacKenzie said. "Honestly, I barely remembered his name back then. He was sort of a face in the crowd."

"I just remember that we weren't very good that year," Krystofiak said. "Tom had a great arm, but he couldn't move very well. We all thought his big sport would be baseball."

Fortunately for Brady, Krystofiak quit football after his freshman year to focus on basketball. That opened the door for Brady to become the starting junior varsity quarterback for his sophomore year. MacKenzie, who coached at Serra from 1979 to 2000, was impressed by sophomore Brady's strong arm and, at 6-foot-2 and 205 pounds, he also had excellent quarterback size.

"The great thing about Tom is that he's still that same guy, he hasn't changed a bit," Harke said. "The same person he was in high school. Just a great, down-to-earth guy. I've seen him a few times since high school, and he's really friendly."

Brady won the Serra starting varsity job by his junior year. For his two years as a starter from 1993-1994, he completed 236 of 447 passes (52.8%) for 3,702 yards and 31 touchdowns. The Padres, playing out of the West Catholic Athletic League – one of California's toughest leagues – went a combined 11-9 and never made the playoffs.

Nevertheless, Brady earned *Blue Chip Illustrated* and *Prep Football Report* All-American selections. He also garnered all-state and all-Far West honors, as well as the Serra Most Valuable Player award. All the while, he carried a 3.5 grade point average and drew scholarship interest from approximately 75 colleges.

"When you talk to most youth, they're there, but they're not listening. They don't apply what you're telling them," said Tom Martinez, a quarterbacks coach who has worked with Brady since the ninth grade. "My pleasure with him was that he was all ears. He'd listen to what I said, would go off, then come back improved a bunch. All of a sudden the ball came in like a man, all of a sudden he wasn't little Tommy Brady."

Those who have been close to Brady say he is still the humble, All-American guy he always has been. "He is that guy that you'd want your daughter to marry," said

Damon Huard, the Patriots' former third-string quarterback. "He's got that smile on his face, he's really, really easygoing, he's real genuine."

John Kirby was Brady's favorite target their senior season and the tandem hooked up 42 times. Kirby, a Padre receiver coach and teacher who played two seasons at the University of Hawaii, said "I hear him audible and it reminds me of our own little code we started on the JV team, when he saw a DB playing too tight, Tom would pull on his face mask and it would change a short route into a streak. He'd put it right on the money. And he did time after time. Just like he does now. Everything you see and hear now is what we saw and heard in high school. It's just kind of surreal to see it now on TV. To see it on such a gigantic stage."

Serra athletic director Kevin Donahue says "Certainly, he was destined for success. He was the All-American boy. Down to earth. Well grounded. But how in the world can you predict someone will be one of the greatest of all time at anything?"

"I expected him to be a good college quarterback but if anything I thought he'd be a major league baseball player," Kirby said. "He was known as a baseball player."

"He was really adept at throwing the fade pattern," MacKenzie said. "Right on the money. It was God given. In 31 years of coaching I'd never seen someone able to throw like Tom Brady. He was our future, someone we needed to develop and cultivate."

MacKenzie remembers telling Brady at the end of his sophomore year that he had to work out harder in the weight room if he wanted to earn an NCAA Division I scholarship. Brady responded by finding a personal trainer and an off-season coach. He supposedly visited the high school gym to work out two or three times a day.

"He just flat-out outworked everyone," Carter said. "He was a student of the game and he stayed after every practice to throw extra passes."

"Most teen-agers will avoid at all cost what they aren't good at," MacKenzie said. "Tom Brady was the opposite. He'd take to heart what he needed to improve on."

"A lot of times I find that people who are blessed with the most talent don't ever develop that attitude," says Brady. "The ones who aren't blessed in that way are the most competitive and have the biggest heart."

"Everything I heard was that the first thing he did each morning was work out," Ayoob said. "It seemed like he never wasted time. That's why he was so successful."

"Everything I see in him now is what I remember about him back then," Kirby said. "He never saw himself as a high school quarterback star. He didn't let the attention get to him then. If anything, he tried to stay out of the spotlight, just like now. I think that's why we're all so incredibly proud of him. It's really unbelievable not only that he's reached such status but that he's the same old humble Tom that we knew."

"Even after he won his first Super Bowl, he was still coming to see me and I didn't notice one difference to him," said barber Brent Dzygryniuk, who started cutting Brady's hair when he was 12. "He was just humble Tommy."

Brady was drafted in the 18th round of the 1995 Major League Baseball Draft as a catcher by the Montreal Expos, but instead accepted a scholarship to the University of Michigan where he played football. Tom attended classes in Ann Arbor from 1995 through 1999 and majored in organizational studies. A redshirt freshman for the 1995 season, he served as Brian Griese's backup during the Wolverines 1996 National Championship season. Tom appeared in just two games that season and threw only five passes.

He continued to see limited action in 1997, playing in only four games with 12-of-15 passing for 103 yards. During those first three seasons, Brady spent more time standing on the sidelines than on the football field and at one point, he hired a sports psychologist to help him cope with frustration and anxiety. Michigan insiders said Tom even stormed into the office of Head Coach Lloyd Carr and said he wanted to transfer to UC Berkeley.

Brady continued to work hard on his game and his body, memorized the team's playbook, and beat out Drew Henson to become Michigan's starting quarterback in 1998 for all 13 games. He earned All-Big 10 Conference honorable mention, as well as Academic All-Big 10. In his first year as the full-time starter he completed 214 of 350 passes (61.1%) for 2,636 yards and 15 touchdowns. The Wolverines under Brady finished with a 10-3 record and a berth in the CompUSA Florida Citrus Bowl game versus Arkansas. Michigan won the game 45-31 as Tom completed 14 of 27 passes for 209 yards and a touchdown in the victory. He connected with DiAllo Johnson in the end zone from 21 yards out for the eventual game-winning touchdown with 2:25 remaining.

In 1999, Brady remained at Michigan as a fifth-year senior to get more starting experience for the 2000 NFL draft. Now captain of the Wolverines, Tom became one of the top QBs in the Big 10, leading the team to a 10-2 record. He earned All-

Big 10 Conference second-team honors and completed 214 of 341 passes (62.8%) for 2,586 yards, 20 touchdowns, and only six interceptions. Only Jim Harbaugh threw for more yards in a Michigan season. Brady set a school record for most attempts (350) and completions (214) in a season. Only Elvis Grbac had more touchdowns in a season for the Wolverines. Brady was named the Bo Schembechler Award winner as Michigan's Most Valuable Player for the season.

The last game of his college career was also Brady's most spectacular performance. In the FedEx Orange Bowl versus Alabama on January 1, 2000, Tom rallied the Wolverines from a 14-point deficit to win the game 35-34 in overtime. He completed 34 of 46 passes for 369 yards and four touchdowns.

In his five years at Michigan, Brady played in a total of 31 games and started 25. His record as a starter was 20-5. He finished his career with two bowl game victories, 443 completions on 711 attempts for 5,351 yards, 35 touchdowns and 19 interceptions.

NFL scouts had differing opinions on Brady. Though he was accurate and possessed a high football IQ, he didn't run well and threw a poor deep ball. Eventually, New England Patriots coach Bill Belichick selected Tom with the 199th overall pick in the 2000 Draft. NFL Network experts have called the selection "the greatest steal in the history of the NFL Draft." Quarterbacks who where picked ahead of Brady in the draft included Chad Pennington (Jets), Giovanni Carmazzi (49ers), Chris Redman (Ravens), Tee Martin (Steelers), Marc Bulger (Saints), and Spergon Wynn (Browns).

Brady signed a three-year contract, with a signing bonus of $38,500. He had been expecting to be drafted in the third or fourth round and was very disappointed with being selected so late. "We started to hear all those quarterback names and Tommy wasn't getting picked," said Tom Brady Sr., a San Mateo businessman. "He started to get depressed and had to get out of the house for a while. He came back in and the phone rang and it was the Patriots. Tommy started to break down…we got drafted."

Patriots rookie training camp was the next test. When Brady arrived in Foxboro, Massachusetts for training camp in the summer of 2000, the Patriots already had three quarterbacks on the roster. Rookie Brady had no guarantee of even making the team, but he played well enough in training camp and pre-season games to win a roster spot.

"I was so nervous to go out to practice because I was competing every day. I swear to God, I would lose sleep," he said. "I'd wake up and check the weather to see how windy it was going to be because I knew I was going out there and throwing. You'd learn valuable lessons about competition, and I approached every day in practice like it really was the game."

As he did early in college, Brady spent his rookie season holding a clipboard and watching from the sidelines. He started the 2000 season as the fourth-string quarterback, behind starter Drew Bledsoe and backups John Friesz and Michael Bishop, but climbed to number two as the season progressed. He threw only three passes, completing one for six yards. In 2001, Tom got his big break. When Bledsoe sustained a serious injury that resulted in internal bleeding in Week 2, Brady took the NFL by storm as the Patriots' permanent starter.

After an 0-2 start, Brady led New England to an 11-5 finish, good enough for a playoff berth and a first-round bye. In his first playoff start, Tom led New England to a dramatic 16-13 overtime victory over the Oakland Raiders in the Divisional Playoff round. The game was played in a blinding snowstorm and included a controversial call by officials over what appeared to be a Brady fumble that lost the game for the Patriots. The fumble was overturned based on the rarely-enforced "Tuck Rule," opening the door for Brady to march the Pats to the game-tying and game-winning scoring drives.

The following week, Brady suffered an ankle injury in the first half of the AFC championship game against the Pittsburgh Steelers, and was replaced by Bledsoe. Bledsoe lifted the team to a 24-17 victory. But Tom returned the following week against the St. Louis Rams in Super Bowl XXXVI and was named MVP after New England's last second 20-17 victory. After years of studying the throwing motions of Montana, Young and John Elway, the former San Mateo youth star was suddenly a Super Bowl hero himself.

Brady also became the fifth quarterback since 1970 to earn a trip to the Pro Bowl in only his first year as a starter. In his first 162 attempts, he didn't throw an interception, the longest INT-free streak to start a career in NFL history. Tom is the only QB in Patriots history to win 11 of his first 14 starts. He is one of only three QBs that led their teams to the Super Bowl in their first year as starter. He was the third-youngest quarterback (24.5 years old) to start in a Super Bowl (behind Dan Marino and David Woodley). Brady's base salary for 2001 was $298,000. Drew Bledsoe's was $3.4 million. Third-stringer Huard made $525,000.

2002 was a disappointing season for Brady and the Patriots as they finished 9-7 and missed the playoffs. Tom nursed a shoulder injury during the second half of the season and finished with a career-low single season QB rating of 85.7.

After a 2-2 start in the 2003 season, Brady sparked New England to 12 consecutive wins as the Patriots ran the table and won the AFC East. Brady's quarterback rating rose 37 points to 122.9 with 3,620 yards and 23 touchdowns. The Pats defeated the Tennesse Titans 17-14 in the divisional round of the playoffs, decided by Adam Vinateri's 46-yard field goal. The following week, Vinateri kicked five more field goals as New England topped Peyton Manning and the Indianapolis Colts 24-14 in the AFC Championship game to advance to Super Bowl XXXVIII.

The Patriots defeated the Carolina Panthers by a score of 32–29 with Brady named Super Bowl MVP for the second time in three years. He set a new Super Bowl record with 32 pass completions. Tom's performance included a 67% completion rate, 354 passing yards, and three touchdowns. *Sports Illustrated's* Peter King called it the "Greatest Super Bowl of all time."

His second Super Bowl MVP prize was a Cadillac XLR. Brady donated the car to Serra, which auctioned it for $375,000 and used it for school renovations. Tom also signed more than 200 footballs to thank the students who raised the most funds. "He sat there for more than two hours signing everything and anything we needed," Athletic Director Kevin Donahue said. "He said, 'if it's for the Padres, of course I'll do it.'"

For 2004, the Patriots again went 14-2. Brady threw for 3,692 yards and 28 touchdowns and earned his second Pro-Bowl selection. In the playoffs, New England's defense again battered Manning and the Colts for an easy 20-3 victory. Brady threw for 236 yards and two touchdowns in the AFC championship game to crush the Pittsburgh Steelers 41-27.

Before the 2005 Super Bowl, the students at Serra dressed in blue and white and gathered on the football field, spelling out the words "Beat Philly." With their 24-21 victory over the Philadelphia Eagles in Super Bowl XXXIX, the third for New England since 2000, Brady and the Patriots established themselves as one of the great dynasties in NFL history. The Patriots forced four turnovers, and wide receiver Deion Branch, who recorded 133 receiving yards and tied the Super Bowl record with 11 catches, was named the MVP.

Between October 2003 and October 2004, Brady led the Pats to an NFL-record 21 straight wins. An injury-riddled Patriots team heavily relied on him for the 2005 season. Brady finished first among AFC QBs with 4,110 passing yards and third in the league with 26 touchdowns. The Patriots finished with a 10-6 record to obtain their third straight AFC East title. In the playoffs, Brady fueled the Patriots to a 28-3 win over the Jacksonville Jaguars before losing to Denver the following week.

New England finished 12-4 in 2006 with Brady throwing for 3,524 yards and 24 touchdowns. During the post-season, the Patriots defeated the New York Jets 37-16 as Tom went 22-of-34 for 212 yards and two scores. New England beat San Diego the following week to set up another showdown with the Colts. This time, Manning and the Colts got its high-powered offense to the Super Bowl, 38-34.

The zenith of Brady's NFL career was the 2007 season. He led the Patriots to a 16-0 record and smashed many records in the process including a 117.2 passer rating and 50 TD passes. Tom also won a number of NFL awards, including the NFL MVP as well as the Offensive Player of the Year. He was chosen FedEx Express NFL Player of the Week four times and selected AFC Offensive Player of the Week five times. The perfect Patriots beat Jacksonville (31-20) and San Diego (21-12) in the AFC playoffs and, looking to add a fourth Super Bowl to their dynasty, met the New York Giants in Super Bowl XLII.

Trailing 10-7 in the fourth quarter, Brady engineered a scoring drive that resulted in a six-yard touchdown pass to Randy Moss. With only 2:42 left in the game, it looked as if Tom would get his fourth ring, undefeated season and third Super Bowl MVP. But Plaxico Burress's 13-yard scoring pass from Eli Manning with 35 seconds left doomed the Patriots, 17-14.

Brady's domination of the NFL took an abrupt turn in 2008 when he was sidelined most of the year due to debilitating injuries sustained on opening day. He underwent two knee surgeries and two subsequent surgeries to counter infections sustained in post surgery.

In 2009, Tom rebounded to fire 28 touchdown passes and topped the 4,000-yard passing mark for the third time in his career. But the Patriots finished 10-6 and were eliminated in the wild-card round of the playoffs by the Baltimore Ravens 33-14, his first career home playoff loss.

In 2010, Brady again led the NFL in passer rating at 111.0. His 36 touchdowns, 3,900 yards and 65.9 completion percentage sparked another amazing season in which he tossed a career-low four interceptions. But the Rex Ryan-led Jets, a team that New England pounded 45-3 just six weeks prior, eliminated the Pats 28-21 despite Brady's 299 yards and two touchdowns. In February, Tom was named the NFL's MVP for the second time and became the first player in NFL history to receive all 50 first-place votes.

As an encore to his brilliant 2010 season, Brady recorded one of the finest passing exhibitions in pro football history. In the first Monday Night game of 2011, Tom threw for 517 yards and four touchdowns, nearly breaking the single-game passing record of 554 yards set by fellow Bay Area native Norm Van Brocklin in 1951. Brady was 32-of-48 with one interception – his first in 358 consecutive attempts – as New England won at Miami. The four scoring strikes gave Tom 265 touchdowns for his career against only 104 interceptions.

Tom Brady is winning personified. He won both NCAA bowl games he started in college. He is the fastest quarterback to 100 wins and won 111 of his first 145 NFL starts. The Patriots set the record for the longest consecutive win streak in NFL history with 21 straight wins. Tom has played in four Super Bowls, winning three. He won two MVPS, two Super Bowl MVPs, and did not lose in his first 10 playoff games, an NFL record. He holds the league record for most touchdown passes in a season with 50. Brady has the fifth-highest career passer rating of all time (95.2) and he is the only QB to win three Super Bowls before his 28th birthday. He was named *Sports Illustrated's* Sportsman of the Year in 2005.

"He's never going to be spectacular," Tom, Sr. told ESPN. "He won't break nine tackles to pick up three yards. He won't be all that strong or elusive. He's just pretty darn smart. He plays a different game -- he doesn't make a bad pass."

Brady has graced the cover of *Sports Illustrated* 13 times – the most for any football player since his hero Montana. He has been named one of *People's* 50 most beautiful people, featured by GQ and seen with a host of female celebrities. He is the golden boy who last year was the Associated Press Male Athlete of the Year and Esquire's Best Dressed Man in the World. Tom has judged beauty pageants and acted in a movie, but he is also at home sitting with the first lady at a State of the Union address and meeting the Pope at the Vatican. He endorses few companies and once rejected a proposal for a Tom Brady Day in San Mateo. He's been interviewed by "*60 Minutes,*" hosted *Saturday Night Live,* and appeared in animated TV such as *The Simpsons* and *Family Guy*.

Brady dated actress Bridget Moynahan from 2004 until 2006. In 2007, Moynahan confirmed she was pregnant with her and Brady's child. Tom and Bridget ended their relationship sometime in early December 2006, around the time Moynahan became pregnant. Tom was present when John Edward Thomas Moynahan was born on August 22, 2007. John has Brady's first and middle names, though in reverse order. "The people who know him best, like his family, always knew that he would take responsibility and do what's expected as a father because he loves his son very much," said uncle Christopher Brady.

In 2007, Brady put his famous face and rugged good looks to use as a model when he was selected a "Stetson Man," and was featured in an ad campaign for the cologne. Tom reportedly refused to wear the familiar Stetson cowboy hat during the shoot, which sparked some initial controversy,

Events of Brady's personal life are frequently publicized. His romance with Brazilian supermodel Gisele Bündchen was daily news on programs such as *Entertainment Tonight* and *TMZ*. Since 2004, she has been the highest-paid model in the world and the sixteenth richest woman in the entertainment industry with an estimated $150 million fortune. Modeling insiders have argued that Bündchen is the only true remaining "supermodel" and according to *Forbes,* she may become the first billionaire model. Tom married Gisele on February 26, 2009 in an intimate Catholic ceremony in Santa Monica. Two paparazzi photographers claim they were shot at by security guards after Brady and Bündchen renewed their wedding vows in Costa Rica in April. The photographers filed a lawsuit against the couple, seeking over $1 million in damages.

On December 8, 2009, Bündchen gave birth to the couple's first child together, Benjamin Rein Brady, and celebrated the christening in Santa Monica. Giselle announced that his middle name is a shortened version of her father's name Reinoldo. Tom, Giselle, and Benjamin reside in Franklin, Massachusetts.

Thanks to a hot start early in his career, Brady's name is already linked to the ranks of Joe Montana, Steve Young, Terry Bradshaw, Peyton Manning, Brett Favre and other elite NFL quarterbacks. Where will he rank among the NFL's all-time greatest? Count on a lot more winning from Tom Brady.

14

DAN FOUTS

Dan Fouts's brilliant career as a football quarterback took off at St. Ignatius Prep in San Francisco and landed in the Pro Football Hall of Fame in Canton, Ohio. In the NFL's emerging era of quick-strike passing, he piloted aerial attacks to near perfection, bombing defenses up and down the West Coast in the process.

Daniel Francis Fouts was born in San Francisco on June 10, 1951. He grew up a 49er fan with brothers Bob and John and sisters Patty and Nancy but never dreamed he would ever play in the NFL, nonetheless become one of the game's great quarterbacks. Looking back on his football career, Fouts himself admits there were several lucky breaks along the way.

"I stand before you today on the steps of the Hall of Fame to tell you that without a doubt that I am the luckiest man in the world," said Fouts in his Canton enshrinement speech in 1993, with apologies to Lou Gehrig.

The first of these breaks came when Fouts was a young boy. His father, Bob Fouts, was the play-by-play radio announcer for the hometown 49ers and leveraged his contacts to get his son a job as a team ball boy and later as a statistician. The experience gave Dan an opportunity to observe pro football at an early age and gain a firsthand view of what the sport looks like at the highest level. While his pals were watching the 49ers on TV in the 1960s, Fouts was mingling on the sidelines at Kezar Stadium with the likes of veteran quarterbacks John Brodie and Billy Kilmer.

In junior high, Fouts was interested in playing receiver when he joined the local Pop Warner Football League. His father, however, said he should learn to play quarterback or not play at all. Bob Fouts said it was the only football advice he ever gave Dan.

As a ball boy for the 49ers, Fouts was noticed by his future high school coach Vince Tringali, an old-school disciplinarian who played a key role in developing Fouts's tough-minded aggressive approach to football. "A coach just naturally looks all over the field," said Tringali. "And so I noticed this kid on the sidelines throwing the ball back to the referee. I didn't know who he was, but I could see he had a heck of an arm."

Fouts was a youngster wise beyond his years, and was not in awe of even the most iconic NFL players. After all, Brodie and former 49er quarterback Y. A. Tittle were frequent house guests due to his father's position with the team. Dan simply did his job of gathering footballs. Did he dream of someday playing in the NFL himself? "I don't know of any kid who can think that far ahead," he said. "Standing on the sidelines at Kezar, I never really thought much about being on the field. I didn't have any sense of great drama. I was just having a good time watching the game."

In 1965, 14-year-old Fouts enrolled in Marin Catholic High School in Kentfield for his two first years of high school, and made starting varsity quarterback by his sophomore year. He decided to transfer to St. Ignatius College Preparatory High School for his final two years of high school to play for his friend Tringali.

"San Francisco was a great place to learn," Fouts jokingly told *Sports Illustrated* in 1978. "The bus stop near school was five doors from the Black Panther headquarters. Hookers approached me — a little sucker in a letter sweater — while I waited for the bus. I found myself drinking Coke out of a paper sack, like the winos. S.I. [St. Ignatius] was just a few blocks up the hill from The Haight. I'd sit next to a guy on a bus who was reading a whole newspaper in Chinese. I think it's important to have both experiences — the city and the country."

For the 1967 season, SI moved into the stronger West Catholic Athletic League and was not expected to be a contender. Some in the SI family argued that the school should remain in the AAA for fear of being dominated by the Peninsula and South Bay teams. But in that first year in the WCAL, Fouts led the Wildcats to the league championship in his junior year. SI went 6–0 in regular season play, beating both St. Francis and Riordan 26–20, St. Mary's 35–6, Serra 27–7, Bellarmine 28–21 and Mitty 41–0. SI also added a basketball championship in its inaugural WCAL year.

As an all-city senior, Fouts did not get many pass attempts as the 1968 Wildcats featured a run-heavy offense. Local media and college scouts at the time were more interested in Jesse Freitas of Serra High in San Mateo, who was teaming with gifted receiver Lynn Swann. The University of Oregon was the only Pacific 8 (now Pacific 12) school to recruit Fouts. George Seifert, an Oregon assistant who later served as head coach for the 49ers and Panthers, told the young Fouts: "We've got a pro-type offense and you can do the job for us."

Fouts was virtually an unknown when he accepted the scholarship offer but instantly built a reputation for dramatics in his very first collegiate game. He replaced injured Tom Blanchard in the second half against California and sparked the Ducks to a 31-24 win. Dan began to gain national attention as a record-setting quarterback for Oregon, where he and teammate Ahmad Rashad played under future NFL coaches Seifert and John Robinson.

In three seasons, Fouts broke 19 Duck records while passing for 5,995 yards and 37 touchdowns. He earned all-Pac 8 honors in 1973, was elected to the university's Hall of Fame in 1992, and named Alumni Man of the Year in 1993. He also flashed the mental and physical toughness that would become signatures of his play in the NFL. "He's the best, toughest individual and the best college passer I've seen," said Oregon's head coach Dick Enright.

It was the San Diego Chargers -- not the hometown 49ers -- that selected Fouts in the third round of the 1973 NFL draft. Fouts began the season as the backup to Hall of Famer Johnny Unitas, another of Fouts's "lucky breaks." The legendary Unitas had joined the Chargers after 17 spectacular seasons with the Baltimore Colts. Unitas made history in the third game of the season when he became the first player ever to pass for 40,000 career yards. Fouts broke a collarbone in an exhibition game and was unable to play again until the fourth game, against Pittsburgh. As he did with Oregon, Fouts launched his NFL career with instant offense.

Unitas was harassed by the powerful Steeler defense that day, completing only two passes in a first half that put Pittsburgh ahead 38-0. In comes Fouts. He completed 11-of-21 passes for 174 second-half yards and led the Chargers to three touchdowns — one on a 90-yard drive — to bring the final score to 38-21. From that game on,

Unitas's career was over and Dan's was officially underway. Two weeks later, the aging veteran relinquished the starting job to the rookie for good.

As he adjusted to the speed of the NFL game, Fouts showed improvement in each of his first three seasons but the Chargers did not. The team was 2-11-1 in his rookie year and 5-9 in 1974, preliminaries to what is now known in San Diego as the "Bataan Death March" of 1975, during which the team lost its first 11 games. Then in 1976, the Chargers named Bill Walsh offensive coordinator, and Dan's career really began to blossom. This gave him the opportunity to work with one of the best offensive minds in NFL history -- another lucky break. "It was a terrible team," said Walsh, who later became a legendary head coach for the 49ers.

Walsh took over for Tommy Prothro and the San Diego offense was redesigned into a pass-oriented attack that highlighted all of Fouts's skills. Walsh stayed only a year with the Chargers before moving on to a head coaching job at Stanford. "He was such a great teacher," says Fouts. "He worked with me on my fundamentals. You have to have good fundamentals as your base. Once you do, you can concentrate on other aspects of the game, like reading defenses."

Fouts completed 57.9% of his passes for 2,535 yards and 14 touchdowns in 1976, and the Chargers improved from 2-12 to 6-8. Finally, there seemed to be a glimmer of hope of becoming a winning organization.

Walsh – as he left the Chargers – had mutual respect for Fouts. "It took his technical development for people to realize his other qualities — his assertiveness, his leadership, his intelligence. And I'm not sure there is anyone as tough as he is in standing up to the rush. He is naturally courageous. If somebody asked me who the best clutch players were, I'd put Fouts in a category with Bradshaw and Staubach."

After Walsh departed, a higher-paid quarterback named James Harris was acquired by trade from the Rams for the 1977 season. Fouts demanded to be traded. When he was not obliged, he announced his retirement although he was only 26. He protested the NFL's labor agreement in court, hoping to void his contract. Dan testified that the Chargers were not championship contenders while fans and media criticized him roundly. Fouts eventually lost his court case and he rejoined his teammates for the 11th game of the 1977 season, starting in place of the injured Harris. He still knew how to make an entrance, or in this instance a re-entrance, completing 19-of-26 passes for 199 yards in a 30-28 win over Seattle. All was forgiven in short order.

How did Fouts regain the respect of teammates he wanted to leave? "There was no outward reaction from the team," he remembered.

"There were no bitter feelings on our part," says Charger owner Gene Klein, who subsequently signed Fouts to a long-term contract. "Whatever his reasons were for sitting out, I'm sure they were good and proper reasons for him. He was a very purposeful young man."

Dan's good fortune continued in 1978 when Don Coryell signed on as the team's new head coach and the Chargers became an instant contender in the AFC West. Under Coryell, San Diego became known for the quick-strike passing game and the emphasis of the tight end position. This required a tough, smart, strong-armed quarterback. Fouts fit the bill perfectly as the offensive assault dubbed "Air Coryell" was born.

"The thank you I give to you is the most significant because if it wasn't for you and an offense named Air Coryell," he said as Coryell presented him at Fouts's Canton enshrinement. "I most assuredly would not be here accepting this induction to the Hall of Fame."

With Fouts at the controls, Coryell's offense took the Chargers from also-rans to AFC West Champions in 1979, 1980, and 1981. Named both NFL and AFC Player of the Year in 1979, Fouts won the passing title and smashed Joe Namath's record for passing yards gained in a season with 4,082. Few quarterbacks of Fouts's era had the tools to execute San Diego's complex attack, and Coryell believed that Dan was the only QB that could have managed it.

"We're only doing what we do because of Dan," Coryell said. "He has such a flexible mind. He doesn't have all the qualities you'd want in an ideal quarterback. He's not a runner. He's a fine athlete, but he doesn't have the speed. But he is very, very intelligent, and he is extremely competitive and tough mentally. A pro quarterback has to be one of the most courageous persons in sports. He has no chance to prepare himself for a hit the way a running back does. And he's not as big and sturdy. We have an awful time getting Dan to throw the ball away. He wants to take his chances in there, and because of that, he's susceptible to sacks."

Fouts was not a mobile quarterback and the deep passing game led to many hits; his ability to absorb punishing blows and still play at a very high level was rare. He paid a heavy price for his courage. Coryell's primary concern was for Dan's survival. The 6-foot-3, 205-pound Fouts was not as thick as a Terry Bradshaw and got hit more often. He continually aggravated a groin pull much of his career and the hits he sustained often left him too battered to actively practice until late in the week. "We came to the conclusion that he didn't really need a lot of work," says Coryell.

The Charger attack demanded quick recognition from the quarterback, and Fouts had a basketball point guard's gift for identifying the open man. Pass protection was also critical for such an offense. Lucky again for Fouts, the Chargers had an excellent offensive line which included four-time Pro Bowler Ed White, five-time Pro Bowler Russ Washington, three-time Pro Bowler Doug Wilkerson, Billy Shields and Don Macek. San Diego led the league in passing yards an NFL-record six consecutive years from 1978-1983 and again in 1985 under Fouts. They also led the league in total yards 1980-1983 and 1985.

Yet another Fouts lucky break came with the arsenal of receiver talent that the Chargers assembled. Rarely using the shotgun, Fouts would drop back and choose from an assortment of great receivers. Wide receiver Charlie Joiner and tight end Kellen Winslow were the most famous, both now in the Hall of Fame, but John Jefferson, Wes Chandler, and others played large roles. Dan's passing enabled Winslow to lead the NFL in receptions twice (1980-81), while Winslow (1982) and Lionel James (1985) led the AFC in receptions on two other occasions. James set the NFL record (since broken) in 1985 for receiving yards by a running back at 1,027. Jefferson became the first receiver to have 1,000 yards receiving in each of his first three seasons in the league. Both Jefferson (1980) and Chandler (1982) led the NFL in receiving yards. Chandler's 129 yards per game average in 1982 is still a league record. Both Jefferson (1978, 1980) and Chandler (1982) led the NFL in touchdowns. In 1980, Winslow, Jefferson and Joiner became the first trio on the same team to have 1,000 yards receiving in a season. When he retired after 1986, Joiner was the NFL's all-time leader in receptions with 750.

In 1980, Fouts broke his own yardage record with 4,715 yards and then broke it again in 1981 with 4,802. In both 1980 and 1981, Fouts led the Chargers to the AFC championship game, losing both. The Oakland Raiders defeated San Diego 34-27 in 1980 despite Fouts's 336-yard, two-touchdown passing performance. The 1981 AFC title game was played in 59-below-zero wind chill weather. Fouts managed 15 completions for 185 yards and the Chargers' only touchdown, a 33-yard pass to Winslow in a hard-fought loss to the Cincinnati Bengals.

In 1982, Fouts again earned NFL Most Valuable Player, AFC Player of the Year, and All-Pro honors. He averaged an unprecedented 320 passing yards per game in a season shortened to nine games because of a labor strike. That season included consecutive wins against 1982 Super Bowl teams San Francisco (41-37) and Cincinnati (50-34) in which Fouts threw for over 400 yards in each game to lead the Chargers with big plays.

Fouts played in six Pro Bowls in a seven-year span. Despite going to the playoffs from 1979 through 1982, the Chargers never went to the Super Bowl. This has been attributed to poor defense and their unwillingness to run the ball. In Dan's prime the defense was not as stellar but the running game became far better with the addition of Chuck Muncie, traded from New Orleans in 1980, and the drafting of James Brooks from Auburn in 1981. Some say the San Diego defense never had a fair chance as the offense often scored quickly, leaving the defense to spend too much time on the field. It didn't help that Fred Dean, an All-Pro sack leader, was traded away to the 49ers in 1981 in a contract dispute. Dean won the NFC Defensive Player of the Year award that year to help the 49ers to another Super Bowl title and was later inducted into the Hall of Fame.

Late in 1986, when Fouts surpassed the passing yardage record he had seen Unitas set 14 years earlier, he celebrated the accomplishment but maintained the reverence for Johnny U. "He was my idol. I don't want to diminish anything he's ever done."

Overall, the Chargers were 3-4 in the playoffs under Fouts, who threw for over 300 yards in five of those games. One of their more notable wins was the 1982 AFC playoff game known as the "Epic in Miami," where Fouts led his team to a 41-38 victory by completing 33-of-53 passes for a Charger record 433 yards and three touchdowns. His completions, attempts, and yards in the game were all NFL postseason records at the time.

Battered and nearly broken, Fouts retired in 1987. In 15 seasons, he completed 3,297 passes for 43,040 yards, and 254 touchdowns. His total passing yards made him the second most prolific passer in NFL history when he retired. He also rushed for 476 yards and scored 13 touchdowns. He led the NFL in passing yardage four straight years from 1979 to 1982, and became the first player in history to throw for 4,000 yards in three consecutive seasons. Fouts was twice the NFL's MVP. He was only the third quarterback in NFL history to achieve consecutive 30-touchdown seasons, after Steve Bartkowski and Y.A. Tittle.

The six-time Pro Bowler and three-time All-Pro started 171 out of 178 games. He had six seasons over 3,000 yards and played in two of the six greatest passing games in NFL history. His years as pilot of the "Air Coryell" offense led to 42 Charger records and eight NFL records upon his retirement, including most 300-yard passing games with 51. He was inducted into the Pro Football Hall of Fame in 1993, after being elected in his first year of eligibility.

Akin to his father, Dan became a broadcaster in 1988, most recently as an NFL color analyst for CBS and has also worked as a play-by-play announcer and analyst for ABC. His partners have included Ian Eagle, Dick Enberg, Don Criqui, Dick Stockton, James Brown, Verne Lundquist, Jim Nantz, Jack Buck, Brent Musburger and Keith Jackson. Among his career highlights was his work on ABC's "Monday Night Football" alongside Al Michaels and Dennis Miller.

Fouts served for three years as sports anchor for KPIX-TV in San Francisco, where his work earned him two Emmy Awards. In addition to sports reports, he anchored the "Bay to Breakers" and the San Francisco Marathon, and was host of the popular "Hidden Hikes" and "Game Day with Dan Fouts." In 1998, Dan made his movie debut when he and Musburger portrayed themselves in *The Waterboy*, starring Adam Sandler. Fouts and Musberger appeared in the film as ESPN broadcasters for the New Year's Day "Bourbon Bowl" game.

Fouts was among the first athletes signed to endorse Nike products in the early 1970s and he was honored in 1990 when Nike named a building after him at the Nike World Headquarters Walk of Fame in Beaverton, Oregon. Dan has been honored by the California Sports Hall of Fame, San Diego Chargers Hall of Fame, San Diego Hall of Champions, State of Oregon Sports Hall of Fame, and San Francisco Bay Area Sports Hall of Fame.

Fouts and his wife Jeri, along with children Dominic, Suzanne, Ryan and Shannon reside in Sisters, Oregon, where they have been active volunteers in their community. Major contributors to the Sisters Schools Foundation, Dan and Jeri have raised close to $1 million for their local school district. They have also helped raise hundreds of thousands of dollars in the San Diego community over the years through Dan's hosting of such events as the Dan Fouts Celebrity Golf Classic for the March of Dimes, the Dan Fouts Celebrity Bowling Tournament to benefit the Child Abuse Prevention Foundation, and his support of many other charitable organizations in the area.

Fouts was one of the truly outstanding passers of his era. His jersey No. 14 is one of only two numbers retired by the Chargers – the other is Lance Alworth's 19. In 1999, he was ranked number 92 on *The Sporting News* list of The 100 Greatest Football Players. In 2009, he was picked by fans as the "Greatest Charger of All Time" for the 50th anniversary season. But more than the dozens of awards and records he has achieved, Fouts also created great memories for many NFL fans during the 1970s and 80s who will never forget his downfield bombs on those sunny San Diego afternoons.

"I told you I was lucky," said Fouts. "My football career is similar to a roller coaster ride. I've gone from a pro prospect, to a third-round selection, to a rookie quarterback, to a fledgling quarterback, to a struggling quarterback, to a promising signal caller, to All-Pro Almost, to All-Pro, Player of the Year, to potential Hall of Famer, to aging superstar, to ex-quarterback, to certain Hall of Famer, to elected in first year of eligibility. This gold jacket, these steps, this Hall of Fame… as a roller coaster ride it too has been thrilling."

16

JIM PLUNKETT

The life of an NFL quarterback is an unpredictable rollercoaster of touchdown celebrations and bone-crunching sacks. Rarely did an athlete reach the highs and lows – and highs and lows again – of Jim Plunkett. From a welfare childhood filled with family challenges, Plunkett was often knocked down and nearly knocked out. But he kept getting up and, by the time he retired, he walked away with the most prized trophies in all of football.

James William Plunkett was born in San Jose on December 5, 1947, the youngest of three children. He grew up in Santa Clara before the family found less-expensive housing in San Jose. His parents were both blind, having met at a school for the sightless in New Mexico. Jim's mother Carmella was blind since she was 19, brought on by typhoid fever. His father William was legally blind and worked as a Post Office news vendor to provide his family with a minimal but honest living. They occasionally survived on welfare but were not bitter. "My folks were poor and uneducated," Plunkett later said, "but they accepted life for what it gave them."

Despite his Irish surname, Plunkett is largely Mexican-American. Jim's Irish great-grandfather married a Mexican-American woman and gave his surname to their 50% Mexican and 50% Irish son. His son in turn married a Mexican woman and they gave their son the Irish name William Plunkett, although he was 75%

Mexican. William married a Mexican woman named Carmella who gave birth to Jim, which brings Jim's Mexican-American heritage to 87.5%. Although the Irish genes have been greatly depleted by the repeated pairing with Mexican women, the Irish heritage is easily traceable. Despite the clear Irish name and lineage, Jim identifies himself as a Latino because of his dominant genetic Mexican make-up. While he rightly carries an Irish name, he is Mexican-American far more than he is Irish-American.

Young Jim worked a series of odd jobs while growing up, including gas station attendant, grocery store clerk and as a construction laborer to help support the family. In an acknowledgement of his Mexican roots, Plunkett chose the fictional character of Zorro, the Spanish Robin Hood, as his boyhood hero.

Plunkett attended William C. Overfelt High School in the ninth and 10th grades before he transferred and graduated from James Lick High School, both of which are located in East San Jose. Prior to attending James Lick, he showed his talent for tossing the football by winning a throwing contest at age 14 with a heave of over 60 yards. Once he arrived at JLHS, he played quarterback and defensive end for the football team, and also competed in basketball, baseball, track and wrestling.

Leading the Comets to an unbeaten 1965 season as a senior, Plunkett was named to the North squad in California's All-Star Shrine Game and was heavily recruited by colleges. North's roster, however, was so stocked with quarterbacks that Jim was moved to defensive end and played well. Although Plunkett starred at James Lick, he was not the marquee quarterback in the Bay Area. That was Mike Holmgren, out of Lincoln High in San Francisco. Lincoln also produced future coach George Seifert. Jim considered attending the University of Southern California with its rich football tradition but USC chose Holmgren, who never did win the starting job. Holmgren was a Trojan for four years, while fellow San Franciscan O.J. Simpson won the Heisman and his team the national championship. When USC went for Holmgren, Plunkett decided to stay in Northern California. Notre Dame showed interest, but had big plans for Joe Theisman.

Wanting to stay near home and attend a university with strong academics, Plunkett selected Stanford over California, in part because the radical political environment in Berkeley could be hard on athletes. "I rejected California because the Free Speech Movement was underway in Berkeley and I didn't want to be bothered by student protests . . . I knew all along it would be Stanford," he said.

Plunkett's Stanford career nearly ended before it began. A month before his first class in 1966, Jim was told by doctors that the lump he noticed on his neck was a cancerous tumor. In a phone call with assistant coach Rod Rust, Plunkett shared his concerns. The surgery required to remove a malignant tumor would end his football career. Rust assured Jim that Stanford would honor his scholarship. Rust later said that he made that promise impulsively, confident that Stanford would back him. Rust's mother had gone blind and he felt the pain of the Plunkett family's situation. "I worried more about Stanford being good enough for Jim Plunkett," said Rust.

But the prognosis turned out to be wrong. The Plunkett family's prayers were answered when his tumor turned out to be benign. Jim never forgot the generosity shown by Stanford. It was the beginning of Plunkett's intensely loyal relationship with the university. Only his own family means more. "Stanford is in both our hearts," says Gerry Plunkett, Jim's wife. "I see how very much it means to him."

Plunkett had to fight for everything he had at Stanford. He was Mexican-American from a poor neighborhood, the product of an unglamorous high school program with parents suffering from physical maladies. Jim felt out of place with the rich kids and scholars who populated The Farm. He arrived with other young players— Jack Lasater, Bob Moore, and Jack Schultz — who also felt like outsiders. They were from poor or middle-class families, and they wondered how they would ever fit in at a university filled with well-heeled classmates. "We'd all gone to public schools instead of prep schools, and none of us had a lump of cash in our pocket," Lasater recalled.

Plunkett didn't play well for the freshman team, and when his performance didn't improve the next spring, coach John Ralston suggested a switch to defensive end. Ralston had three other quarterbacks plus a keen memory of Jim's fine performance at defensive end in the Shrine Game, and wanted the 6-foot-3, 205-pound Plunkett to consider a switch to that position. Jim promised to think about it. But after he did, he wanted to be a starting QB. He rejected the idea and firmly informed Ralston: "I am a quarterback." Plunkett vowed to work harder and threw 500 to 1,000 passes per day to maintain his quarterback role. "I don't know where I would have gone," said Jim, "but I would have transferred."

"I was extremely quiet when I got to Stanford," said Plunkett. "I wasn't an in-your-face guy." But he also was gifted with unshakable confidence and an appetite for challenges. Teammates never doubted who was in command if they weren't accountable. "You got the look from Jim," recalls wide receiver Randy Vataha, "and the look was not comfortable."

Ralston redshirted Plunkett in 1967, extending his career at Palo Alto to five years. The year of practice and no play helped Jim considerably. He out-worked his competition and won the 1968 starting quarterback job as a sophomore. In his Stanford debut, Jim was spectacular as he completed 10-of-13 passes for 277 yards and four touchdowns, never relinquishing his hold on the starting spot. He hooked up with Gene Washington and led the Indians to a 20-0 pasting of California in the Big Game. He threw for 14 touchdowns and set a Pacific 8 Conference (forerunner to the Pac-12) record with 2,156 yards passing. Plunkett's arrival ushered in an era of wide-open passing and pro-style offenses in the Pac-8, a trend that continues today.

Jim's junior year was even better when he set league records for touchdown passes (20), passing yards (2,673) and total offense (2,786), ranking third nationally in total offense and fifth in passing. This display of offensive firepower led Washington State coach Jim Sweeney to call Plunkett "The best college football player I've ever seen."

After his junior year, Plunkett became eligible to enter the NFL draft, which would have given him a chance to earn a large roster bonus for himself and his mother. Despite his success on the gridiron, his financial situation had not improved from his poverty-stricken childhood. His father had passed away and, even with his scholarship, Jim needed to take a series of construction jobs to make ends meet. A pro bonus would come in very handy and might even provide Plunkett with the means to finally buy his mother a home of her own. He passed up the chance at an early paycheck, however, so that he could set a good example to the Latin youth he had tutored and urged to stay in school.

"Coach Ralston, all our coaches, and my teammates have been building something at Stanford for the past couple of years," Plunkett explained. "If I were to leave now, I would always have the feeling that I would let them down before our goals were reached. Besides, we are always telling kids today not to drop out, to finish school, to set targets and to work toward them. What would they think if I were to drop out now for professional football?"

Plunkett remained at Stanford, guiding the Indians to an 8-3 season and the 1970 Pacific 8 championship. Jim played magnificently and there was significant Heisman Trophy debate throughout the season. The rest of the Stanford cast was anything but ordinary. The defense included linebacker Jeff Siemon and tackle Pete Lazetich who became first-team All-Americans the following season. But Plunkett, with his strong chin and powerful arm, was the face of Stanford's success. "The team was full of an awful lot of talented guys as well as egos," said strong safety Schultz. "But there was no hint whatsoever of jealousy for all of the accolades and attention being heaped on Jim. He also shined the light back on everybody else."

Back-to-back winning seasons had been previously marred by key losses, and Plunkett's crew was down to its last chance to win a championship. It was never "just football" to them, Schultz recalled. "We had experienced an awful lot of disappointment," including two straight defeats to USC on late field goals. "We didn't want to live through that again."

Upsetting the Trojans would be no easy task. Southern Cal had reached the Rose Bowl in each of the past four years, and conference rival UCLA was formidable as well. Stanford, on the other hand, had finished in the Top 20 only once since 1955.

The 1970 Stanford-USC game was scheduled for October 10. One day before the showdown, Stanford Stadium was the target of a bomb threat. Police searched the stadium, found nothing, and the game proceeded under extra security. The only bombs were those thrown by Plunkett, who passed for 275 yards and one touchdown, a 50-yard strike to tight end Bob Moore. Stanford had overcome the frustrating losses of the two previous years and defeated the Trojans 24-14, the Indians' first victory over the Trojans in 13 years. Two weeks later, Stanford beat UCLA for the first time in eight years. Wins over Oregon State and Washington nailed down the Pac-8 title and a January 1 Rose Bowl berth.

The 1970 season was dubbed the "Year of the Quarterback," as Archie Manning of Mississippi, Rex Kern of Ohio State, Lynn Dickey of Kansas State, Bill Montgomery of Arkansas, Dan Pastorini of Santa Clara, Ken Anderson of Augustana, and Joe Theisman of Notre Dame all enjoyed outstanding seasons. Plunkett was a long-shot Heisman candidate compared to the other famous quarterbacks. But his stellar performances week after week as well as a low-budget marketing campaign by the SU athletic department increased Jim's visibility.

Growing up in New Jersey, Theisman's name was pronounced Thees-man, but the Notre Dame sports information office convinced him to change it to Thys-man, as in Heisman, to promote his candidacy. But it was a dream year for Plunkett. First, he defeated the mighty Trojans to get Stanford into the Rose Bowl. Then USC beat Theisman and Notre Dame, further increasing Plunkett's Heisman chances.

When the Heisman vote was announced, Plunkett won by a wide margin. Theismann finished second to Jim in the balloting (2,299 to 1,401), but in the early going, Manning was Plunkett's primary competition. Not only was Manning playing faultlessly, but Manning-mania engulfed the South. Plunkett received the news of his Heisman victory at close hand, as he was in New York City to appear on a television show. Jim knew the award would mean a lot to the Mexican-American kids who already looked upon him as hero. "Yes, they can take pride in the fact that someone of their race has won it," said Plunkett. "I think it will help the Mexican-American community." When he arrived back in San Francisco, a large contingent of Stanford fans was waiting at the airport to greet him.

"Up to that point, it was certainly the biggest thrill in my life," Plunkett says. "And Bob Murphy was very proud of the fact that while everybody else was spending X number of dollars to hype their candidate, he spent 179 bucks on fliers. That's true."

"When I found out I'd finished second to Jim," said Theismann in 1984, "I was genuinely crushed." Plunkett, shy and modest, took a different view: "I wanted the Heisman, but my whole life wasn't centered on it."

Plunkett helped return the Indians to national prominence. He was once asked what was more important to him, the Heisman or the Rose Bowl. Pasadena seemed a longshot, an honor seemingly owned by powerful USC, who had played so well there under coach John McKay that the stadium was practically their second home field. The question had hardly been asked by the interviewer when Jim quickly replied, "The Rose Bowl, because I can do that with my team." Ralston said "That tells you something about Jim Plunkett. Tears came to my eyes."

Aside from his quarterbacking excellence, there was something that set Plunkett apart from his peers. He remained exceptionally devoted to his family and often returned home to San Jose. The fact that his fellow students did not puzzled him. "I don't understand why they don't go home more," he said. "Even if I just go inside the house and tell my mother I'm going to sack out, she at least knows I'm there – and she's happy."

His totals for that Heisman-winning season were 191 completions in 358 attempts for 2,715 yards. Plunkett threw for 18 touchdowns and ran for an additional 183 yards and three more TDs. He led Stanford to an 8-3 regular-season record with his strong arm and had the finesse to go with it.

Former UCLA coach Tommy Prothro said that "Plunkett is the best drop-back passer I've seen in college football. He has real strength and good speed. If you go all out to blitz him, he'll eat you alive." Oregon State coach Jerry Frei gave him the most succinct and genuinely sincere compliment: "I'm just happy to see him graduate."

Plunkett was the first Latino to win the Heisman Trophy and is still the last Bay Area player to win the award, 41 years later. Aside from the Heisman, he captured the Maxwell Award for the nation's best quarterback and was named Player of the Year by United Press International, The Sporting News, and Sport Magazine. In addition, the American College Football Coaches Association designated him as their Offensive Player of the Year. He won the W.J. Voit Memorial Trophy, awarded each year to the outstanding football player on the Pacific Coast, in both 1969 and 1970.

Plunkett never called attention to his humble beginnings. "Jim doesn't want sympathy, that his family didn't have much, or was on welfare," explained Murphy. "But he realizes now that it's going to stay with him and that he'll have to accept it." At an awards dinner, artist Tommy McDonald presented a portrait of Plunkett to the young Stanford star. "I wish," said McDonald to Jim. "I could give my eyes to your mother for a few hours so she could be here to see this."

But Plunkett's dream season was not over. His Heisman-winning season powered Stanford to their first Rose Bowl in nearly two decades. There, they faced Woody Hayes' powerhouse Ohio State squad, tabbed by the oddsmakers as a 10-point favorite. Jim was once more an underdog. In the history of the Rose Bowl, there may never have been a bigger underdog than Stanford was against the unbeaten and untied Buckeyes. Some said that year's Ohio State roster was one of the strongest in all of college football history with six All-Americans – fullback John Brockington, tight end Jan White, middle guard Jim Stillwagon, and defensive backs Jack Tatum, Tim Anderson, and Mike Sensibaugh. But as Plunkett once theorized, "I kind of like the role of an underdog. I don't know if that has anything to do with my past, but it's something that seems to make me strive for higher goals."

Plunkett triumphed again, leading Stanford to a stunning 27-17 victory on January 1, 1971. Before an energized crowd of 103,838 fans, Jim completed 20-of-30 pass attempts for 265 yards and ran for another 49 yards on the ground. The Indians had kept their Rose Bowl vow and finished eighth in the country in the process. The huge victory is credited with returning the Stanford football program to prominence, and Jim's performance helped established a template for what soon became a college football staple: offenses dedicated to passing the ball.

Not surprisingly, Plunkett was named Rose Bowl Player of the Game. Eight days later he led the North squad to a Hula Bowl win. Again, he gained Player of the Game honors. "Thus far, I believe, Jim Plunkett is the best college quarterback I have ever seen," said TV analyst Bud Wilkinson.

At Stanford, Plunkett piled up three seasons of record-breaking statistics, all since eclipsed by other Cardinal players. Stanford went 22-8-2 in those years, and Jim says his best game was the Rose Bowl victory. As a sophomore in 1968, he passed for 2,156 yards, a Pac-8 record. He shattered the record in '69 and again in '70. With a career total offense of 7,887 yards, Plunkett set an NCAA record that lasted 13 seasons. He also set NCAA records for most pass attempts (962), most completions (530), most passing yards (7,544), and most touchdown passes (52). When he connected for 22-of-36 passes for 268 yards against Washington, he broke the national career passing mark of 7,076 yards held by Steve Ramsey of North Carolina. In 1970, he won 28 awards including a consensus All-America selection.

The pre-Plunkett Stanford coaching staff placed great emphasis on running the ball. And in three of the four seasons before Plunkett's emergence, Stanford had gone 5-5. The coaches realized the game was changing and their difference maker appeared right on time. "It was almost a miracle," says White, "that Jim Plunkett showed up at Stanford exactly as we were searching for a new football identity." Prothro had called him the "best pro quarterback prospect I've ever seen" and Jim certainly looked like an NFL player.

Plunkett was attractive to NFL teams in the 1970s due to his excellent arm strength, passing precision, and his leadership experience from five years at Stanford. In 1971, he was drafted with the No. 1 overall pick by the last-place New England Patriots. The Patriots, 2-12 in 1970, placed Jim front and center for their team future. Plunkett still owns the distinction of being the only player of Hispanic heritage to be selected with the first overall pick in the NFL draft.

A prototypical dropback passer who loved to throw long, Plunkett directed New England to a 6-8 season in 1971, their best record in five years. His first game was a 20-6 win over the Raiders in the first regular season game at Schaefer Stadium in Foxboro. The Patriots also shook up the AFC East standings, as Jim's 88-yard fourth-quarter touchdown pass to former Stanford teammate Vataha on the final day of the season dropped the Baltimore Colts to a 10-4 record behind the 10-3-1 Miami Dolphins. Two weeks before, the Pats defeated the Colts, and Plunkett engineered a 34-13 victory over the Dolphins. Jim finished with 2,158 yards and 19 touchdowns in 1971, winning AFC Rookie of the Year honors.

Plunkett and the Patriots were intent on continuing the team's resurgence in 1972, but instead took a huge step backwards. Jim's touchdown total dipped to eight, interceptions rose sharply to 25, and New England's record sank to 3-11. He was sacked six times in one game at Pittsburgh, on his way to 97 sacks over the next three seasons as the team went 15-27. Plunkett seemed bitten by the jinx that sometimes afflicts Heisman winners, suffered from numerous shoulder problems and had to undergo surgery. "In 1972 my confidence ran into a stone wall," Plunkett said. "I'd never been in a losing situation before."

Oklahoma's Chuck Fairbanks replaced John Mazur as Patriots head coach in 1973 and installed an offense that had Plunkett running the ball on option plays and he continued to absorb punishing hits. He struggled with injuries and a shaky offensive line for the rest of his tenure in New England. Although Jim passed for 19 touchdowns and led the Pats to a 7-7 record in 1974, injuries took their toll. "Years of getting my butt kicked," he recalls.

After knee and shoulder surgeries and limited play in 1975, Plunkett asked to be traded. Earlier that year, the Patriots drafted quarterback Steve Grogan, who became a fixture in New England for 16 seasons. New England traded Jim to the 49ers in 1976 for quarterback Tom Owens, first-round '76 and '77 draft choices, and Houston's '76 and '77 first-round picks.

Plunkett seemed almost born to be the 49er quarterback. When he was traded to San Francisco, it was a widely publicized story of optimism. He was born and raised in the Bay Area and was still young. There was still enough Heisman-type passing skills from his Stanford days to believe that a native son's return home would launch a return to contention for a franchise that had been out of the hunt for years.

Under new coach Monte Clark, Plunkett engineered a dazzling 6-1 start. The San Francisco media was frenzied. All of his Indian promise seemed to be surfacing at Candlestick. With the Raiders off to a strong start, the idea of an all-Bay Area Super Bowl had local fans full of excitement. That year's Super Bowl was scheduled for Pasadena's Rose Bowl – the site of Plunkett's greatest triumph. All seemed right again for the former Stanford hero. Maybe those New England years of losing were but an aberration in his career. "I really thought I was going to be the savior," Plunkett said, "but all I did was put more pressure on myself."

Suddenly it all came apart again. San Francisco fell flat – four straight losses and five of the last seven. An 8-6 record was respectable, but the Niners missed the playoffs behind the Los Angeles Rams. Before family and friends in Northern

California, Plunkett had another frustrating 5-9 season with the 49ers in 1977 and was cut by the team during the 1978 pre-season.

A popular conclusion is that Plunkett was a big-time bust with the 49ers, but he returned a glimmer of hope to their fans. He filled a dismal period between John Brodie and Joe Montana. As his Oakland record proved, he could have led San Francisco to success under the right circumstances. A lack of supporting talent and coaching was at least as much to blame for the failures of 1976-77 as Plunkett himself. He never did team with O.J. Simpson, who was acquired in 1978. The idea of a Plunkett-O.J. "dream ticket" seemed a nice idea, but the 1970s 49ers could only be cured by a new coach like Bill Walsh and a new quarterback like Montana.

After the 49ers released him in August of 1978, 30-year-old Plunkett considered quitting football. He had played seven seasons with New England and San Francisco with only one winning record and had the injuries as a constant reminder. But two weeks later, Raiders Managing General Partner Al Davis signed Jim as a backup QB to a three-year contract worth $465,000. "I'd never been a Raider fan," he explained. "Growing up, the 49ers were always my team. I didn't like that Raider silver-and-black color scheme or the team's attitude."

"It surprised me that he was able to come back because I thought physically he had been so punished that he couldn't come back - and he certainly did," said New York Giants general manager Ernie Accorsi.

For two years, Plunkett's presence on the Raider roster was practically non-existent. As the third-string quarterback, he didn't play at all for the 9-7 Raiders in 1978. The next season, he threw only 15 passes. But in 1980, Ken Stabler was dealt to Houston and Pastorini, one of those 1970 Year of the Quarterback names from Santa Clara, was brought in. During training camp in 1980, Jim asked to be traded because he again expected zero playing time.

The Raiders ignored his request and in Week 5, Plunkett's resurrection began. He got his opportunity when starter Pastorini suffered a broken leg against Kansas City. Though the 33-year-old Plunkett threw five interceptions in the 31-17 defeat, he got the start the next week for the 2-3 Raiders, who thought rookie Marc Wilson was too inexperienced. On the verge of desperation, Oakland called on Plunkett to start for the remainder of the season.

Plunkett stepped into the fray and rallied a team of castoffs much like himself to a second-place AFC West finish. In his first game as a starter, Plunkett's performance startled almost everyone as he completed 11-of-14 passes with one touchdown and no interceptions as Oakland defeated San Diego 38-24, beginning one of the greatest comeback stories in the history of the NFL. Plunkett didn't stop there. He passed for 18 touchdowns and 2,299 yards during the season, guiding the Raiders to nine victories in their last 11 games and a wild-card spot in the playoffs.

In the postseason, Plunkett led Oakland past Houston, Cleveland, and San Diego to face the highly-favored Eagles in Super Bowl XV. Jim rallied the Raiders to a dominant 27-10 victory over Philadelphia, throwing for 261 yards, three TD passes and earning Super Bowl MVP honors. Completing 13-of-21 passes, Plunkett fired two scoring strikes to Cliff Branch and an 80-yarder to Kenny King, accounting for all of Oakland's touchdowns. The Raiders became the first wild-card team in NFL history to win a Super Bowl.

"I'm proud of that game," Plunkett said of Oakland's 1981 Super Bowl victory. "Many people felt I was washed up, and I wasn't sure they were wrong. After 10 years and struggling with New England and San Francisco, that first one meant a lot to me." With a Super Bowl MVP in hand, Jim's comeback season was complete. He was voted the NFL's 1980 Comeback Player of the Year.

"It was the spirit of the redeemed," wrote the editors of *The Football Encyclopedia* about the unlikely champion Raiders, "of those who had come back from the garbage pile to smell the roses."

The Raiders followed up their Super Bowl win with a 7-9 season in 1981. Competing for starts with Wilson, Plunkett appeared in nine games, completing 53% of his passes for an offense that managed only 17 points per game. In strike-shortened 1982, Jim started all nine games and elevated the Oakland offense to 29 points per game as the 8-1 Los Angeles Raiders won the AFC West by two games. In the playoffs, Plunkett completed 24-of-37 passes for 386 yards, including a 64-yard bomb to Branch as LA crushed the Cleveland Browns 27-10. But the Raider attack sputtered the following week against the New York Jets. Plunkett threw for 266 yards including a 57-yard touchdown, but the Jets "Sack Exchange" defense caused five Los Angeles turnovers and New York won 17-14.

When starter Wilson went down hurt in 1983, Plunkett again came off the bench, and again sparked the team, this time with his greatest season as a professional. He started 13 games and won 10, completing 60.7% percent of his passes for 2,935 yards and 20 TDs. Now 36 years old, he still manned the pocket with courage, getting sacked 42 times in 13 games. The Raiders finished 12-4 and captured another AFC West title. In the playoffs, LA pounded the Pittsburgh Steelers 38-10 and the Seattle Seahawks 30-14 led by Marcus Allen's 138 rushing yards per game.

The 1984 Super Bowl versus the defending champion Washington Redskins matched former Heisman competitors Plunkett and Theisman. Again, Plunkett emerged victorious as he passed for 172 yards in the Raiders' 38-9 rout of Washington, at that point the biggest blowout in Super Bowl history. Jim connected with Branch on a 50-yard bomb and a 12-yard TD. Allen, with 191 yards and two touchdowns, was named the game's MVP.

Plunkett spent most of his last three seasons injured or as Wilson's backup. From 1984 to 1986, he made only 17 starts. He played for the last time in 1986 at the Los Angeles Coliseum in a loss to the Indianapolis Colts despite his three-yard touchdown pass to Todd Christianson. Jim sat out all of 1987 with a shoulder injury and his NFL career ended when, at 40, his injuries and pain settled the issue and Oakland released him. Plunkett is currently the fourth-leading passer in Raiders history.

For his NFL career, Plunkett completed 1,943 of 3,701 passes for 25,882 yards with 164 touchdowns, retiring as an all-time Raider great. His career included 19 fourth-quarter comebacks and 23 game-winning drives, but also contained 380 sacks. "He has to be one of the great comeback stories of our time," said Davis.

Plunkett is still connected to the Raiders. During the NFL season, the once-reticent Plunkett co-hosts the team's weekly TV program, *The Silver and Black Show*, does a post-game radio show, and is a co-host of other Raiders TV broadcasts. He sometimes sits with Davis during games. He owns a Coors Distributorship in Stockton. Jim is an avid golfer, tennis player and also gives corporate motivational speeches. "I'm much better [as a speaker] now, I can guarantee you," he says.

In November 1991, Stanford retired Plunkett's No. 16. Although 12 Stanford players have been inducted into the Pro Football Hall of Fame, his was only the second Stanford number to be retired, the first being the legendary Ernie Nevers' No. 1. Jim was also named the first recipient of the Leukemia Society of America's Ernie Davis Award.

Plunkett's knees were replaced a few years ago with titanium and Teflon. That and 15 other surgeries have made it difficult for him to stand or walk too long. But he still continues his involvement on behalf of the Vista Center for the Blind and Visually Impaired in Palo Alto. There are also Stanford-oriented events on his schedule, such as a dinner he hosts each September for quarterbacks on the Cardinal roster. For years, he has opened the guesthouse at his home to Stanford athletes who could not find affordable housing.

Jim and his wife Gerry and daughter Meghan still maintain Atherton as their residence. For questions about what drives Jim, there is just one answer: "I love my wife. I love my daughter." It hasn't all been good times for the Plunkett family. Perhaps the most powerful expression of loyalty from Jim's Stanford teammates occurred during their pain when the Plunketts' 25-year-old son Jimmy died in 2008. "Bob [Moore] and Jack Schultz came to our house every day," Gerry recalled.

"We've all tasted what life has to deliver," says Schultz. "Some of it has been wonderful and some of it has been absolutely horrific. And we've known that we're there for each other."

"Those were wonderful days for me," Plunkett says. "I played in the NFL for 17 years, went to college for only four. And my best friends and associates are the people I went to Stanford with, to this day."

Jim, Gerry and Meghan filmed a 2009 episode of the TV program *Dog Whisperer* featuring the pit bull that had belonged to Jimmy. After Jimmy's death, Meghan chose to keep the dog with her to honor her brother. When the dog began to show aggression, Meghan was concerned. "Our daughter was very upset; she didn't want to feel she was letting Jimmy down," said Jim. "The show became kind of a tribute to him."

Plunkett keeps his Heisman in a trophy room along with photos and memorabilia at his home, a reminder of his brilliant career. When Gerry recently won her sixth Stanford Women's Golf Club championship, she reportedly joked with friends that maybe they should cover up her husband's Heisman for just one day to emphasize her moment in the sun. But nothing did ever cover up the trophy. And Plunkett's loyalty to Stanford has never wavered. For 21 years he has hosted a golf tournament to raise money for athletic scholarships.

Stanford and 49er coach Jim Harbaugh, who has a reverence for football tradition, is emphatic about Plunkett's identity now. "He's iconic," notes Harbaugh, "but he lives it with such little fanfare. He gives of his time, his energy, his money, and he's got a genuine humility. He's a good guy."

Plunkett is the only eligible quarterback to start and win two Super Bowls without being inducted into the Pro Football Hall of Fame in Canton, Ohio. Despite struggles in his Patriot and 49er years, occasional "Jim Plunkett for the Hall of Fame" talk surfaces. Davis, at recent Raider press conferences, got aggressive and said Plunkett "should be in the Hall of Fame by far over many who are in the Hall of Fame."

Davis says that Plunkett, in his mind, is better than John Elway, who's third all-time in most statistical categories and has won two Super Bowls but also lost three. "You look at him against Elway, you look at him in Super Bowls, you look at him in the Rose Bowl at Stanford, you look at him with the Heisman Trophy," said Davis. "John came on and won two Super Bowls at the end that have stars on them for maybe not doing it the right way."

Plunkett compiled an 8-2 career NFL playoff record and is often presented as a classic comeback story -- from fallen prospect to the ultimate winner of nearly every important trophy in football. He led the Raiders to two Super Bowl championships and also won a Super Bowl MVP. He has the distinction of being the first minority player to quarterback a team to a Super Bowl victory and the only Hispanic to be named Super Bowl MVP. Jim became one of only four players to win the Heisman Trophy and Super Bowl MVP -- Roger Staubach before him, Allen and Desmond Howard after him.

Plunkett won Stanford's only Heisman Trophy and quarterbacked the Indians to a Rose Bowl championship and the game's MVP award. He was drafted No. 1 overall by the New England Patriots, won the 1971 AFC Rookie of the Year and also played for the 49ers and Raiders.

He was a tall street kid from San Jose, a Mexican-American with an Irish name. He settled on Stanford partly because he wanted to stay close to his parents, both of whom were blind. But despite all his football success, Jim Plunkett is that rare humble celebrity who praises friends and respects others, who hasn't abandoned the values he learned during childhood poverty. Plunkett's life has been a series of triumphs and tragedies and a feature film based on his life is in progress. His against-the-odds story attracted scores of fans, including some who were only casual football followers. His father died before his junior season and Jim made certain there was time to spend with his mother no matter how great the football pressures. "People had read about my parents, about my family life growing up," said Plunkett. "I got so many great letters. Some of them said my story gave them a new sense of purpose in life. I still feel good when I think about it."

20

FRANK ROBINSON

Hall of Fame outfielder Frank Robinson combined power hitting and athleticism to become an offensive force, smashing 586 home runs and batting .294 in a career that spanned 21 seasons. He is the only player to win MVP awards in both major leagues and also won Rookie of the Year, Triple Crown and World Series MVP honors. But for all his trophies and accolades over a sparkling career, Robinson is most proud of his Presidential Medal of Freedom, presented to him in 2005 by the President of the United States.

Frank Robinson, Jr. was born on August 31, 1935, in Beaumont, Texas, the son of Ruth Shaw Robinson and her third husband, Frank Robinson, Sr., a local railroad worker. Frank Jr. was the last child born to his mother, who already had 10 children from prior marriages. When her husband left the family, Ruth moved four-year-old Frank and the family from East Texas to Northern California, eventually settling in West Oakland.

One of baseball's most intense players and known for quickness, Robinson explained that "When you sit down at the table to eat with 10 kids, you better be quick."

Robinson grew up in a poor multicultural neighborhood where he starred as a youth athlete on the streets and playgrounds. Frank played baseball all day long every day in the summer, coming home for dinner only after darkness fell. "When I was growing up in Oakland, we played from sunrise to sunset," he remembers. "And we played on concrete. It's what you did."

Robinson attended Tompkins elementary school in West Oakland. He was given the nickname "pencils" because of his thin legs and he told everyone in grade school he'd grow up to be a pro baseball player. This from someone whose family could not afford to buy him his own glove until he was 14.

With no father or coaching to cultivate his natural talents, his batting ability impressed George Powles, one of his teachers that recruited 14-year-old Robinson for his Doll Drug Company team. A year later, Frank's American Legion team won the first of two national championships. The team would eventually send 14 of its 25 players into professional baseball.

Robinson also played basketball and continued to learn under Powles' coaching at Oakland's McClymonds High School, where he was one year behind teammate and future Boston Celtics basketball legend Bill Russell. Powles coached baseball, basketball, and football at McClymonds from 1947 to 1975. He's been described as "a guy who had the smarts to become a major-league manager but who instead chose to mentor kids in working-class Oakland and motivate them to succeed."

Powles saw great opportunities for African-American athletes to play at the highest level thanks to doors opened by Jackie Robinson. "I learned more about baseball from George than I did from anybody in the big leagues," Robinson said in an interview with the alumni magazine of San Francisco State, Powles' alma mater.

Robinson had told a guidance counselor at McClymonds that he wanted to play major league baseball. His dream became reality after his high school graduation in 1953 when Frank was signed by the Cincinnati Reds. The Reds were actually scouting another player – JW Porter. They signed both players with Porter getting a substantially higher bonus. He was out of baseball six years later.

Though he grew up poor, Robinson was raised in an integrated neighborhood in Oakland where few examples of racism and prejudice occurred. Attitudes changed when he reported to the Reds' minor league team in Ogden, Utah. Now 18, he was assigned to Class C in the Pioneer League as a third baseman. He made two errors in his first two games and was quickly shifted to left field.

"Ogden was in a Mormon state, and though I didn't know it, at that time the Mormon religion insisted that Negroes were inferior beings," he described in his book *Extra Innings*. "I got my first taste of racial bigotry in Ogden." He was restricted from patronizing the hotels or restaurants frequented by white players. An avid movie fan, a local theater denied Robinson entry to see a film. While the white players from the Ogden team lived in private homes, Frank and his black teammates lived in a hotel and he had to wait for special black cabs to ride to the ballpark. All the while, he had to endure the racial taunts and obscenities shouted by fans and opponents.

In 1954, Robinson was promoted through the Reds minor league system, playing for the Tulsa Oilers of the Texas League and the Columbia, South Carolina, Reds of the South Atlantic League. In Columbia, he was exposed to the racial segregation of the South, especially while traveling. Focused on improving his game, Frank ended the 1955 season with an impressive 25 home runs and 110 runs batted in.

Cincinnati officially promoted Robinson to the major leagues in 1956, debuting with the Reds at an annual salary of $6,000. In his first big league at-bat, he blasted a double off the outfield wall. By the time that first season had ended, Robinson had completed one of the most remarkable rookie years in major league history, hitting .290, crushing 38 home runs and driving in 83 runs.

Crowding the plate, fearlessly competing with pitchers and running the bases aggressively, Robinson tied Wally Berger's rookie record of 38 homers, made the National League All-Star team, led the NL with 122 runs scored, and was hit by pitches a record 20 times. The Reds set a new NL record with 221 homers, climbing 16 games in the standings to finish only two games out of first place. Frank was unanimously named the National League's Rookie of the Year.

For the next decade, Robinson was the clear leader of the Reds. Batting .322 in his second year, Frank was one of eight teammates selected to the All-Star starting lineup in 1957 and was the only outfielder who wasn't removed by Commissioner Ford Frick after rumors arose of ballot-stuffing by Cincinnati management. Frank attended Xavier University in Cincinnati during the off-season.

"Pitchers did me a favor when they knocked me down," said Robinson. "It made me more determined. I wouldn't let that pitcher get me out. They say you can't hit if you're on your back, but I didn't hit on my back. I got up."

An arm injury dropped Robinson's batting average down to .269 in 1958, but Frank contributed defensively by winning the Gold Glove Award in left field. Shifted to first base full-time in 1959, Frank was selected but did not play in the first of that year's two All-Star Games. He erupted in the second game with three hits, including a home run.

Later that season, a hard slide into Milwaukee Braves third baseman Eddie Matthews ignited one of the most infamous brawls in baseball history and the first between black and white star players. Booed by fans, Robinson responded in Game 2 of the doubleheader with a grand slam against the Braves and robbed Matthews of a hit. He finished 1959 with a sizzling 36 home runs, 125 RBI, a .311 batting average, and 106 runs scored.

Continuing his power surge, Frank won his first of three straight league slugging championships with a .595 slugging average in 1960. A young civil rights advocate, he also began carrying a handgun in response to numerous death threats. He was even arrested for threatening a Cincinnati restaurant cook who had refused to serve him.

In 1961, Robinson led the Reds to their first National League championship in 21 years with his first MVP season, hitting .323 with 37 home runs, 124 RBI, and 117 runs. His .611 slugging percentage led the league and he swiped 22 bases in 25 attempts, tops in stolen base percentage. He was especially clutch in the stretch run. Robinson was so dangerous after being knocked down that Phillies manager Gene Mauch began fining any of his pitchers who pitched Frank inside. Robinson's third straight slugging title came in 1962 (.624), when he also led the league with 51 doubles and 134 runs. He hit .342 with 39 homers and 136 RBI, and finished second in total bases and batting average.

"He was not afraid of getting hurt," said Hall of Fame pitcher Bob Gibson. "I don't care how many times you hit him…you could not get him away from that plate."

Hampered by injuries again in 1963, Robinson saw his offensive output temporarily decline. He snapped his slump by choking up on the bat and swinging downward at the ball. His speed and hustle gave him a career-high 26 steals. Healthy again in 1964, Robinson rebounded by hitting .306 with 29 home runs and 96 RBI. The power fully restored in 1965, Frank crushed 33 homers and drove in 113 runs as he re-entered the prime of his career.

Cincinnati shocked the baseball world in 1965 when General Manager Bill DeWitt unexpectedly traded Robinson to the Baltimore Orioles for pitchers Milt Pappas and Jack Baldschun. The deal was among the most unpopular in Reds history, and the team would struggle until Johnny Bench, Pete Rose, and Joe Morgan formed the

"Big Red Machine" three years later. DeWitt called Robinson "an old thirty," and was eventually fired.

Making his American League debut in 1966, Robinson was a smashing success, leading the Orioles to a World Series sweep of the favored Los Angeles Dodgers. The first Triple Crown winner since Mickey Mantle in 1956, Robinson topped the AL with 49 home runs, 122 RBI, a .316 batting average, a .637 slugging percentage, and 122 runs scored. He capped his monster season with two home runs off Dodger ace Don Drysdale in the '66 World Series. When he was voted Most Valuable Player, he became the first and only player to win the award in both the National and American Leagues.

"We waited for him that spring," said Orioles teammate Brooks Robinson. "Well, we'd heard about him but you know how it is… you say here comes the guy with the reputation. Well show me. He showed us all right. He's got to be the best hitter I ever played with."

Robinson drove relentlessly toward a second straight Triple Crown in 1967 until he was again injured late in the season. Carl Yastrzemski won the Triple Crown that year and Frank finished second in batting (.311) and slugging (.576), third in RBI (94), and fourth in home runs (30) in only 129 games. Injuries continued to hamper him in 1968, but Robinson rebounded in 1969, leading the Orioles to the AL pennant while hitting .308 with 32 home runs, 100 RBI, and 111 runs.

"Going over the hitters it was decided that we should pitch Frank Robinson underground," said former Yankees pitcher Jim Bouton.

While in Baltimore, Robinson took an active role in the civil rights movement. He originally had little interest in joining the NAACP because of the public appearance obligations. But after seeing Baltimore's segregated housing and discriminatory real estate practices, he reconsidered. Frank became an enthusiastic speaker on racial issues.

"I don't see why you reporters keep confusing Brooks (Robinson) and me," he once said to Baltimore reporters. "Can't you see that we wear different numbers?"

June 26, 1970 was a career highlight for the slugger when Robinson hit grand slams in consecutive innings. He finished the season with 25 homers, 78 RBI, and a .306 batting average, his last .300 season. In 1971, Frank cracked 28 home runs, drove in 99 runs, and hit .281, leading Baltimore to its fourth World Series trip in six years. On September 13, 1971, Frank became the 11th member of the 500 Home Run

Club. The Orioles were playing a double-header against the Detroit Tigers. In the first game, Frank hit his 499th career home run followed by his 500th in the nightcap.

For 1972, Robinson was traded to the Dodgers in a six-player trade. He hit only .251 with 19 homers in 103 games for Los Angeles before moving on to the Angels in a seven-player deal the following off-season. Frank rebounded in 1973 to .266 with 30 round-trippers and 97 RBI in Anaheim.

As a player with the Angels, Robinson was managing in winter leagues, fully intending to make baseball history by becoming the first African-American manager in the major leagues. When the punchless Indians acquired him on waivers late in 1974, rumors of a managerial change soon surfaced. Frank hit 22 homers and after the season, the Indians promoted Robinson to player-manager for opening day 1975. He hit a home run in his first at-bat that lifted pitcher Gaylord Perry and the Indians to a win.

In 1976, Robinson gradually removed himself from the lineup to focus on managing and guided the Indians to their first winning record (81-78) since 1968 and only their third winning season since 1959. On September 18, Frank played in his final game. Despite the early success, he was fired as manager when Cleveland started slowly in 1977. He taught hitting for the Angels the rest of the season and also coached in Baltimore and managed at minor league Rochester through 1980. Robinson returned to the majors and managed the San Francisco Giants from 1981 through August 1985, contending in '81 and '82 in the NL West despite a nondescript roster.

In 1982, Robinson was a first-ballot inductee into the National Baseball Hall of Fame, representing the Baltimore Orioles. Robinson is also a charter member of the Orioles Hall of Fame (along with Brooks Robinson), and a member of the Reds Hall of Fame, inducted into both in 1978.

Frank returned to Baltimore as a coach in 1986. He was promoted to manager after Cal Ripken, Sr. started the season 0-6. The losing streak continued to a record 21 losses before the Orioles finally won. Frank energized the team in 1989, leading the O's to first place by the All-Star break and second place by the end of the season – they were not eliminated until the final weekend against Toronto. The Orioles had faced the Blue Jays earlier that season, managed by Cito Gaston, the first game in MLB history to feature African-American managers from both teams.

In 1999, Robinson ranked Number 22 on *The Sporting News* list of The 100 Greatest Baseball Players and was nominated as a finalist for the Major League Baseball All-Century Team. In 2003, The Cincinnati Reds erected a bronze statue of Frank at Great American Ball Park.

Robinson was awarded the Presidential Medal of Freedom on November 9, 2005, by President George W. Bush. The Medal is the nation's highest civilian award for distinguished service to the United States. The ceremony took place in the East Room of the White House. Frank was one of several people to receive the award, including boxer Muhammad Ali, Jack Nicklaus, and Aretha Franklin.

"It doesn't get any better than this," said Robinson after the ceremony ended. "It's a tremendous honor to be presented the medal from the president along with all the other recipients. It's mind-boggling. I stayed away from injuries. Fortunately, I had a lot of good teammates and we had success. And that's what it is all about."

When President Bush read Robinson's accomplishments, which included winning the Most Valuable Player in both the National and American Leagues and being the first African-American manager in the majors, Robinson fought back tears. At that moment, he said he was thinking about all the black baseball players who paved the way for him to be successful.

"I think about the Negro League players," Robinson said. "You think about Jackie Robinson breaking the color barrier. You think about Roy Campanella, Willie Mays – those guys in the old days when they had to take the rough times on and off the field. They made it easy for me to accomplish what I've been able to do."

On April 13, 2007, Robinson accepted the inaugural Jackie Robinson Society Community Recognition Award at George Washington University. In March 2008, he was awarded the Major league Baseball Beacon of Life Award, bestowed upon an individual whose career embodies the spirit of the civil rights movement.

Excerpts from Frank Robinson's 1982 Hall of Fame Induction Speech

"I don't see anyone playing in the major leagues today who combines both the talent and the intensity that I had. I always tried to do the best. I knew I couldn't always be the best, but I tried to be."

"A lot of people have said to me what makes you go, what makes you tick, what makes you so determined. And I have a lot of thoughts on it. I've expressed them. But maybe as I stand here today and reflect back to Oakland, California when I was a youngster, and all I can remember is a young man standing on first base as a ground ball hit the shortstop and I went into second base with a nice slide and I got up and my pants were torn. I looked down and had the raspberries bleeding a little bit. I didn't think too much about it 'til I got home and my mother scolded me about that about tearing the pants and I just said, "there's nothing to it, mom." But I think that was the stage that set the determination in everything the way I played the game. And a lot of people say there's nothing wrong with that, that's the way baseball is supposed to be played your suppose to slide in if there's a forceout at second base."

"I was blessed I think to come across a man that set the foundation for my baseball career and made it my life in general, and that man a lot of you will not recognize the name is George Powles. He was my sandlot coach, and high school coach, American Legion coach in Oakland, California. And he was a dedicated man. He gave to the youth of Oakland his time, his knowledge and his ability that he knew what it would take to play baseball. And what he taught me was how to play the game of baseball the way it should be played and that is to give 100 percent at all times. Do whatever you can do to win a ballgame, short of hurting anyone intentionally. But also I think the biggest thing that he gave to me, and the youth of Oakland was he also taught us how to lose and accept it. Not be happy about it, but how to accept it graciously. Because we all can't win all the time and you have to be able to accept defeat and build from that. George Powles gave me the foundation I'm still building on. And I just want to give him his just dues, and I want to say to George Powles, thank you for all the youth of Oakland because I know they appreciate it like I did and still do. And he is still a good friend of mine, and he still comes out to the ballpark and builds up my confidence."

"I didn't mind the trade (to Baltimore). I honestly didn't, but I was shocked and I was hurt at first because that was the first time I felt like I had failed. And I really took a while to recover from that. But after I thought about it for awhile, I said, "hey look, your going to a good ball club. They've been close twice. You go over there and just do what you're capable of doing. Maybe you can help them win." And I really didn't realize at the time, until I got there, what a great situation I was walking into. Not only was I walking into a good ball club, and being associated with some outstanding individuals, such as Brooks Robinson, Boog Powell, Jim Palmer, people like that."

"Without help, and prayers, I wouldn't be standing here today. Because for a young boy in Oakland, California playing on an asphalt baseball field, he didn't dare dream. Not even dare think. Wouldn't even dare let the thought enter his mind that he would one day be standing up here. Being inducted into the Hall of Fame. But it has happened. And I thank the Lord for giving me the God given talent to play the greatest game in this country."

Dodger Jackie Robinson has long been one of Frank's heroes. "I was 11 when Jackie came up," Robinson said. "I was old enough to understand that what he'd done had provided me the opportunity to realize my dream and play in the major leagues if I was good enough."

Frank Robinson's unique blend of talent and intensity helped him fully realize his dreams, hitting 586 home runs over a brilliant 21-season career, most of them in Cincinnati and Baltimore. He was the only player to win MVP awards in both leagues. He hit .300 nine times, 30+ homers 11 times, and fell just 57 hits short of 3,000. A 12-time All-Star, Frank led the Reds to their first pennant in 21 years, led the Orioles to their first pennant and World Championship and then became the first African-American manager in the majors. Both the Reds and the Orioles have retired Frank's No. 20 – the first Oriole to have his number retired.

Gifted as they were, former McClymonds High School basketball teammates Bill Russell and Robinson made overall contributions that were socially enriching as they were athletic. After Hall of Fame coach Red Auerbach stepped away from the Celtics bench in 1966, it was Russell who took over as player-coach, thus becoming the first African-American head coach in any major U.S. pro sport. Nine years later, Robinson debuted as Major League Baseball's first African-American manager with the Indians.

After 37 seasons as a player and manager, Frank began working in the Major League Baseball commissioner's office. He resides in Culver City with his wife of 50 years and children Frank III and Nichelle. Frank is also the author of three books. In a May 2010 interview with the *Washington Post*, Robinson described his newest role in Commissioner Bud Selig's office.

"I'm spearheading the commissioner's office on diversity on the baseball side. We handled it on the business side. Now he wants it to be overall with the baseball side of it, the front office and throughout the system for baseball.

"It entails looking at the numbers of minorities in the organization and what positions they hold and the authority they have. If you have 25 people on your staff in the minor leagues and only have one or two minorities, that's not a good number. It's just to remind them and to point it out to them that they have to do better. I'm not here to tell them who to hire and who to fire. I just want to remind that the commissioner would like an even playing field, and over time they should do better at their hiring of minorities in the organization."

Frank Robinson was without a doubt one of Major League Baseball's greatest all-around players. His sparkling batting statistics are remarkable considering he battled both injuries and some of the greatest pitchers in history, primarily in the 1960s. He still ranks in the all-time Top 10 in home runs and many other batting categories. As the first African-American to manage a big league team, he created a legacy of opening doors for other minorities as managers and executives and also provided inspiration to hundreds of players as both a teammate and coach.

20

GARY PAYTON

Considered one of the NBA's greatest point guards, Hall of Famer Gary Payton became the first player in league history with 20,000 points, 5,000 rebounds, 8,000 assists and 2,000 steals. The milestone is a tribute to Payton's wide assortment of basketball skills that included scoring, passing, rebounding, and some of most tenacious defense the league has ever seen. Nicknamed "The Glove," Payton was also the first to be selected to the NBA All-Defensive Team nine times.

Gary Dwayne Payton was born July 23, 1968 in Oakland, the son of Alfred and Annie Payton. His father cooked in restaurants in Hayward, Fremont and Oakland and also worked at a cannery. Gary grew up in the West Oakland projects, which steadily worsened between the birth of the Paytons' fourth child Alfred and their fifth, Gary. The neighborhood was sometimes a battleground where Annie and Al fought against street life and its drug-related temptations. It was an ordeal the Paytons never expected to face.

"The other kids we never worried about," said Annie. "But we were worried about Gary getting out of here. Things changed so much by the time he came along, and he was the kind of kid who was easily led."

Throughout most of his childhood, Gary played basketball on the Jefferson Elementary School playground, around the corner from the Payton house. His favorite player as a kid? George "Ice Man" Gervin of the San Antonio Spurs. In the classroom, young Payton lost interest easily, clowned during class and often got in trouble. Gary had four older brothers and sisters whom Payton credits with inspiring his feistiness.

Al Payton was the perfect father to raise the competitive yet unfocused basketball prodigy. Reared in Mississippi by a great aunt on old-fashioned Southern values, Al was a stern disciplinarian who played college basketball at Alcorn A&M College. In recognition of his no-nonsense ways, the kids he coached during summers in the Oakland Neighborhood Basketball League named him "Mr. Mean" and he even wore the nickname on his license plates.

When Gary was 10 years old, Al reportedly won $30,000 on a gambling bet and moved the family to East Oakland near High Street. During Payton's adolescence, East Oakland was divided out like territories to the drug gangs. Dealers hung out and sometimes even shared meals at the Payton household. Gary speaks openly of his life-long association with East Oakland street hustlers. "I probably knew every dealer in Oakland," he said. While he always connected with them as friends, he never approved of their lifestyle.

To keep his son detached from East Oakland's booming drug business, Al used a natural outlet that Gary loved – basketball. The Paytons' living room became an ever-growing shrine to Gary's basketball exploits: autographed balls, portraits and over 80 trophies jammed their shelves. The awards collection began when Gary was in the sixth grade and his father entered a team in the ONBL, called "The Family" and Al made it very clear he was the daddy.

Payton attended Claremont Junior High and raised his grades to a B average while playing baseball and basketball. Although only five-foot-two by the end of seventh grade, Gary was fast and could score in several ways. Al found summer youth tournaments for Gary and frequently drove all night to San Diego, Las Vegas and Phoenix. It was during those summers that Al drummed into his son's head the importance of defense and passing. Whenever Gary didn't defend or pass to his liking, Al would resort to the ultimate form of punishment – he'd pull his son out of the game.

"With Gary, I knew he loved to play," said Al. "So if he did something wrong, I sat him down. Once I sat him down and put him back in, he'd take it out on the opponents. I had him on a very tight schedule…I made him take vitamins, eat his vegetables and kept him off the streets. Discipline. That's why he's so good."

All the practice and all the games and all the tournaments essentially turned Gary into an Al Payton twin. The talk and walk, the attitude and hard-nosed style of play, and his love for flashy cars all were inherited from his father. Al even preceded Gary in wearing a single diamond earring. "Gary was the baby, and Al put a lot of time and effort into him," Annie said. "And Gary listens to him. Whatever Al says, Gary will do."

At 14, Payton prepared to follow his friends to nearby Fremont High School. Shortly before registration, a boy was stabbed to death during a fight on the Fremont playground, and the Payton family quickly took action. Their petition to have Gary transferred to Skyline High School was accepted after aggressive lobbying by his father. Al informed his son that he'd be heading up the Skyline hill instead of down the street for his high school education.

Skyline High School sits above all the street crime of East Oakland. The school is part of a prosperous, mostly white neighborhood atop the East Bay Hills, which offer spectacular views of Oakland and San Francisco Bay. It is a place of restaurants, clothing shops and organic food markets, a completely different world a few miles from the inner city that looms below. Skyline has one of the city's more renowned curriculums but never had won a title in the Oakland Athletic League (OAL). Al was more concerned with books than basketball.

Gary's father gave him a 1967 Chevrolet with the license plate "MR ICY" in high school. Gary burned out two engines driving up the steep, windy road to Skyline High, but Al replaced them. If his son needed $100 sneakers, Al bought them. Gary also had clothes when he wanted them and money in his pocket every day. Al worked as a Hayward restaurant chef in the morning, another shift at a restaurant in Oakland in the evenings, and occasionally took part-time work at a local cannery - all so his youngest son would never go wanting. "Money changes people's minds," Al said. "I made sure Gary never had to sell drugs to get any."

OAL basketball games are often played with armed security guards in attendance and are no longer held at night. Oregon State coach Jim Anderson said he scouted a tournament where six police units were called to calm a raucous crowd—and that was before a game. The Paytons frequently served as Gary's entourage and bodyguards. Wary of surprise attacks, Al and Alfred escorted Gary to and from all his Skyline games. "You talk about rowdy," says Payton. "In Oakland, the players were on you. The refs were on you. The stands were on you. You had to talk back or you were a sissy; you'd get run out of the league. Afterward? Yeah, it was kind of a struggle to get out of the gym. Cops had to be everywhere."

In his sophomore year, Payton's grades slumped and he was declared academically ineligible. Payton was suspended from the team for half of his sophomore season for bad grades and a worse attitude. "I messed up—fighting, trashing teachers and coaches, everybody," he says.

Skyline finished that season a disappointing 1-9 in league play. After consecutive one-day suspensions for clowning around in class, a Skyline teacher finally put in a call to Gary's father. Enraged, Al stormed into his son's math class and humiliated Gary into submission. "Gary wanted to go to class and be a comedian," Al recalled. "Because he was a basketball player, he didn't think he had to do anything else. I went in there and told his classmates, 'I'm going to show you all that he's not a little man, he's a little baby.' And I kind of spanked him in front of everyone. That was that. Even in college, all anyone had to do was say, 'I'm going to call your father,' and Gary would straighten right up."

For two months, Al met with teachers three times a week to confirm his son's efforts. Gary got to school every day at 5:00 am for a special study group. "I started growing up," he said. He met Pam Sims, a 4.0 student and gifted athlete who later earned a full athletic scholarship to Stanford University. Payton's hard work in academics paid off when it became obvious that a collegiate basketball career was in his future. At the same time, the NCAA raised minimum academic requirements for its student-athletes. If Gary wanted to play in college, he had to get – and keep – good grades.

Al Payton was clearly the inspiration for his son's patented trash talk. Eldest sister Sharon, an accomplished trash-talking softball player who raised Gary while their parents worked, kept the banter going. Older brothers, Greg and Alfred, who played some college ball at San Francisco State, also encouraged a verbal approach. "As far as talking on the court was concerned," Gary says, "the whole family was behind me on that."

In 1985, Payton finished his junior year with 18.3 points, 10.3 assists, and 4.1 rebounds per game as the Titans finished 19-7 and won the OAL championship for the first time in 20 years. Fred Noel, Payton's Skyline coach, said "When Gary first came up, he was the cockiest mother - you just wanted to kick him in the butt. I learned that he will do anything necessary to play basketball." In the Northern

California title game, the Titans lost to Logan High on a buzzer beater shot. In 1986, Skyline finished 20-5 and repeated as OAL champs. The Titans again reached the CIF championship game and again lost, this time to De LaSalle by one point.

Talk is cheap, if it isn't backed up. Payton spoke freely, but he also had the talent to win. He and Foster led Skyline to two OAL titles and a combined 39-12 record during their junior and senior years. For 1985-86, Gary averaged 20.6 points, 6.9 rebounds and 10.5 assists and was named all-California. He remains the Titans' all-time leading scorer with 2,172 points.

Still, when college recruiters looked at Payton in 1986, many of them saw him as a risk. "He had an air, like a guy who might cause trouble," said former UCLA coach Jim Harrick. Foster signed with the Bruins—and transferred to UTEP—but Walt Hazzard, UCLA's coach at the time, already had a first-rate point guard in Pooh Richardson. Most scouts visiting Skyline were there for Foster, but Noel urged them to consider Payton.

St. John's University coach Lou Carnesecca noticed Payton at summer tournaments in Phoenix and had high interest in Gary. Carnesecca led him to believe Payton would receive a St. John's scholarship. Gary also had offers from Division I schools such as Stanford, North Carolina State, New Mexico State and Oregon State. But Payton was attracted to the excitement and the glamour of New York City and chose the Redmen. A press conference was scheduled but Carnesecca called Noel to revoke his scholarship offer minutes before Gary's announcement.

Oregon State had been Annie's first choice but she had been outvoted. Al felt comfortable with Oregon State's Ralph Miller after a visit to the Paytons' house. The veteran Beaver coach told Gary "I'm not calling anymore. If you want to come, you call me. If you don't call, Oregon State will go on."

Payton made that phone call, but wasn't yet thrilled to be a Beaver. The St. John's episode had dented his confidence. "Gary was devastated," Al said. "But it made him a better ballplayer. He wanted to prove Carnesecca made a mistake. Gary just kept getting better and better, hoping he'd get a chance to play St. John's."

Payton moved into the dorms in Corvallis, Oregon, largely an unknown quantity. But that didn't last long. The development of Gary may have been Miller's best coaching at OSU. They made an unlikely couple but Payton, the rapping streetwise trash-talker floor general, and Miller, who's been around as long as basketball's founding fathers, both wanted to win. Miller insisted that Gary lose his outrageous haircut but let him keep his earring and his on-court demeanor, and turned over the keys to his team if Payton promised to play tough defense. Miller vowed to Gary that he would start only if he learned to guard people.

Payton kept that promise and immediately set out to become the best player in college basketball. That famous lockdown defense combined with a relentless ability to attack the basket would re-write the OSU record books. "I was really scared when I went to Oregon State," Payton admitted. "I wasn't sure I could play at the college level. Losing the scholarship to St. John's like that put ideas in my head. I began to think nobody wanted me, and wondered why."

He shaved his head and, as a freshman in 1987, won the last Defensive Player of the Year award ever earned by a Pacific 10 Conference player. Miller said "He might have walked in a little questioning, but after the first week, he was sure he could play. From the first time he walked on the floor, it was clear he had talent."

Payton was his trash-talk best with Bay Area enemies California and Stanford. "Get someone out here who can guard me!" he screamed at the Cardinal bench when Stanford's physical tactics "got under my skin." He maintained a running verbal feud with Golden Bear fans during visits to Berkeley.

"I started talking back, and it was like thousands against just Gary - who's going to win?" Payton says. "It hyped me up. If somebody talks to me from the crowd, I can talk back because I can back it up. As soon as I do something good, they're going to shut up."

A Payton family fan club of 50 showed up in full force to a game against Cal at Harmon Gym in Berkeley. The woofing in the stands turned the game into a sideshow. Reportedly, Oski the Cal Bear mascot approached the family with a frosted layer cake. Thinking the cake was a fake, Annie Payton bolted from her seat and taunted Oski, "Throw it at me! Throw it at me!" The cake sailed over Annie's head and hit Greg, a minister. Oski was suspended for the rest of the season.

Payton sometimes chewed out his own Beaver teammates as well as Pac-10 opponents. Gary was 6-foot-4 and 180 pounds, most of it steel wire and sandpaper. Some say the biggest surprise of all is that nobody has ever smashed his face to pieces. "A shack bully," is how Washington State coach Kelvin Sampson once described Payton. "He's like a bounty hunter, always out there looking for you. But I think he gets more respect than any player in the league."

Payton's defensive skills sometimes overshadowed the fact he was also a natural scorer. He once scored 58 points in a 98-94 overtime win over USC to come within three points of the Pac-10 single-game scoring record set by Lew Alcindor in 1966-67. Afterward, USC coach George Raveling said "That was as good a one-man performance as I've ever seen in the conference— be it Walton, Jabbar or whomever you want to name."

In the 1989 Far West Classic, Payton scored 15 of his team's first 22 points against Boston University. On the final two nights of the tournament, against Louisiana Tech and Oregon, he made the game-winning shots to cap performances in which he had 35 points and 12 assists, followed by 30 and 13. "This is a great player," said Boston University coach Mike Jarvis. "Does he have any relatives?"

"I've loved my days at Oregon State," says Payton. "If I had gone to New York, maybe I'd have made All-America two years ago, but who knows what trouble I might have gotten into in the big city? Here, I settled down, slept a lot, started to take care of my body. The trash-talking and stuff — I've calmed down. At this level it's all business."

Throughout his four-year career at OSU, he became one of the most decorated basketball players in Beaver history. During his senior year, Payton was featured on the cover of *Sports Illustrated* as the National Player of the Year in 1990. He was a consensus All-American in 1990, three-time All-Pac-10 selection, and was named the Pac-10 Conference's 1987 Freshman of the Year.

Payton was voted MVP of the Far West Classic tournament three times and was the Pac-10 Player of the Week nine times. He also was named to the Pac-10's All-Decade Team. Gary ended his collegiate career as Oregon State's all-time leader in three pointers, assists, steals, and points with 2,172, an average of about 18 per game. During his OSU career, the Beavers made three NCAA Tournament appearances and one NIT appearance. He was elected to OSU's Sports Hall of Fame in 1996. Payton started every game for four years and ended his Oregon State career No. 2 on the all-time NCAA career leaders lists for steals and assists. When reminded he passed on Payton, Carnesecca said "When I make a mistake, it's a real whopper."

Ready for the next level, Payton was selected with the No. 2 overall pick in the 1990 NBA Draft. Derrick Coleman was picked first and then Gary was chosen by the Seattle Supersonics. The Sonics paid a private detective to perform a background check on Payton, the highest pick in team history.

Entering the NBA to star-studded expectations, Payton struggled during his first two seasons in the league, averaging 8.2 points per game during that span. He started all 82 games as a rookie for the 41-41 Sonics. He finished the year ranked 12th in assists and 20th in steals, outranking all NBA rookies in both categories.

Soon after signing his rookie contract, Payton purchased automobiles for himself and his parents, a condominium on Lake Union and other luxuries. He made $13.5 million in his first six years with the Sonics, including $2.1 million in 1990-91. Payton lived as large as he wanted. He signed the second-richest endorsement contract, after David Robinson, that Nike has ever awarded an NBA rookie. Payton planned to set up his father and brother Alfred with a chain of sports bar/restaurants in Oakland, Corvallis and Seattle. They would be named Payton's Place.

In 1992, the Sonics named George Karl their new head coach. Karl at first did not understand some of the street game that Gary brought. By adding his shaved head to those belonging to expressive Seattle teammates Xavier McDaniel and Sedale Threatt, Payton never lacked for conversation topics with hostile NBA crowds. Payton named the trio the "Three Bald Heads." "I may not talk as much as I did in college," Payton said, "but I will express some things."

Payton soon expressed himself to be one of the NBA's top point guards, as he and "Man-Child" Shawn Kemp formed "Sonic Boom" – one of the most thrilling tandems of all time. Gary became the mastermind of high-flying alley-oop plays to Kemp, which became one of the most exciting highlights in sports. Payton earned his "The Glove" nickname when his cousin called him during the 1993 Western Conference playoffs and told him he was covering Kevin Johnson like a glove. He also became known as "GP" and "The Mouth."

Payton earned one of his nine All-NBA team selections when he was chosen to the All-NBA third team in 1994. Payton would go on to make the All-NBA first team in 1998 and 2000, All-NBA second team in 1995, 1996, 1997, 1999, and 2002 and All-NBA third team in 1994 and 2001.

Payton's defensive skill was once described by Kevin Johnson: "You think of guys with great hands, like Maurice Cheeks and Derek Harper. Gary is like that. But he's also a great individual defender and a great team defender. He has all three components covered. That's very rare."

In 1993-94, Payton led the Sonics to the best record in the Western Conference. Seattle, however, was upset by Dikembe Mutombo and the Denver Nuggets in the first round of the playoffs. All of his stats improved as Gary's career progressed. In 1995-96, he took his third trip to the NBA All-Star game. He was now a major threat beyond the three point line. Along with Kemp, he led the Sonics to the second-best regular season record at 64-18. By season's end, he was the leader in steals with 2.85 per game, ranked 10th in assists with 7.5 assists per game, 10th for total minutes, and 12th in minutes averaged per game.

Even in the NBA, Payton was still known for his trash talk. His trademark open-mouth, bobbing-head style on the court led to Gary receiving the third-most technical fouls of all time (behind Jerry Sloan and Rasheed Wallace). Payton often named John Stockton as his most difficult opponent and Tim Hardaway's crossover dribble as the most difficult move to defend. Gary was a member of the gold medal-winning 1996 and 2000 U.S. Men's Olympic Basketball Teams. He has been on the cover of *Sports Illustrated* six times: three times as the featured cover story and three times in a secondary role.

The Supersonics reached the 1996 NBA Finals under Karl and lost in six games to Michael Jordan's Chicago Bulls. Payton is considered one of the best defensive opponents of Jordan and the two players had a high-profile rivalry throughout the '96 Finals. Jordan and Gary were the only two guards to have won the NBA Defensive Player of the Year award since 1989, and despite their different positions (shooting guard and point guard), they were well-matched for other reasons. Both were prodigious "trash talkers" and had legendary competitiveness. Payton was quick and strong as an ox, making him the kind of player who could frustrate Jordan defensively. Gary, at 6-4 and with a tough physique, was one of a handful of point guards with the size and body type to guard Jordan.

Midway through the Finals, Karl assigned Payton to play defense as a shooting guard instead of his normal point guard assignment in order to defend Jordan. Though the Bulls won the series, Payton's defense held Jordan and the Bulls to their lowest offensive output in an NBA Finals game. In his first three NBA Finals, Jordan averaged 36.3 points per game and had scored at least 30 points in 14 of his 17 games. In the '96 Finals, however, Jordan averaged 27.3 points per game and scored more than 30 points in only one of the six games.

The Sonics won Game 5 by 21 points and Payton held Jordan to 26 points – Jordan's second-lowest Finals total of his career up to that point. In Game 6, which the Bulls would win to capture the championship, Payton played 47 minutes and Jordan missed 14 of his 19 shots and was held to a Finals-low 22 points.

NBC commentator Bill Walton said Payton "outplayed" Jordan during the second half of the series, and that Karl would "rue" the decision to "hide [Payton] from the king" in the early games of the series. During this series, Payton and his Sonics also held Jordan's Bulls to the lowest-scoring quarter in their NBA Finals history.

Payton married Skyline alumnus Monique James on July 26, 1997. They live in Oakland and Las Vegas and have three children: Gary Jr., Julian, and Raquel, a sophomore at St. John's University. Payton also has another son named Gary Payton II with a different mother.

In addition to his flair for the dramatic, Payton refined his fundamentally sound game and thrived in the post to beat opponents with turnaround jumpers, head fakes, and a step-back three-pointer. During the 1999-2000 season, GP put it all together to average 24 points, nine assists, and seven rebounds per game in one of the best all-around statistical performances in NBA history. The Seattle Mayor's Office declared June 6, 2000 as "Gary Payton Day." Skyline High School retired Payton's No. 20 jersey in Oakland at a Warriors-Sonics game.

Although Payton was still one of the top point guards in the NBA in the early 2000s, Sonics management made questionable general manager and coaching decisions. His braggy attitude, along with other factors, earned Gary a reputation as difficult and volatile which was further fueled by various fines and suspensions handed out to him by team management during Payton's last few years in Seattle.

Seattle discarded Kemp while he was still one of the best power forwards in the league. In the middle of the 2002–03 season at the trade deadline, Payton was dealt to the Milwaukee Bucks in a five-player trade that sent all-star Ray Allen to Seattle. Payton played the remaining 28 games with the Bucks.

As an unrestricted free agent prior to the 2003–04 season, Payton, along with former Utah Jazz star Karl Malone, signed with the Los Angeles Lakers to try to win their first NBA Championship. According to his agent, he turned down a $35 million contract with the Portland Trail Blazers to sign with the Lakers for the mid-level exception. Gary was a veteran who signed cheaply for a last, best shot at a title. But Payton and Malone did not hop aboard the Laker dynasty train merely for the honor of it. Both had considerable talent left. In his last season in Utah, Malone averaged 20 points and almost eight rebounds per game, and Gary had similar totals in points and assists.

Despite injuries to Malone, Shaquille O'Neal, and Kobe Bryant during the regular season, the Lakers won 56 games and the Pacific Division. Los Angeles then beat Houston, San Antonio, and Minnesota en route to the 2004 NBA Finals, where they lost to the Detroit Pistons in five games.

The Sporting News noted in a 2000 article that "Durability always has been one of Payton's strong suits. He has missed only two games in 10 seasons and is generally counted on for nearly a full game's worth of nonstop motion, despite chronic back pain that requires extensive stretching and regular applications of heating packs." Malone was the only player to log more minutes of playing time than Payton in the 1990s, and since the 1990–91 season, no one played more minutes than Gary. *Sports Illustrated* called Payton's 2003–04 season the best season ever by a point guard age 35 or older, and Gary continued to play at a high level even as he advanced in age.

Prior to the 2004–05 season, the Lakers traded Payton along with Rick Fox to the Boston Celtics for Chris Mihm, Jumaine Jones and Chucky Atkins. Gary planned on a another season in LA, but ultimately reported to Boston and began the season as the starting point guard.

On February 24, 2005, the Celtics traded Payton to the Atlanta Hawks in a swap that brought former Celtic Antoine Walker back to Boston. The Hawks released Gary immediately after the trade and he returned to the Celtics a week later as a free agent. Payton started 77 games for Boston as they won the Atlantic Division crown. In he playoffs, Gary and the Celtics were eliminated in the first round by the Indiana Pacers.

For his 16th NBA season, Payton signed a one-year, $1.1 million contract with the Miami Heat on September 22, 2005. He played in the same backcourt as superstar Dwayne Wade and was reunited with Walker and O'Neal. After all of his fantastic basketball accomplishments, Gary finally won his first NBA Championship on June 20, 2006, when Miami defeated the Dallas Mavericks in Game 6 of the NBA Finals. Down two games to none, Payton hit two crucial shots in that series: a game-winning shot in Game 3 and the Heat's final basket in Game 5's one-point victory.

In 2006, the 38-year old Payton re-signed with defending champion Miami for a one-year, $1.2 million contract. During his final season, he climbed higher on several career leaderboards. Gary moved into eighth place in NBA games played, passed John Havlicek and Robert Parish to move into seventh in career minutes, and passed Hal Greer and Larry Bird to become the 21st-highest scorer in NBA history.

Since Payton's career ended in 2007, he has been described as one of the all-time greatest point guards. Gail Goodrich, who played alongside legend Jerry West, said "Gary Payton is probably as complete a guard as there ever was." All-star point guard Kevin Johnson considers Gary "certainly...amongst the best ever" and "just as intimidating...maybe even more so than all-time greats Magic Johnson, Isiah Thomas, Tiny Archibald and Maurice Cheeks." When asked to rate the best players in each position of the late 1990s and early 2000s, former coach Karl said of Payton "I don't know who else you'd take at point guard. Some say Jason Kidd. Well, every time Gary went nose-to-nose with Kidd, Gary won that matchup."

Besides the 2006 championship, Payton's amazing career was highlighted by nine All-Star appearances, the Defensive Player of Year award in 1996, and two Olympic Gold Medal teams. He was also selected to the NBA All-Defensive first team nine consecutive seasons (1994-2002), an NBA record.

Payton is currently third all-time in career steals, fifth all-time among guards in defensive rebounds, 12th in offensive rebounds, and 10th in total rebounds for a guard. Among players considered point guards, Gary ranks third in defensive rebounds, fifth in offensive rebounds, and fourth in total rebounds, behind Kidd, Oscar Robertson and Magic Johnson. Gary is the only point guard to have won the NBA Defensive Player of the Year award. Payton also managed to make the playoffs a whopping 15 times, playing in the Finals three times.

The Sporting News said in 2000 that Payton was "building a case as the best two-way point guard in history," and asked "If you weigh offense and defense equally, is Payton the best ever?" When comparing Gary to the all-time greats, it has been said that "Payton arguably is the best defender of them all, and his offensive game is better than most." In the second half of his career, GP showed another side to his value. Durability. In 17 seasons, Payton missed only 11 games, and at one point held the longest active streak for consecutive games played (over 300). Of the games he did miss, most were due to suspensions. Gary was always willing to play through injury, often starting games wearing bandages across his abdomen or lower back.

Payton's cantankerous demeanor and nonstop trash talk may have also turned off some teammates, opponents, and media types. But Gary became much less volatile in his later years, and many players, including O'Neal and Walker, have loved playing with GP. In Los Angeles, Boston, and Miami, he was recognized as a spiritual leader and mentor for many of the younger players. Of his barking, Gary has stated "I never take it too far...I just try to talk and get their mind off the game, and turn their attention on me," adding that "sometimes I get accused of trash talking even though I'm not. [Referees and spectators] immediately figure you're trash talking. But I could be talking to a guy about what's going on or asking about his family."

One of Payton's core philosophies is that "mental toughness" is as much a part of basketball as on-court play. In addition, Kidd has lauded Payton as a "mentor" for the way he schooled Kidd growing up on nearby Oakland playgrounds. Gary has said that his mental toughness was developed in his days learning basketball in Oakland. "You learned that you can be friends before the game and after the game. But once the game starts, it's all about business. No jive."

Payton has made numerous charitable contributions of both time and money to various communities. He created *The Gary Payton Foundation* in 1996 to provide safe places for sports and to help underprivileged Oakland youth stay in school. He hosts an annual charity game as part of his foundation. Gary and Monique have been active in fundraising endeavors for HIV awareness, the March of Dimes, the Boys & Girls Clubs of America and the Make-a-Wish Foundation.

Payton also donated Miami Heat tickets to underprivileged children. At Christmas time in 2003, he took 10 families from the Ronald McDonald house in Los Angeles and let each of the 40 children have a $100 shopping spree at FAO Schwarz toy store. For Christmas 2005, he gave 60 children $100 Toys-R-Us shopping sprees as part of the Voices For Children program. In 1999, Gary wrote an autobiographical children's book entitled *Confidence Counts* as part of the "Positively for Kids" series, illustrating the importance of confidence through events in his own life. In July 1999, Payton was named to *The Sporting News* "Good Guys In Sports" list. Gary hosted a charity radio show in 1998 on Seattle's KUBE. He played hip-hop music including The Roots, Raekwon, Outkast, and Cam'ron.

Since the Seattle Supersonics moved to Oklahoma City to become the Thunder, Payton has expressed a directive not to have his jersey retired in Oklahoma City as part of Thunder history. He wishes instead for it to remain in Seattle, where he achieved the height of his success and popularity. Gary is currently working on supporting efforts to bring an NBA team back to Seattle and has stated that he wants to be involved with team management. During the 2008–09 season, Payton served as a studio analyst for NBA TV and as an occasional substitute analyst on

The NBA on TNT. Gary has also appeared in *White Men Can't Jump* (1992), *Eddie* (1996), *Like Mike,* and *The Breaks.*

Payton is a proud symbol of prosperity for Oakland's youth. In 2008, the Oakland School Board honored Gary for his work on Back-to-School and "Attend and Achieve" projects. He told the small audience that he had enjoyed being a part of these efforts so much that he planned to "do a lot more in the future."

Payton knows what it likes to come from the streets. In his youth, he hit the books and open teammates often enough to forge a multi-million dollar career. He dealt passes instead of drugs and pushed fast breaks instead of dope. That's the message Gary delivers to youngsters at the East Oakland Development Youth Center and during summer basketball camps in Seattle. He does the same during frequent visits to old teachers, counselors and coaches at Skyline High School. "I made a big impact on the kids here, I guess," Payton says. "So I come back as often as I can."

Known as one of the greatest lockdown defenders of all time, Gary Payton is scheduled to be inducted in the National Basketball Hall of Fame in 2012. With his wiry strength, physical style of play, and non-stop trash talk, Payton's intensity drove him to stardom in high school, college, the Olympics, and the NBA. He was a rare athlete that could get into the head of even the legendary Michael Jordan. Best known for his 13-year tenure with Seattle and holder of Sonic records in points, assists, and steals, Payton will undisputedly go down as one of the best all-around guards in NBA history.

24

RICKEY HENDERSON

One of baseball's most productive and durable players, no player scored more runs, stole more bases, drew more walks or electrified more fans than Oakland's hometown hero Rickey Henderson. Nicknamed "The Man of Steal" because of his incredible ability on the base paths, his amazing combination of both speed and power made him the greatest leadoff hitter in baseball history.

Rickey Nelson Henley, named after singer-actor Ricky Nelson, was born in Chicago to parents John and Bobbie Henley on Christmas Day, 1958. Bobbie had gone into labor late on Christmas Eve during a Chicago snowstorm and she phoned John to come home and drive her to the hospital. John said no, he didn't want to rush home right away. Rickey's father was playing poker — and winning. As for Rickey, he was born in the back seat of an Oldsmobile on the way to the hospital. He later joked, "I was already fast. I couldn't wait." Two years later, John left the family. In 1965, Bobbie and seven-year-old Rickey moved out west for a new start in California.

As a child learning to play sports in Oakland, Henderson attended the local elementary school and played baseball at Bushrod Park. He even became friends with Oakland Athletics owner Charles O. Finley as a boy. "Seems like that's where he spent most of his time," said Bobbie. "He just wanted to be out there running around doing something. Baseball gave him something to do that he liked."

In the sixth grade, Rickey earned his first trophy. "I got the huge trophy," he said. "It was for the kid in the area that excelled in sports – football, basketball, baseball, track. I felt so proud. I was the King of Bushrod." Henderson developed the ability to bat right-handed although he was a naturally left-handed thrower — a rare combination for baseball players. He later said "All my friends were right-handed and swung from the right side, so I thought that's the way it was supposed to be done."

Hank Thomasson was a local baseball coach who took an interest in young Rickey Henley. He pushed him, even picking him up for practice or games. Most weeknights were spent at practice, with weekend games at Bushrod Park, Golden Gate Field and Fruitvale Field. The playgrounds had many leagues growing raw talent in that era including the Police League, Pony League, Babe Ruth and Connie Mack.

"We played at all the local ballparks, all over Oakland — and a lot of the ballparks in Berkeley and Pinole, too," Henderson said. "I came out of the neighborhood where we always felt it was kind of tough to get scouts to come see kids play. I was one of the lucky ones that got an opportunity. James Guinn saw me play, and he decided that I had the ability to be a professional baseball player."

"I watched Rickey play with Hank Thomasson's team," Guinn says. "What was really outstanding was his speed. I'm a speed man. If a kid can run, I'm interested because speed helps everything else. I thought he had unlimited potential, and I wrote that in my scouting report."

Rickey's first love was football, specifically breaking long runs into the end zone. He was a running back and whether the game was flag or touch or tackle, he ran hard. Catching him was like trying to grab a lightning bolt. "Personally, I thought Rickey was kind of rough in baseball," Dave Stewart said of his former teammate as a youth and with the A's. "Football seemed like a more natural fit for him."

Baseball took several years for Rickey to master. It was initially a summer pastime, a way to burn off energy until football started. Arriving as a freshman at Oakland Technical High School, Rickey didn't bother with baseball until others turned him toward the diamond. "Baseball seemed too slow," Henderson said. "And it wasn't a contact sport."

Family and friends told Rickey he could play multiple sports — and be good at all of them. A counselor at Tech started her own incentive program. She offered pocket change to kids who played for the school, a little more for those who produced — money for hits and steals and runs. From that moment on, Rickey focused on baseball, basketball, and was an All-American running back in football with a pair of 1,000-yard rushing seasons. In 1974, Bobbie married Paul Henderson in Rickey Henley's junior year and the family adopted the Henderson surname.

Rickey began his senior year at Tech considering several college football scholarship offers including Arizona State. As a senior he rushed for 1,100 yards and returned a kickoff 98 yards for a touchdown. In baseball, Henderson soon settled into the role that defined him. After batting second for the Bulldogs, coach Bob Cryer installed Rickey at the top of the order. Already having batted leadoff in youth leagues, Henderson walked, hit, and ran his way to the All-Oakland Athletic League Team for the third time, batting .435 with 30 stolen bases.

"It just didn't suit me to have to wait around to get a chance to come up and hit," Henderson says. "I always wanted to be the first one to grab a bat. I was comfortable being the first man up. I wanted to be the first one with a chance to get a hit, and I knew that gave me a chance to come up more than anybody else."

Upon graduating in 1976, the 5-foot-9 Henderson received over a dozen football scholarship offers and turned them down on the advice of his mother, who argued that football players had shorter careers. Rickey, blessed with speed and explosiveness, was eventually drafted by his hometown Oakland A's. The Athletics selected him in the fourth round of the 1976 Major League Baseball Draft. Later that year, Henderson married his high-school sweetheart, Pamela. Rickey promised himself that he would return to football if he did not make the majors within four years. "My dream was to play football for the Oakland Raiders," Henderson said. "But my mother thought I would get hurt playing football, so she chose baseball for me. I guess moms do know best."

After accepting a $10,000 signing bonus from Oakland, Rickey spent the first season of his minor league career with the Boise A's of the Northwest League. In 46 games, Henderson batted .336 with 29 steals in 36 attempts and hit three home runs and two triples. His defense, however, was disappointing and Rickey vowed to improve his throwing accuracy. His salary for the 1976 season was $500 per month.

In 1977, Henderson spent the season with the Modesto A's under manager Tom Trebelhorn. He batted .345 in 134 games with 104 runs during his record-setting season with Modesto. Rickey, along with Darrell Woodard, nearly broke the league record for team stolen bases. The Modesto A's finished the season with 357 stolen bases, just shy of the league record of 370. While Woodard tied the single-season player mark with 90 steals, Henderson broke the record by swiping 95 and was awarded the Sundial Trophy, given to the Modesto's Most Valuable Player. He became the fourth professional player to steal seven bases in one game.

Henderson spent the 1978 season with the Jersey City, New Jersey A's of the Eastern League. Rickey led the league with 81 steals and also led all outfielders with four double plays and 15 assists. After the season ended, he played winter ball for the Navojoa Mayos of the Mexican Pacific League. He played in six games for the team, which won its first championship. Rickey remembers a night at a Mexican disco when he wore a pair of heels about four inches high. Suddenly, men ran in yelling with guns and started shooting. Henderson ducked under a table as gunfire filled the room. When the shooting ended, he looked down and saw a bullet had pierced the heel of his shoe. "If tall heels hadn't been popular, Rickey might have had his career ruined," he said.

Henderson started the 1979 season with the Ogden A's of the Pacific Coast League. In 71 games for Ogden, he batted .309 and stole 44 bases. The 20-year-old outfielder made his major league debut with last-place Oakland on June 24, 1979, getting two hits and a stolen base in four at bats. He batted .274 with 33 steals in 89 games. Rickey was as strong a Rookie of the Year candidate in 1979 as either of the co-winners — John Castino and Alfredo Griffin. Henderson, however, did not receive a single vote for the award.

In 1980, Finley hired manager Billy Martin and his exciting brand of "Billy Ball" propelled Rickey to stardom. Martin was a Berkeley native and a former World Series-winning player and manager with the New York Yankees. He loved aggressive managing, frequently greenlighting Henderson on steals, hit-and-runs, squeeze plays and double steals. Rickey became only the third player to steal 100 bases in a season: Maury Wills's 104 steals in 1962 and Lou Brock's 118 in 1974 preceded him. His 100 steals set a new American League record, surpassing Ty Cobb's 96 set in 1915. That winter, Henderson played in the Puerto Rican Professional Baseball League and his 42 stolen bases broke that league's record as well.

"At the time, I probably didn't recognize what it stands for over a long period of time," Henderson said. "I think I was having fun, you know, just stealing bases. It was based upon (Martin) wanting it. (Martin) had a strategy, and he told me the strategy, and we worked together and achieved that. That year, every day I came to the ballpark, I couldn't even care if I got a hit. My job was that I've got to steal a base."

Martin also managed Henderson with the Yankees in 1985 and 1988. Martin, Rickey says, taught him more about the game of baseball than anyone else in his career. If Martin were alive in 2009, he likely would have been Henderson's choice to introduce him at the Hall of Fame. Billy died in a pickup truck crash on Christmas Day 1989, Rickey's 31st birthday. Henderson still misses Martin, the man he called a father figure. Martin taught him how to prepare, how to play defense and how to perfect his leading and sliding techniques. And most importantly, how to respect and love the game. "You don't have that now," Rickey said. "The motivation, the heart. Kids don't understand the generations that made this game. You know, the sacrifices and what the game really means to you."

In 1981, Henderson was a Most Valuable Player candidate when he batted .319, led the league in hits, and again in steals with 56 in a strike-shortened season. He finished second to Milwaukee Brewer Rollie Fingers in the MVP voting. Rickey's fielding that season earned him his only Gold Glove Award. In his first taste of post-season action, Rickey hit .182 in the AL Division Series against Kansas City and .364 in the American League Championship Series against New York.

On August 27, 1982, Henderson shattered Lou Brock's MLB record of 118 stolen bases set in 1974 and finished the season with an astonishing 130 steals, a record that hasn't been approached since. That season, Rickey stole a stunning 84 bases before the All-Star break — a full 21 more than any player in history. In comparison, no one has stolen 84 bases *in an entire season* since 1988. Henderson's 130 steals outpaced nine of the American League's 14 *teams* that season.

Many baseball insiders think Henderson's awesome record of 130 steals will never be broken. "I don't see it happening," said Boston Red Sox outfielder Carl Crawford, who has stolen at least 50 bases five times. "You never say never, but there's only one Rickey. You've got to have a guy that always gets on base, and hits mostly singles so he can steal. But with Rickey, he hit so many homers, too. When you think about it, it's just insane what he did. That number is so big, it doesn't even cross my mind."

As his muscular frame developed, Henderson continued to improve as a hitter. He elevated his power-hitting ability, which eventually led to another record – most home runs to lead off a game. During his career, Rickey hit over 20 home runs in four different seasons, with a high of 28 in 1986 and again in 1990. Henderson adopted an exaggerated crouch as his batting stance, which reduced his strike zone without sacrificing power. Sportswriter Jim Murray described Rickey's strike zone as being "smaller than Hitler's heart."

"I found that if I squatted down real low at the plate... I could see the ball better," he said, describing his approach to *Sports Illustrated* in 1982. "I also knew it threw the pitcher off. I found that I could put my weight on my back foot and still turn my hips on the swing. I'm down so low I don't have much of a strike zone."

In 1983, Henderson eclipsed 100 steals for the third time in his career with 108 stolen bases. His 66 thefts in 1984 topped the AL for the fifth consecutive season, and he was second in the league with 113 runs. Following the '84 season, he was traded to the Yankees with Bert Bradley for five players: Tim Birtsas, Jay Howell, Stan Javier, Eric Plunk, and Jose Rijo.

Henderson took his blend of power and speed to New York in 1985. At the top of the order for the Yankees, he batted .314 with 146 runs scored in only 143 games. He cracked 24 homers, drove in 72, walked 99 times, stole 80 bases, and was caught just 10 times. Rickey had a career-best .516 slugging percentage and .419 on-base percentage. Henderson became the first player in major league history to reach 80 stolen bases and 20 home runs. He won the Silver Slugger Award and was third in the MVP voting behind teammate Don Mattingly and Wade Boggs. As an outfielder, he proved himself to be versatile, moving from left to centerfield (he later returned to his preferred left field). For his flashy catches, Rickey earned the nickname "Style Dog."

In 1986, Henderson smashed an AL record nine leadoff homers in one season and posted career highs in homers (28), at-bats (608) and RBI (74). His 130 runs topped the major leagues for the second consecutive year. Rickey again achieved an 80/20 season, as did the Reds' Eric Davis, and they remain the only players to do so in major league history. He led the league in steals for the seventh straight year and was the first player to lead the AL in runs scored for consecutive seasons since Mickey Mantle in 1960-61.

Henderson missed 67 games due to injuries in 1987 and had one of his poorer seasons. His lackluster performance drew criticism from the New York media, which had never covered Rickey or his eccentricities kindly. Yankees owner George Steinbrenner issued a press release claiming that manager Lou Piniella wanted to trade Henderson and questioned Rickey's effort. Still, Henderson had a career-best on-base percentage (.423), and was fifth in the league in steals (41) despite playing only 95 games.

The 1987 season was the only one from 1980–1991 in which Henderson did not lead the league in steals. Seattle's Harold Reynolds topped the AL with 60 steals. Reynolds often tells the story of getting a call from Henderson after the season: "I say, 'Hey, what's going on, Rickey?' I think he's calling to congratulate me, but he says, '*Sixty* stolen bases? You ought to be ashamed. Rickey would have 60 at the break.' And then *click*, he hung up."

Henderson rebounded in 1988 to lead the AL in steals with 93, scored 118 runs, and hit .305. Though only in New York for four and one-half seasons, Rickey set the Yankees' franchise record with 326 stolen bases. He also made his seventh straight All-Star appearance. His fifth-inning score on July 17 vs. Chicago was his 1,000th career run. Henderson swiped four bases in a game three times and was successful on an amazing 44 of his last 46 attempts.

It wasn't until a 1989 mid-season trade to Oakland that Rickey established himself as one of the game's greatest players. His 52 steals and 72 runs in only 85 games sparked the A's to the postseason and his 126 walks were the most by any AL hitter since 1970. With a record eight steals in five games against Toronto, he was named MVP of the ALCS. Henderson hit .400 while scoring eight runs and delivering two home runs, five RBI, seven walks and a 1.000 slugging percentage. Leading the A's to a four-game sweep over the San Francisco Giants for their first World Series title since 1974, Rickey hit .474 with nine hits, scored 12 runs and slugged .895 including two triples and a homer.

Henderson had now been a major league player for 12 seasons and according to former teammates, Rickey was a fun-loving unique personality, not at all selfish and egotistical as many had assumed. Among his favorite pre-game rituals, however, were flexing and swinging a bat in his underwear in front of a full-length mirror saying, "Rickey's the best." He was also a constant clubhouse game-player: cards, dominos or anything else to ignore meetings that review opposing pitchers. Henderson refused all scouting reports of pitchers he was about to face.

Once in the 1980s, the Yankees sent Henderson a six-figure signing bonus check. After a few months passed, an internal audit revealed that the check had not been cashed. Brian Cashman, then a low-level executive with the club, called Henderson to ask if there was a problem with the check. "No problem," Rickey said. "I've got it framed on the wall."

Longtime scout Charlie Metro remembered the havoc caused by Henderson. "I did a lot of study and I found that it's impossible to throw Rickey Henderson out," he said. "I started using stopwatches and everything. [He] can go from first to second in 2.9 seconds and no pitcher-catcher combination in baseball could throw from here to there to tag second in 2.9 seconds, it was always 3, 3.1, 3.2. The runner that can make the continuous, regular move like Rickey's can't be thrown out, and he's proven it."

In 1990, Henderson finally won the American League MVP award and helped Oakland to another pennant. He finished second in the AL in batting average with a mark of .325, losing the batting crown to Kansas City's George Brett on the final day of the season. Reaching safely by a hit or a walk in 125 of his 136 games, he led the AL in runs (119), on-base percentage (.439) and in steals (65). Rickey scored in the first inning 33 times, and the A's were 26-7 in those games. He hit .294 in the ALCS vs. Boston and hit .333 with three steals in the World Series but the A's were swept by the underdog Cincinnati Reds. Three of his five hits went for extra bases and he added a spectacular catch in Game 2 at Cincinnati.

Hall of Famer Dennis Eckersley, Henderson's former teammate with the A's, remembers Henderson loving day games because he could "look at his shadow and admire it on the way to first base."

On May 1, 1991 at the Coliseum, Henderson stole the 939th base of his career against New York, becoming the greatest base thief in history with one more steal than Lou Brock totaled from 1963 to 1979. Rickey's achievement was somewhat overshadowed when 44-year-old Nolan Ryan set a record that same night by throwing the seventh no-hitter of his career. Two years earlier, Ryan had also achieved glory at Rickey's expense by making him his 5,000th strikeout victim.

"First of all, I would like to thank God for giving me the opportunity. I want to thank the Haas family, the Oakland organization, the city of Oakland, and all you beautiful fans for supporting me," said Henderson after becoming the all-time steals king. "Most of all, I'd like to thank my mom, my friends, and loved ones for their support. I want to give my appreciation to Tom Trebelhorn and the late Billy Martin. Billy Martin was a great manager. He was a great friend to me. I love you, Billy. I wish you were here. Lou Brock was the symbol of great base stealing. But today, I'm the greatest of all time."

Because his idol was boxing great Muhammad Ali, Henderson decided to use the words "greatest of all time." These words have since been taken by many to support the notion that Rickey is selfish and arrogant. But years later, Henderson revealed that he had gone over his planned remarks ahead of time with Brock and the Cardinals Hall of Famer "had no problem with it. In fact, he helped me write what I was going to say that day." On the day of the speech, Brock later told the media "He spoke from his heart." Lou and Rickey have had a friendly relationship ever since their first meeting in 1981. Brock pronounced the young speedster as the heir to his record, saying "How are we gonna break it?"

"As soon as I said it, it ruined everything. Everybody thought it was the worst thing you could ever say," said Henderson with mixed feelings about his record-breaking comments. "Those words haunt me to this day, and will continue to haunt me. They overshadow what I've accomplished in this game."

Henderson missed 45 games in 1992 due to an assortment of injuries but still finished second on the club with 77 runs scored and led the A's with 95 walks, 48 steals and a .426 on-base percentage. In the ALCS, Rickey hit .261, walked four times and added two steals against Toronto. He became the first man in baseball history to steal 1,000 bases when he swiped third base at Detroit on May 1. Rickey finished with fewer than 50 steals for just the third time in his career and did not win the stolen base title for the first time since 1987. He finished the year with a bang in his final at-bat of the regular season on October 4, singling for the 2,000th hit of his career.

In July 1993, the Athletics traded Henderson to the playoff-bound Toronto Blue Jays for Steve Karsay and José Herrera. Rickey had an outstanding four months with the A's and at the time of the trade, he was leading the club in average (.327), runs (77), homers (17), walks (85), stolen bases (31), on-base percentage (.469) and slugging (.553). On July 5 vs. Cleveland, Henderson became only the second player in major league history to open both games of a doubleheader with a homer. His first homer for Toronto came versus the A's in his first game back at the Coliseum.

Henderson stole his 1,066th base, breaking the world stolen base record established 10 years earlier by Yutaka Fukumoto of the Hankyu Braves in Japan's Pacific League. He ended up with 114 runs and 120 walks and closed out the year with 17 consecutive stolen bases. In the postseason, Rickey batted only .120 with four walks and four runs plus two steals in the ALCS vs. Chicago. He then hit .227 in the World Series with five walks, six runs, and a steal against Philadelphia. Henderson was on second base — causing pitcher Mitch Williams to use a slide-step and hurry his delivery — when Joe Carter hit his historic walkoff home run to end the 1993 World Series.

After winning his second World Series ring with Toronto, Henderson re-signed as a free agent with Oakland for the third time in December 1993. In 1994, his opening day start in Milwaukee was his 11th for Oakland, tops in A's history. On April 13, Rickey played in the 2,000th game of his career becoming only the 159th player to reach that mark. He played in 112 games with Oakland with nine home runs and 54 RBI and stole 32 bases in 42 tries. Henderson led the majors with a .382 average with men on base and averaged 4.36 pitches per plate appearance.

Henderson signed with the San Diego Padres in the 1995 offseason, where he again finished in the Top 10 in the league in walks, on-base percentage, steals and runs. He batted .333 in the 1996 NLDS versus St. Louis. "I don't know how to put into words how fortunate I was to spend time around one of the icons of the game," said former Padres All-Star closer Trevor Hoffman, a teammate of Henderson's. "I can't comprehend that yet. Years from now, though, I'll be able to say I played with Rickey Henderson, and I imagine it will be like saying I played with Babe Ruth."

In 1997, Rickey split the season between the Padres and the Anaheim Angels. The Angels traded pitchers Ryan Hancock and Steven Agosto to the Padres for Henderson. Rickey was also among the first to have aliases on the road. The Padres had no idea how to contact him after trading him in 1997 to the Angels. "I called the hotel and I asked for Snoop Doggy Dogg," Padres general manager Kevin Towers said. "The operator thought I was crazy, and no one was registered under that name. Then I asked for Ice-T. Nothing. Cool Papa Bell. Nope. Then I asked for Richard Pryor, and she said, 'Oh, Mr. Pryor is here. Let me connect you.'"

Rickey once boarded the Padre bus, and started walking towards the back. Hall of Famer Tony Gwynn, seated near the front, stopped Henderson and said, "Rickey, you sit up here. You've got tenure."

"Ten?" Henderson said defiantly. "Rickey got 20 years in the big leagues."

Henderson was ready to sign a $1.1 million contract with Oakland in 1998 when he demanded a suite on the road. Athletics general manager Billy Beane told him such clauses were against club policy but Rickey insisted. "Tell you what," Beane said. "As general manager I get a suite on the road. I don't make a lot of trips. I'll give you my suite whenever I don't go." In January 1998, he signed as a free agent with the A's, the fourth different time he played for the franchise.

In his 20th major league campaign, 39-year-old Henderson posted his 12th and final league-leading season, when his 66 steals in 1998 made him the oldest steals leader in history. He also scored 101 runs and led the AL in walks with 118. He scored the 2,000th run of his career vs. Cleveland. On December 13, Henderson was signed by the New York Mets as a free agent.

In 1999, Henderson ranked 51st on *The Sporting News* list of The 100 Greatest Baseball Players and was a nominee for the Major League Baseball All-Century Team. During the '99 season, he batted .315 with 37 steals and was seventh in the NL in on-base percentage at .423. He wore No. 24, which had not been regularly worn by a Mets player since Willie Mays retired in 1973. Following the Mets' loss in the NLCS, the New York media made much of a card game between Henderson and Bobby Bonilla. Both players had been removed from the lineup, and they reportedly left the dugout before the playoff game concluded. Rickey is an avowed card shark and competition junkie. He will play almost anything with scoring, especially if it involves a friendly wager.

"One time," says Mariners catcher Ben Davis, who played with Henderson on the Padres, "Rickey came walking into the clubhouse with this denim outfit and big suede hat. And he goes, 'Rickey got a big ranch [in California]. Rickey got a big bull. Rickey got horses. Rickey got chickens and everything...and Rickey got a 20-gallon hat.'"

2000 was Henderson's 22nd major league season. With a swipe of second on opening day, Rickey joined Ted Williams as the only players to steal a base in four decades. In May, he was released by New York and quickly signed by Seattle. In his second game as a Mariner, Henderson hit a leadoff home run and became one of four players to homer in four different decades. Despite the late start, Rickey finished fourth in the AL in stolen bases with 31. In May, Henderson drew his 2,000th career walk, accomplished only by Babe Ruth and Ted Williams.

"In 2000," said former Mariner Alex Rodriguez, "Rickey was scuffling down the stretch, and there was some speculation that he wouldn't even be on the postseason roster. Rickey would say, 'Don't worry about Rickey. Rickey's an October player. Rickey's a postseason player.' And he was. He helped us beat Chicago. Sometimes he'd come back to the dugout after an umpire called him out, and I'd go, 'Rickey, was that a strike?' And he'd go, 'Maybe, but not to Rickey.'"

Many stories have been told about Henderson over the years, both the player and person. He is well known for his malapropisms, for referring to himself in the third-person, and for talking to himself at length at the plate. Rickey has been known to speak to his bats, asking them which one has the next hit inside them. He once fell asleep on an icepack and contracted a case of frostbite in August. Henderson once defended his position during a contract dispute: "All I'm asking for is what I want." One off-season, in search of a team, he left a message on Towers's voicemail that went like this: "Kevin, this is Rickey. Calling on behalf of Rickey. Rickey wants to play baseball."

Rickey was asked if he owned a Garth Brooks album. "Rickey doesn't have albums," he answered. "Rickey has CDs." Another time he bragged that his Manhattan apartment had such a great view he could see "the Entire State Building." He once settled a feud with Yankees manager Lou Piniella, saying "Let bye-byes be bye-byes."

A free agent in March 2001, Henderson returned to the Padres and signed a minor-league contract. He was called up in April after injuries to outfielders Gwynn and Mark Kotsay and Rickey broke three all-time records and reached an additional career milestone. He broke Ruth's record of 2,062 career walks, Ty Cobb's record of 2,246 career runs, and Zack Wheat's record of 2,328 career games in left field. On the final day of the season, he collected his 3,000th career hit, a leadoff double off Rockies pitcher John Thomson. It was also Gwynn's last major league game. Rickey had originally wanted to sit out the game so as not to detract from the occasion, but Gwynn insisted that Henderson play.

Henderson finished the 2001 season with 25 stolen bases, ninth in the NL. It marked Rickey's 23rd consecutive season in which he stole more than 20 bases. With Gwynn at 3,141 hits, it was just the second time in MLB history that a pair of teammates each had 3,000 career hits; Ty Cobb and Tris Speaker had previously played together for the 1928 A's.

In 2002 — his 24th major league season — Henderson played for the Boston Red Sox and became the oldest centerfielder in major league history (43) when he filled in for starter Johnny Damon. The Red Sox agreed to pick up the tab on the suite Rickey was renting at the Boston Ritz-Carlton, which cost $10,000 a month. Henderson signed a minor league deal that included an invitation to spring training and a $350,000 salary after he played his way onto the Boston roster with an impressive spring. Rickey played sparingly for the Red Sox, hitting .223 with five homers, 16 RBIs, eight stolen bases and a .369 on-base percentage, 38 points above the league average.

Over 24 seasons in the major leagues, Henderson never spent his meal money. Before each road trip, MLB players get an envelope filled with cash to cover meal expenses. Rickey would take the envelopes home and put them in shoe boxes. Whenever his daughters, Angela, Alexis, or Adriann did well in school, Henderson would allow them to choose an envelope from a shoe box, a little game he called "Pick It." The jackpot was getting an envelope from one of those 13-day, four-city trips. The girls would keep the money. "They do what they want with it," he said. "It gives them motivation for their school and something to do, like a job."

As the 2003 season began, Henderson was without a team for the first time in his career. He signed with the Newark Bears of the independent Atlantic League in April for one last shot at the major leagues. Rickey knew that he could still play baseball. He could still lay off pitches dangerously close to the strike zone, still make a pitcher perspire just by taking that confident lead off first base, and he could still fly.

Henderson finally got a chance at a 25th season when the Los Angeles Dodgers signed him over the All-Star break. In 30 games in Los Angeles at the age of 44, he amazingly hit two homers, batted .208, and stole three bases without being caught. Rickey played his last major league game on September 19, 2003; he was hit by a pitch in his only plate appearance, and came around to score his 2,295th run. After leaving the Dodgers, Henderson started his second consecutive season with Newark in the spring of 2004. In 91 games he had a .462 OBP, with more than twice as many walks (96) as strikeouts (41), and stole 37 bases while being caught only twice. In 2005, Rickey signed with the San Diego Surf Dawgs of the Golden Baseball League, another independent league. This was the GBL's inaugural season, and Rickey helped the team to the league championship. In 73 games he posted a .270 batting average, a .456 OBP, and 73 walks.

After his last major league game in 2003, the 10-time American League All-Star ranked among baseball's top 100 all-time home run hitters and was the all-time leader in walks. In addition to the career steals record, Henderson also holds the single-season record for stolen bases (130 in 1982) and is the only player in AL history to steal 100 bases in a season, having done so three times. His 1,406 career steals is 50 percent higher than the previous record of 938 by Lou Brock. Rickey holds the all-time franchise stolen base record for both the A's and Yankees, and was among the league's Top 10 base stealers in 21 different seasons. In a game in 1977 he stole seven bases, tying a major league record. Most baseball experts agree he was the greatest leadoff man in the history of the game, certainly of his era. He amassed 3,055 hits, 2,190 walks, 510 doubles, was three homers shy of 300, batted .279 lifetime, and posted an incredible .401 career on-base percentage.

"If you're one run down, there's nobody you'd ever rather have up at the plate than Rickey," says Mariners coach Rene Lachemann, a former Oakland coach. "You didn't want to walk him, because that was a double — he'd steal second — but if you didn't throw it over the plate, he wouldn't swing. And if you did throw it over the plate, he could knock it out of the park."

In 2005, *The Sporting News* updated their 100 Greatest Players list and Henderson had inched up to 50th and was a nominee for the Major League Baseball All-Century Team. The Mets hired Rickey as a special instructor in 2006, primarily to work with hitters and teach base stealing. Henderson's impact was noticeable on José Reyes, the Mets' current leadoff hitter. "I always want to be around the game," Rickey said in May 2007. "That's something that's in my blood. Helping them have success feels just as good." He has periodically been a special instructor in the Athletics' spring training camps. In 2010, Rickey coached base stealing (most notably with Rajai Davis and Coco Crisp) and outfield drills.

Henderson finally conceded his "official retirement" on July 13, 2007. "I haven't submitted retirement papers to MLB, but I think MLB already had their papers that I was retired." Characteristically, he added, "If it was a situation where we were going to win the World Series and I was the only player that they had left, I would put on the shoes."

Henderson was a headfirst slider. In 2008, he discussed his technique at length with *Sports Illustrated*: "I wanted to know how to dive into the base because I was getting strawberries on my legs. I was thinking about head-first versus feet-first, and wondering which would save my body. I felt that running was more important to me, so I started going head-first. I got my technique from airplanes. I was on a plane and asleep and when we landed we bounced and it woke me up. Then the next flight I had the same pilot and the plane went down so smooth. So I asked the pilot why, and he said when you land a plane smooth, you get the plane elevated to the lowest position you can and then you smooth it in."

On January 12, 2009, Henderson was elected to the National Baseball Hall of Fame in his first year on the ballot, receiving 94.8 percent of the vote. This was the 13th highest vote percentage in major league history. Statistician Bill James was once asked if he thought Rickey was a Hall of Fame caliber player and said "If you could split him in two, you'd have two Hall of Famers."

His enshrinement came that summer in Cooperstown. "As a kid growing up in Oakland, my heroes were Jackie Robinson, Willie Mays, Hank Aaron, Reggie

Jackson," he said in his induction speech. "What about that Reggie Jackson? I stand outside the ballpark in the parking lot, waiting for Reggie Jackson to give me an autograph ... I said, 'Reggie, can I have an autograph?' He would pass me a pen, with his name on it. I never got an autograph." Jackson was sitting behind him, cracking up with Robin Yount and various other Hall of Fame alumni.

"In closing, I would like to say my favorite hero was Muhammad Ali. He said at one time, quote, 'I am the greatest,' end of quote. That is something I always wanted to be. And now that the Association has voted me into the Baseball Hall of Fame, my journey as a player is complete. I am now in the class of the greatest players of all time. And at this moment, I am.....very, very humble. Thank you."

The Athletics retired Henderson's No. 24 on August 1, 2009 at the long-awaited Rickey Henderson Day, also attended by Pam and daughters Angela, Alexis, and Adriann. "He's the greatest leadoff hitter of all time," Oakland GM Beane said. "And I'm not sure there's a close second."

Henderson epitomized the leadoff position, and after he was done playing, no one has come close to duplicating it. There still hasn't been a player to steal 90 bases since Henderson stole 93 in 1988. "I always wanted to start the game, be the first one to get a hit, be the first one to score a run. I used the stolen bases and the walks in order to get on base to try and come across the plate, score runs and give my team an opportunity to win."

Henderson stole all those bases and scored all those runs and played in over 3,000 games not only because of his body strength, but also because of his brain. Rickey could tell from the faintest, most undetectable twitch of a pitcher's muscles whether he was going home or throwing over to first. He understood that conditioning isn't all about strength, but also about flexibility. And more than anyone else in the history of the game, he understood that baseball is entirely a game of discipline — the discipline to patiently work endless counts your way, the discipline to understand that your goal is to get on base, and the discipline to understand that a season is more important than a game, and a career more important than a season. Rickey later became known for his showboating with his slow motion home run trot and "snatch catches," in which he would flick his glove out at incoming fly balls, then whip his arm behind his back after making the catch. Henderson was sometimes hated as an opponent, but beloved as a teammate.

"One of my favorite teammates of all time," Brian Johnson said. "I grew up in Oakland, and he was an icon to me. When I was in San Diego, I lockered next to him, and my biggest fear was that he was a bad guy. It was a breath of fresh air to find out he was the nicest guy, a genuine good guy and a great teammate."

"One of the best teammates I've ever had," Rodriguez said. "He made the game fun every day."

On October 3, 2009, Rickey Henderson Field was officially christened to honor one of Oakland Tech's most famous graduates. Rickey attended the dedication ceremony with his family and close friends, and gave a speech about what the new diamond meant to him and the community. Maybe now, he said, local youths might become more involved with baseball, allowing them to pursue and realize their own dreams as a teenage Henderson did many years ago.

Henderson had a funny way with math. When told by reporters that former Padres teammate Ken Caminiti said that 50 percent of all major leaguers used steroids, Henderson said "Well, Rickey's not one of them. So that's 49 percent right there."

"Wherever Rickey's been," said former teammate Dave Stewart, "he's always been the life of the party. Always."

"A lot of stuff [people] had me doing or something they said I had created, it's comedy," said Rickey. "I guess that's how they want to judge me, as a character."

"He rises to the occasion — the big moment — better than anybody I've ever seen." said manager Tony LaRussa. "In the clubhouse, on the plane, on the buses, Rickey was anything but the egotistical superstar who kept to himself. He was right in the middle of all the conversations, cutting up. He is so much better a teammate than is the perception. If you asked anybody on those Oakland teams, I would bet you'd find that everybody liked Rickey as a person."

Henderson completed his career with two World Series Championship rings, from 1989 in Oakland and 1993 in Toronto. Ten times he was an All Star, three times he won Silver Slugger Awards, and in 1990 he was the American League MVP. He finished in the Top 10 in the MVP voting six times. He smashed a record 81 leadoff home runs and won a Gold Glove in 1981. Bill James wrote in 2000, "Without exaggerating one inch, you could find 50 Hall of Famers who, all taken together, don't own as many records, and as many *important* records, as Rickey Henderson."

As of 2011, Rickey Henderson is the all-time leader in runs scored and stolen bases, ranks fourth all-time in career games played, and 21st in hits. His record for most career walks has since been broken by Barry Bonds. Rickey hit only .279, but his on-base average was a sparkling .401. His awesome 25-year career elevated Henderson to the Top 10 in many all-time leader categories. Rickey's high on-base percentage, power hitting, and baserunning totals made him one of the most electric players of his era. He was further known for his intense passion for playing baseball and a confident, charismatic and quotable personality that baseball fans everywhere will never forget.

Bay Area Legends

24

JEFF GORDON

Long before NASCAR championships, Daytona 500s, and Talladega nights, it was in Vallejo that Jeff Gordon first got hooked on speed. He is one of the lucky few who found his calling at an early age and took it to the limit.

Jeffrey Michael Gordon was born on August 4, 1971 in Vallejo. Gordon's parents are Carol and William G. Gordon and he also has an older sister named Kim. When Jeff was barely a year old, Carol and Bill divorced. Soon after, Carol met John Bickford, who worked at Carol's medical supply company. Baby Jeff was a handful for a single mother and John was not only willing to lend a hand, he dedicated his life to helping Jeff become one of the greatest race car drivers in history.

At three years old, Gordon was small for his age but he was quick, agile, and elusive. He showed uncanny balance and coordination. While his playmates were rolling out Big Wheels and tricycles, he had the training wheels off his two-wheeler. He was biking, skate-boarding and roller-skating, often joining older bike-riding boys to ride and race around the block.

By the time Jeff was four years old, John and Carol were married. Jeff's new stepfather John – a former motorcycle racer – bought him a BMX bicycle. John modified it when Jeff's feet couldn't reach the pedals. He encouraged his stepson to enter BMX races. Gordon often competed against boys twice his age and size, but still won his share of races. Carol became concerned that he would be injured in the frequent collisions at these races.

"They were hauling the older kids away in an ambulance with broken arms, broken legs, cracked ribs, so I complained to John, 'Isn't there something we can do that's a little bit safer than this?'" John's trade was engineering and building controls for customized wheelchairs and later started his own business. John considered various forms of racing and concluded that it would be safer to buy Jeff his own race car – at four years old.

A few days later, John appeared in the driveway with two miniature cars – quarter-midget racers to be exact – one for Jeff and one for Kim. The cars were about six feet long and were powered by one-cylinder 2.8 horsepower engines. Jeff's midget racer also had the name "Gordy" painted on its tiny hood - the nickname given to him by family and friends.

From that moment on, Gordon began a legendary career born of his stepfather's vision. Although his sister never caught the "racing bug," Jeff quickly demonstrated that he had a natural talent for driving. Within a few weeks, Gordon was lapping a vacant lot against a stopwatch. "I didn't bring the cars home to push the kids into racing," says Bickford. "I just wanted to give Jeff a chance to see if he liked it."

John's old passion for motorcycle racing helped get Jeff ready to compete. Gordon would take his quarter midget car out to a parking lot and would race nearly every day after school. Jeff began racing quarter midgets when he turned five and won races although he could barely read or write. "We'd take that car out every night after I got home from work and run it lap after lap," John said. "Jeff couldn't seem to get enough of it."

The Roy Hayer Memorial Race Track (formerly The Cracker Jack) in Rio Linda is noted as the first track Gordon ever competed on. He traveled northeast to Sacramento, south to San Jose and eventually to regional and national events as he developed his driving talent. These events were safer than BMX, and because Jeff was lighter than the other drivers – many of whom were teens – he could coax an extra mph or two out of his car. He earned plenty of "Fast Time" ribbons in the qualifiers, but he usually left the track without a trophy since the older boys knew how to keep him in back of the pack.

"I ran Rio Linda, Sunnyvale, Visalia, Pomona . . . mainly around the Sunnyvale-Fremont area, and Rio Linda, which was a dirt track we'd go to some weekends. In fact, the very first time I ever got into a race car was at Rio Linda," Gordon said.

In practice, Carol drove the other car to bother and block Jeff so he could hone his skills. He soon learned how to "read" quarter midgets and developed a series of passing moves. Jeff was now able to stand on the gas pedal and keep it floored throughout a race. By the time he was six, he was winning. Gordon would run laps against John's stopwatch and expect improving times. "He'd never really get mad at me," Bickford says now, "but he'd sure get mad at that stopwatch."

At the nearby Solano County fairgrounds in Vallejo, John asked management's permission to mark off a makeshift track, as long as Jeff didn't practice while the fairgrounds were being used. It was nothing more than a section of barren parking lot, overgrown with weeds and littered with trash bins. Rollercoasters and other amusement rides stood in the horizon. Bickford coned off a rough oval along the underbrush so young Jeff could practice a few laps in his racecar. From those first rough laps made around the county fairgrounds parking lot, he eventually graduated to indoor events held inside the fairgrounds' exposition hall.

By age six, Gordon had won 35 main events and set five track records. Winning again and again in the weekend events, Jeff developed a reputation as the kid to beat. Not only did he drive very aggressively, he had a sixth sense for the feel of the vehicle and could articulate these observations to John, who made the necessary mechanical adjustments.

Jeff turned seven in 1978 and recorded the fastest time in every qualifier he entered, won 35 races, and set speed records at five different California tracks. Gordon won the first of three Quarter Midget National Championships that year. At 8, he took the checkered flag 52 times, including the Grand National Championship in Denver. Some drivers – even those with wins under their belt – would pull out of events when they heard Gordon was running. No teenage racer likes losing to an 8-year-old. Many promoters even began offering trophies for 2nd and 3rd place, unprecedented at this level before Jeff's arrival.

With his family's supervision, he began touring the nation in search of new races. He would fly to weekend races while John drove his cars from track to track, and then fly home in time for school on Monday. Jeff was winning so frequently in quarter midgets that at age nine, he was beating drivers 17 and older. "I really felt comfortable and confident in those cars," Jeff remembered. "I felt that I could win just about every time out."

Meanwhile, the family lived and slept in their car. They also slept in their pickup and the cheapest of motels. They eventually bought a used motor home. For the next several years, from California to Illinois, Jeff dominated pre-teen and teenage quarter midget and go kart competition. By age 12, he had won hundreds of races. The rising star signed autographs for adoring fans, and his parents even sold "Jeff Gordon" T-shirts. He also took up waterskiing as a break from racing. Waterskiing fulfilled his need for speed and after just a few weeks at a training school, his coaches told Carol and John that their boy was as good as some pros.

Gordon advanced to racing 60 mph go karts, which were powered by 10-horsepower engines and ran on larger tracks. The other racers, ranging from 15-year-olds to adults, were angered that a child was competing against them. At first they tried to alienate and intimidate Jeff but he competed in 25 races and won them all. Some parents were so upset that Gordon was beating their children some thought he was a midget or was just not telling the truth about his age. After his second quarter midget championship, it was obvious to John and Jeff that he needed bigger and better challenges.

"We were always trying to prepare for the next opportunity – that would be the way to say it," Bickford says. "I think all parents have a certain level of concern, but if he chose skydiving I'd be more worried than racing."

In 1984, Bickford considered purchase of a 100-mph sprint car for his 13-year-old son while shouts of "child abuse" rose from youth racing circles. Sprint cars look small but weigh 1,000 pounds and have 700-horsepower engines shoehorned into them. John had a sprint car built to accommodate Jeff's small frame. The idea was for Gordon to practice on deserted roads until he was legally old enough to enter events. Jeff, who quickly mastered his car and was ready to race it, started to grow impatient.

While most boys his age were busy playing video games or talking on the school bus, Jeff was attending business meetings with sponsors and risking his life racing against opponents twice his age. When the opportunity arose to race a sprint series in Australia, he jumped at it. In February of 1985, John and Jeff discovered Florida's sprint car laws. They obtained entry to an event in Jacksonville and drove cross-country for the race. Race officials were stunned when they saw how young and small Gordon really was. John convinced them that his stepson was competent and that they could not prevent him from competing. Ironically, the event was canceled due to a thunderstorm. Jeff, however, began entering and challenging for the lead in Florida All-Star events. He finished as high as second and attracted the attention of ESPN, which produced a short feature on him.

Jeff's extraordinary high-speed skill at 14 was so apparent that his parents were faced with a difficult decision. Put Jeff's career on hold to attend Vallejo High School and stay close to family and friends, or sell John's business and move to the racing mecca of Indiana. Vallejo was great, but Jeff needed to race against adults to improve and he couldn't do that in California because of age restrictions. "It was one of those crossroads in life you come to where you're going to have to make a commitment to something, whether it's your life or your kid's life," said Bickford. "And I felt the potential in our family lied in our ability to do what it took to advance the kid."

As Vallejo's brand new Marine World went up in 1986, Gordon and the family moved out. The difficult decision was made to help accelerate Jeff's career. They moved from California to Florida and then they relocated to Pittsboro, Indiana, near Indianapolis. Open-wheel racing was very popular in the Midwest and there were lots of races. Jeff could now legally race sprint cars in Indiana with his parents' permission. Indiana was the heart of sprint car country and the family needed to be near chassis builders and within reach of dozens of racetracks.

John and Carol were not wealthy people. After selling John's business, they kept a close eye on their shrinking checking account. After relocating to Indiana, things were far from easy. John built and maintained Jeff's car and traveled around the Midwest while the family sometimes could not cover expenses at home. They struggled to make ends meet, surviving on Carol's paycheck, Jeff's prize money, and jobs John picked up working on other cars. In an interview with *Newsweek*, John said that the family "slept in pick-up trucks and made our own parts. That's why I think Jeff is misunderstood by people who think he was born to rich parents and had a silver spoon in his mouth."

Gordon attended Tri-West High School in Lizton and raced locally on weekends. He adopted Bloomington Speedway as his home track and became one of its most consistent winners. From Florida to Oregon and beyond, Jeff won at the highest levels of short-track, open-wheel racing. He joined the United States Auto Club (USAC) at 16 and was the youngest driver to ever get licensed. Gordon won three sprint car track championships before he was old enough to get a driver's license.

He was the 1989 USAC Midget Rookie of the Year and received national attention due to his age and amazing driving abilities.

Despite his schedule, Jeff always made time to study and keep his grades up. He took a drivers education class although he had already won a hundred races. Even with his new-found fame, he maintained a low profile at school, keeping most of his racing accomplishments to himself when possible. He enjoyed his high school sporting events, attending many and always cheering for his school's teams. He joined the cross country team in high school to stay in shape for racing. Often, he'd leave school early on Fridays in favor of travel to tracks like Eldora and Winchester. Gordon was voted Tri-West prom king and graduated in 1989. On the day of his graduation, he got his diploma and quickly changed into his racing gear for a dirt track race in Bloomington that night.

"Pittsboro is a small town, he went to high school there, went to the prom, went to graduation, and he was racing all over the place right there close to Pittsboro," Bickford said. "Right there six miles away was Indianapolis Raceway Park, and he raced on TV and the kids would see him and they'd talk at school. They'd go to the different dirt-track races he won, and he'd see them at school the next day. It was a town that really got behind him. I mean, heck, they named a street after him, they've got an overpass on Interstate 74, and all that stuff. He's a big deal to them. It's just different."

By 1989, Gordon became an 18-year-old regular on ESPN's *Thursday Night Thunder* broadcasts, and his name was often mentioned with other young drivers who might make the jump to a big-money circuit. That same year, he met former racer Ray Evernham, now a mechanic and team manager. "The very first time I saw Jeff he looked about 14 or 15 years old. His mother was with him, and he had a briefcase in one hand. He called me Mr. Evernham. He was trying to grow a mustache and when he opened his briefcase, he had a video game, a cell phone and a racing magazine in it. I asked myself, 'What am I getting myself into?'"

At 19, Gordon won the 1990 USAC Midget Car championship and became the youngest champion ever. In 21 USAC races, Jeff was the fastest qualifier 10 times and won nine races. He was now ready to take the final step in his racing career, which meant he had to specialize in one racing category. He was already well-known in every corner of the racing world and sponsors began lining up. Jeff's options included open-wheel (Indy Car) racing and stock-car racing – the two most lucrative categories. John then suggested that Jeff go to Rockingham, North Carolina and attend the Buck Baker driving school. Not for sprint cars, but for 180-

mph NASCAR stock cars. ESPN filmed a segment about Jeff's experience there and in exchange, Baker taught Gordon for free. After taking his first lap in a stock car, Jeff fell in love and vowed to master his final racing challenge.

Coincidently, NASCAR owner Hugh Connerty was at Baker's School that same day. He managed a team sponsored by Outback Steakhouse and Evernham was his young crew chief. Believing the pairing of Gordon and Evernham could make an outstanding combination, Connerty signed Jeff for the remainder of the 1990 season. Hugh secured some funding for a car through Outback, and it was ready for the Busch Grand National race in Charlotte. Gordon was always the youngest driver on the track and he was finishing most races in a very unusual position for him – near the back of the pack. The teenager ran in four Busch Series races and did well enough to attract the attention of Bill Davis, an owner with greater resources.

At the age of 20, Gordon became the youngest driver to win the USAC Silver Crown, and a season championship. He also won four Crown National midget car races that season and took home more than $100,000 in prize money. In 1991, Gordon and Connerty amicably parted ways when funding became difficult to secure. Conversations started between Jeff and Davis and the two entered into a one-page agreement for the '91 season. Gordon continued racing in the 1992 NASCAR Busch Series and ended the season by capturing the title of Busch Series Rookie of The Year, driving the #1 Carolina Ford car. He set a NASCAR record with 11 poles in a single season.

Gordon's popularity put him on the radar of Rick Hendrick, an elite owner of several NASCAR teams and one of the largest automotive chains in the country, Hendrick Automotive Group. Hendrick noticed Jeff driving extremely loose at Atlanta Motor Speedway that year. Seeing how undisciplined he was driving against a field of seasoned competitors, he predicted the young star would crash. Instead, Gordon outmaneuvered Dale Earnhardt and Harry Gant to take the checkered flag. Soon after, Jeff became a member of the Hendrick Motorsports family, one of the most successful teams in NASCAR history.

The new team was formed following the signing of Gordon's contract on May 8, 1992. It began with Jeff, John, Ray, and Jimmy Johnson (then General Manager of Hendrick Motorsports). In June, Evernham officially started building the team and organizing the shop. Jeff signed the deal of a lifetime, putting him into the elite circle of NASCAR teams. The rest is history. Jeff became an integral part of the Hendrick Motorsports family which has continued the winning tradition ever since.

Gordon now felt ready to graduate from the Busch Series and enter Winston Cup competition -- the elite series of NASCAR sanctioned events. Meanwhile, he and Evernham, whom Davis had also hired, were forming the kind of close bond driver and crew chief need to win. At the age of 21, Jeff raced in the final event of the 1992 season at Atlanta. This race also happened to be the very last for Richard "The King" Petty, the all-time NASCAR wins leader. Looking back on this race, it seems like the torch had been passed from one great legend to a future one: Jeff "Wonderboy" Gordon.

In his first six NASCAR seasons, Gordon won 42 races and earned nearly $25 million in prize money. With all the winning came a new lifestyle of success including the big houses, the boats, the planes, the businesses, and the charity foundation. He owned a garageful of exotic cars even though he spent most of his time being driven around in a tinted-windows Suburban. Corporations lobbied for his endorsement as he created a generic, mid-American public personality. He'd typically pull himself from the car after each victory and carefully thank 'the crew of the awesome #24 DuPont Chevrolet Monte Carlo" and a host of associated sponsors.

It was around this time that Gordon was picked up by the mainstream media. He was a new NASCAR personality and often discussed his abilities with cool self-confidence. Worst of all, he was from California. The Southerners – the sport's core fans – rooted for veterans like Dale Earnhardt or Darrell Waltrip – rugged, homegrown men who built the sport from dogged determination and hard work and sacrifice and in whom fans saw something of themselves. In Gordon they saw nothing of themselves. He had been programmed his whole life to race and was falsely perceived to have been privileged, even spoiled. Jeff also represented the new NASCAR, and change was bad.

Gordon's much-anticipated first full Winston Cup season began in 1993. Jeff's number 24 car, sponsored by DuPont Automotive Finishes, featured a dazzling array of colors and his team soon became known to NASCAR fans as the Rainbow Warriors. As part of his corporate image shift, Jeff also cut the mullet and shaved his thin mustache. During the season, his tendency to push cars too hard and crash made many question young Gordon's competency to compete safely at such a level. He responded by picking up the Rookie of the Year award, scoring a Daytona 500 qualifying race and earning a respectable finish in the 1993 Winston Cup point standings.

At Daytona, Gordon amazed spectators when he won his 125-mile qualifying race. It had been almost 30 years since a rookie had won this event. The victory was so unexpected – even by Jeff – that he had no idea how to get from the finish line to Victory Lane. It was the most embarrassing and thrilling day of his young career. During the celebration, he received the customary winner's kiss from Miss Winston, Brooke Sealy. That day she and Jeff began a romance that lasted all season. Because of rules about dating drivers, they kept it hidden. They were later married. They seemed perfectly suited as Brooke was a model and a devout Christian. By then Gordon had embraced a vigorous Christianity, and the two of them went everywhere together and prayed together beside his car before each race. They married in 1994 and lived in Huntersville, North Carolina, until 1998 when they moved to Highland Beach, Florida.

Gordon proved that his qualifying win was no fluke when he led early in the Daytona 500, something no rookie had ever done before. Jeff stayed among the leaders all day but slipped back to fifth during the final laps and it was apparent he had much to learn. Jeff's best finish in '93 was second (Coca Cola 600 and Miller 400) and he won one pole. He ended up 14th in the standings, good enough for Rookie of the Year honors.

Gordon's first official Winston Cup victory came in Charlotte at the 1994 Coca-Cola 600 – NASCAR's longest and most difficult race. Jeff had recently moved the family to western North Carolina so the win was a nice housewarming. The season got off to a fast start at the Busch Clash, an all-star race between the previous year's pole winners. Jeff showed his experience as he patiently trailed Earnhardt and Brett Bodine. At the opportune moment, Jeff blasted past them for the win. He again ran strong at the Daytona 500, finishing fourth behind winner Sterling Marlin.

Jeff finished eighth in the Winston Cup point standings for the 1994 season, as Earnhardt captured the Cup for the second straight year. Because the two stars looked different, spoke different, acted different and drove so differently, it was only natural for fans to choose sides. This sparked a rivalry among fans that lasted throughout the 1990s. The more passionate their fans got, the more NASCAR items they bought to fly their colors.

Gordon won his first NASCAR Cup Championship in 1995 – the pinnacle of the stock car racing universe. At 24, he was the youngest-ever Cup Champ. At this time, seven-time champion Earnhardt, coined Jeff's nickname of "Wonderboy." Most of the other drivers welcomed him with both respect and contempt. Gordon didn't care – all he could see was that next stopwatch time. He clinched the Cup by battling Earnhardt in the final race of the season. Jeff had a seemingly insurmountable lead in the standings, only to have Earnhardt come roaring back in the final weeks. With one race left, Gordon clung to a small 34-point lead. When he eventually finished far enough ahead of The Intimidator, he claimed his first NASCAR championship. At the awards banquet in New York, he offered a special toast to Earnhardt which many viewed as a symbolic passing of the torch. Gordon had earned his first championship the year after Earnhardt won his last.

Gordon was bringing new fans into the nationalized sport by the thousands, broadening NASCAR's new appeal to the North, East and West. Even Gordon skeptics could appreciate his role in growing NASCAR's popularity and media coverage. He was now one of the richest drivers in any category. In 1996, Jeff won a remarkable 10 races but still lost out by 37 points. Jeff believed he was NASCAR's top driver – and so did just about everyone else in the sport. During the offseason, he began focusing on adding a second Cup to his collection.

"I don't feel I'm a step above anyone on this team," he said in 1996. "I'm just another link in the chain. We travel together, work together, struggle together, lose together, and win together. Sure, I'm the guy the reporters want to talk to on Sunday, and I'm the guy who holds up the giant cardboard checks when we win, but I'm not naive or vain enough to think that I'm the sole reason we're successful. Racing is a team effort — always has been, always will be."

Gordon won his first Daytona 500 in 1997, becoming the youngest driver in history to win the storied race. Daytona had long been the elusive prize for Earnhardt, who had contended often but never won. Dale seized an early lead and was running strong when he came out of a turn too high and nicked the wall. Earnhardt swerved and bumped Gordon, who maintained control of his car. Unfortunately for the Intimidator, the two cars behind him plowed into his car and he was knocked out of the race.

Jeff scored three additional wins early in 1997. He traded paint with Wallace at the Food City 500 to win by a length and survived a spinout to edge Bobby Hamilton at the Goody's 500. He also won at Darlington for his third major of the year, earning a $1 million bonus from Winston. Jeff took the checkered flag in 10 races for the second straight year and held off Dale Jarrett and Mark Martin to claim his second NASCAR Cup championship.

From 1993 to 2000, Gordon carried a DuPont rainbow scheme that inspired the team nickname. Throughout the years, he has occasionally featured different paint, such as *Jurassic Park* in 1997, *Star Wars: The Phantom Menace* in 1999, and Snoopy in the 2000 Brickyard 400. In 1997, Jeff signed a long-term contract with Pepsi that is still in place today.

In 1998, Jeff failed to defend his Daytona 500 title but won 13 times – including a streak of five races in a row – and captured his second Brickyard 400. He dominated the competition to claim his third NASCAR Cup championship at the age of 27. No driver under 30 had ever won more than two.

Gordon is a Christian. He has talked about how in the early 1990s he got curious and followed some drivers to a weekly chapel, which is how he first started to learn more about God. A humanitarian, Jeff founded The Jeff Gordon Foundation in 1999, an organization that helps children dealing with life-threatening and chronic illnesses. With other sports celebrities such as Lance Armstrong, Tony Hawk, Andre Agassi, and Muhammad Ali, he set up a charitable organization in 2007 called Athletes for Hope, whose purpose is to help other professional athletes actively participate in charitable issues and support the community.

Jeff opened the 1999 season with an outstanding performance at Daytona. With 10 laps remaining, Jeff zig-zagged onto the apron to pass leader Wallace, and then held off Earnhardt the rest of the way. As Gordon headed toward Victory Lane, the Intimidator bumped Jeff's fender and waved. It was the ultimate salute from NASCAR's most legendary driver. For the season, Gordon collected seven wins, seven poles, 18 Top 5 finishes, 21 Top 10s, and finished sixth in the Cup standings.

That September, Evernham left HMS to become an owner. It was the break-up of NASCAR's most successful driver/crew chief combination. Jeff hated to see him leave, but Evernham had accomplished everything and more in the pits. Other Rainbow Warrior departures followed. Brian Whitesell assumed the role of crew chief but was replaced for 2000 by Robbie Loomis, formerly the Petty Enterprises crew chief. The jury was out on the Gordon-Loomis partnership heading into the new year. Was Evernham truly irreplaceable?

Gordon delivered a disappointing performance during the 2000 Sprint Cup Series after he and Evernham split. Loomis quickly became the target of abuse from Jeff's fans. In a sport where only a few feet separate crew from fans, the new crew chief was roundly booed. Fortunately, the team began to mesh in the second half, recording Top 10 finishes in all but one of their last 11 races. He finished ninth in the standings with three wins, three poles, 11 Top 5 finishes, and 22 Top 10 finishes.

Gordon and Loomis proved skeptics wrong in 2001 by winning six races (including a third Brickyard 400) to earn an amazing fourth NASCAR Cup championship. Jeff started and finished the year strong, separating himself from Ricky Rudd and Dale Jarrett halfway through the season. He won the championship going away, and became only the third driver to win four Cup championships in NASCAR history, second only to Petty and Earnhardt.

Gordon entered the 2002 season as defending champion, but the good times soured quickly. Prior to the Darlington race in March, Brooke filed for divorce, citing marital misconduct after seven years of marriage. Rumors ran wild, causing distractions for Jeff and his team. "For some reason, no matter what happens in my life," said Gordon during the divorce proceedings. "I always seem to have a piece of my heart that says everything is going to be OK."

Gordon moved out of the Florida mansion he and Brooke had occupied since the 1990s and he crashed on couches or slept in his motor home most of the season. Brooke was asking for temporary and permanent alimony, the primary house, the Porsche and the Mercedes 600, use of the boats and the plane, and money to pay the salaries of the chef, the maids, and the groundskeeper. Jeff countersued his wife, denying marital misconduct in Palm Beach County Circuit Court. He added that he should not have to equally split the couple's estate because he risked his life to earn it. The divorce proceedings clearly affected his performance on the track. The Gordons eventually reached a settlement that guaranteed Brooke at least $15.3 million.

Through it all, Gordon placed high enough in races to stay within contention of the point chase, but he could not get back to Victory Lane. By the end of August he had gone 31 races in a row without a win – his longest drought since he was a rookie. Finally, he won at Bristol and then again a week later at Darlington. He capped the '02 season at Kansas City with one more victory, but finished fourth to Tony Stewart for the Cup championship. He recorded his 60th Winston Cup win and his 300th start, and he reached the $50 million mark in career winnings.

Gordon continued to pile up points early in 2003, winning the Virginia 500 and recording eight Top 5 finishes through the Brickyard 400. He went cold in August and early September, and dropped out of contention for the title. Jeff rebounded to score seven Top 5s in his final nine starts – including back-to-back victories at the Subway 500 and MBNA 500. The late-season surge lifted him to fourth in the standings behind champion Matt Kenseth, his teammate Johnson, and Dale Earnhardt, Jr.

The 2004 season was a huge rebound for Team Gordon. Jeff won the Brickyard 400 in August, his fourth Indy win. He is the only NASCAR driver with four Brickyard 400 victories, and one of only five drivers to have four victories at the historic track. Gordon won at Talladega the week before, won the next weekend at Infineon, and followed that up with a victory in the Pepsi 400 at Daytona, his second consecutive restrictor plate win.

In October, the Hendrick organization was shaken to its core when 10 employees perished in a plane crash. The victims, on their way to the race in Martinsville, included Rick Hendrick's son, Ricky, a former driver and a good friend of Jeff's. Gordon dedicated the rest of the year to Ricky's memory and came within a hair of winning his fifth championship. He finished third in the final three races, and only a lucky pit stop by eventual champion Kurt Busch kept him from becoming number one. If the old points system remained in place, Jeff would have captured another title. Still, 2004 was his second-best season in terms of prize winnings, as he banked $6.4 million, raising his total net worth to $155 million.

He started 2005 by winning at Daytona for the third time in his career. Inconsistency would plague him throughout the rest of the year. A late rally put him in position to qualify for the points chase, but in the final race at Richmond, Gordon made contact with the wall and failed to qualify. Although out of contention for the Nextel Cup championship, Jeff finished the year strong, winning for the seventh time at Martinsville. It marked the first time since 1993 that he had not finished in the Top 10. Loomis eventually resigned and was replaced by Steve Letarte, a longtime Rainbow Warrior.

Four years after the much-publicized divorce from Brooke, Gordon married Ingrid Vandebosch on November 7, 2006, in a small private ceremony in Mexico. The couple first met in 2002 through a mutual friend, but did not become an item until 2004. Jeff had announced their engagement in June at a wine country croquet event at Meadowood Resort in St. Helena.

Gordon won two races in 2006 and drove consistently, especially late in the season. In all, he recorded 14 Top 5 finishes. His "comeback" was achieved on NASCAR's 1.5-mile tracks. He won at Chicagoland Speedway — the first there for HMS. Jeff finished the year sixth in the Cup standings while Johnson won his first Cup championship.

Jeff's climb back to the top continued in 2007. He enjoyed his finest season since the 2001 championship, winning six times and finishing second behind Johnson in the Cup standings. It was a season full of highlights. Among the most memorable was his win at Phoenix, which tied Earnhardt for sixth place on NASCAR's all-time victory list. During Gordon's victory lap, he held a black #3 banner out of his car window. In May at Darlington, Jeff won for the seventh time at that track. Gordon earned the pole at Talladega, his 60th career pole (and third consecutive in 2007), passing Darrell Waltrip's record of 59 to become the modern pole leader. Jeff and his wife welcomed their first child, daughter Ella Sofia Gordon, on June 20, 2007.

By 2008, Gordon had competed in 545 NASCAR races, with 81 victories, 67 poles, 244 Top 5 finishes and 331 Top 10 finishes. Gordon became the first driver to reach $100 million in career winnings for the Cup series.

When he slumped in 2008, fans tried to understand why. Why couldn't this four-time champion win? Some blamed the fact that Gordon had a newborn at home. The #24 team could not keep any momentum going. Jeff failed to win a race for the first time in 15 years, but he managed to finish in the Top 10 overall. His fans had a tense moment during the UAW Dodge 400 in Las Vegas when he spun and hit an inside wall with tremendous force with four laps left. Jeff later said it was one of the hardest hits of his life. He later lobbied with other drivers to install steel-and-foam SAFER barriers on the inside track walls. Gordon finished seventh in the 2008 Chase for the Sprint Cup, 368 points out of first place. He finished winless for the first time since 1993.

Jeff's 2009 got off to an encouraging start when he outran Stewart at the end of the Gatorade Duel in Daytona. That earned him the third position for the Daytona 500. Gordon ran well but had to overcome tire problems that pushed him back to a 13th-place finish. He placed well in ensuing races and actually led the points standings during the spring. Gordon ended his 47-race winless streak, winning the Samsung 500 for his 82nd career victory and his first at Texas Motor Speedway. He held off teammate Johnson for the win and extended his points lead to 162 points.

The 2010 season kicked off in February at Daytona and Gordon cut a tire on the final lap and finished 26th. One of the major questions heading into 2010 was Gordon's sponsors. DuPont signaled its intentions to scale back on motorsports sponsorships as the season began. For the first time in his Cup series career, Gordon and Hendrick were actively searching for a new primary sponsor for the #24 car. In October, Jeff and Rick announced a three-year partnership with The AARP Foundation's Drive To End Hunger charity.

Gordon required a backup driver, Scott Pruett, at Watkins Glen because his wife was due to give birth the weekend of August 8, 2010. On August 9, Ingrid delivered their son, Leo Benjamin Gordon. At Texas, he was running strong, until an altercation occurred with Jeff Burton. Jeff wrecked under caution flags and he was upset with Burton, causing them to have a physical fight. He would finish 37th. In the Ford 400, he started 11th and finished 37th due to engine failure. He went winless again for only the third time in his career.

Gordon started the 2011 season in Daytona driving the #24 "Drive to End Hunger" Chevrolet Impala. He started the race in the second position but after an unfortunate multi-car accident, finished 28th behind Johnson. In February, Jeff finally headed back to Victory Lane, the longest winless streak of his career now in his rearview mirror. Overcoming several potentially disastrous incidents, Gordon passed Kyle Busch with eight laps left and stretched his lead from there, ending his winless streak at 66 races at the Subway Fresh Fit 500 in Phoenix. "It feels so amazing. I can't tell you how amazing this feels," Jeff said. "It's been a long time, I know, and I'm going to savor this one so much."

After Top 5 finishes at Martinsville, Talladega, and Kansas, Gordon added another 2011 victory in June at the Five Hour Energy 500 at Pocono, finishing just ahead of both Kurt and Kyle Busch. Two weeks later, it was Kurt who won the Toyota/Save Mart 350 at Infineon while Jeff finished second. In July, Gordon led for 36 laps at the Brickyard but placed second behind winner Paul Menard. As of September, Jeff was third in the standings and had won three times with 10 Top 5 finishes, raising his career statistics to 85 victories (third all-time), 70 poles, 284 Top 5 finishes and 392 Top 10s.

Gordon was honored by *People's* "50 Most Beautiful People" list in 1997. He occasionally appears on television and has co-hosted *Live with Regis and Kelly* ten times on days when Regis Philbin was unavailable. In January 2003, Jeff became the first NASCAR driver to host NBC's *Saturday Night Live*. In 2005, he played himself in the feature film *Herbie Fully Loaded*. In 2009, he voiced a character on the animated series *Speed Racer/Next Generation*. In 2010, Jeff was the guest celebrity on an episode of ABC's *Extreme Makeover: Home Edition*. Jeff also appears in PlayStation 3 videogame *Gran Turismo 5* as himself, providing tutorials on NASCAR racing.

Gordon owns a private jet, a British Aerospace BAE-125-800, with a tail number matching his car number, N24JG. He also owns a Lazzara 106 yacht called the 24 Karat. Jeff began his wine experience in 1999 and his enthusiasm for fine wine has continued to grow. Working personally with Briggs & Sons Winemaking Co. of Calistoga, he launched the Jeff Gordon Collection of Wines in the fall of 2005 with a 2004 Carneros Chardonnay, followed by vintages of Napa Valley Merlot and Cabernet Sauvignon.

Gordon, who turned 40 in 2011, said he expects to race at least through 2015. The retirement issue has come up as Hendrick Motorsports seeks additional sponsorship for his team for next season. "Even though I feel like I am making a commitment to myself, the team and sponsors for four or five years, that doesn't mean I am going to be winning races four or five years from now," said Jeff. "Ella, she is just starting to realize what I do and get into it. Four or five years old is a great time for them to be able to experience that."

"This is probably more home in a way," Gordon says of Vallejo compared with his Indiana experience. "I have a lot of family here and friends I grew up with from elementary school. I didn't race seriously here. Most of the friends I have around here are friends I went to school with. To me, truly more of my memories of growing up are here. My memories of racing and getting to that next level are Indiana. So it's just different. It's hard to really describe how the differences are. I think it's because I get to see my cousins and my dad and a lot of different friends. I don't have family in Indiana."

Gordon's greatest asset has been superfast processing of visual information paired with the incredible feel he has for his vehicle. Time seems to slow down for Gordon similar to dominant athletes like Wayne Gretzky and Michael Jordan. Adjustments he makes with that extra millisecond makes him a truly unique driver. Jeff is perhaps the only Sprint Cup driver who is a legitimate threat to win on any type of course or track. He has perfected the bump-and-run on short tracks, is a master at restrictor-plate racing on the super speedways, and can use the worst track conditions to his advantage. His open-wheel experience also gives him a huge edge.

NASCAR fans fought amongst themselves over who Jeff Gordon really was. Millions believe he's the best American driver who ever lived and an equal number think he's a slick corporate pretty boy. It didn't help that he was from California and that his name wasn't Robby, Ricky, or Dale. They said he was too small and too young. No one raced the legendary Earnhardt harder, and no two drivers had more respect for each other. It didn't matter that the racing world said Gordon was finished with the breakup of the crew on the #24 car and the departure of Evernham. In the end, all that matters is that Jeff Gordon is one of the all-time greatest NASCAR champions, and it still remains to be seen just how many more races and championships he can win.

25

BARRY BONDS

The son of an All-Star and the godson of a legend, Barry Bonds was born to play baseball. When Bonds smashed Hank Aaron's all-time home run record in 2007 and retired later that season, it was a triumphant finale to a Hall of Fame career for one of the game's most feared sluggers. He worked tirelessly to master the art of power hitting and won an incredible seven MVP awards. Bonds was an athlete's athlete and sparkled among even elite players. His contentious personality, however, and a cloud of steroid suspicion have forever tarnished his legacy of excellence.

Barry Lamar Bonds was born in Riverside on July 24, 1964 to Patricia Howard and Bobby Lee Bonds. Bobby, who spent 23 years with the Giants organization, started his big league playing career with San Francisco in 1968. Bobby and Pat moved from Riverside to San Carlos and raised Barry, Rickey, and Bobby Jr. at 175 Lyndhurst Avenue. As if being the son of an all-star major leaguer wasn't enough, Barry had the further distinction of having Hall of Famer Willie Mays as his godfather.

Bobby went on to have an outstanding pro career. He played for several teams after the Giants, and no matter where in the majors he was sent, he produced. He smashed at least 25 homers and stole 30-plus bases for five different clubs, and is one of only four players to have stolen 300 bases and slammed 300 homers during his career. Cracking a grand slam in his first big league game for the Giants, Bobby was a three-time Gold Glove outfielder who blasted 332 home runs and stole 461 bases.

From an early age, Barry was consumed by baseball. When he was four years old, his mom Pat would take Barry and Rickey to Candlestick Park and the boys would play in the locker room and dugout. At five, Barry was not your typical first grader. Bobby arranged for Barry's own Giants uniform so he could stand in the outfield between his dad and Mays during batting practice. While other boys could only watch from the stands, Bonds would chase fly balls with Bobby and Willie. As he told *Sports Illustrated,* "I was too young to bat with them, but I could compete with them in the field." Bonds may have gotten his speed from his aunt, Rosie Bonds, a former Olympic hurdler. He is also a distant cousin of Hall of Fame slugger Reggie Jackson.

Bonds attended Junípero Serra High School in San Mateo and excelled in baseball, basketball and football. Other legendary Padre alumni include NFL stars Tom Brady and Hall of Famer Lynn Swann. As a freshman, Barry played baseball on Serra's junior varsity team during the 1979 season. The fleet centerfielder provided plenty of offense on the varsity diamond over the next three years and graduated with a career .404 batting average. Serra coach Dave Stevens said that the first time he saw Bonds play, he "ran with such speed and grace and his bat was so quick."

Bonds hit .467 during his senior year, and earned high school All-American honors. "Serra High School, to me, was my most enjoyable time for me in my entire life. That was the only time I was free. We just played baseball because it was fun."

The hometown Giants drafted 18-year-old Bonds in the second round of the 1982 MLB draft, one year after Bobby retired. But the Giants and the Bonds family were unable to agree on contract terms. Tom Haller's final offer was $70,000. Bonds's minimum to go pro was $75,000, so Barry instead headed to the desert to develop his game and earn a college degree.

Bonds attended Arizona State University in Tempe on a baseball scholarship. As a sophomore in 1984, he batted .360 and stole 30 bases. In 1985, Barry was a *Sporting News* All-American when he hit .368, smashed 23 home runs and drove in 66 runs. Bonds tied the NCAA record with seven consecutive hits in the 1984 College World Series and was later named to the All-Time College World Series Team in 1996.

Bonds finished his Sun Devil career with a .347 average, 45 home runs and 175 RBI. He was selected to the All-Pac 10 Conference team all three years. During college, he played part of one summer in the amateur Alaska Baseball League with the Alaska Goldpanners. He graduated from Arizona State in 1986 with a degree in criminology.

"I liked the hell out of Barry Bonds," said former Arizona State coach Jim Brock. "Unfortunately, I never saw a teammate care about him. Part of it would be his being rude, inconsiderate, and self-centered. He bragged about the money he turned down and popped off about his dad. I don't think he ever figured out what to do to get people to like him."

Bonds was again drafted in 1985, this time sixth overall by the Pittsburgh Pirates. He spent the remainder of the year playing for the Class A Prince William Pirates in the Carolina League. Barry finished the season batting .299 with 13 home runs and 76 hits in 71 games. For 1986, Bonds was promoted to the Hawaii Islanders of the Class AAA Pacific Coast League. He hit .311 in 44 games for Hawaii, earning a quick call-up to Pittsburgh.

Before Bonds arrived in the major leagues in Pittsburgh, Pirate fan attendance at Three Rivers Stadium was pitiful, with 1984 and 1985 ticket sales below 10,000 per game for the 81-game home schedule. Barry made his major league debut on May 30, 1986 at 21 years of age. His much anticipated big league premiere fizzled with an 0-5 performance versus Orel Hershiser and the Los Angeles Dodgers.

Standing 6-foot-2 and weighing 185 pounds when he first joined the Pirates, Bonds batted and threw left-handed. By the end of the '86 season, he led all National League rookies with 16 homers, 36 stolen bases, 65 walks and 48 RBI in 113 games. Barry finished sixth in the NL Rookie of the Year voting and became just the second Pirate to record 20 homers and 20 stolen bases in a season, stealing 36 bases in 43 attempts. Bothered by his lackluster .223 batting average and 102 strikeouts, Bonds vowed to improve in both areas. He displayed solid defensive skills as Pittsburgh's centerfielder, collecting 10 assists and committing just five errors. The Pirates, meanwhile, finished last in the NL East, 44 games behind the New York Mets.

In 1987, Bonds split his time between left field and center field with the arrival of centerfielder Andy Van Slyke. The Pirates experienced unprecedented fan enthusiasm with Bonds on the team and set the club attendance record of 52,119 in the 1987 home opener. Reducing his strikeouts, Barry's average climbed to .261

with 25 home runs and 32 steals. Pittsburgh went 80-82, an improvement of 16 wins from '86. With Bonds and Van Slyke in the outfield, the Pirates had an athletic defensive tandem that covered large chunks of the Three Rivers outfield.

Barry and Susann "Sun" Margreth Branco, the Swedish mother of his first two children, eloped to Las Vegas, Nevada on February 5, 1988. The couple had met in Montreal, Quebec in 1987.

Bonds became Pittsburgh's everyday leftfielder in 1988 to help minimize his average throwing arm – Barry's only shortcoming as a player. In left field the remainder of his career, Bonds compensated for his lone flaw with a quick and accurate release. The Pirates broke another record with 54,089 attending the 1988 home opener. Barry again improved, hitting .283 with 24 home runs and fit well into a highly respected lineup that now featured Bobby Bonilla, Van Slyke and Jay Bell.

In 1989, Bonds contributed 19 homers, 32 steals, 93 walks and 14 outfield assists for the fifth-place Pirates. Following the season, trade rumors surfaced that Bonds would be traded to the Dodgers, but no such trade occurred. Later that season, Bobby and Barry Bonds passed the father-son tandem of Yogi and Dale Berra for most career home runs.

Pittsburgh improved its win total by 21 games in 1990 to win the NL East title at 95-67. Bonds won his first Most Valuable Player award, hitting .301 with 33 home runs and 114 RBIs. His 52 stolen bases were third in the league. Barry also won his first Silver Slugger and Gold Glove Awards. His first "30-30" season enabled Bonds to join his father on the exclusive list of players who surpassed 30 homers and 30 steals in the same season. In October, the Pirates earned their first postseason berth since winning the 1979 World Series. The Cincinnati Reds, however, were looking to end a similar playoff drought and defeated Pittsburgh in six games en route to winning the '90 World Series. Bonds managed only three singles and a .167 batting average in the NLCS.

In spring training of 1991 in Florida, Bonds scolded a Pirates official because photographers were taking shots of him and then he became difficult with instructor Bill Virdon. Bucs manager Jim Leyland confronted Bonds. "One guy's not going to run this club," Leyland said. "If you don't want to be here, get out of here." Barry showed up the next day and apologized.

Bonds produced another outstanding season in 1991, blasting 25 homers and driving in 116 runs, and again won Gold Glove and Silver Slugger awards. He finished second to the Atlanta Braves' Terry Pendleton in the MVP voting. The Pirates slugging outfield of Bonds, Bonilla and Van Slyke led the team to two straight divison titles but again performed miserably in the playoffs, hitting .200 (15 for 75) in a seven-game loss to Atlanta.

In 1992, Bonds won his second NL MVP award. While hitting .311 with 34 homers and 103 RBIs, he carried the Pirates to their third straight National League East crown. Pittsburgh again faced the Braves in another seven-game NLCS. Bonds fielded a Game 7 hit by Francisco Cabrera and attempted to throw out Sid Bream at home plate. But the throw to catcher Mike LaValliere was late and Bream scored the series-winning run. The Pirates were denied a trip to the World Series for the third consecutive season. Barry hit .261 in the NLCS with a home run in Game 6.

Following the loss, Bonds and star teammate Doug Drabek were expected to command salaries too large for Pittsburgh to re-sign them. In 1991 and 1992, Bonds cemented his status as one of the game's finest all-around players. He made only three errors in the outfield each season, earning a Gold Glove award each year. Yet, despite helping the Pirates capture their second and third consecutive Eastern Division titles, Bonds struggled during the postseason. In 20 NLCS games from 1990-92, Bonds hit .191 with one home run and three RBI.

"The fans have always embraced me here in Pittsburgh, always," said Bonds. "I don't ever remember having any bad times here in Pittsburgh. That's just the Pittsburgh media. It's depressing all the time. That's just how it is. I don't think the people take it to heart."

In December 1992, free agent Bonds left Pittsburgh and signed a six-year, $43.8 million contract with the Giants, making him the highest-paid MLB player in terms of both total value and average annual salary. For Bonds, it was a dream situation calling him back home to San Francisco, with his father as hitting coach and a private suite on the road. Bonds intended to wear No. 24 and after receiving Mays's blessing, the Giants unretired it. But public outrage from fans and media was overwhelming and Barry switched his jersey to No. 25, his dad Bobby's number in San Francisco.

Bonds sizzled in a spectacular first season in San Francisco, batting a career-high .336 with 46 homers and 123 RBI. The Giants won 103 games, but lost the division title to Atlanta, who won 104 in what some refer to as "the last great pennant race."

Barry won a slew of awards in '93 including his third MVP award in four years. Bonds had own public relations rep, masseur, trainer, and a private part of the locker room where he kept a recliner and a big-screen TV. He did not stretch, eat or pose for pictures with the team.

"Barry does a lot of questionable things," former Giant teammate Jeff Kent told *Sports Illustrated*. "You just hope he shows up for the game and performs. I learned not to think about it or worry about it or analyze it. I was raised to be a team guy and I am, but Barry's Barry."

In the strike-shortened season of 1994, Bonds hit .312 with 37 home runs and an NL-leading 74 walks, finishing fourth in the NL MVP voting. He won his fifth consecutive Gold Glove. Meanwhile, Barry's marriage to Sun dissolved. The divorce became a recurring media item. Bonds had his Swedish spouse sign a prenuptial agreement in which she "waived her right to a share of his present and future earnings," which was upheld in court. They had two children (Nikolai and Shikari) and separated in June 1994, divorced by December and had their marriage annulled in 1997 by the Catholic Church. Bonds had been providing his wife $20,000 per month in child support and $10,000 in spousal support at the time of the ruling. Barry also had an extensive relationship with Kimberly Bell from 1994 through May 2003, and purchased a home for Bell in Scottsdale, Arizona.

In 1995, Bonds hit .294 with 33 homers, stole 31 bases and drove in 104 runs, his third "30-30" season. He exceeded both marks in 1996, when he became baseball's second-ever "40-40" player with 42 homers and 40 steals. Barry duplicated the feat Jose Canseco accomplished eight years earlier and walked a league record 151 times. Bonds also became only the fourth player to collect 300 home runs and 300 stolen bases in his career, joining Mays, Andre Dawson, and Bobby Bonds on that exclusive list.

Bonds hit 42 homers and drove in 101 runs in 1997, propelling the Giants to the playoffs. Again, he struggled in the postseason - going 3-for-12 at the plate as Florida swept San Francisco. Barry tied his father for most "30-30" seasons, and he placed fifth in the MVP balloting.

Bonds married his second wife, Liz Watson, on January 10, 1998 at the San Francisco Ritz-Carlton Hotel with 240 guests. They lived in Los Altos Hills with their daughter Aisha. Bonds also owns a home in the exclusive gated community of Beverly Park in Beverly Hills.

In 1998, Bonds hit .303 with 37 home runs and drove in 122 runs, won his eighth Gold Glove, and became the first player ever to eclipse 400 home runs and 400 steals. With two out in the ninth inning against the Arizona Diamondbacks in May, Barry became only the fifth player in baseball history to be given an intentional walk with the bases loaded. Nap Lajoie (1901), Del Bissonette (1928) and Bill Nicholson (1944) were three others in the 20th century who received that rare honor.

"You walk Barry," said Greg Maddux, winner of 355 games in his major-league pitching career. "Just walk him."

Baseball statistician Bill James ranked Bonds as the best player of the 1990s, adding that Craig Biggio of Houston was a distant second. In 1999, with statistics through 1997 being considered, Bonds ranked No. 34 on *The Sporting News* list of The 100 Greatest Baseball Players, making him the highest-ranked active player. When the list was revised in 2005, Bonds was re-ranked No. 6 behind Babe Ruth, Mays, Ty Cobb, Walter Johnson, and Aaron. James wrote of Bonds, "Certainly the most unappreciated superstar of my lifetime... [Ken] Griffey has always been more popular, but Bonds has been a far, far greater player. When people begin to take in all of his accomplishments," James predicted, "Bonds may well be rated among the five greatest players in the history of the game."

In 2000, Bonds hit .306 with a career-best .688 slugging percentage and hit 49 home runs in just 143 games while drawing 117 walks. But Barry was 3-for-17 (.176) against the New York Mets as the Giants were eliminated in the divisional round of the playoffs.

Bonds was always an exceptional athlete and always possessed the drive to push himself to be the best. Barry turned 36 in 2000 and began training with Greg Anderson who introduced him to a company called BALCO. Founded by Victor Conte, BALCO supplied an elite group of athletes with nutritional supplements that Conte claimed would enhance their performance. Bonds began to use BALCO products later revealed to contain androgenic steroids and other performance enhancing drugs.

Bonds was indicted for supplying false statements to a federal investigation and obstruction of justice in the banned substances investigation of BALCO. Bonds has always maintained that he never knowingly took steroids. He contends he did what his trainer advised, and used creams and supplements without knowing they contained steroids or Human Growth Hormone (HGH).

In 2001, Bonds produced one of the most historic seasons in baseball history. Utilizing his phenomenal hitting ability, tremendous knowledge of the strike zone and discipline at the plate, he set major-league records with 73 home runs (one every 6.5 at-bats) and 177 walks. Bonds's slugging percentage of .863 broke Ruth's 80-year-old single-season record, and his on-base percentage of .515 represented the highest mark in over 40 years. Along with his .328 batting average and 129 runs scored, he easily became the first player to win four MVP awards.

Bonds launched his 500th home run on April 17 against Terry Adams of the Dodgers. On October 4, he tied the previous single-season record of 70 set by Mark McGwire in 1998 by homering off of Wilfredo Rodríguez. He then hit numbers 71 and 72 off of Chan Ho Park the following night. Bonds added his 73rd off of Dennis Springer on October 7. The last home run ball was later sold to toy manufacturer Todd McFarlane for $450,000. McFarlane previously bought Mark McGwire's 70th home run ball.

"In my lifetime, I haven't seen anybody like him, with the career he's had and the things he can do — and he's getting better at this time in his life," said former All-Star Tim Raines. "To me, what he did last year was probably the most remarkable thing that's ever happened in the game. To walk 170 times *and* hit 73 home runs? It was like: The only time he swings, he hits a home run. When they throw him a strike, he hits it out of the ballpark. And when they throw a ball, he doesn't swing. I don't think anyone has ever been in a zone like that. The guy has almost hit eighty home runs in a year and a week. He's got as many home runs in one year as I've got my whole career, in 23 years."

Bonds's record of 73 home runs in 2001 came just three years after McGwire, who has also been tied to performance-enhancing drugs, broke Roger Maris's single season record of 61 homers. Bonds denied taking steroids at anytime in 2001 when he was pursuing the season home-run record. He enjoyed his largest base of support at AT&T Park in San Francisco where fans cheered as he shattered records. On the road, he was booed mercilessly and seen as a selfish villain who used steroids to smash homers.

Contrary to the laws of nature – though in accordance with the laws of illegal performance-enhancing substances – Bonds's batting achievements increased dramatically as he headed toward 40. This is widely believed to be the result of his consumption of anabolic steroids to increase his size and strength. The change in Bonds's appearance from the end of the previous season was undeniable. Giants management, unwilling to anger their volatile star with unproven allegations, instead chalked up Bonds's new look to the muscle growth, skull development, back acne, and jaundice that all men naturally experience in their late 30s.

After the record-breaking season, Bonds re-signed with the Giants with a five-year, $90 million contract in January 2002. His rigorous off-season conditioning program prepared him for the start of each season, and his hitting remained laser-like. He crushed 46 home runs, won the NL batting title with a career-high .370 average and struck out only 47 times. Barry drew a record 198 walks, 68 of them intentional. He slugged .799 and broke Ted Williams' major league record for on-base average with .582. Bonds also hit his 600th home run on August 9 at home against Kip Wells, making him just the fourth player to reach that milestone. At age 38, he became the oldest player ever to win his first batting title. At the end of the year, Bonds received an unprecedented fifth MVP award.

After the Giants clinched a playoff spot in 2002, Bonds finally overcame his history of playoff ineffectiveness. He batted .294 in the NLDS with three homers and four RBI as San Francisco edged the Braves in five games. The Giants then defeated St. Louis in the NLCS in five games with Bonds hitting .273, including a homer and six RBI. Although San Francisco eventually lost the World Series to the Anaheim Angels in seven games, Bonds was spectacular, batting .471 with four homers, 13 walks and six RBI. Despite the disappointing loss – the closest Bonds ever got to a championship of any kind – he tied the record for most home runs in a single postseason with eight. He also set a new MLB record with a World Series slugging percentage of 1.294.

After battling lung cancer and other health complications, Bobby died in August 2003. "It appeared to be inevitable, but nobody thought it would happen this soon," former Giants manager Dusty Baker said. "I lost a childhood hero. We grew up in the same town, my dad was his coach and his mom babysat me when I was young. He was a great friend."

Before their next game, the Giants observed a moment of silence and a video tribute to Bobby, who spent more than two decades with the club as a player, coach, scout and front-office employee. "Bobby has meant so much to this organization for such a long time," said Giants President Peter Magowan.

Bobby had been in failing health for nearly a year. In addition to chemotherapy to combat the cancer, he had surgery for a brain tumor in April and open-heart surgery in July after spending time in the hospital in early June with pneumonia. Orlando Cepeda recalls Bonds telling him when Barry was playing at Arizona State that

"My son is going to be the best ever. I said, 'Bobby, that's what everybody thinks about their son!'"

Despite his loss, Barry remained strong at the plate in 2003, slamming 45 home runs and winning the NL MVP yet again. He hit .341 and at .529, his on-base percentage was well above .500 for the third consecutive year. Bonds also stole the 500th base of his career, making him the first member of the "500-500" club. The Giants won the NL West, but Bonds's postseason struggles re-emerged. He batted just .222 with no home runs and two RBI in the NLDS against the Marlins, who defeated the Giants in four games.

In 2003, Bonds became a suspect in an anabolic steroids supply scandal when Anderson was indicted by a federal grand jury in the United States District Court. This led to an assumption that Bonds used performance-enhancing drugs during a time when there was no mandatory testing in Major League Baseball. In his defense, Barry issued a statement that he used a clear substance and a cream as nutritional supplement oil and a rubbing balm for arthritis. A close associate of Anderson and Conte, Bonds was called to testify before the grand jury. At the time, he denied knowingly using steroids.

In 2004, Bonds had perhaps his best season. He hit .362 en route to his second National League batting title, and again broke his own record by walking a staggering 232 times. He slugged .812, fourth-highest of all time, and broke his on-base percentage record with .609. Bonds passed Mays on the career home run list by hitting his 661st off of Ben Ford on April 13. He hit number 700 off of Jake Peavy on September 17. Bonds hit 45 home runs and struck out just 41 times, putting himself in rare territory as few major leaguers have posted more home runs than strikeouts in a season. Bonds won his fourth consecutive MVP award and his seventh overall, four more than any other player in history. On July 4, he tied and passed Rickey Henderson's record with his 2,190th and 2,191st career walks.

As Bonds approached Aaron's career record of 755 home runs, the media asked Aaron for his opinion of Barry. He stated that he was a fan and admirer of Bonds and avoided the controversy regarding whether the record requires an asterisk due to Barry's alleged steroid usage. He felt recognition and respect for the award was something to be determined by the fans.

Maddux said of Bonds in 2004: "He's always been the best player in the game. Is he the best ever? What do I know? I only know what happened in the 1990s. He's always been a complete player. He didn't have to hit 30 extra home runs to convince me of that."

Barry's salary for the 2005 season was $22 million, second-highest to Alex Rodriguez. But Bonds sustained a knee injury, multiple surgeries, and extensive rehabilitation. He was not activated until September 12. Upon his return, Bonds resumed his high-caliber performance at the plate, hitting home runs in four consecutive games from September 18 to September 21 and finished with five round-trippers in only 14 games.

Bonds refused to sign the license agreement with the MLB Player's Association, meaning that Barry doesn't appear in MLB video games and forced game makers to replace him. As a result, Barry was replaced by "Jon Dowd" in MVP Baseball 2005.

The book *Game of Shadows*, written by Lance Williams and Mark Fainaru Wada, was released in March 2006 and became a hot topic for Bay Area and national sports media and fans. *Sports Illustrated* featured the book on its cover and released its first public excerpts. With substantial documented evidence, the book alleges Bonds used stanozolol and a host of other steroids, and was perhaps the tipping point for the change in public opinion regarding Bonds's steroid use.

Game of Shadows detailed how athletes received performance-enhancing drugs from BALCO. The authors alleged Bonds turned to steroids after the 1998 season because injuries had taken their toll on his career and he was jealous of the attention McGwire received from breaking Maris's record. When McGwire, a far less outstanding all-around player than Bonds, became the face of the sport and its new home-run king, Bonds's sense of outrage drove his motivation to new heights.

According to the book, Bonds maintained a regimen of mixing human growth hormone, testosterone, insulin, anabolic steroids, trenbolone (a steroid to improve the muscle tone of beef cattle), and "Mexican beans," a fast-acting steroid that exits the body quickly, since the 2000 season. The book contained excerpts of grand jury testimony that were supposed to be sealed and confidential by law. The authors have been steadfast in their refusal to divulge their sources and at one point faced jail time.

In May 2006, former *Sports Illustrated* writer Jeff Pearlman released a revealing biography of Bonds entitled *Love Me, Hate Me: Barry Bonds and the Making of an Anti-Hero*. This book also contained many allegations against Barry. Pearlman describes Bonds as "a polarizing insufferable braggart with a legendary ego and staggering ability," and included over 500 interviews, but none with Bonds himself.

In 2006, Bonds earned $20 million (not including bonuses), the fourth highest salary in baseball. He had earned approximately $172 million during his career, making him baseball's all-time highest paid player. On May 7, Bonds grew closer to second place on the all-time home run list, hitting his 713th career home run at Citizens Bank Park in Philadelphia off Jon Lieber in a nationally-televised game. The towering shot — one of the longest in Citizens Bank Park's brief history – traveled an estimated 450 feet and hit the third-deck facade in right field.

On May 20, Bonds caught Ruth, hitting home run number 714 to deep right field to lead off the second inning. The home run came off A's pitcher Brad Halsey in Oakland. Bonds was quoted after the game as being "glad it's over with" and stated that the media should be focused on Albert Pujols, who was on a blistering home run pace.

On May 28, Bonds passed Ruth, hitting his 715th career home run to center field off Colorado pitcher Byung-Hyun Kim. The ball was hit an estimated 445 feet into center field where it went through the hands of several fans but then fell onto an elevated platform in center field. Then it rolled off the platform where Andrew Morbitzer, a 38-year-old San Francisco resident, caught the ball while he was in line at a concession stand. On September 23, Bonds surpassed Aaron for the NL career home run record with his 734th round-tripper, his final homer of the season.

In 2007, the *New York Daily News* reported that Bonds had tested positive for amphetamines. Under baseball's substance abuse policy, players testing positive were to submit to six additional tests and undergo treatment and counseling. The policy also stated that players were not to be identified for a first positive test, but the *Daily News* leaked the test's results. When the MLB Players Association notified Bonds of the results, he initially attributed it to something he had taken from the locker of Giants teammate Mark Sweeney, but would later retract this statement and he publicly apologized to Sweeney.

Bonds signed a revised one-year, $15.8 million contract on February 15 and reported to Giants spring training on time. Public opinion remained divided as he neared Aaron's hallowed record during that season. Aaron decided that he would not attend any possible record-breaking games. Most people believed that Bonds obtained his out-of-this-world power hitting at such a late stage in his career, at least in part, from the use of steroids. There was also no denying that Bonds's devotion to strenuous training, along with his natural athletic ability, enabled him to remain one of the most feared hitters in the game well into his 40s.

Barry finally smashed Aaron's all-time home run record of 755 in August, 2007. On August 4, Bonds homered off Clay Hensley of the San Diego Padres to tie Aaron's mark at AT&T Park. Bonds greeted his teammates, his wife Liz, and daughter Aisha Lynn behind the backstop. Nikolai was a batboy for the Giants and a fixture next to his dad in the dugout during games. Hensley was the 445th different pitcher to be taken deep by Bonds. Ironically, given the cloud of suspicion that surrounded Barry, the tying home run was hit off a pitcher who'd been suspended by baseball in 2005 for steroid use.

On August 7, Bonds crushed a 435-foot home run, his 756th, against Mike Bacsik of the Washington Nationals, setting a new all-time record for career homers. Bonds launched a 3–2 pitch into the right-center field bleachers and greeted Nikolai with an extended bear hug after crossing home plate. A brief video was then shown on the AT&T scoreboard in which Aaron graciously congratulated Bonds for surpassing the record he owned for 33 years. Aaron hoped that "the achievement of this record will inspire others to chase their own dreams." Barry made an emotional statement on the field with Mays at his side and thanked his teammates, family and his late father.

Matt Murphy, a 22-year-old Mets fan from Queens, New York, was the fan who ended up with the record-breaking ball. Murphy was quickly protected and escorted away from the crowd by a crew of San Francisco police officers. Commissioner Bud Selig was not in attendance in this game but Selig called Bonds later that night to congratulate him on breaking the record as did President George W. Bush. On August 24, the city of San Francisco celebrated Barry's accomplishments with a large rally at Justin Herman Plaza. The tribute included videos from Lou Brock, Ernie Banks, Ozzie Smith, Joe Montana, Wayne Gretzky and Michael Jordan. Speeches were made by Mays, Giants teammates Omar Vizquel and Rich Aurilia, and Magowan. Mayor Gavin Newsom presented Bonds the "Key to the City" of San Francisco and Giants vice president Larry Baer gave Barry the home plate he touched after slamming his 756th career home run.

Home run ball No. 756 was presented for auction on August 21. Bidding closed with a winning bid of $752,467 on September 15 after a three-phase online auction. The high bidder, fashion designer Marc Ecko, created a website to let fans vote for what should be done with the ball. Of Ecko's plans, Bonds said "He spent $750,000 on the ball and that's what he's doing with it? What he's doing is stupid." Ten million voters told Ecko to brand the ball with an asterisk and send it to the National Baseball Hall of Fame and Museum.

Bonds finished 2007 hitting .276 with 28 home runs and 66 RBI. Though he turned 43, he led both leagues with 132 walks. On September 21, the Giants confirmed that they would not attempt to re-sign Bonds for the 2008 season. Barry played his last game on September 26. He went 0-for-3, stinging a ball that was caught at the warning track in left-center field in his final at bat. Bonds officially filed for free agency in October. His agent Jeff Borris said "I'm anticipating widespread interest from every Major League team." But no team signed him during the 2008 or 2009 seasons. On December 9, 2009, Borris told the *San Francisco Chronicle* that Bonds had played his last major league game.

Bonds's awe-inspiring career accomplishments place him among the greatest baseball players of all time. To accompany his unprecedented seven MVPs and eight Gold Gloves, Bonds completed his amazing career with the most home runs (762), most walks (2,558), and most intentional walks (688) in baseball history. He averaged 34.6 home runs over 22 seasons. He led the National League in walks 12 times, on-base percentage 10 times, and slugging seven times. Bonds went "30–30" five times and remains one of only four members of the "40–40" club. Bonds is the lone member of the "500–500" club. He is a 14-time All-Star that also won NL batting championships in 2002 and 2004.

Fans of both the Pirates and Giants have called for the teams to retire their respective uniform numbers worn by Bonds. His No. 24 Pirates jersey is available to players, most prominently worn by Brian Giles from 1999–2003; it is currently worn by Pedro Alvarez. The Giants have not reissued nor retired Bonds's No. 25 since he left the team.

In retirement, Bonds has had frequent legal entanglements. In 2007, he was indicted on charges of perjury and obstruction of justice for allegedly lying to the grand jury during the government's investigation of BALCO. The trial began March 21, 2011. He was convicted on April 13, 2011 on the obstruction of justice charge. The verdict followed a highly–publicized 12-day trial. Bonds posted a statement on his website saying "Despite the charges that have been filed against me, I still have confidence in the judicial system...And I know that when all of this is over, I will be vindicated because I am innocent."

In 2009, Liz Watson filed for legal separation, citing irreconcilable differences. In 2010, she withdrew her separation proceeding and filed for divorce. Later that year,

19-year-old Nikolai was arrested and charged with five misdemeanors stemming from a confrontation with Sun, who questioned him about jewelry that was missing from their Menlo Park home. Menlo Park police say that Bonds apparently followed his mother into a bedroom, began to throw furniture around, spat in her face, and prevented her from leaving the house. The prosecutor said Sun refused to cooperate in the case against her son, resulting in a plea deal. Barry accompanied him to San Mateo County Superior Court. Nikolai was sentenced to the four days already served in jail, a $2,130 fine and was ordered to undergo 32 hours of anger management training.

Bonds, who once asked, "Where is it written that we're supposed to pretend we don't realize we're good?" is widely considered a me-first player. He resented and ignored what he labeled a "white media." When asked about fan criticism for a lack of hustle, Bonds once said that "I don't care what they think. They ain't out here. If you're better than me, then you can come out here and put my uniform on and do it." Barry, however, did have a softer side. In 1996, San Francisco Mayor Willie Brown declared a "Barry Bonds Day" to thank the slugger for his fund-raising work for underprivileged kids.

Today, a dark cloud still casts a shadow on many of Bonds's greatest achievements due to allegations that he used performance-enhancing drugs. Throughout his Hall of Fame career, Barry had a contentious relationship with the news media, managers, coaches and teammates. He was never given a known nickname by teammates. Bonds was awed and respected by the baseball world as a hitter but resented by many as aloof, a prima donna, and for exhibiting rude behavior. Still, many of those same teammates admitted to calling Bonds "the greatest player I have played with or ever will."

Possessing perhaps the best vision and strike zone recognition in baseball history, Barry Bonds was one of the most feared sluggers of all time. Gifted at reading the trajectory of fly balls as they jumped off hitters' bats, he used his speed to protect left field. Although his arm was never the strongest in the league, it was accurate, as evidenced by Barry's 123 assists. Bonds earned seven NL MVP awards. He also won eight Gold Glove Awards and hit .298 for his career with 2,935 hits, 1,996 RBIs, and 514 stolen bases. He is the all-time leader in home runs (762), and consecutive seasons with 30+ home runs (13), and holds the single-season record with 73. Barry and his late father Bobby, both blessed with speed and power, head the list of father-son duos with 1,094 career home runs and 975 stolen bases, barely missing the "1,000-1,000" milestone.

In retirement, Bonds spends most of his time at his Beverley Hills estate. "My history is San Francisco," said Bonds. "That's my father, my godfather. Every friend in the world that I grew up with is there. There's no place in the world like San Francisco for me, right now. I don't know if there ever will be."

31

HELEN WILLS

Arguably the most dominant women's tennis champion of the 20th century, Helen Wills was an eight-time Wimbledon winner, a seven-time U.S. Open champ and a two-time Olympic gold medalist. Known for her steely demeanor and unflappable temperament on the court, Wills earned the nickname "Miss Poker Face." During a 158-match stretch from 1927 to 1933, she did not lose a single set. Wills captured 31 total Grand Slam titles, and became the first American female athlete to enjoy international stardom.

Helen Newington Wills was born in Centerville, now part of Fremont, on October 6, 1905. Wills spent her childhood in Berkeley and received her introduction to tennis from her father, Dr. Clarence Wills. Helen also developed her early game at the Byron Hot Springs resort and attended grammar school in Byron. By age six, she was still a small and relatively fragile girl, hardly a young sportswoman. Helen, however, was blessed to have parents that got their daughter interested in outdoor activities, particularly swimming and horseback riding. When she was eight, Clarence bought her a tennis racket and played with Helen every day. "I can remember when, as a beginner, I was delighted with any ball as long as it would bounce," she remembered.

Wills attended Head-Royce School in Oakland – one of California's top prep schools – for her high school education. For her 14th birthday, her parents gave her a membership to the Berkeley Tennis Club, and Helen took advanced lessons. Her trademark concentration, power, and speed quickly developed, and she began competing on the national circuits in 1920. Wills was a bit of a fanatic, playing every day and bent on defeating every opponent. Helen would take on the pretend role of American champion "Little Bill" Johnston while she practiced. As she hit balls, she would silently chant "Now I'm Johnston, now I'm Johnston." Soon after, she no longer needed to use her imagination. Now she was Helen Wills, and soon the real Johnston came out to the BTC to practice with her.

Hazel Hotchkiss Wightman, holder of 43 national titles, met Wills in the summer of 1920 when Helen was still 14. Wightman worked with her for six weeks in Berkeley and then continued the following summer when Wills and her mother traveled east as Wightman's guests. Wightman was among the few people who got along with Helen comfortably. Wightman's secret for bringing out Helen's inner personality was to treat her as an unqueenly and imperfect human being. "Helen was really an unconfident and awkward girl," said Wightman. "I thought of Helen as an honestly shy person who was bewildered by how difficult it was to please most people."

Former men's world champion William Tilden once wrote about the young Berkeley star in a 1921 article, saying that "I have no doubt but that in a few years Helen Wills of California will add her name to the list of champions already made famous by such players as Molla Bjurstedt Mallory, Mary K. Browne and May Sutton Bundy."

On the corner of Domingo and Tunnel near the Claremont hotel, the Berkeley Tennis Club was founded in 1906 and has been home to some of the world's greatest tennis stars. Don Budge, who was the No. 1 player in the world for five years during the 1930s and the first man to win all four Grand Slam events in a single year, called the BTC his home. Other stars who have played here over the years include Arthur Ashe, Rod Laver, Ken Rosewall, Stan Smith and Billie Jean King (who is also a member). Wills grew to love the sport and became dedicated to playing – and winning – every day.

At 15, Wills's dedication helped her capture the 1921 U.S. National Junior Championship in her first attempt as a five-foot tall pigtailed teenager. In 1922, she won another Junior title, and saw France's Suzanne Lenglen, the most famous tennis player of the era, for the first time. Helen finished second in the 1922 U.S.

Open and teamed with Marion Zinderstein Jessup to claim the doubles championship. By the end of 1922, Wills was ranked third among American women. Amazingly, she had grown seven inches and gained 25 pounds within a three-year period. She was ready to embark on one of the finest decades of tennis success ever achieved by a man or a woman.

Already a junior champion, Wills scored her first major championship victory at age 17 by dethroning defending champion Mallory at the 1923 U.S. Open in Forest Hills, New York. Six thousand spectators, one of the largest galleries to ever witness a women's tennis match, turned out to see if the beautiful California teenager – "Helen of the Pigtails," or "The Girl of the Golden West" – could defeat the seven-time champion Mallory. Wills needed just 33 minutes for the 6-2, 6-1 victory and began a lengthy tenure at the top by receiving the No. 1 U.S. ranking after her victory. She was the second-youngest U.S. Open winner.

"My feelings, as the last ball traveled over the net, and as I realized that the final match was mine, I cannot describe," she recalled of her first U.S. Open title. "I felt that here was a prize for all the games I had ever played."

Wills made that trip to New York with her mother, who provided the emotional support that her daughter needed. Helen was a quiet and reserved girl who admitted in later years that she found escape in painting and tennis. The presence of her mother provided Wills with both mental strength and friendship. A hero's crowd and a band had awaited her at Oakland's 16th Street train station on her triumphant return from New York. After being congratulated time and again by fellow passengers along the cross-country journey, she couldn't bear the thought of such a mob scene. Helen and her mother quietly disembarked at an earlier East Bay stop and hired a car to drive them back to Berkeley.

Wills was suddenly a smashing sensation. At the beginning of the 1923 season, the *New York Times* wrote that "women's tennis in this country seemed in a bad way. Mrs. Mallory held such absolute sway, defeating her opponents with such uninterrupted regularity, that little interest was taken in the matches." Helen breathed new life into the normally staid East Coast scene and drew new fans to women's tennis. They grabbed and shouted at Helen as if she were a movie star. They vigorously applauded errors by her opponents. No one could quite get used to the idea of a beautiful woman athlete – that wasn't supposed to exist in the 1920s. "Women don't show to advantage on the track or in the field," sportswriter Paul Gallico wrote. It was even believed that some women of the era who excelled in sports did so because it was the only way to attract attention.

Helen's physical gifts and focus were already passing into legend. Sportswriter Grantland Rice wondered how the teen could be so "intensely serious, unemotional, stoical – not only for a girl of her age, but for a human being of any age." Shortly after Helen returned to Oakland, the U.S. Lawn Tennis Association announced plans to send the new American champion to Europe to face world champion Lenglen. Helen's father Clarence told reporters that the offer of a European tour was pleasing, but only if such a trip did not interfere with his daughter's studies. Tennis, he said, was "just for fun."

Wills graduated from Head-Royce and won an academic scholarship to the University of California at Berkeley, just a few miles north of the club. She intended to study fine arts. Helen was not a typical college freshman, having recently dethroned Mallory, the longtime queen of American tennis. Wills went on to be honored as a Phi Beta Kappa at Berkeley, one of the most prestigious honor society awards. She also became the first female Cal athlete to earn a school letter.

On September 17, 1923, a fire started at midday in the scrubland of Wildcat Canyon in the Berkeley hills. Wills was on campus when she noticed the burning smell in the air. The fire continued to leap forward and the electricity went out at homes west of the university – including at the Wills residence on Shattuck Avenue – before those inside had any idea what was happening. Anxious residents, gripped by panic, rushed into the streets.

Helen's Kappa Kappa Gamma house survived but the nearby Delta Zeta Tau and Alpha Sigma Delta houses weren't as lucky – both burned to the ground. Instead of retreating, Wills hurried to the front and provided water and coffee to firefighters and escorted rescued residents to relief stations. Just as she was on the tennis court, Helen remained calm and focused. Late in the afternoon, she and a few sorority sisters climbed a hill to track the progress of the fire. Suddenly, Helen's right eye – and then her whole head – caught fire. She screamed in pain, hopping and pulling at her eye, with the other girls screaming uncontrollably. Wills walked into an emergency room for blistered feet and eye pain. News of the tennis champion's admittance quickly spread, leading to speculation that she "had suffered an injury that would result in the loss of the sight of one eye." Helen, always shy and awkward around strangers, laughed at the rumor. Her doctor told her the pain would pass and her eyesight would be fine.

The following morning, Wills stepped out of her parents' house with a large bandage over her eye and surveyed the devastated neighborhood just across from Live Oak Park.

More than a thousand houses had been damaged, with at least 500 completely destroyed. Fifty city blocks had been transformed into black, desert-like terrain, survived only by lines of brick chimneys. Twenty-five people had been reported missing, and more than 50 injured. Neighbors sat sobbing outside their wrecked homes.

Helen soon after visited her beloved courts at the Berkeley Tennis Club and was relieved to find the club unharmed. She preferred the Berkeley club to Forest Hills, and was confident she would also prefer it to the All-England Club at Wimbledon. She got a kick out of playing against the men there, the golden Berkeley hills rising up around them, the afternoon sun on her shoulders. New members always would "laugh at the idea of playing a child and a girl at that" and then she would whip them, sometimes without the loss of a game. All she wanted, she later realized, was a "sunny day, white balls, fresh white tennis clothes, a good-natured opponent, and a brisk game." She knew of only one way to describe such a perfect blend of desires: "heaven."

Wills traveled to Europe for the first time to play at Wimbledon in 1924, losing to Britain's No. 1 ranked player Kitty McKane Godfree in the finals, her first and only singles loss at Wimbledon. Later in the season Helen repeated as U.S. Open Champion and claimed two gold medals at the Olympic Games in Paris. It marked the last time tennis was played at the Olympics until 1988. Helen won the singles gold without the loss of a set and added a second gold medal by taking the doubles with Wightman, who was almost 20 years her senior. Wills also teamed with Wightman to win the 1924 Wimbledon doubles crown. They were never defeated. Wightman's commanding cries "Run, Helen!" were so memorable at Wimbledon that the English made it part of their tennis vernacular.

Time magazine, which featured Wills on its cover in 1926 and 1929, said "There was nothing frivolous about 'Little Miss Poker Face.' She stood her ground like a tank, drilling out bullet serves and powerful baseline drives." Strong from the baseline but unafraid of ambushing her opponents at the net, Helen was a tireless opponent. Like her flamboyant European role model Lenglen, Wills used men as her practice partners to help overpower her competitors. On both the forehand and backhand, she was able to drive the ball with speed, pace, and depth, and had a serve that could pull her opponent wide of the service box. Though Helen didn't often attack the net, she was also a capable volleyer.

After claiming her third consecutive U.S. Open Championship in 1925, Wills made her way to France in 1926 to pursue her painting and her education. She was also ready for the Lenglen challenge. The media went into a frenzy at the prospect of Lenglen, the top female player in the world, asserting her superiority over the 20-year-old American who had already won three U.S. titles. Wills and Lenglen dominated the inter-war years, together winning 30 grand slam titles between 1919 and 1938. Yet they played each other only once, and it was not in one of those majors. Billed as "the match of the century," it took place at the Carlton Club in Cannes on February 16, 1926 in a tournament final.

The encounter was given added spice by the contrasting characters and styles of the two women. The favorite Lenglen, almost 27 and the reigning French Open and six-time Wimbledon champion, was renowned for her glamour, grace, flamboyance and strategic brilliance. Wills was a highly-touted up-and-comer, more statuesque, physically stronger, but with a quiet and serious personality. There was a prizefight atmosphere, with tickets scalped at a then-shocking rate of $50. Roofs and windows of nearby buildings were crowded with spectators, including the King of Sweden.

Lenglen won the match 6–3, 8–6 after being down 2–1 in the first set and 5–4 in the second set. Wills had set point in the second but a disputed line call cost her the point and she went on to lose the match. For the only time in her career, Helen showed strong emotion on the court, raising her voice to argue with the linesman. It was a closely fought battle that alerted the tennis world that Wills was ripe to capture Lenglen's crown. After the match, Lenglen's father advised her that she would lose her next match to Helen if they met again soon and Lenglen avoided Wills for the remainder of the spring. Before the rivalry could gain traction, Lenglen turned professional, and the two never met again.

Wills noted that although she lost the match, she gained perspective on necessary changes to her game, which relied on peppering her opponents into submission with strong ground strokes. Despite the loss, Helen did meet another significant person at Cannes. A young businessman in the crowd, financier Frederick Moody, introduced himself to Helen after the match. Wills traveled to France in 1926 to participate in the French Open for the first time. Unfortunately, she required an emergency appendectomy that ended her tournament and forced her to withdraw from Wimbledon. The appendix caused her to miss out on all three 1926 majors.

Though their styles and personalities differed, Wills shared similarities with Lenglen as well, as both practiced with men instead of women. Both players also became noted for their fashion choices. Wills displayed grace, beauty and glamour both on and off the tennis court, but had a look unlike the bohemian bandanna and flowing coat sported by Lenglen. Wills advocated sensible clothing on the courts and blamed trailing hemlines for women's ineptitude at the net. She termed them "a mental as well as a physical hazard" and always wore a knee-length pleated skirt during play. She typically wore a white sailor suit, white open neck blouse, white shoes, and a white visor – a trend-setter for her day.

In 1927, a revived Wills became unbeatable and began her streak of not losing a set until the 1933 Wimbledon Championships. Her first victory at Wimbledon came in 1927 and made her the first female American victor there since May Sutton in 1905. Not only did she win all three Grand Slam events that year, she did so without conceding a set. She was unbeaten in 180 matches during her most dominant period, not even losing a set in 158 singles matches played from 1927 to 1933. During this stretch she captured all seven of her U.S. Open titles, five of her eight Wimbledon titles, and four French championships, finally losing her first set to Dorothy Round in the 1933 Wimbledon final, a match Wills won 6-4, 6-8, 6-3.

Like Lenglen, Wills had achieved international celebrity with her success, and despite her introverted personality, won over several famous fans. She took tea with the British Prime Minister, was the subject of poetry by Louis Untermeyer and counted King Gustaf V of Sweden and Charlie Chaplin among her admirers. In 1930, Chaplin remarked that the most beautiful sight he had ever seen "was the movement of Helen Wills playing tennis."

Wills wrote a coaching manual, *Tennis* (1928), her autobiography, *Fifteen-Thirty: The Story of a Tennis Player* (1937), and a mystery, *Death Serves an Ace* (1939, with Robert Murphy). She also wrote articles for the *Saturday Evening Post* and other magazines.

She was already quite famous when she married Moody in December 1929. She won approximately one-half of her major championships as Helen Wills and one-half as Helen Wills Moody. Wills was an artist and painted throughout her life. She was delighted to be chosen as the model for Diego Rivera's two-story mural "The Riches of California," commissioned for $2,500 in 1930. Helen and Frederick invited Rivera and his wife, painter Frieda Kahlo, to a celebratory tea after the mural's unveiling at the San Francisco Stock Exchange.

She often faced Helen Jacobs – also from Berkeley – in Grand Slam finals. Wills beat Jacobs in the French final of 1930, the Wimbledon final in 1929, 1932, 1935 (despite trailing 5-2 and match point in the third set) and 1938 and the U.S. Open semis in 1927 and the final in 1928. Jacobs's one victory over Wills was in the U.S. Open final in 1933 when Helen had to withdraw in the third set due to an injury that forced her out of competition for two years. At the time, Jacobs was leading in the third set. The defeat snapped Helen's streak of seven consecutive U.S. Championships crowns in seven attempts. Because she felt the press and fans treated her harshly at that U.S. Open, Wills vowed never to play in Forest Hills again.

Wills was reported to be an introverted and detached woman. On court, she rarely showed emotion, ignored her opponents, and took no notice of the crowd. Godfree, who inflicted the only defeat Wills suffered at Wimbledon during her career, said "Helen was a very private person, and she didn't really make friends very much." Because of her stoic and utterly unflappable demeanor and unchanging expression, sportswriter Grantland Rice bestowed on Wills the nickname "Little Miss Poker Face." As her success and unpopularity with the public increased, she was also called "Queen Helen" and "the Imperial Helen."

Alice Marble, one of the many opponents who felt ignored by Wills, dubbed her the Garbo of the tennis tour. Helen nonetheless lived a very public and, at times, storybook existence. The lack of emotion on court was interpreted by many as an aloof coolness and did not endear her to the news media or spectators. "When I play," she said. "I become entirely absorbed in the game. It may be a form of concentration." Her focus was legendary. She claimed to be unaware of game points, set points and even match points. According to her biographer Larry Engelman, she adhered to a mantra, "Every shot, every shot, every shot." In her autobiography, she said, "I had one thought and that was to put the ball across the net. I was simply myself, too deeply concentrated on the game for any extraneous thought."

Between 1923 and 1933, Wills won 17 of her 19 Grand Slam singles titles and was runnerup in the other two. This was at a time when players did not compete in the Australian Open because of the travel time and distance. She also competed in the 1932 Olympic Arts Competition. Her game had become truly formidable. She continued to practice against men, which helped to maintain the powerful, athletic and unflagging play that dominated all challengers. As late as 1933, she played and beat eighth-ranked American male player Phil Neer 6–3, 6–4 in an exhibition match.

"I love the feel of hitting the ball hard, the pleasure of a rally. It is these things that make tennis the delightful game that it is," said Wills.

Wills divorced her first husband Frederick in 1937 and married professional Irish polo player and film writer Aiden Roarck two years later. She then became known as Helen Wills Moody Roarck.

After taking a year off to recuperate, Wills came back to win the 1935 and 1938 Wimbledon titles, beating Jacobs both times. The 1938 Wimbledon final was a contrast in styles between Moody's booming forehand and Jacobs' powerful serve and deceptive topspin. The match began as one for the ages, with the two champions trading points to a 4-4 tie in the first set. Jacobs then suffered an ankle injury, which forced her to limp through the next eight games as she lost in straight sets. After the match Jacobs said she had "never been more sorry about anything in my life." For Wills, it was a record eighth Wimbledon championship that raised her career record there to 50-1. Her record stood for 52 years before it was broken in 1990 by Martina Navratilova.

Later, Wills spoke highly of Jacobs as a tennis player. They didn't mix socially as they had different circles of friends, and Wills lived in California while Jacobs was based mainly on the east coast. Wills also said in her autobiography *Fifteen Thirty* that the view often expressed by the press that there was a feud with Jacobs was incorrect. The idea was attractive to the press of course: girls with the same name, living in the same area, at even living in the same Berkeley house, as the Wills family vacated it before the Jacobs family moved in.

Wills was named Associated Press Female Athlete of the Year in 1935, but bothered by back pain and a disinclination to turn professional, she retired from tennis altogether by 1938. Helen's career records are breathtaking. She won an astounding 31 Grand Slam titles (singles, women's doubles, and mixed doubles) during her career, including seven singles titles at the U.S. Open, eight singles titles at Wimbledon, and four singles titles at the French Open. Had the Australian Open been a Grand Slam event during her era, she undoubtedly would have won several more Grand Slam titles. Excluding her defaults at the French Championships and Wimbledon in 1926, Wills reached the final of every Grand Slam singles event she played during her career. She was the No. 1 ranked women's tennis player in the world for eight years between 1922 and 1933. From 1927 to 1933, Helen won 180 straight matches, including a 158-match streak in which she did not lose a single set. Her career record was 398-35, a .919 winning percentage. Only Steffi Graf and Margaret Court have won more Grand Slam singles titles. Helen was also successful when representing her country. From 1923 to 1938, she won 18 of 20 Wightman Cup singles matches and two Olympic gold medals in Paris.

Budge, 11 years her junior, called Wills "one of my idols." Like Moody, Budge was born in the Bay Area. "I remember riding to Berkeley on my bicycle to watch her practice," he said. Budge was one of those who teamed with her in mixed doubles. "She hit the ball harder than most, except maybe Steffi Graf. Her footwork didn't have to be great. She would control the play because she hit the ball so hard."

Wills focused on art after retirement, giving exhibitions of her paintings and etchings in New York, London and Paris galleries. She personally drew all of the illustrations in her book *Tennis*. For Wills, who confessed to suffering the intangible pangs of "a restless heart," tennis and painting were the best antidotes for her. She maintained an artist's studio at her residences in San Francisco and later in Carmel, once sold 40 paintings for $100 each and illustrated her own articles for *The Saturday Evening Post*.

When asked in 1941 about whether Wills or Lenglen was the better player, Elizabeth Ryan, who played against both of them, said "Suzanne, of course. But Helen Wills Moody owned every kind of shot, plus a genius for knowing how and when to use them." Godfree, who played both several times and was a two time Wimbledon champion during Lenglen's absence, also stated that Lenglen was "by far" the better player.

George Lott, a 12-time winner of Grand Slam doubles titles and a contemporary of Wills, once said, "Helen's expression rarely varied and she always tended strictly to business, but her opponents were never in doubt as to what she held: an excellent serve, a powerful forehand, a strong backhand, a killer instinct, and no weaknesses. Five of a kind! Who would want to draw against that kind of hand?"

Wills followed the game closely in her senior years, watching matches on television, and she never seemed to have lost her competitive edge. "She admired Martina Navratilova greatly as a tennis player who broke her record," said Jeanne Cherry, a Los Angeles tennis historian. "I once asked her how she felt about Martina breaking her record, and she said, 'Well, you know, she pumps iron.'" It had taken more than half a century for a woman to win more Wimbledon singles titles than Wills.

"Whatever Helen did, she had to be the best at it," said Edward Chandler, a San Francisco attorney who was a lifelong friend of Wills. "She never really seemed to replace tennis. She stopped playing at 82, but she was outspoken in her admiration for Chris Evert, she despised Jimmy Connors for the way he behaved and she was very happy to see Pete Sampras come along, because he seemed a throwback to the older school."

In 1994, Wills gave this rendition of what ended her career in an interview with *Inside Tennis* reporter William Simon: "Well, it was during the war and my husband was at Fort Reilly, Kansas. I was walking my big police dog, Sultan. A little dog came barking wildly out of a house and grabbed my dog by the throat. Those little fox terriers have no sense. They're just wild. So my poor dog was being chewed to pieces. But in the fight, my index finger on my right hand was bitten. My poor old finger, the finger next to the thumb. The thumb is very important in tennis. So that was the end of my career. I couldn't manage. I never mentioned this before to anyone."

Wills was inducted into the International Tennis Hall of Fame in 1959. In 1981, she was inducted into the Bay Area Sports Hall of Fame. She remained an avid tennis player into her 80s. Following failing health for several years, Helen died at age 92 of natural causes on New Year's Day 1998 at Carmel Convalescent Center. She had no children and there were no known family survivors. Her ashes were scattered at sea, and there was no service. At the time of her death in 1998, Wills bequeathed $10 million to the University of California at Berkeley to fund the establishment of a Neuroscience institute. The result was the Helen Wills Neuroscience Institute, built in 1999 and now home to more than 40 faculty researchers and 36 graduate students.

One of the most gifted, inspiring and influential women to have ever played tennis, Helen Wills was also a highly accomplished painter, a successful writer, and an excellent horsewoman. Perhaps the greatest female tennis player of the 20th century and the first American-born woman to achieve international celebrity as an athlete, she rubbed shoulders with kings and prime ministers, was painted by Diego Rivera, and was admired by the rich and famous. Wills spent 364 consecutive weeks as the No. 1 U.S. player from 1927 to 1933. She again rose to No. 1 in 1935 and again in 1938. In total, Wills captured the top spot for nine years. She had an effortless and graceful game paired with intense focus. Helen, who never appeared for a match without her signature stark white visor, created a legacy of inspiration for generations of American women.

32

O.J. SIMPSON

Never in the history of sports has an athlete risen so high only to fall so far. From a beloved football star, broadcaster, actor and corporate spokesman, O.J. Simpson transformed himself into one of the most villainous and despised men in America. You already know how his story ends. It was in San Francisco that it began.

Orenthal James Simpson was born at Stanford University Hospital on July 9, 1947 to Eunice Durden and James Lee Simpson, the third of four children. He was raised along with brother Truman, and sisters Shirley and Carmelita in the rugged Potrero Hill neighborhood of San Francisco. The family lived in various Potrero projects, staying longest at 906 Connecticut Street. Simpson's grandparents were from Shreveport, Louisiana and Wilmot, Arkansas. An aunt suggested the name Orenthal, supposedly the name of a French actor she admired.

Baby Orenthal struggled to walk. Doctors diagnosed the boy with rickets – a vitamin D and calcium deficiency that weakened his legs and left him bowlegged and pigeon-toed. To achieve normal walking, surgeons would have to break and reset his legs or fit him with braces. The Simpsons could afford neither. Eunice, who worked as an orderly at a hospital, made him wear a pair of shoes connected by an iron bar for a few hours almost every day until he was five. He did end up bowlegged – and later a sprinter who could run the 100-yard dash in 9.3 seconds.

A bank janitor and cook, Jimmie Lee Simpson led an openly gay lifestyle, and was known in the neighborhood as a Castro cross-dresser. Jimmie Lee left Eunice in 1952 to raise the four children on her own when Orenthal was only four. Eunice was already working full-time – and now overtime – at the hospital. Simpson began to hate the name Orenthal, so he started calling himself "O.J." His early interest in sports was encouraged by his mother and, paired with his determination and physical gifts, he craved competition from an early age.

"I remember once when he was a little boy, he was watching the Rose Bowl on TV," Eunice said. "He told me he'd play in that game someday. How could I believe him? He didn't even have his shoes on the right feet."

In grammar school, Simpson discovered the Potrero Hill Recreation Center where neighborhood boys played basketball, baseball, and football. Although children called him "Pencil Pins" because of his thin legs, he was soon picked first in almost every sport. O.J. saw his first major league baseball game at 11 in 1958 when Willie Mays and the New York Giants moved west to Seals Stadium. He remembered when Eunice, his Uncle Hollis and a lot of neighborhood folks were looking forward to seeing the new team in town.

"All the white teachers in school seem to get just as excited about Mays and the Giants as my mother and uncle," he said. "People smiled when they talked about him. There was so much adulation."

But Simpson was a troubled child. He struggled in school and once described his neighborhood as "your average black ghetto." Adolescence was tough on him as well as he was cut from his youth football team and joined his first street gang – the Persian Warriors – at age 13 in 1960. Another boy that joined was childhood friend Allen "A.C." Cowlings and the pair were participating in gangfights soon after.

There were few opportunities for poor black kids in Potrero. As a youth, Simpson joined several gangs, provoked fights, crashed school dances, stole auto parts, gambled, and skipped school. "I was in a lot of street fights," he recalled. "Maybe because I usually won. I was proud I was a tough scrapper. We had our gangs. They were full of guys who didn't know right from wrong and couldn't have cared less.... We didn't care about anything good. We didn't know about anything good."

Simpson once told biographer Bill Libby, "I had a lot of hatred and defiance in me. I could easily have come to a bad end if I hadn't gotten a break. " Meanwhile, Simpson's athletic talent was developing at the PHRC. O.J.'s formative years were spent in the projects and at the gym playing sports. A Potrero neighbor said, "Black kids were welcome at that gym and that's where most spent their time."

"I never infringed on people," Simpson said in a 1976 interview with *Playboy*. "I only beat up dudes who deserved it. At least once a week, usually on Friday or Saturday night. If there weren't no fight, it wasn't no weekend."

Although Simpson's brushes with the law were mostly petty, he was jailed at a San Francisco juvenile detention center at 15. Police held him for a weekend after a gang fight over liquor stolen from a local store. When he arrived home on Monday, he expected a beating from his father, a common strategy used by Eunice when things got out of control. But this time someone else was waiting at the Simpson home: Willie Mays himself.

Mays, the star centerfielder of the San Francisco Giants, had been asked to intercede by Lefty Gordon, the PHRC supervisor. He took young Simpson with him for a day in the life of a pro athlete. He never discussed gangs or jail or getting into trouble. Instead, he brought an awed Simpson to his massive home in swanky Forest Park, one of the city's finest districts. It was an ordinary day, filled with errands like picking up laundry, but it was that house that left an impression on O.J. "To have that hero pay attention to me, it made me feel that I must be special, too. He made me realize that we all have it in ourselves to be heroes. I wasn't that much smaller than him and I was almost as fast. He was human, a regular guy, but he was almost a god."

Simpson attended Galileo High School, located in San Francisco's Russian Hill and Marina District neighborhoods. He made the school's football team originally as a tackle and later as a running back. O.J. was also the leader of a different kind of gang – a social group known as The Superiors that organized school dances and events. In the springtime, Simpson also played on the baseball team and ran track.

Marguerite Whitley was Simpson's high-school sweetheart; O.J. stole her from best friend Cowlings. Whitley described Simpson's early life in a 1968 *Look* magazine interview. "He was a beast," she said then. "He was pretty horrible. If there were other fellows who wanted to talk to girls, he'd make them stay away. He'd been a terrible person, right on the edge of trouble. Just awful. I sensed something good in him, but I don't think it really showed. He lived on the brink of disaster."

Simpson was on the verge of making his own breaks as a raw but explosive running back at Galileo. As he improved, he was willing to brag to anyone, including one of

America's greatest athletes. One Sunday after the 49ers had lost to the Cleveland Browns at Kezar Stadium, Simpson and his friends stopped for ice cream. To their amazement, Jim Brown, the NFL's leading rusher, suddenly appeared.

"I really first met him when I was just a kid in San Francisco," said Simpson. "It was after a 49er game – I was a big fan of (Hugh) McElhenny and Joe Perry – and a bunch of us had gone across the street from Kezar Stadium to an ice cream parlor where we hung out after games. We were just messing around in there when who should walk in but Mr. Jim Brown himself.

"Well, you know how kids are. We started fooling around, mumbling things, and finally I just walked right up to him and said, 'Mr. Brown, someday I'm going to break all your records, wait and see.' I know it sounds unbelievable now, but I was just kidding around. Brown hardly looked at me. He just kind of walked away smiling."

The NFL was an impossible dream for a projects kid at Galileo High, one of the worst teams in the city. But Simpson's talents did not go unnoticed. Football occupied his time productively and the Lions coaching staff worked hard at developing his remarkable abilities. They knew they had an exceptional athlete on their hands – with an exceptionally bad attitude. Coach Jack McBride remembers O.J. as "a very lazy student" but worth redeeming. When Simpson and two friends were caught gambling before a big game, McBride delivered a scolding that O.J. never forgot: "Even though I felt bad about it at the time, and I was a little mad at him, he told me that no one was going to give me anything in the world. He said, 'If you want something, you'll have to work for it and act like you deserve it. If you want respect you're going to have to act respectable.'"

Simpson eventually became a star at Galileo, earning All-City honors in his senior year. In 1964, the Lions took on mighty St. Ignatius, winners of 23 straight games. As expected, Galileo trailed, 25-10. But then Simpson took over the game, scoring touchdowns of 90, 80 and 60 yards for the biggest upset in San Francisco high school history. In his finest GHS game, he gained over 300 yards in 17 carries. But by season's end, Simpson did not receive a single college scholarship offer.

Meanwhile, Eunice continued to hold the family together. "There were always three meals on the table," said boyhood friend Jon Greenberg. "The house was kept up, and he always had a mother at home he could go to." When he was inducted into the Hall of Fame, Simpson singled out his mom. "You just don't know what it is to be eight years old and all your friends think you have the best mother in the world."

Simpson's grades failed to meet admission requirements for four-year universities, including his dream school – the University of Southern California. Unable to outrun or out-talk his C-minus average, he briefly considered enlisting in the Army after high school but then appeared headed to Arizona State. O.J. got as far as the airport before Marguerite tearfully persuaded Simpson to stay in San Francisco for another year and enroll at City College.

From 1965 to 1966, Simpson attended classes at City College of San Francisco, a member of the California Community College system. He was a record-setting running back and defensive back and was named to the Junior College All-American team as a running back. He also ran on the track team. As a Ram, Simpson wore No. 32, set national JC rushing records and was named Conference Player of the Year twice. In two dominating seasons at CCSF, O.J. ran for 2,445 yards and 54 touchdowns, averaging 9.2 yards per carry. His career rushing record stood for 27 years.

Those who knew him and saw him play with the Rams had no doubt he would go on to the NFL. "We all knew where he was going," said defensive lineman Kevin Devine, now with the San Francisco Fire Department. "At that time, all the kids who came to City played against each other in high school. We couldn't even tackle him."

It was no secret to opponents that O.J. was destined to be a great player. He set national records and once rushed for 304 yards and six touchdowns in one game. Teams knew to target him. "Laney tackled Simpson every play, whether he had the ball or not," Devine said. When Cowlings dropped out of high school, O.J. convinced him to get his G.E.D. and attend City College. Cowlings went on to become all-City at CCSF and an NFL player for nine seasons. "Back then O.J. set a pretty good example," Cooney said.

At CCSF, O.J. began crafting the wholesome image he would later be known for. "He'd wander the sidelines at halftime, talking to people and telling stories," Devine said. "At parties, you'd see him drinking milk." Despite the team's winning record and Simpson's dazzling running style, few students attended the Friday afternoon games.

Simpson still ranks fourth overall in career rushing yards and eighth for a City College single season with 1,365 yards. All of the players ranked above him in today's CCSF record books required 12-game seasons while O.J.'s teams played a nine-game schedule. After two years at CCSF, Simpson was heavily recruited and received 50 college scholarship offers to play football. On June 24, 1967, 20-year-old O.J. married Marguerite, his 18-year-old high school sweetheart. They would have three children together, Arnelle, Jason, and Aaren.

Simpson chose Southern Cal, the only school he ever wanted to play for and one steeped in football tradition. He majored in sociology. As a player and as a person he was still raw. He once said that he went to USC so he could learn which fork to use at dinner. But he had one overwhelming advantage – he could run with a football better than anyone.

At 6-foot-1 and 210 pounds, Simpson gained national prominence as a two-time All-American halfback for the Trojans. O.J. led the nation in rushing with 1,451 yards and 11 touchdowns in 1967. He also ran on the USC 440 sprint relay team that broke the world record at the NCAA track championships in Provo in June 1967 and ran the 100-yard dash in 9.3 seconds.

It was at USC that Simpson became "The Juice." With the strength to break tackles and the magic moves to embarrass defenders, Simpson's runs were jaw-dropping. O.J.'s most electrifying Trojan moment came against unbeaten UCLA. His scintillating 64-yard broken-field touchdown run gave USC a 21-20 victory and lifted the Trojans to a Rose Bowl win over Indiana. Simpson had been a serious contender for the Heisman in his junior year at USC but finished second to UCLA quarterback Gary Beban. Dick Belsky wrote that O.J. "was the finest and most explosive running back to come out of college football in a decade. Some thought he might be the most prized collegian in football history."

In 1968, he rushed for an all-time NCAA record 1,709 yards and 22 touchdowns, earning the Heisman Trophy, the Maxwell Award, and the Walter Camp Award. *Sport* magazine named Simpson its "Man of the Year" in February of 1969, the first time the award had gone to a college player. O.J. still holds the record for the largest margin of Heisman victory, defeating the runner-up by 1,750 points.

In both 1967 and 1968 he led the Trojans to the Rose Bowl, scored 35 touchdowns, and gained 3,295 yards in only 22 games. O.J. ran for more than 100 yards in 17 of his 21 games at Southern Cal and topped the 200-yard mark five times. "Simpson was not only the greatest player I ever had – he was the greatest player anyone ever had," said John McKay, his coach at USC. Although O.J. was "All-World" at USC, he did not graduate.

After the triumphs of Galileo, CCSF, and USC, Simpson moved into the pro football ranks in 1969. Under the rules of the NFL draft, the team that finishes the season with the worst record chooses first. Heisman-winning Simpson was selected No. 1 overall in the 1969 draft by the 1-12-1 Buffalo Bills. Before he played a single game, Chevrolet signed him to a three-year, $250,000 endorsement deal.

As a highly heralded NFL rookie, O.J. was now polishing a public image that made millions. "I became very aware of my image," Simpson recalled in a book of his own, *OJ: The Education of a Rich Rookie*. "After taking so long to find out who I was, I didn't want anyone else to misunderstand me. I didn't want to be O.J. Simpson, running back. I wanted to be O.J. Simpson, a good guy. I'm happy to admit it: I really enjoyed being liked. I loved it when kids stopped me for autographs. I loved it when people recognized me on the street. I loved it, I think, because I could at last recognize myself."

Despite his soaring success, Simpson reportedly required constant reassurance, the validation of cheering crowds and fawning fans. He could recognize himself only by a reaction by others. He told writer Pete Axthelm about a vacation trip to France. "Over there I was just another tourist who didn't speak the language. Nobody knew me and I felt alone and lost."

Simpson's transformation from college golden boy to professional superstar occurred in Buffalo, a scrappy, blue collar city in an economic downturn. Back in 1969, Buffalo was a bleak scene of brutal winters and lost jobs. The city needed a spark, a savior of sorts, and it came in the form of O.J., the prize draft choice of the Buffalo Bills.

Simpson did not want to come to Buffalo at first, and said he preferred playing on the West Coast to "make as much money" as he could. But tight-fisted Bills owner Ralph Wilson quickly ponied up a four-year deal worth $100,000 a year, a staggering amount at the time. More than 2,000 people screaming "O.J., O.J." showed up at the airport in Buffalo to watch Simpson walk off the plane. Within hours, he had 340 requests for personal appearances. O.J. quickly upgraded Buffalo's image, at least as a sports town.

"A lot of bad things were happening to Buffalo at the time," said Larry Felser of the Buffalo News. "And the town already had an inferiority complex. But O.J. became the personification of success and notoriety – that Buffalo was indeed a good place after all. He was our validation."

O.J. was not an immediate success and did not win Rookie of the Year acclaim in 1969. His first three years with Buffalo were frustrating as the Bills went 9-33. Head coaches John Rauch and Harvey Johnson didn't believe in building their offense around Simpson and incredibly, he was used sparingly as a running back. When Lou Saban took over in 1972, he recognized what McKay had found at USC – O.J.'s ability to make people miss. The more he carried, the better he got. Saban built a talented offensive line for the San Francisco speedster to get the football early and often.

Simpson immediately responded with huge ground-gaining performances. His per game average was 10 yards more than any other NFL running back. "The Juice" powered one of the league's top rushing offenses, and he ran behind the famed "Electric Company" offensive line. Blockers included Hall of Famer Joe DeLamielleure, Reggie Mackenzie and Dave Foley. Simpson led the NFL with 1,251 yards rushing in 1972 as the Bills improved to 4-9-1.

O.J. is perhaps best remembered for his sensational 1973 season when he became the first player in NFL history to rush for over 2,000 yards and broke the single-season rushing record held by Jim Brown. With 219 yards in Week 13 against the New England Patriots, Simpson's season total reached 1,803 with one game left. With a 200-yard performance in the snow at New York's Shea Stadium, Simpson totaled 2,003 yards, better than 143 yards per game. He was voted the 1973 NFL Most Valuable Player and awarded the Hickok Belt as the Professional Athlete of the Year. Although the 2,003-yard season has been surpassed since, no other player accomplished the feat in only 14 games.

Simpson was now far more than just a football player. He became a professional "good guy," an actor always playing the warmhearted, ever-smiling Juice. O.J. the myth was shaped not by Connecticut Street in San Francisco, but by Madison Avenue in New York. He came along at just the right time, when the civil rights battles of the '60s had created a new level of racial tolerance. Married with two children, he had a healthy look, a bright smile, the right nickname – all of it non-threatening. Said sports columnist Ron Rapoport of the Los Angeles Daily News: "Madison Avenue was looking for a breakthrough black man and he was it."

After injuries "held" him to 1,125 yards in 1974, Simpson had another banner season in 1975, rushing for 1,817 yards and an NFL record 23 touchdowns while catching passes for 426 receiving yards. Away from football but within sports, he won the 1975 American Superstars competition. He won his final rushing title in 1976 with 1,503 yards. Despite all the rushing success of O.J. and the Electric

Company, the Bills never won a playoff game, managing only a 32-14 first-round loss in 1974 at Pittsburgh.

Simpson's celebrity allowed him to meet and date beautiful women. Marriage was no obstacle, according to friends. While married to pregnant Marguerite, he met Nicole Brown in 1977 when she was 18 years old, a homecoming princess fresh out of Dana Hills High School. She was a waitress at a Beverly Hills restaurant where he dined, and they struck up a relationship immediately. No matter that expectant Marguerite was home, fully aware of his escapades. "My wife knows I'm under control," O.J. told *People* magazine in 1978. Simpson also hosted *Saturday Night Live* later that year.

O.J. maintained a race-neutral style, which included dating white women, and while it drew criticism in both black and white circles, Simpson always appeared comfortable. He'd later say with pride that Hertz's research found that American consumers considered him "colorless." He told the *New York Times* that his biggest accomplishment was that "people looked at me like a man first, not a black man."

Injuries limited Simpson to seven games with the Bills in 1977 and at season's end, he was traded to the 49ers for five draft choices, including a first-rounder. With daughter Arnelle now nine years old and son Jason seven, O.J. had returned to San Francisco for the 1978 season, but it was anything but a happy homecoming. He separated from Marguerite in October. Simpson's younger daughter Aaren drowned as a 23-month-old infant the following August in their new Rockingham mansion pool while in the custody of Marguerite. O.J. blamed her for the death and expressed difficulty dealing with the loss. "I don't know how long it will take me to get over, but I know I need to keep busy."

On the field, chronic injuries and poor rosters netted O.J. only 1,053 yards and 3.8 yards per carry over his final two seasons. He officially retired following the 1979 campaign. Simpson was named NFL Player of the Year in 1972, 1973 and 1975. He was both All-AFC and All-Pro five straight years from 1972 through 1976. He played in six Pro Bowls, winning MVP honors in the 1973 game.

Simpson's career achievements for 11 NFL seasons confirm a Hall of Fame career. He rushed for 11,236 yards, added 2,142 more on 203 pass receptions, returned 33 kickoffs 990 yards, and amassed 14,368 total yards. O.J. scored 76 touchdowns. He led the NFL in rushing four times in a five-year span and finished his career as the No. 2 all-time rusher, now No. 11. Simpson also broke the single-game rushing record with 273 yards in a game and ran for more than 200 yards in a game six times. He was the first NFL player to run for 2,000 yards in a season.

In retirement, the famous, likable, and good-looking Simpson now had unlimited endorsement opportunities similar to Michael Jordan in the 1990s. RC Cola, Schick, Foster Grant, Wilson, and Treesweet were just some of the brands that hired him to pitch their products. He settled back into Los Angeles, where it all began at USC. He was still O.J., only his helmet and pads were replaced by a briefcase and business portfolio that included ownership of restaurants, stores and real estate on both coasts.

Simpson became a commentator for ABC's *Monday Night Football* and a movie actor, including appearances in all three *Naked Gun* comedy films. He also starred in "Roots," the immensely popular TV docudrama. While football came easy for Simpson, broadcasting and acting did not, and he was criticized at first for grammar and clarity. However, his bubbling personality kept him popular with viewers. Even during his playing career, O.J. always wanted to be an actor and had small roles in TV shows like *Dragnet* and *Medical Center*. He also appeared in *The Towering Inferno*, *Capricorn One*, and the cable series *1st & Ten*. He accumulated many small parts though no one ever confused him with Olivier or Poitier.

In Hertz commercials, a well-dressed O.J. ran to catch a rent-a-car, smiling as he hurdled airport hazards and flashed past a cheering old lady. He was an African-American man casually interacting with white men and women. Simpson's image remained neutral, which catapulted him to a level of financial success unknown to any athlete of his time. He was an attractive African-American who did not clench a militant fist, but rather extended an open hand in friendship. There was a Mr. Clean image he presented while few knew of the darker side that existed in his youth.

With his film career accelerating in the early 1980s, Simpson sought to be the same kind of star on the silver screen he had been on the football field. He dreamed of performing like Dustin Hoffman, playing complex roles and winning Oscars. A *U.S. News* writer who interviewed him regularly recalled that O.J.'s Hollywood fantasies revealed how "naive and sheltered" he really was. He was a limited actor, seemingly able to play only one role: himself. "The 30-second commercial format was perfect to capture O.J. Simpson," pointed out ad executive Mark Morris. In longer formats, he simply lacked the necessary depth.

Divorce proceedings continued with Marguerite. The amicable parting was highlighted by a $500,000 payment of from O.J. to Marguerite and thousands more per year in support for their two children. Marguerite once said "I have been shoved out of the way, pushed and stepped on by more than one beautiful woman. I admit I'm jealous."

Simpson's divorce became final in 1980 and he married Nicole on February 2, 1985 at the Rockingham mansion with 400 guests. In August, O.J. was inducted into the Pro Football Hall of Fame. Simpson paused during his acceptance speech when he began talking about his mother Eunice. "She drove me 700 miles so I wouldn't miss my first Little League game," said Simpson, crying. He credited Eunice with his success and she responded by saying "I didn't really think he'd turn out the way he did, but he always said you'd read about him in the papers someday and my oldest daughter would always say, 'Yeah, in the police report.'"

Simpson and Roger Staubach became the first Heisman Trophy winners to be inducted into the Pro Football Hall of Fame. Early in his career with Buffalo, Simpson said he considered quitting. But Bills coach Lou Saban, who introduced O.J. at the ceremony, redesigned his offense for Simpson. Saban said he received his inspiration from his mother. "She said, 'Louie, don't be stupid. Give O.J. the football. I just regret he wasn't able to play on a championship team," said Saban.

Meanwhile, Simpson's father Jimmie Lee revealed he was an AIDs patient, shortly before Sydney Brooke Simpson, the daughter of Nicole and O.J., was born on October 17, 1985. Jimmie Lee passed away in 1986, two years before Sydney's brother Justin Ryan Simpson arrived on August 6, 1988.

Even in a sea of Hollywood stars, O.J. and Nicole made a striking pair. He was athletically handsome and age-defying. She was blond and attractive, and a workout warrior. They openly kissed at parties, sporting events and charity benefits. They dropped into the hottest nightspots of West LA. They drove Ferraris and summered at his house in Laguna Beach. They vacationed, on Hertz, in Hawaii, Vail, Aspen, and Mexico. Nicole wanted to enroll in a junior college, but was discouraged by Simpson, who wanted her to be available at all times. She found herself socializing in the most exclusive cliques of Los Angeles.

"We moved into a $5 million residence in the exclusive area of Brentwood," she later said in a court document. "We had a full staff to assist us. The house was extensively remodeled a few years ago, and no expense was spared.... We also spent our summers at a $1.9 million Laguna Beach house, which is situated on the sand. This house was never rented but only kept for our own enjoyment during the summer and at other times during the year. [O.J.] and I maintained a bicoastal lifestyle. We have an apartment in New York, which I used several times each year, sometimes for as long as one month at a time.... Whenever we traveled on commercial airlines, we flew first class. However, it was not unusual to travel by private jet, such as on trips to Las Vegas."

Acquaintances have described celebrity-filled parties at Rockingham, where guests played pool and tennis and participated in scavenger hunts. The couple's two children completed this seemingly perfect portrait. But old habits die hard, and those who know Simpson well said that women remained eager to please him wherever he went. Usually, they were in their early 20s.

About this time, another side to Simpson began appearing behind the tall gates to his Brentwood estate. This became apparent in the predawn hours of New Year's Day 1989. Police were summoned to Rockingham Avenue at 3:30 am, and found Nicole outside the house, her eye blackened and her lip bloodied.

According to the police report, Nicole rushed across the lawn, wearing a bra and sweatpants, and collapsed against the gate-release button. "He's going to kill me, he's going to kill me," she yelled, running to officers who responded to the call. "You never do anything about him; you talk to him and then leave." She said Simpson hit and kicked her as he yelled, "I'll kill you," police said. O.J. then appeared from the house wearing a bathrobe and screamed at police, "I don't want that woman sleeping in my bed anymore." Threatened with arrest, he yelled, "The police have been out here eight times before, and now you're going to arrest me for this? This is a family matter. Why do you want to make a big deal of it? We can handle it."

Simpson pled no contest. He was placed on two years probation, paid a fine of $470, and ordered to undergo counseling and perform community service. O.J. was allowed to attend his required counseling by telephone, so that his traveling schedule would not be affected. Hertz never wavered on his contract as their spokesman and his football broadcasting career continued uninterrupted. Son Jason, meanwhile, enrolled as a freshman at USC.

Nicole confided in friends and family regarding beatings by Simpson, who did not appreciate her flirtatious association with other men. O.J. denied ever hitting Nicole and said that her injuries came as a result of friendly "wrestling." After what was described as a "rocky marriage," Nicole filed for divorce in 1992. The divorce created new problems, this time financial, as Simpson cited business and investment losses. His net worth was still valued by a judge to be more than $10 million.

"I knew he beat her," says an agent who was in the same social circle. "It was common knowledge. A lot of his friends knew it – not just the 1989 incident, but all the beatings. They all tried to keep it quiet. In the small circle these athletes socialized in, people just didn't ever go public with this information. They protected him."

The judge ultimately awarded Nicole alimony of $9,000 a month and monthly child support of $15,000. She moved into a $700,000 townhouse less than two miles from the large house on Rockingham Avenue she had shared with O.J. and kept one of the Ferraris. Their beautiful lives now proceeded independently.

Simpson still made movies, including a third *Naked Gun* film, but his acting career had clearly slumped. In television, he primarily appeared on NBC's NFL pre-game show, but he eventually lost his prized role on *Monday Night Football*. He often made personal appearances, mainly for Hertz, and continued to generate a lot of income. O.J. was still phenomenally recognizable and well-liked, but he was no longer a superstar and no longer young.

Nicole continued to work out, shop and frequented the local restaurants. She was now a fixture in affluent Brentwood Gardens, although some thought that she was somewhat "out of her element" among the young actors and actresses. She was, after all, 35. On Thursday nights, she often danced until 2 a.m. at Renaissance, a club in Santa Monica.

In October of 1992, the year Nicole and O.J. were officially divorced, she consulted a therapist named Susan Forward, who has written about obsessive love. Forward now says "He beat her all through their marriage, and after they were separated, he would stalk her." According to Forward, Nicole was a classic battered wife: blaming herself, overly dependent, unable to break away. But even after the divorce was final, they continued to see each other.

Paula Barbieri, a 25-year-old Victoria's Secret model, began dating Simpson in the early 1990s. He once told a reporter it was strange getting used to someone with her own life and schedule; neither of his ex-wives ever worked. Simpson, at age 46, stopped seeing Barbieri toward the end of 1993. When a friend of O.J.'s ran into Barbieri on a plane, she made a joke about ex-wives and said, "I'm out of it, I'm leaving him alone. I have elected to let him find whatever he needs to find."

By December of 1993, O.J. was trying desperately to resurrect his marriage with Nicole. At Theodore's, Simpson told the shopgirls that he aimed to get back together with Nicole and that whatever failed between them had been his fault. The Simpsons appeared to be dating and even attempting a reconciliation. Friends went out to dinner with them. Sometime shortly after the Super Bowl in January, O.J., Nicole and their children chartered a yacht in Florida called *Miss Turnberry* and luxuriated for a couple of days at $10,000 a day.

A broadcasting colleague remembers going out with O.J. and Nicole and other friends during Super Bowl week. "It was really lovely," he said. "I thought they were getting along well. I didn't get any impression other than that they were still in love, that they wanted to get back together. I got that impression from her as well as him. They were putting the marriage back together, and the vision in O.J.'s mind was that they were going to remarry. He had even recently stopped seeing other women, which for O.J. was a sign of real commitment."

But there were additional aspects to their renewed courtship. There have been reports of neighbors overhearing fighting at Nicole's condo. Given the couple's history, it's natural to assume their arguments had again become violent. Unless treated, spousal abuse often continues unchecked.

The last time Nicole and O.J. were seen together was at a dance recital on June 12, 1994 with their children. Later that day, she was found on her doorstep brutally murdered – knifed to death – along with her friend, Ron Goldman.

Goldman's co-workers at Theodore's and at Mezzaluna doubt that he and Nicole were involved in a relationship. "He would have told us," said Jodi Kahn, a salesperson at Theodore's. "My god, the things he told us anyway. Nicole would have been a remarkable achievement. You have to understand, these young guys are in awe of a woman like Nicole," Kahn said. "It was just enough to be near her." But Nicole and Ron's relationship was something more than a casual acquaintance. Neighbors remember seeing Goldman at Nicole's playing with the children and he was also seen driving Nicole's Ferrari. "Small town, man," said a local business owner to a magazine reporter. "O.J.'s car? O.J.'s around here a lot, too, you know. Not cool."

Los Angeles police believe that Simpson and Goldman intersected tragically on the night of June 12. But for all the details that connect them, nobody is sure that the meeting was anything but coincidental. On that tragic Sunday, O.J. played golf early at Riviera Country Club, and in the afternoon he and Nicole attended

Sydney's dance recital at Paul Revere Junior High, though they did not sit together. Afterward, Nicole took the children to Mezzaluna to meet friends for dinner. O.J.'s whereabouts at that time are unknown, though one of his lawyers said he was at home preparing for a late-night flight to Chicago for Hertz promotional work.

After Nicole arrived home that evening, she phoned Mezzaluna to announce she had left a pair of sunglasses. Goldman told the manager that he would return them when he finished work. He clocked out at 9:33 p.m., had a beer and then walked to Nicole's home several blocks away. There were no known witnesses to what happened next between Nicole's doorstep and a locked outer gate on a pleasant stretch of South Bundy Drive. At 12:10, just as O.J.'s American Airlines flight was leaving LAX, the bodies were discovered. In the Hollywood tradition of celebrity death, floral bouquets appeared at the gate.

Shortly after O.J. checked into the Chicago O'Hare Plaza Hotel, a Los Angeles police officer phoned to tell him that Nicole had been murdered. O.J. then made about 10 calls from the room, including one to a woman believed to be Barbieri. According to witnesses at the hotel, O.J. was frantic as he checked out and rushed back to the airport. The moment he returned to his house, Simpson was greeted by police and handcuffed. Attorney Howard Weitzman had the police un-cuff him. Speculation grew quickly and pointed to his involvement. O.J. was now a suspect, and promised to turn himself in to police.

The LAPD, who to that point handled the case with precision, then bungled Simpson's arrest. With one of crime history's most highly visible suspects in their sights, the police lost track of him for most of the next 24 hours. O.J. went to Nicole's funeral Thursday morning and was scheduled to return that afternoon with heavy security. From the media coverage, he supposedly was the man shielded from reporters by a long coat as he entered his front door between a pair of other men. However, police later learned that the man being shielded was a decoy.

Robert Shapiro, who replaced Weitzman as Simpson's attorney, was told on Friday morning that warrants had been issued for O.J.'s arrest. Shapiro arranged for a surrender at police headquarters. At that time, Cowlings and two doctors tended to Simpson at the Encino home, one for depression. Simpson ignored surrender deadlines set by police. Their patience exhausted, police arrived in Encino to make the arrest. Shapiro then discovered that Simpson and Cowlings had disappeared while in an upstairs room conferring with the two doctors.

In an angry press conference, Commander David Gascon declared Simpson a fugitive and all of Southern California, including airport officials and border patrols, was put on notice. Shapiro then announced that O.J., in addition to being a fugitive, was suicidal. He said that Simpson had drafted his will and had written three letters, one to his mother, another to his children and a third to the public. O.J.'s friend Robert Kardashian held a press conference to read the letter addressed to the public. In it Simpson said "First, everyone understand I had nothing to do with Nicole's murder." He ended by saying, "Don't feel sorry for me. I've had a great life, great friends. Please think of the real O.J. and not this lost person. Thanks for making my life special. I hope I helped yours."

Less than an hour later, a white Ford Bronco was spotted in Orange County. Officers from multiple police agencies began pursuit. Close to 100,000,000 people watched as a "low-speed chase" on Interstate 5 was broadcast live across America. Cowlings, who was driving, warned police through his cell phone that Simpson had a gun to his own head. Pursuers backed off and ushered the Bronco along freeways and surface streets.

Bystanders flocked to the freeways where the Bronco was traveling, hanging signs that said "GO OJ," "Don't Squeeze the Juice" and other greetings. Drivers honked horns and pedestrians ran onto the freeways. Friends went on TV and radio and tearfully pleaded with Simpson to surrender peacefully. Helicopters tracked his every move. O.J. and Cowlings motored on at a polite pace, reaching Simpson's house shortly before 8 p.m. After a 50-minute stalemate during which Cowlings was gesturing furiously, Simpson left the Bronco and entered his house. He had $8,000 in cash, a fake beard and mustache, his passport, and a loaded pistol. He was allowed to use the bathroom, call his mother and drink a glass of orange juice before taken into custody — arrested for double murder. Cowlings was arrested for aiding and abetting a fugitive, and then released on $250,000 bond.

Sources say the heated arguments with Nicole were mostly about money. And within the last year O.J. had told a close friend and co-worker that he hoped Nicole would marry again so that he could be relieved of the alimony. But could he murder for money? What if this native of the San Francisco projects, a former gang member, saw a handsome young man driving a Ferrari that he had bought for his ex-wife? Did he seek revenge for the unfairness?

Simpson is clearly more complex than the image his celebrity projected. But he believed he had simple goals: to own a large home, to become an American hero regardless of color, and to be liked. O.J. had achieved all of that. Then, in 1994,

Nicole Brown supposedly told him she would never reconcile. Friends say it was perhaps the only occurrence in his adult life that Simpson had ever been told no. What happened next, Los Angeles police contend, was he became a man who lost complete control of his senses.

As O.J. was charged, processed, and jailed, Americans were divided on what actually happened. People had a need to wrap their mind around this famous person and that evil deed. Could Simpson have committed this horrible crime, one carried out as their children, Sydney, 8, and Justin, 5, slept a few feet away? Could Simpson have plotted one or both of these murders, boarded a plane and played out an alibi that had been arranged in advance? Could he have returned home, attended a visitation for the woman he murdered and then her funeral? Could he have done all that? Could anyone?

Simpson emerged from the dramatic chase without shooting himself, but most believed he was dead regardless. Never again would he be the smiling pitchman who wanted to be liked. He is viewed differently, with thoughts of fascination mixed with horror. This was never supposed to be part of the image he worked 46 years to create. The new O.J. would never be able to return to the same private life that existed just two weeks ago.

For Americans that watched Simpson hurdle through airports or interview NFL players as a sideline reporter for NBC, the disintegration of this man was stunning. Previous domestic violence allegations just never stuck, although they should have. "It was perplexing," said a former NBC Sports employee, a woman. "People at NBC Sports used to always remark about the beating, shaking their heads and saying, "Here's a man who used to beat his wife, and none of America cares or remembers.' People refused to believe it because they thought he was such a nice guy."

Details of the pre-trial investigation were leaked to the media and nearly all of them tightened the net on Simpson. A bloody glove found at the crime scene matched one found at O.J.'s house; some of the blood spilled matched Simpson's type; there was blood found on his clothes, possibly in a washing machine O.J. might not have known how to operate.

Simpson's trial was an eight-month media extravaganza, often called the "Trial of the Century." It was covered gavel-to-gavel through courtroom cameras and educated all of America on such topics as Crime Scene Investigations, forensics, the LAPD, domestic violence, the legal process, and families of the victims. New television programs – even networks – were created involving legal analysts and judges as well as made-for-TV crime dramas.

Simpson pleaded in court, "Absolutely, positively, 100 percent not guilty" to begin the proceedings. Americans were then introduced to a colorful cast of characters, including Lance Ito, the judge of questionable competence; Kato Kaelin, Simpson's lazy houseguest; Marcia Clark, the prosecutor with ever-changing hair and wardrobe; and Johnnie Cochran, the slick defense lawyer. Famed trial lawyer F. Lee Bailey and Barry Scheck were also added to O.J.'s "Dream Team" defense counsel.

When the prosecution requested Simpson try on the killer's gloves, he couldn't squeeze his sprawled hand inside. Cochran said "If the glove doesn't fit, you must acquit." The defense continued to poke holes in questionable police work and tainted evidence. When asked on the witness stand whether he'd planted any evidence to frame Simpson, LAPD Detective Mark Fuhrman invoked his Fifth Amendment right not to incriminate himself. Much of the trial included establishing the fact that Fuhrman had made racist comments years before. The Brown and Goldman family attended many of the proceedings

Simpson was acquitted in criminal court on October 3, 1995. In a subsequent 1997 civil trial, where standards of proof are lower, Simpson was found liable for the deaths of Nicole Brown Simpson and Ronald Goldman. He was ordered to pay the families compensatory and punitive damages totaling $33.5 million. However, most of O.J.'s fortune went to defense costs and there's been little call for his acting skills or celebrity endorsements since the trial, leaving Simpson to live on only his NFL pension.

"You'll never be able to hear O.J. Simpson's name or even watch the great vintage footage of O.J. Simpson as one of the very greatest players who ever lived without thinking of this tragedy," said NBC's Bob Costas, a broadcast teammate of Simpson's. "But that's the consequence of what happened."

"Nobody will ever think of him as a football player again. Clearly what has taken place since 1994 will forever be O.J. Simpson's legacy and whatever he did in a sporting sense becomes totally secondary," said ABC broadcaster Al Michaels.

People in Potrero Hill had a hard time accepting what happened to their local hero. A resident of the community said "When you've been touched so positively by a man of his stature and see all the warmth that resided in him over the years, it's hard to think of him as anything else." The football field that dominates the second block of Galileo High School had been named in honor of it greatest star – O.J. Simpson. In 1995, after the trial, the field was subsequently renamed "George White Field." An O.J. jersey still hangs over the school trophy case.

As Simpson's mother had attended his Hall of Fame enshrinement, she often appeared to support O.J. in court. Throughout his career, O.J. maintained a close relationship with Eunice. Friend Michelle Metcalf said there was a special bond between O.J. and his mom. "He would say 'My mama. My mama would inspire us to stay in school' and this and that. He had a wonderful love for his mother."

His acting and sports announcing careers abruptly ended. From the spokesmen that big corporations lined up to pay millions, Simpson became someone that nobody wanted. The State of California claimed he owed $1.44 million in past due taxes and filed a tax lien in his case in 1999. In 2000, he moved into seclusion near Miami, Florida.

In 2001, Simpson's anger again got him into trouble with police. He was arrested in Miami-Dade County in a road rage incident. O.J. faced up to 16 years in prison, but was quickly acquitted on two charges. Simpson's Miami home was searched by the FBI on December 4, 2001 on suspicion of ecstasy possession and money laundering. The FBI had received a tip that O.J. was involved in a major drug trafficking ring after 10 other suspects were arrested. Simpson's home was thoroughly searched for two hours, yet no illegal drugs were ever discovered. No arrest or formal charges ever stemmed from this incident. However, investigators uncovered equipment capable of broadcasting pirated satellite television signals which eventually led to Simpson being sued in federal court.

In 2002, Simpson was again arrested in Miami-Dade County for speeding and failing to comply with proper boating regulations. In 2004, satellite television network DirecTV accused O.J. in a Miami federal court of stealing its broadcast signals. The company later won a $25,000 judgment, and Simpson was ordered to pay $33,678 in attorney's fees and costs. He was also ordered later that year to surrender his income from autographs.

In 2007, Simpson led a group of men into a room at the Palace Station Hotel in Las Vegas and took sports memorabilia at gunpoint. O.J. told police he re-claimed items stolen from him, and denied any hotel room break-in and denied that he or anyone else carried a gun. But along with three other suspects, Simpson was arrested and charged with multiple felony counts, including criminal conspiracy, kidnapping, assault, robbery, and using a deadly weapon. Bail was set at $125,000, with stipulations that he have no contact with the co-defendants and that he surrender his passport.

By October of 2007, all three of Simpson's co-defendants plea bargained with the prosecution for reduced charges in exchange for testimony that guns were used in the robbery. After the hearings, a judge ordered that O.J. be tried for armed robbery and other crimes. On October 3, 2008, Simpson was found guilty of all felony charges. His counsel moved for new trial based on judicial errors and insufficient evidence and declared they would appeal to the Nevada Supreme Court if necessary.

On December 5, 2008, 61-year-old Orenthal James Simpson was sentenced to 33 years in prison with the possibility of parole in 2017. In 2009, the Nevada Supreme Court denied a request for bail during Simpson's appeal. He is now serving his sentence as Nevada Department of Corrections inmate #1027820 at the Lovelock Correctional Center.

33

OLLIE MATSON

Hall of Fame running back Ollie Matson was one of the NFL's most exciting and versatile stars of the 1950s and 1960s. Physically, he had it all – 6-foot-2, 220-pound size, sprinter speed, and brute strength. On the field, he did it all – rushing, receiving, blocking, returning kicks, and even defending as a punishing defensive back. His athletic exploits at San Francisco's Washington High, the University of San Francisco and at the 1952 Olympics made him a local legend well before his NFL glory.

Oliver Genoa Matson, Jr. was born on May 1, 1930, in Trinity, Texas, a small town about 90 miles northeast of Houston. Ollie grew up in Depression-era America, a time of simple living, sacrifice, and prejudice. His parents were Ollie Sr. and Gertrude Matson, a Houston elementary school teacher. Segregation was the Texas law of the land during Matson's grammar school years. Schools, libraries, water fountains, and public bathrooms were separate for whites and African-Americans. Interracial marriage was against the law. Poll taxes kept minorities – and poor whites – away from voting booths. Walt Jourdan, a childhood friend of Ollie's for 60 years, said Matson didn't often discuss his Texas years. "Most of us in those days didn't want to talk about where you came from because there weren't a lot of good memories. They didn't treat us too well. We didn't go back unless there was a funeral."

The combination of Southern racism and brisk war-time manufacturing on the West Coast sparked an exodus of African-Americans to Northern California, whose black population multiplied nine times during the 1940s. The Matson family moved to San Francisco in search of a better life in 1944 when Ollie and his twin sister Ocie were 14 years old. The family settled in the Western Addition neighborhood, sandwiched between Van Ness Avenue, Golden Gate Park, the Upper and Lower Haight neighborhoods, and Pacific Heights. Within a few years, Ollie established himself as one of the city's exceptional prep athletes at George Washington High, where bright new sports facilities were built in 1940.

Inspired by world heavyweight champion boxer Joe Louis, Matson originally wanted to be a boxer but that idea was vetoed by his mother. He pursued football, basketball and track instead. By his senior year he had an unusual combination of size and speed, so fast that he was nicknamed "Mercury" Matson.

"When I was a youngster, I didn't have the money, and my family didn't have the money to buy a football," said Matson. "We had to take a can and wrap it up and we played with it. So in playing with this can, I used to tell my mother, 'I'm going to be a football player.'"

"My mother had different aspirations. She said, 'No son, you are going to be a doctor.' I said, 'No, I can't be. I want to be a football player.' So we went on and I proved to her that I was a football player. But, I think the most significant thing in my life is that there were many people that I have met that had the faith and courage that I could do a lot of things."

In 1947, Matson broke the Washington High School record for touchdowns. The following spring he shattered a high school record in the quarter-mile and qualified for the final U.S. Olympic trial heats in the 400-meter sprint, and barely missed making the team. After graduation from Washington High in 1948, Matson attended classes at City College of San Francisco, where he was one of the "City College Seven," a group of African-American student-athletes that formed a close bond on and off the field. According to Jourdan, "Most of us were born in the South or our parents came from the South." Coming to California was "about becoming something." In an era when most Americans didn't attend college, the "CC7" all earned degrees and enjoyed successful professional careers, including Rotea Gilford, who later became the deputy mayor of San Francisco, and Burl Toler, the first African-American referee in NFL history.

The 1948 City College football team posted a perfect 12-0 season, allowing less than five points per game. Matson set a new national junior college touchdown record on the way to attaining Junior College All-American status. He also played basketball at CCSF. Though he was recruited by several major universities with enticing offers in 1949, Ollie chose to study history and play football at the University of San Francisco, largely because Gertrude felt confident that he would get a quality education at the private Jesuit institution. Matson played football for USF under head coach Joe Kuharich, who later coached Matson in four of his NFL seasons.

"Ever since Matson enrolled at the University of San Francisco in 1949, newswriters have searched for adjectives to describe this man," said Kuharich. "The fleet-footed Ollie Matson, winged-footed Ollie Matson, mercurial Ollie Matson, Matson the magnificent. I know that Matson has thrilled many with his long runs and his great exploits on the gridiron."

While at USF, Matson became a member of Kappa Alpha Psi fraternity and was a three-year football starter. The Dons also had a 25-year-old public relations director named Pete Rozelle, who would later become a Hall of Fame commissioner of the NFL. At USF, Matson continued to show signs of explosiveness on the football field. Teammate Bob St. Clair said "If you were behind in a game you always had a chance. He was always a threat…if he broke through the middle or around the end he was gone." But as one of the team's two African-American players (Toler was the other), he faced obstacles his white teammates did not.

For a 1950 road game in Tulsa, Oklahoma, USF was asked to leave their two African-American players behind. The team took the higher ground and ignored the request, but Matson and Toler couldn't dine at the same restaurants or stay at the same hotel as their white teammates and some Tulsa fans were openly hostile. Wide receiver Ralph Thomas said that weekend's game was an "ugly display of people…that's all you heard all night long…the only thing that separated us was a chain link fence."

"I got hit with everything: fists, elbows, knees," Matson told *The Saturday Evening Post* in 1966. "Finished that game with two black eyes, a bloody nose and my face puffed up like a pound cake. I scored three touchdowns, and they were all called back."

Matson's star continued to rise at USF. In his junior year he was the number one rusher in the nation until slowed by leg and knee injuries. But he came back stronger than ever the following season, as did the Dons. As a senior in 1951, Ollie led the nation in rushing yards with 1,566 and touchdowns with 21. Matson's yardage total almost broke the NCAA major-college record (he was short by four yards) and was the second-most yards ever gained until USC's O.J. Simpson rushed for 1,709 yards in 1968. Somehow, with all these sparkling offensive achievements, he finished ninth in the Heisman Trophy voting and was recognized only as a defensive back on All-American teams. Dick Kazmaier of Princeton walked away with the Heisman that season.

"They weren't ready for me," Matson said in 2001 of the lack of Heisman respect. "But I'm not angry. Those were the days when we were growing up, so you have to take the bitter with the sweet. My days at USF were just beautiful."

Kuharich told a *Sporting News* reporter in a 1951 interview, "No one can match his speed. Yet his power is as sharp as any plunging fullback. He is not Mr. Outside or Mr. Inside. He is Mr. All Outside and Mr. Inside. He is Mr. All Sides and Mr. Everywhere. To this add his blocking, his pass protection and terrific defensive work and you have something that's never been duplicated in a generation."

With the future of the USF football program flickering due to heavy debt, the Dons powered their way through an undefeated season in which their average victory was 31-8. Though rarely mentioned among the elite college football powers, USF went undefeated and untied in 1951 with an extremely talented team that included nine future NFL players, three of whom are enshrined in the Pro Football Hall of Fame – Matson, Gino Marchetti, and St. Clair, an offensive tackle who later played for the San Francisco 49ers. No other college team has placed three of its members in the Hall of Fame. A 10th member of that team – linebacker Toler – would have made it to the NFL, but was injured so seriously in the 1952 All-Star game that he never played for the Cleveland Browns, the NFL team that drafted him. Instead, Toler became the first black NFL official.

"I thought he was a real gentleman, a great guy, fairly quiet," said Marchetti of Matson. "He wasn't the kind of guy to smoke, have a few drinks with the guys. He was a good person, loved his mother."

Despite its perfect 9-0 record, the 1951 USF team was not invited to a bowl game. It was later reported that the Southern bowl institutions — Orange in Miami, Sugar in New Orleans and Cotton in Dallas — with all of their repulsive bigotry, let it be known that they would only invite an all-white team to play in their grossly prejudiced affairs. Orange Bowl officials hinted to USF that the Dons would be "oh so welcome" to the Miami celebration if they attended without Ollie Matson and Burl Toler. A bowl game could have given USF enough money to keep its football program afloat. Informed of this "invitation," every single Caucasian member of the San Francisco team yelled out a resounding "no" to the Orange Bowl.

That Dons team was destined forever to carry the slogan "Unbeaten, Untied and Uninvited." One of the public justifications for the snubbing was a weak USF schedule, partly a result of major local teams such as Stanford and California avoiding them, but other forces were clearly present. The University of the Pacific, whom the Dons had destroyed 47-14 that season, were invited to the Sun Bowl.

Matson told *The New York Times* in 2001 that when Kuharich told the players that they might be invited to the Orange Bowl if Matson and Toler did not play, defensive star Marchetti said, "No, we ain't going to go without Burl and Ollie. We didn't talk about it, we didn't vote on it, you never heard another word. When we rejected it, it was 100% backed up by the club and the school."

The 1951 Dons, with their 9-0 record, are considered by some to have been one of the finest college football teams ever because it consisted of more excellent players than any intercollegiate squad in history. And yet USF never played major college football after that season, dropping a program in the red by more than $70,000. "We could have been the best team in the country that year," said Matson, who rushed for an NCAA-record 3,166 yards in three years as a starter for the Dons. "It was just unfortunate we ran across all those situations."

The Chicago Cardinals selected Matson as the third overall pick in the 1952 NFL draft but Ollie delayed signing in order to compete as an amateur track athlete in the '52 summer Olympic Games in Helsinki, Finland. At Helsinki, he captured a bronze medal in the 400-meter run with a time of 46.8 seconds and a silver medal as a member of the U.S. 400-meter relay team.

Ollie then returned to football, and over the next 14 years, he became one of the most versatile and productive all-purpose backs in NFL history, playing for the Cardinals, Los Angeles Rams, Detroit Lions and Philadelphia Eagles. He also returned kickoffs and punts, and played some defensive back early in his career. Not a month after the Olympic closing ceremonies, Matson reported to training camp for the Cardinals, and got off to a quick start.

At 6-feet-2 inches and 220 pounds, Ollie was exceptionally strong. But opponents feared his speed even more. "Speed and quickness, that's what you need to return kicks," he once said. "I was big, but I was swift for that size. I could either run around you, over you or through you. I didn't do a lot of hard cutting like Gale Sayers did. But we both had that peripheral vision to know where guys were going to be, and we had that speed to get there."

Later compared to 1990s running back Bo Jackson, Matson was an unusually big man for an offensive back of his era. With that huge, muscular body traveling at the speed of a sprinter, Ollie was extremely difficult to bring down. Add exceptionally good peripheral vision, and Matson could cut and swerve to avoid tacklers coming at him from all angles. He ran with a smooth, gliding style that made it appear he wasn't going at full speed. Sometimes the defenders were fooled too, and before they could gather themselves to make the tackle, he would explode past them. Matson could run a power play to the inside, a slant off-tackle, or a sweep or pitchout to the outside. He also took great pride in carrying out his play-action fakes with full effort, as if he were getting the ball.

When Matson first signed to play with the Cardinals in 1952, he was hailed as the fleet-footed ball carrier that would hopefully lead Chicago out of the NFL's basement. He was one of only three African-American Cardinals. In his first season of professional football, he made All-Pro as a defensive back and shared Rookie of the Year honors with Hugh McElhenny of the San Francisco 49ers. Ollie was also used on offense and compiled 531 total yards from scrimmage for Chicago and ran back 20 kickoffs for 624 yards, a 31.2 average, and two touchdowns.

"In 1952, he entered the National Football League as the number one draft choice," said Kuharich. "For 14 years he faced the most difficult competition in the country. And, believe me, I think that Matson has the respect of each and every teammate and each and every competitor that has ever faced him in competition. I can't help but tell you that this is an All-American, an All-Pro and the type of man that brings glory to each and everyone that has ever been associated with him."

Just as Matson's football career got started, he was drafted into the Army. He missed the 1953 season while he served as an infantryman at Ford Ord in Monterey, California, but was able to return the following fall. Once back in a football uniform in 1954, he was an All-NFL performer, year in and year out. That same year he earned a teaching credential and married his high school sweetheart, Mary Paige.

Matson led the league in all-purpose yards in 1954 and 1956, in punt return yards and return average in 1955, and in yards per kickoff return in 1958. He was voted first-team All-Pro in each of his first five NFL seasons. Despite making Kuharich their head coach and having Matson get as many touches as possible, the fortunes of the erratic Cardinals didn't change. In his six years in Chicago, the Cardinals compiled a 22-48-2 record and had only one winning season, 7-5 in 1956. Matson's season highlights included a 105-yard kickoff return against the Washington Redskins and the Most Valuable Player award in the 1956 Pro Bowl after scoring two touchdowns.

The great open field runners, like McElhenny, Sayers and Barry Sanders, occupy a special place in NFL history. Any time they touched the ball, there was a feeling that something special was about to happen. Matson also understood it. As he told *Sports Illustrated* for a cover story in 1957, "I'm disappointed if I don't make a long run in a game because I know people come and pay their good money to see me make long runs, and I like to please them." In 1958, Ollie led the NFL in kickoff returns, running back 14 kickoffs for 497 yards (a 35.5 average), and two touchdowns.

On February 27, 1959, in one of the biggest trades in NFL history, Matson was dealt to the Los Angeles Rams for eight players and a future draft pick. The Rams and their young general manager Rozelle were so intent on acquiring Ollie that they gave the Cardinals seven members of their 1958 roster, their second draft choice that spring of 1959, plus a player to be delivered during the 1959 pre-season. Yet many observers felt this was really a fairly balanced swap of talent since the multi-talented Matson was worth much more than average pro football players. Rozelle, who was 32 years old when he fashioned the big trade, sent a telegram to NFL Commissioner Bert Bell the next day notifying him of the deal. Eleven months later, in January of 1960, Rozelle succeeded Bell as NFL commissioner at about the time that the Cardinals moved from Chicago to St. Louis.

No welcoming committee greeted the Matsons when they arrived in Los Angeles. Ollie and his wife were shown houses at night to conceal their race from white neighbors and the cold reception followed him to the Rams, where his skills were misdirected or underutilized by three coaches in four losing seasons. As Mary Matson told an *L.A. Times* reporter in 2002, "One black for nine whites? In those days?....Lots of people in Los Angeles never got over that."

In the same interview, Mary said "If we worried about everything that happened to us, we would be dead," and true to form, the Matsons soldiered on and created opportunities with the move. The Los Angeles duplex would become their base for life and the first of many real estate investments. Bruce Matson said, "(Ollie) believed in investing his money, but he wasn't a spendthrift. When he got paid he took a meager amount for himself and sent the rest back home…he would buy property off-season because his salary alone wasn't enough to cover everything."

Ollie and Mary lived in the same mid-city Los Angeles home from the time he played for the Rams until his passing. The site, known as the "Ollie and Mary Matson Residence," was nominated as a City of Los Angeles Historic-Cultural Monument. The home was transformed into an historic museum and interpretive center by students of Los Angeles Trade Technical College in 2008.

Matson was tabbed as the star that could deliver the Rams a long-awaited championship. Through no fault of his own, Ollie did neither. Yet little of the luster was lost from one of the most brilliant pro football careers ever. He spent four years with the Rams, all losing seasons. Despite the losses, Matson strived to be the best player possible. He frequently put in extra time after practice running pass routes with the backup quarterbacks. Most running backs can catch a screen pass, or a check-down in the flat. Few, like Matson, were also significant downfield receiving threats out of the backfield. With his tremendous speed, the linebackers and safeties usually couldn't stay with him.

Matson was an important figure in American sports integration in the 1950s, and his trailblazing ways ran in the family. His nephew, national sports writer Art Thompson III, said that Ollie's mother was responsible for integrating another American institution, with help from her famous son. For years, Gertrude Matson had watched the Rose Bowl Parade disappointed at the absence of African-American representation. So in 1963, she held a series of group meetings to enter an African-American sponsored float into the next year's procession. Brad Pye, who was involved in the planning, said the parade committee "really didn't want us in."

"In 1964, my grandmother was the first African-American to have a float in the Rose Parade," said Thompson. "She was watching the parade and wondered why there weren't any black people in it. She said, 'I'm going to get a float in the Rose Parade.' She solicited my uncle. He funded the whole thing. It won a prize, too."

When the entry deadline was missed, the committee rejected an extension until Matson stepped up and guaranteed the $25,000 needed to advance the project. As a result, "Freedom Bursts Forth" ran in the Rose Bowl Parade on January 1, 1964, just as Lyndon Johnson began pushing the watershed Civil Rights Act through Congress. The float money reflected a generosity which took many forms. Though he was typically introverted, Matson and his wife were active hosts and Ollie's barbecue skills received especially high praise. Youngest son Bruce Matson said "Every day we had people over. We fed more people than you could shake a stick at...they never said no to people."

In 1961, Matson was named to the NFL's all-decade team for the 1950s. After his stint with the Rams, Matson spent the 1963 season in Detroit before again reuniting with Kuharich in Philadelphia in 1964 for his final three seasons. With Kuharich's help, Matson rebounded in 1964 and was the runner-up for the NFL's Comeback Player of the Year award.

Late in the 1966 season, Matson made his final appearance as a player back in the Bay Area. On a rainy day and a muddy field at San Francisco's Kezar Stadium, the Eagles rallied to defeat the 49ers, 35-34. Due to the inclement weather, Ollie was slated to play only on the kickoff-return team. But an injury to starting running back Timmy Brown on the opening kickoff thrust Matson into fulltime duty and he scored the winning touchdown with a leaping catch of a pass thrown by Philadelphia's King Hill.

In August of 1967, Matson announced his retirement from the NFL. He played 14 seasons but only twice was he on a winning team. He scored 74 touchdowns: 40 rushing, 23 receiving, six by kickoff return, three by punt return, and one by fumble recovery. Over his brilliant career, Matson rushed for 5,173 yards and caught 222 passes for another 3,285 yards. Altogether, he gained 12,884 yards on rushing, receptions, and returns, second only to the legendary Jim Brown at the time of his retirement. Matson also set a record with nine touchdowns on kickoff returns that stood until 2009.

The greatness Matson achieved in National Football League stadiums must be considered an individual accomplishment. He seemed to consistently play on teams with average to below-average talent around him. Enemy defenses almost always concentrated on Ollie alone. Yet his career statistics remain exceptional. Matson was frustrated by the fact that he never played on a team that even reached the playoffs. "I had all the records," he said. "But gee whiz, that didn't mean anything to me. I wanted to be on a team where I could go to the championship. But my whole life, it seemed every team I'd get on that looked like it had a chance, it would go the other way."

At 36, Matson stepped out from under the spotlight of pro football intent on spending more time with family. His daughter Lisa said, "People wanted him to become an actor after he retired but acting wasn't his thing. He said 'I lived out of a suitcase all those years…I don't want the limelight now.'"

Ollie III, a high school teacher and coach who lives in Baltimore, said his father wanted to be an NFL coach, but this wish came "about ten years too soon," as African-Americans weren't offered management positions at that time. But Matson didn't stew over the injustice. "He lived life his way, on his terms, so he just accepted it….My dad was a trailblazer. And that's the way it was for a lot of people during his time. They made things better for all of us and people coming afterward." Ollie III, Matson's oldest son, was a stellar athlete in his own right and grew to be 6-foot-6. He chose basketball over football despite being recruited by Notre Dame, Oklahoma, and other college football powers.

Matson was elected to the Pro Football Hall of Fame in 1972, his first year of eligibility, and was enshrined July 29, 1972. He entered the Hall in the same class as his college teammate Marchetti, Lamar Hunt, and Clarence "Ace" Parker. He was presented in Canton, Ohio by Kuharich, his longtime coach with USF, the Cardinals, and the Eagles.

"As I look through the stadium here today I see quite a number of young people and I would like to say to you, don't quit," said Matson in his enshrinement speech. "Don't always go and ask for something without working for it. Because this life is not that way, you only get out of life what you put into it. And I put a lot in it, and now, I'm receiving a lot."

"Figures do not show his true value," Ray Richards, the Cardinals' coach from 1955 to 1957, once said of Matson, who was named to the Pro Bowl six times and was All-Pro seven times. "When he is in the lineup, somehow the whole team is inspired."

Today, the legacy Ollie left behind continues to capture the hearts of fans of all ages. His spectacular runs, preserved on old black and white film, are some of the NFL's signature moments of that era. When Matson gained entry into the Hall of Fame, his children didn't know how accomplished their father was because he rarely mentioned his football career. Daughter Barbara (King), now an office manager living in Oklahoma, said "He wasn't the type of person who talks about himself or what he's done….A lot of things about him I found out later in life, reading books and magazines."

"As I have said many times in the age of the specialists, Matson was the complete football player," said Kuarich as he introduced Ollie in Canton. "I have admired this young man. I have applauded each and every exploit that he has had on the gridiron, but I must go beyond that. This is a true American example of the type of young man that should compete in football that should represent his country in any and every endeavor. I salute Ollie Matson for all of these reasons and I know that his teammates those at the University of San Francisco from '49 through '51, and those that were his teammates in Chicago, Los Angeles, Detroit, and Philadelphia stand today in reverence of a great professional football performer, and a true All-American man."

In retirement, Matson's involvement in sports continued. After scouting for the Philadelphia Eagles for a year, he became a Physical Education teacher and football coach at Los Angeles High School in 1968. Ollie followed in the footsteps of his mother, who had seeded an appreciation for education that was passed on to his children, all of whom have college diplomas. Bruce, now a dentist living in Houston, said, "My parents strongly believed in education. They sacrificed and sent us to private schools. Football or basketball alone won't bring you to the Promised Land."

After a few years at L.A. High, Matson was hired as assistant football coach at San Diego State, which made him the first African-American to hold a coaching position at that university. Matson's hiring gave the SDSU backfield the unique opportunity of being mentored by a Hall of Fame running back. On a part-time basis, Ollie still scouted for the Eagles. Matson stayed with San Diego State for the 1974 and 1975 seasons and was inducted into the College Football Hall of Fame in 1976. With this designation, he became the only athlete ever to win Olympic medals and enter into both the pro and college football halls of fame.

In 1977, Matson took a job as a special-events supervisor at the Los Angeles Coliseum. In this capacity he led tours and oversaw parking, ticketing, and guest attendance during numerous grand scale events, including LA Raiders and UCLA Bruins games, and the 1984 Summer Olympics. Ollie retired in February, 1989. He also had a lifelong commitment to the well-being of America's youth. He taught inner-city kids how to run, throw, and maintain focus through Operation Champ, a Great Society program that provided a positive outlet for at-risk youth. When Ollie III's Little League couldn't afford umpires, Matson supplied the necessary funds. Ollie refused to do beer commercials because he felt that alcohol endorsements sent the wrong message to children, and he made numerous appearances at Boys and

Girls Clubs in Fresno. Earl Watson, who hosted the clubs, said, "A lot of athletes wouldn't go there unless the press was there," but "every time I asked him he went out of his way to help me....It meant so much to the kids. He was very sincere about dealing with kids."

King described her father's life after retirement as industrious - and structured. Matson kept himself busy gardening, tending to his rental units, and doing charity events, and his schedule ran like clockwork. He woke up every weekday at 4:30 a.m. to run a few miles at the L.A. High track near his house. Saturday was golf. Sunday was barbecuing. By 11 Sunday morning the chicken or ribs were hot and ready in the kitchen. Bedtime was early. "When the sun went down he'd disappear...he wouldn't say good night. Everyone that knew him knew what was going on."

Thompson said in 2010 that Matson had been bedridden for several years due to a form of dementia. He said Ollie hadn't spoken in four years. His affliction was a type of dementia that doctors attributed to the head injuries that he suffered during his football career. A 2009 study commissioned by the NFL reported that Alzheimer's disease or similar memory-related diseases appear to have been diagnosed in former NFL players at a significantly higher rate than for other men. The studies reported that it was 19 times the normal rate for men ages 30-49. Matson suffered from Chronic Traumatic Encephalopathy (CTE) in his later years, which is a result of numerous hard hits to the head he sustained during his football days.

Decades of unconditional love were repaid to Ollie in the last several years of his life, as he battled dementia. For a time, he was cared for by his wife Mary, even as her own health declined. She passed away in February 2007, after 52 years of marriage. Thereafter, Matson had personal caregivers and the daily attention of his daughter Lisa, a nurse who lived with him. In addition, he received rotating visits from his other three children, who flew in from around the country.

At age 80, Matson died in the Los Angeles home he had purchased in 1959 on February 19, 2011 of respiratory failure, surrounded by family. He was survived by two daughters, Lisa Lewis and Barbara King; two sons, Ollie III and Bruce; a twin sister, Ocie Thompson; eight grandchildren; and two great-grandchildren.

"He was the best at everything," said Thompson. "He was the best at barbecue. We'd have pingpong tournaments growing up, he'd pop in and kill everybody. He was the man. He had a full and productive life. He always had a smile and a handshake. He was a warm and very friendly person. I've never seen him get angry. Never, ever. Whether it was barbecuing, listening to his collection of Dinah Washington and Sam Cooke albums, winning games of skill, giving sage advice to the younger generation or just maintaining a calm steady hand ... we all felt his positive influence. If you were around him, you'd never know he was one of the greatest athletes to come out of the city. He didn't carry himself that way."

College football hero, Olympic medalist, NFL star and Pro Football Hall of Famer. He was Ollie Matson, who in his heyday was touted as the "Fastest Man in Cleats," a seven-time All-Pro who was equally deadly to a defense as a runner or a receiver. In his prime he was one of the most dangerous men in the league when poised to return a punt or a kickoff, and in his rookie year, was the Chicago Cardinals' best running back and best defensive back in the same season.

Kuharich, who coached Matson in college and in the pros, called him "the best all-around football player I've seen or coached." Dick Evans, an Eagles defensive coach, called him, quite simply, "the greatest athlete I've ever seen."

Bay Area Legends

34

MAX BAER

Possessing perhaps the most powerful right hand in boxing history, Max Baer was crowned world heavyweight champion in 1934. The "Livermore Larupper" was a character unlike any other fighter of his time. Baer's lethal punching power combined with a clown-like personality and 72-12 record made him perhaps the most popular boxer between Jack Dempsey and the rise of Joe Louis. Baer was also a source of pride for Jewish people at a time when Nazis began persecution of European Jews.

Maximillion Adelbert Baer, better known as Max Baer, was born on February 11, 1909 in Omaha, Nebraska. His parents were Jacob Baer, who was Jewish, and Dora Bales, who was of Scots-Irish ancestry. Max's eldest sister was Frances, his younger sister Bernice, his younger brother was boxer-turned-actor Buddy Baer, and his adopted brother was August Baer.

The Baer family moved to Durango, Colorado before Bernice and Buddy were born, only to find the winters unbearable. In May 1922, the family purchased a new car, piled in and began the long drive to the milder climates of California, where Dora's sister lived in Alameda. They drove more than a thousand miles along unpaved roads. Jacob's expertise in the butcher business led to numerous job offers around the San Francisco Bay Area. While living in Hayward, Max took his first job as a delivery boy for John Lee Wilbur. Wilbur ran a grocery store on B Street and bought meat from Jacob.

The Baers lived temporarily in Hayward, San Leandro and Galt before settling in Livermore in 1926. Livermore was an authentic cowboy and rodeo town, surrounded by miles of acres of rolling hills and rangeland. It was an ideal region for sustaining cattle herds that provided fresh meat to the rapidly growing Livermore and Pleasanton area.

In 1928, Jacob bought the Twin Oaks Ranch in Murray Township where he worked with Frances's husband to raise over 2,000 hogs. Max dropped out of school in the eighth grade to help his father on their ranch full-time. Baer often credited his working as a butcher boy, carrying heavy carcasses of meat, sledge-hammering cattle with one blow, and working at a gravel pit for developing his well-muscled frame, broad shoulders, and feared right-hand punch.

By the age of 18, Baer was already six feet tall and weighed 190 pounds. Encouraged by friends to learn boxing, he set up a makeshift gym on his father's ranch and built up his punching power. Max eventually moved to Oakland in pursuit of finding a manager, taking a job at a local factory to support himself. The factory owner's son, J. Hamilton Lorimer, became his first manager. With Lorimer backing him, Max fought in his first professional boxing match in Stockton on May 16, 1929, knocking out Chief Caribou in two rounds.

Now 6-foot-2, Baer won 22 of his first 24 fights as a professional, nine with first-round knockouts. His conditioning, combined with his tremendous power, made him a formidable foe. He fought 16 more times in 1929, losing only when was disqualified for tossing an opponent to the mat. Max was again disqualified in his first match of 1930, this time for "stalling." He rebounded by wining his next seven fights – six by knockout – and secured a fight with Les Kennedy, one of the best boxers in California. Still raw and unpolished at 20, Max was unable to counter Kennedy's professional, experienced style and lost a ten-round decision.

Despite the Kennedy loss, Baer's aggressive style and knockout punch continued to make him a big draw on the West Coast. In his next major fight, Max was matched against Frankie Campbell, brother of baseball player Dolph Camilli. Campbell had recently defeated Kennedy. But Baer was now in supreme condition and becoming smarter in the ring. Max fought Campbell in San Francisco on August 25, 1930, and with only two blows, knocked him out. Campbell was unconscious on the canvas and doctors failed to revive him after hours of trying. After nearly an hour,

Campbell was transported by ambulance to a nearby hospital, where he died of massive brain hemorrhaging. An autopsy revealed that Baer's devastating blows had knocked Campbell's entire brain loose from the connective tissue holding it in place within his cranium.

Baer was charged with manslaughter when Campbell died. Ultimately acquitted of criminal charges, Baer was suspended from fighting in California for a year. The death of the promising Campbell created an outrage among anti-boxing forces, prompting the California Commission to also suspend the referee and several others involved. Max was so badly shaken and frightened by the tragedy that he quit boxing altogether for another four months, his longest period of inactivity. Baer gave purses from succeeding bouts to Campbell's family and helped put his children through college, but lost four of his next six fights, partly because of his reluctance to go on the attack. In his next match, he lost a ten round decision to Ernie Schaaf. The Campbell incident earned Max the reputation as a "killer" in the ring and was even used for promotional purposes to make the young Californian seem dangerous.

Max was matched against New Zealand fighter Tom Heeney, his first internationally known opponent, who had once battled Gene Tunney for the heavyweight title. Heeney was well beyond his prime, however, and Baer had an easy time annihilating him inside of three rounds. This led to a fight with Tommy Loughran, the lightning-quick future Hall of Famer and former light heavyweight champion of the world.

Baer faced Loughran on February 6, 1931 and the fight proved to be one of the most important bouts of Max's career. Though Loughran's talent and experience dominated Baer in a 10-round unanimous decision, he took the time to give Max some coaching points after the fight. Tommy told Max that he would go a long way if he would learn to quit looping his punches and straighten them out to provide a quicker route to the target. He also advised Baer that he was telegraphing his punches.

Meanwhile, former world heavyweight champion Jack Dempsey, who refereed the bout between Loughran and Baer, took notice of Baer. Dempsey and Max became great friends and remained so for the rest of their lives. Dempsey often acted as a mentor to Max and even promoted several of his fights. Baer fared better after Dempsey took him on as a protégé. Dempsey taught Max how to shorten his punches for greater efficiency and how to upgrade his defense.

Though Baer lost to contenders Johnny Risko and Paolino Uzcudun, he showed more patience and better technique, showing that he heeded the advice of Loughran and Dempsey. The hard work paid dividends as Max won 10 consecutive fights within a 10-month period. Included among the wins were rematches with Risko, Kennedy, and Heeney, as well as two decisions over contender King Levinsky.

By the summer of 1932, Max was finally a legitimate contender for the heavyweight championship of the world. On August 31, 1932, he fought a rematch with Schaaf. Though he fell slightly behind on points in the early going, Baer paced himself for a long fight and started slugging in the ninth round. In the final seconds of the 10th round, Baer hit Schaaf in the temple with what some witnesses claimed to be the hardest right hand that ever connected in boxing. Schaaf was saved by the bell. Several minutes passed before Schaaf was revived enough to stand under his own power.

Because the bell rang before the referee could complete his count, Baer was not credited with an official knockout, but Max did win the 10-round decision. Schaaf was never quite the same after that bout, complaining of headaches and his comeback began slow and weak. Six months after the Baer fight, Schaaf died in the ring after taking a left jab from massive Italian Primo Carnera. Although Carnera was now vilified as a "man killer," others claimed that Schaaf died as a result of damage previously inflicted by Max. The death of Campbell and accusations over Schaaf's demise profoundly affected Baer, even though he remained a devastating force in the ring. While outwardly maintaining his clowning and even profiting from his "killer" image in public, Baer was internally shaken by these deaths.

In 1933, Baer knocked out veteran contender Tuffy Griffiths in seven rounds, and was matched with former world champion Max Schmeling on June 8. A skilled boxer with a solid right-hand punch, Schmeling was considered the top contender for Jack Sharkey's heavyweight crown. The German Schmeling became a controversial boxing figure due to his association with Nazi leader Adolf Hitler. In the best fight of his career, Baer defeated Schmeling in front of 60,000 spectators at Yankee Stadium.

At the fight's opening, he charged out aggressively and took immediate control of the fight. Lucky to survive the early rounds, Schmeling used his superior technique to gain a slight scorecard lead by the middle rounds. In the ninth, Baer seemed full of energy and went on the attack. The 10th featured more of the same until Baer connected with a right-hand smash that sent Schmeling flying into the ropes. Another right cross moments later dropped the German. Barely able to rise at the count of nine, Schmeling was essentially beaten except to attempt to block Baer's storm of bombs. Baer again sent the German tumbling against the ropes and a hard rabbit punch from Max cracked the disoriented Schmeling on the back of the head, causing referee Arthur Donovan to stop the fight.

With Hitler listening on radio in Berlin, Baer wore the Star of David on his trunks which Max swore to wear in every future match, a demonstration of pride for the Jewish people at a time when Nazi persecution of German Jews was just beginning. Schmeling was Hitler's favorite German boxer, and Max immediately became the champion of Jews and those who despised the Nazis' racial policies. When Baer KO'd Schmeling in the 10th round he growled at him "That's for Hitler!"

Baer's film debut was *The Prizefighter and the Lady* in 1933 opposite Myrna Loy and Walter Huston. In this MGM movie, he played Steve Morgan, a bartender that the Professor (Huston) aspires to be a boxer. Steve wins a fight, then marries Belle Mercer, played by Loy. He starts training seriously, but it turns out he has a huge ego and an eye for women. Featured were Baer's upcoming opponent Carnera and Dempsey as himself, acting as the referee. The film ends with a fictional bout between Baer and Carnera, the matchup fight fans were desperately calling for in real life.

On March 29, 1934, *The Prizefighter and the Lady* was officially banned from German theaters by Joseph Goebbels, Adolf Hitler's Minister of Propaganda and Public Entertainment, even though it received favorable reviews in Nazi publications. Baer told reporters in Lake Tahoe that "They didn't ban the picture because I have Jewish blood. They banned it because I knocked out Max Schmeling."

The boxing world agreed that Max Baer was now a top heavyweight contender. Shortly after the Schmeling fight, world champion Sharkey lost his title by knockout to Carnera. Carnera's behemoth size made him a freak show draw, but Baer was the most famous active heavyweight in the world at the time. The long-anticipated fight finally took place on June 14, 1934, at Madison Square Garden Bowl in Long Island City, New York. At the pre-fight weigh-in, Max's zany behavior perplexed Carnera but certainly satisfied the press. He plucked hairs from Carncra's chest, reciting, "He loves me; he loves me not." He also reached out and tickled Carnera, shouting, "Boo, you big palooka!" Baer would be at a rare size disadvantage, giving up more than 50 pounds in weight and at least three inches in height to the Italian brute, making Carnera the betting favorite.

Before a crowd of 50,000, Baer knocked the giant Carnera down 11 times in 11 rounds, and claimed the world heavyweight championship title. Max came out of his corner cautiously, keeping his distance as Primo tried to chase. When Baer's wild right hand caught the champion flush, the momentum seemed to turn instantly. Carnera crashed to the canvas and appeared weak and groggy when he rose. Sensing a first-round knockout opportunity, Baer went on the offensive, putting together a series of vicious punches that knocked Primo down twice more. Carnera survived the round, but wandered into the wrong corner. Exhausted by his futile efforts to knock out the giant, Baer tried desperately to finish Carnera off in the second, but the pair ended up clenching and wrestling for the next several rounds.

Having steadied himself, Carnera eventually began to use his size and reach. Primo was never known as a technical boxer but, against the exhausted Baer, he had enough skills to gain a scorecard lead after nine rounds. Toward the end of the 10th, a roundhouse right from Max turned the tide once again, sending Primo sprawling across the ring. The battered Carnera made it to his feet just in time to hear the bell. He came out for the 11th, but went down twice more before the referee stopped the fight. Including the wrestling falls in the middle of the fight, Primo hit the deck 11 times in 11 rounds. Max Baer was the new NYSAC and NBA World Heavyweight Champion.

At the height of his popularity, Baer starred in movies and lived a high society life. He was romantically linked to many movie stars, chorus girls, and Broadway actresses before marrying in 1935. Nicknamed "Madcap Maxie," and the "Livermore Larupper," Baer held the title of World Heavyweight Champion from 1934 into 1935. Max was a popular champion, charismatic and exciting and his clowning antics in and out of the ring were a nice diversion for a public suffering the tumultuous struggles of the Great Depression. But Max's increasingly carefree lifestyle caused the champ to neglect serious training after winning the title. Baer instead lounged about in his riches, fame, and many female companions. While he gave popular boxing clinics and exhibitions, he stayed away from the professional ranks for almost a year. In the meantime, an unlikely contender by the name of James J. Braddock established himself as a credible challenger for Max's crown.

A poverty-stricken part-time boxer who worked at the New Jersey ports to support his family, Braddock was thought to be washed up. But when he won three consecutive fights against quality names in the division, the press nicknamed him the "Cinderella Man" because of his rags-to-riches situation. Schmeling's ties to the Nazis prohibited a rematch with Baer. Scouted as nothing more than a journeyman,

Braddock was hand-picked by Baer's camp because he was seen as an easy payday for Max.

On June 13, 1935 at Madison Square Garden Bowl, Baer fought Braddock. Braddock, 30, took a few heavy hits from the powerful 26-year-old champion. But Braddock kept coming, wearing down Baer who seemed perplexed by Braddock's ability to take a punch. Overconfident and under-trained, Baer found himself having an unexpected tough time against his smaller opponent. Braddock, meanwhile, fought the fight of his life. The challenger used constant movement and a stiff left jab to keep Max unsettled. Baer tried to throw his haymaker right hand, but Braddock knew to look out for it and the champion usually missed by a mile.

Unable to compete with Braddock's conditioning and technical precision, Baer could do little else but gasp for breath and make faces at his opponent. The champion fouled on occasion and, when warned by the referee, made theatrical gestures of apology to the crowd and Braddock. After a grueling back-and-forth battle, Braddock won as a 10-to-1 underdog with a unanimous decision, in one of the great upsets in ring history. The fight has since become a boxing legend. Baer had given away the World Heavyweight title to Braddock in his first defense. He fought with an injured right hand, and his lackadaisical training, and joking effort cost him the fifteen-round decision. He had been champion for one year. Max demanded a rematch, which he was never granted.

Baer's career, however, was far from over. For the next six years, he compiled a record of 30-4. In interviews after the Braddock loss, Max admitted that he had failed to train correctly for the fight and that he knew he needed to refocus on boxing. He promised fans to be better prepared for his next match on September 24, 1935 versus an undefeated sensation from Detroit by the name of Joe Louis. At this early point in his career, Louis had beaten some tough opponents – including Carnera – but had yet to get in the ring with a fighter as dangerous as Baer. At Yankee Stadium, 88,150 fans paid $1,000,832 to see the two power punchers – the most profitable U.S. fight in nearly 10 years.

Though both fighters landed hard hits as expected, Louis scored with punches that were quicker, compact, and more accurate. Baer again appeared out of shape, breaking his promise to train diligently. His punches were loopy and ineffective and at no point did the "Brown Bomber" seem intimidated by Baer's fabled power. Both men traded punches for three rounds, with Louis clearly getting the best of Max. In the fourth round, looking exhausted after taking a storm of punishment from Louis, Baer dropped voluntarily to his knees. It was the first time Max had gone down in 48 professional fights. He rose to fight on, but was quickly flattened to the canvas by a Louis combination. Though Max made it to one knee, he could not rise in time and suffered his first knockout loss. During the fight, Baer returned to his corner and said he could not breath. Dempsey said "I conned him into the ring…I told him I'd kill him with the water bottle if he didn't go back out there and get knocked out." Baer subsequently announced his retirement from boxing.

As with many boxers, Baer's initial retirement did not last long. He returned to fighting in 1936 despite weighing in at an all-time high of 226 pounds. Baer dominated a six-round decision against Tony Souza. The Souza fight was the first of 18 matches Baer fought inside of three months, as Max toured America fighting locals from Salt Lake City, Boise, San Antonio, Tulsa, Vancouver, Twin Falls, and other cities.

On April 15, 1937, Baer faced England's heavyweight champion Tommy Farr – his first ranked opponent since Louis. Farr defeated Baer in 12 rounds, Max's first loss in 23 outings. Baer avenged the loss less than a year later, knocking down Farr two times on the way to a 15-round decision, and followed the victory with a first-round knockout of Ohio's Hank Hankinson.

On June 1, 1939, Baer fought Lou Nova in the first televised heavyweight prizefight. Having regained his status as one of the leading fighters in the division, Max fought up-and-comer Nova at Yankee Stadium before 16,778 fans. In an exciting battle, Max suffered severe facial swelling and cuts that forced the referee to stop the fight in the 11th round. Though many concluded that Baer was finally finished as a world class boxer, he scored four consecutive knockout wins within the following 12 months, including a seventh-round KO of hard-hitting contender Tony Galento. On April 4, 1941, Max briefly showed shades of his old fighting prowess, flooring Nova with a right hand in the fourth round of their rematch. In later rounds, however, Nova took control of the match. After Max went down twice in the eighth, the referee awarded the fight to Nova by TKO. Max never again fought professionally and instead retired to his Sacramento home.

Baer boxed in 84 professional fights from 1929 to 1941. His career record was 72-12-0 with 52 knockouts, which makes him a member of an exclusive group of boxers who have won 50 or more fights by knockout. He is rated No. 22 on *Ring Magazine's* list of 100 Greatest Punchers of all time. Max was inducted into the Boxing Hall of Fame in 1968, the World Boxing Hall of Fame in 1984, and the International Boxing Hall of Fame in 1995. A 1998 issue of *Ring Magazine* ranked Baer No. 20 of "The 50 Greatest Heavyweights of All Time." The International

Boxing Hall of Fame Official Record Book said that Max fought with perhaps "the most powerful right hand in heavyweight history."

Baer acted in nearly 20 movies, including *Africa Screams* with Bud Abbott and Lou Costello in 1949. A clown in and out of the ring, Max appeared in a popular vaudeville act and on his own TV variety show. He appeared in Humphrey Bogart's final movie, *The Harder They Fall* (1956), opposite Mike Lane as Toro Moreno, a fictionalized version of Primo Carnera. Baer additionally worked as a disc jockey for a Sacramento radio station, and also as a wrestler. Max performed a successful nightclub act both individually and with "Slapsie" Maxie Rosenbloom. He also served as a physical conditioning instructor for the Air Force, public relations director for a Sacramento automobile dealership, and referee for boxing matches.

Baer married twice, briefly to actress Dorothy Dunbar from 1931 to 1933, and then to Mary Ellen Sullivan on June 29, 1935 until his death. Max and Mary Ellen had three children: Max Jr. (born 1937), James (1941), and Maude (1943). Max was also romantically linked to Jean Harlow, Mae West and Greta Garbo.

On November 21, 1959, Baer was scheduled to appear in television commercials before returning to his home in Sacramento. After refereeing a boxing match in Phoenix, Baer traveled to Los Angeles and checked into the Roosevelt Hotel in Hollywood. While shaving, he suffered a heart attack and called the front desk requesting a doctor. The desk clerk said "a house doctor would be right up." "A house doctor?" he replied jokingly, "No, dummy, I need a people doctor."

Doctors gave Max medication and a fire rescue squad administered oxygen. Baer's chest pains subsided and he showed signs of recovery when the 50-year old fighter was stricken with a second attack. Just a moment before, he was joking with the doctor, saying he had experienced lighter attacks earlier in Sacramento. Then he slumped on his side and died within a matter of minutes. His last words were "Oh God, here I go."

Max Baer's funeral was one of the largest ever attended in Sacramento. Among his mourners were four former world champions, politicians, and Cub Scouts. There were women in mink stoles and diamonds, women in cotton house dresses, and in slacks. Hundreds of other mourners were unable to fit into the funeral home, but crowded around the outside. Some climbed car roofs and nearby scaffolding. Joe Louis and Jack Dempsey were among Max's pallbearers. The cemetery service was concluded by an American Legion firing squad, recognizing Baer's service in

World War II. He was laid to rest in a garden crypt in St. Mary's Catholic Cemetery in Sacramento.

Baer's obituary made the front page of the *New York Times*. He was an active member of the Fraternal Order of Eagles. Known for his kind heart and colorful personality, Max was loved by his fellow Eagles. When Max died, the Eagles created a charity fund as a tribute to him and to fight the disease that killed him. Max Baer Heart Fund's primary goals are to assist in heart research and education. Since the fund started in 1959, millions of dollars have been raised for universities, medical centers and hospitals across the United States and Canada.

The 2005 movie *Cinderella Man* portrayed Braddock as the hero who fights Baer in the ultimate challenge match. Critics took issue with director Ron Howard's portrayal of Baer as cruel and intimidating, when he is remembered as popular and amiable. Before the match, Baer is heard saying to Braddock's wife "You're too pretty to be a widow." According to Baer's family and historians this malice never took place. The final climatic scenes between Max and Braddock have people hating the bragging bully Baer while cheering on the beloved "average Joe" Braddock.

The film also portrays Baer as a womanizer and jokester, which was accurate, but those who knew him describe a happy and friendly man, always looking for the lighter side of a brutal sport. It was exactly this perspective and positive attitude that made him so likable for those suffering during the Depression era. His friends and family members are justifiably angered that the man they knew as warm, generous and gentlemanly should be portrayed so falsely. Since Max was unable to defend himself from his portrayal in *Cinderella Man*, the task of rehabilitating his father's reputation has fallen to Max Jr., also known as Jethro Bodine of the *Beverly Hillbillies*.

Today, Baer is remembered mostly for his defeat of Schmeling, the heavyweight champion of the Nazis, who were shocked to see a Jewish fighter beat their hero. He grew up and lived in Livermore and is remembered by the town that he loved. Throughout his career he insisted to be introduced as "Max Baer of Livermore, California" Today, there is a sports park named Max Baer Park in Livermore, which he always considered his hometown. There is also a park in Sacramento named after him. He was honored by induction into the Bay Area Sports Hall of Fame in 1988.

Max Baer came to international heavyweight prominence in an era when boxing was one of the nation's most popular sports. When the downtrodden American public desperately needed a good laugh, he provided the comedy. With each new antic in the ring and every story that surrounded him, his immeasurable charm, joyful personality, and sledgehammer right hand entertained fans. He did not intentionally injure or kill anyone. In reality, Max was one of America's most beloved boxing champions.

Bay Area Legends

34

DAVE STEWART

Nicknamed "Smoke" because of his blazing fastball, Dave Stewart's career is a lesson in perseverance. He rose from a troubled Oakland youth to a star athlete at St. Elizabeth High. He climbed from a six-year minor leaguer to a big leaguer. He soared from a struggling injured reliever to one of the most dominant starting pitchers in all of baseball. His intensity and no quit attitude became an inspiration to teammates, young players, and fans across the Bay Area.

Stewart was the backbone of the Oakland A's pitching staff during their three American League championships from 1988 to 1990. He became only the ninth pitcher in MLB history to win 20 or more games for four straight seasons and was part of three World Series championship teams. He won two games and earned World Series MVP honors in 1989 as he helped bring a championship to his hometown Oakland.

David Keith Stewart was born in Oakland on February 19, 1957 to parents Nathalie and David Stewart. Dave was the youngest of seven children, which included five sisters. When Dave was three, Nathalie and David moved the family into a house on Havenscourt Boulevard, between 66th and 67th Avenues. In 1962, a construction project began a few blocks from the Stewart home.

The city of Oakland, seeking an identity and reputation distinct and separate from that of San Francisco, built the Oakland-Alameda County Coliseum, a new stadium for the 1966 Raiders and eventually a major league baseball team. Two years later, the Kansas City Athletics moved into town and played their first game at the new park on April 17, 1968.

Nathalie worked at the cannery down the block; David, who passed away in 1972, was a longshoreman. "My father didn't want me to be a ballplayer," says Dave. "When I was nine, he told me, 'You can't make a living hitting a ball with a broomstick.' He was a hardworking man. There'd be three-day stretches when we didn't see him if a ship came in, because he wanted to make sure we were provided for. I have five sisters, so I was taught sports by my older brother, Gregory."

At Sunday school at the Havenscourt Community Church one day in 1961, four-year-old Dave met a boy named Wornel Simpson. "From that moment on, we were best of friends," says Simpson. "When we were in high school, we used to sit at home and dream about the future. I was prone to the books, he was the athlete, but we had a shared dream—to make a lot of money, then use it to help others from our community. Little did we know that someday he'd be a superstar pitcher and I'd be a financial planner, doing just what we always dreamed."

Stewart grew up in a tough neighborhood that was made even tougher, he regretfully acknowledges, by his own belligerence. "I was a menace as a kid," he recalls. "A fighter, a rebel without a cause. They couldn't contain me. My mom kept switching me to different, stricter schools, but I didn't get any better. For some reason, and I'm still not sure why, I just didn't like people in general. I loved my family—there were seven of us, five girls and two boys—but I couldn't get along with anyone else. I suppose a part of it was that I would look at other kids and see they had more than I had. I'd had to work after school regularly since I was 12. Even in high school, where I played football, basketball and baseball, I pumped gas after practice."

All around Stewart as he grew up were the sights, sounds and temptations of East Oakland, one of the city's poorest neighborhoods. Across the street from the Carr clubhouse was the former headquarters of the Black Panthers. Dave remembers the Panthers in their berets and leather jackets. "A bunch of them used to play basketball and shoot pool there," he says. "They were part of the neighborhood. One night the cops opened fire on my grandmother's house because they thought [Panther leader] Bobby Seale was hanging out there. My grandmother and aunt were in there, and if you'd seen all the bullet holes through the building, you'd realize it's a miracle they lived." A mile from his house was the clubhouse of the Hell's Angels, and The Symbionese Liberation Army was also quartered in the neighborhood.

"My circle of friends stayed with our own dreams because we had strong family backgrounds and because we were always playing sports, especially at the Boys Club," says Stewart. "My parents had strong values of right and wrong."

"I was tempted by the street life. I admit I experimented a little. But every time I got to the brink of getting in trouble, I pulled back. Sure, there was a lot of stuff happening on the street; the projects across 14th Street housed one of the biggest drug operations in the country. But it wasn't hard staying away from drugs or trouble. I had the Boys' Club and sports. There was a heck of a lot more good available to me than there was bad."

Stewart used to visit this branch of the Oakland Boys Club nearly every day until he signed his first professional contract. Stewart and future A's teammate Rickey Henderson once played American Legion ball together. "What you see in Stewart is a toughness typical of Oakland kids," says Hall of Famer Joe Morgan. "Not just street toughness, but competitive toughness. For every Joe Morgan or David Stewart, there are a dozen guys that were as good who didn't make it. You learn to persevere."

By his junior year at St. Elizabeth High, Dave became "just a different person. A P.E. teacher named Bob Howard would talk to me by the hour about trying harder, about doing something with myself. And then, during that time, I was influenced by Wornel. I'd known him since I was four, and he'd never done anything bad in his life. He was as good as I was bad."

A three-sport star athlete at St. Elizabeth, Stewart won high school All-America honors as a catcher, linebacker, and tight end. As a forward for the basketball team, he averaged 16 points per game. Upon graduation in 1975, Dave was offered 26 scholarships to play college football but turned them all down to sign with the Los Angeles Dodgers, who drafted him in the 16th round of the 1975 amateur draft. For several off-seasons he took classes at Merritt College and Cal State-Hayward, and says he will someday fulfill a promise to his mother and get a degree, "even if I'm an old guy on a campus full of kids."

The Dodgers quickly converted Stewart from catcher to pitcher in 1975. Because he could throw a 95-mph fastball, he officially became "Smoke" Stewart when the rookie reported to the Northwest League's Bellingham Dodgers in Washington. Dave made 22 appearances with an 0-5 record as last-place Bellingham finished 25 games out of first place. His next year in Class A ball wasn't much better, as 19-year-old Stewart managed only a 1-3 record with a disastrous 6.90 ERA in 28 appearances.

In 1977, the Dodgers reassigned Stewart to a different Class A league, this time in Clinton, Iowa of the Midwest League. The change of scenery paid off as he posted a spectacular 17-4 record with a 2.15 ERA and Clinton won a divisional title. Team officials in LA took notice of Dave's breakout season and gave him a late-season starting opportunity with their AAA Albuquerque Dukes affiliate. Stewart responded with six strong innings and the victory.

Stewart reported for his fourth year in the minors in 1978 with Class AA San Antonio of the Texas League, posting a 14-12 record and a 3.45 ERA. The 21-year-old right-hander made a brief major league debut at Dodger Stadium on September 22, 1978, pitching two scoreless innings of relief against the Padres at the end of the season.

He returned to the minors encouraged by his big league appearance. But in 1979, the Dodgers again sent Stewart to Albuquerque where he was battered by Pacific Coast League hitters and finished with an 11-12 record and a 5.24 ERA. Dave gave up nearly 11 hits per game, his worst since Bellingham. He rebounded in 1980, winning 15 games and dropping his ERA to a respectable 3.70.

Stewart resurfaced in the majors again in 1981 and produced a 13-11 record with the Dodgers over the 1981 and 1982 seasons. For his first major league victory, Dave relieved Bob Welch in '81 against the Giants at Candlestick Park, pitching two scoreless innings as the LA came from behind to win 4-3. He played a small relief role in the Dodgers' 1981 World Series championship over New York.

Unfortunately for Stewart, there wasn't much to go with the smoke. "The only way you can get by with nothing but a fastball is in short relief," he said. The Dodgers tried him there, spelling star closer Steve Howe. They also tried him as a middle reliever and a spot starter. In 1983, "Stew" showed improvement as he appeared in 46 games, going 5-2 with a 2.96 ERA. But after nine seasons, LA's patience with Dave ran out.

The Dodgers traded Stewart to the Texas Rangers in August of 1983 with Ricky Wright and $200,000 for future teammate Rick Honeycutt. Rangers manager Doug

Rader wasted no time putting Stewart into the starting rotation, and he finished the year with a 5-2 record and a dazzling 2.14 ERA in eight late-season starts. But in 1984, Stewart regressed to 7-14 and clashed with Rader over a new pitch he was fiddling with: the forkball. Dave was convinced he needed something to go with his fastball and curve but Rader did not agree. "He had his point of view and I had mine," Stewart said. We never got it settled, and he was the boss."

Banished to the Ranger bullpen, Dave's struggles became worse on and off the mound. During spring training in 1984, Stewart told a Texas newspaper he had known all along that former Dodger teammate Howe was using illegal drugs. He even admitted covering for Howe when he was questioned by manager Tommy Lasorda and other players. Dave admits now he was wrong in shielding Howe. "I certainly wouldn't do it that way again," he said. "With all Steve's gone through, I probably hurt him more than I helped him. It was a mistake."

In 1985, Stewart again made headlines – and again for the wrong reasons. He was arrested in a parked car on a skid-row Los Angeles street with a 6-foot-3 prostitute named Lucille... who turned out to be a transvestite. Dave said he didn't know "Lucille" was a man. Lewd conduct charges were eventually reduced to soliciting and Stewart was fined $150 with a year's probation. Only two days after his arrest, he was scheduled to accept the Dallas-Fort Worth Baseball Writers "good guy" award at the annual banquet. Showing his inner strength, Stewart appeared at the dinner, publicly apologized, and candidly answered all questions.

"It's part of growing up, I guess," he later said. "I was going through a period where one bad thing after another seemed to be happening to me. I've learned a lesson. Now I try to do what's right, knowing that sometimes I'll fall short. Some people might think of me as a hypocrite when I speak against drugs, since I'm the guy who protected Howe. And if I'm talking to a class, they can say, 'Hey, he was the one with the prostitute.' The thing is, I know I'm a sinner. But I do try. I also know you never finish growing."

"What bothers me is that those who won't forget it are saying one can't ever make a mistake," said Stewart towards the end of his career. "I did, and I admit it. I'm ashamed. But if you dig deep enough, you'll find something in everyone that he is ashamed of. If that incident has had something to do with my lack of recognition, I don't care now. I got back to basics. What is important? Three things: Am I respected by my teammates, am I respected by my community, and am I happy with that? I am."

Stewart hit rock bottom in Texas. He was 0-6 in 42 appearances in 1985 and was traded to Philadelphia in September for Rick Surhoff. Arm injuries also surfaced. In the off-season he had surgery to remove two small bone chips from his pitching elbow, but the Phillies released him early in 1986 after only eight appearances. At that point, Dave had spent five full seasons and parts of two others in the major leagues and had nothing but a losing record (30-37), an injured arm and a bad reputation to show for it.

On May 23, 1986 – 11 years after he left – Stewart came home. Almost out of baseball, he was a free agent no team wanted except the Oakland A's, hoping that home cooking would reverse his fortunes. But Stew was knocked around for 13 runs in his first 22 innings out of the A's bullpen in June and was headed nowhere. Meanwhile, manager Jackie Moore was suddenly fired, and six days later, Tony LaRussa was hired to replace him. LaRussa, desperately in need of starters, consulted Oakland pitching coach Dave Duncan and decided to give Stewart a shot as a starting pitcher.

LaRussa had not yet joined the team when he called Stewart on July 4 in Milwaukee and told him, "If you want the ball on Monday, you've got it." Dave wanted it and wanted it badly. On July 7, in LaRussa's debut as manager, Stewart beat Roger Clemens and the Red Sox 6-4 in Fenway Park before a national television audience. Stewart successfully locked down his new starting role with the A's, posting a 9-5 record and a 3.74 ERA over the last three months of the season. Oakland finished fourth in AL West, 16 games behind the California Angels.

The forkball, something Smoke was crucified for in Texas, became his career savior. Duncan encouraged Stewart to add a forkball (also known as a split-fingered fastball) to his repertoire, which made his fastball – still traveling in the 90s – all the more effective.

In 1987, Stewart not only continued his success in the Oakland rotation, he suddenly became one of the best pitchers in the majors. He won 20 games, the most in MLB that season, and became the first A's hurler with 200 strikeouts in a season since Vida Blue in 1971. Only 16 months after the Phillies cut him, Stewart incredibly finished third in the Cy Young Award voting behind Clemens and Jimmy Key. On a fragile pitching staff vulnerable to illness and injury, Dave did not miss a start and also became a genuine stopper, with 13 of his 20 victories following A's defeats. Oakland finished 81-81 that season.

The pitcher the A's gambled on paid quick dividends beyond their wildest dreams. Stew became known as a hard worker and a clubhouse leader but, as catcher Mickey Tettleton describes him, "absolutely the nicest guy you're ever gonna meet."

"Now that the season is coming to an end, I'm starting to realize that, hey, I've really had a good year," said Stewart of his 1987 season. "I'd never even dreamed of winning 20 games. I knew that if I got the chance I could be a good pitcher, but you never know."

His new-found national stardom continued as he again won 20 or more games in each of the next three seasons (1988-1990) and led a powerful Athletics club to the World Series each of those years. Stewart's teammates included Henderson, Dave Parker, Carney Lansford, Terry Steinbach, and the "Bash Brothers" – Mark McGwire and Jose Canseco. Remarkably, he pitched over 250 innings in each of those four seasons, posting an amazing 41 complete games.

The 6-foot-2, 200-pounder had records of 20-13 in 1987, 21-12 in 1988, 21-9 in 1989, and 22-11 in 1990. He was named the right-handed pitcher on *The Sporting News* American League All-Star team in 1988, when he had a 3.23 ERA and led the league with 14 complete games and 275 2/3 innings pitched. In 1990, he was the AL leader with four shutouts, 11 complete games, and 257 innings. "I love it when he goes out there," said Henderson. "He puts his heart and soul into every game."

Stewart elevated his game even higher when he went 6-0 to start the 1988 season. He finished 21-12 with a 3.23 ERA in 275 innings which included a major league-leading 14 complete games. The A's won 104 games and ran away with the AL West championship. In the playoffs against Boston, Oakland swept the Red Sox in four games behind two strong starts by ace Stewart and shutout relief by Dennis Eckersley, the ALCS MVP.

The A's, like all of baseball, were surprised to see Los Angeles upset the heavily-favored New York Mets in the National League Championship Series. Surely Oakland – with its mighty star-studded lineup – would crush this band of misfits and castoffs known as the '88 Dodgers. In Game 1, Stewart delivered another quality playoff start. He was in line for the win, allowing three runs in eight innings as the A's clung to a 4-3 lead. Eckersley, who rarely allowed walks or home runs, did both in the ninth as Kirk Gibson's walkoff home run won the game for the Dodgers. Oakland never recovered, scoring just seven runs in the rest of the series as LA won the world championship in five games.

In 1989, Stewart reached the pinnacle of his career. He was named an AL All-Star and in the World Series, Dave started and won two of the four games while giving up just three runs. This time, the A's offense produced 29 runs in four games as Oakland swept San Francisco in the "Battle of the Bay." Stewart pitched eight innings in Game 1 and a complete game in Game 3. With a 2-0 record and an ERA of 1.69, he was named the World Series MVP. "It wasn't until this World Series that Stew finally got recognized for what he is," said LaRussa.

"I spent a lot of days as the eighth and 10th man on staffs," said Stewart, "dreaming about being the number one guy, pitching in the World Series. Here I am, doing what I always wanted to do."

Minutes before Game 3 on October 17, television cameras shook at Candlestick Park as ABC broadcasters Al Michaels and Jim Palmer discussed the game. The infamous Loma Prieta earthquake postponed the series for 10 days, which actually had a beneficial effect on Stewart's stats and MVP award. Smoke would not have pitched a second game if there had been a quake-less sweep.

Just hours after getting the win in Game 3 of the World Series, Stewart hurried to the ugly wreckage of the collapsed Nimitz Freeway that killed 39 people and became such a familiar image to people across America. He helped carry supplies and water for victims and emergency crews. Dave's late-night visits to this site became a habit, and he stayed on the scene until 4:30 am that first night.

"The police let me go in near the workers," said Stewart. "I just stand and watch and try to boost the spirits of those people working all night, the people trying to find bodies and cleaning up the rubble. Some nights I didn't plan to be here, but when I couldn't get to sleep, I'd drive over and stand for an hour or two, then go home and go right to sleep. I haven't figured out why I'm drawn here, except that for me this isn't something to gawk at like a tourist. This is part of my life."

In the eyes of his Oakland neighbors, the 1989 World Series belonged to Dave Stewart, and his MVP meant Most Valuable Person. "The A's winning the Series really means something to Oakland," said former Oakland mayor Lionel Wilson. "Whereas had the Giants won, it wouldn't really have meant as much to San Francisco. And the fact that David Stewart won it for his hometown makes it most important, because David Stewart is the symbol of what Oakland can—and will—be."

"I won those games for my teammates and for myself, but I also won them for my community," remembered Stewart. "I won them for that guy over there, and those kids on the corner, and that elderly woman next to them. I won them for the parks-and-recreation people, the teachers, the police, my Little League coach and all the people who helped shape my character and baseball skills. There are more than 300,000 people in this town who tonight can say, 'We're Number One,' and mean it." When Eckersley touched first base to end the Series, Stewart rushed toward the outfield and embraced Henderson, his hometown pal. "We've done it," said Dave. "*We* is what this feeling is all about, Rickey, and for you and me at this moment, old friend, we is just a little more special. It's ours."

Immediately upon receiving his World Series winners' bonus, Stewart donated 20% of it to the Earthquake Relief Fund. Dave's primary concern was raising money for Oakland's recovery. "I've got some fund-raising ideas, and I'm sure the club will have some too," he said in October of '89. "I also know that I'll get any cooperation I ask for from my teammates."

On June 29, 1990, Stewart added another jewel to his pitching career. He no-hit the Blue Jays in Toronto, the first no-hitter by an African-American since Jim Bibby in 1973 and the last A's no-hitter until Dallas Braden pitched a perfect game in 2010. In a game that started minutes after Dave's masterpiece finished, Dodger Fernando Valenzuela no-hit the St. Louis Cardinals at Dodger Stadium – the first time in Major League history that no-hitters had been thrown in both leagues on the same day. Coincidentally, ESPN broadcast both games back-to-back that night.

The last of Stewart's four consecutive 20-plus-win seasons came in 1990. With 22 more victories, he helped the A's win their third straight ALCS, again beating the Red Sox. Stewart (2-0) was named the series MVP, allowing only two runs in 16 innings. Oakland's offense again sputtered in the World Series, managing only eight runs in four games as the decidedly underdog Cincinnati Reds swept the Athletics. Eric Davis, Chris Sabo and the "Nasty Boys" bullpen led Cincinnati. Stewart produced a complete game performance in Game 4 and allowed only one earned run.

After his historic 84-45 stretch, Stewart suffered arm problems in 1991 and 1992, and managed only a 23-21 record. Stew was also a part of the 1992 Oakland team which lost in the ALCS to the Blue Jays. Toronto, which went on to win the World Series that year, impressed Dave as an organization and signed him in 1993. He had a 12-8 record despite spending six weeks on the disabled list with recurring arm trouble.

The Blue Jays made it to the ALCS once again in 1993 and defeated the Chicago White Sox in six games. Fighting off injuries, Stewart won Games 2 and 6, allowing just three earned runs in 13 innings. He earned ALCS MVP honors for the second time in his career. In the World Series against Philadelphia, Dave lost Game 2 and took a no-decision in Game 6 as Joe Carter's walkoff home run gave Toronto their second straight championship.

Stewart remained with the Blue Jays for the 1994 season but struggled to a 7-8 record and 5.87 ERA. The season was shortened by a players strike. Stewart, who has lived through the strike of '85 as well as '81 and '94, knows that it is difficult to win over a hostile public that only wants to hear "play ball," not points of principle. "In '81, I was young and just really was going with the flow," Stewart said. "This time I feel like I'm a part of the flow. I want to be involved."

"A lot of people will always look at strikes, especially in the entertainment industry, as a money issue, something having to do with greed," Stewart said. "But those attitudes too often have to do more with envy and jealousy. People are just not trying to understand."

He closed out his career in 1995 at home in Oakland, losing seven out of his last 10 decisions. "I thought he had the same mound presence out there," said general manager Sandy Alderson, who brought Smoke back to the A's after two seasons with the Blue Jays. On July 17, Stewart lasted just two innings, giving up eight runs to the lowly Brewers at Milwaukee County Stadium, in what would be his final game in the big leagues. He retired shortly thereafter.

Stewart started 18 career postseason games, compiling a stellar 2.84 ERA and a 10-6 record, which included an 8-0 ALCS record with a 2.03 ERA. Including the postseason, Stewart posted a 9-1 head-to-head career record against Clemens. Stewart was an imposing force on the mound, whether in the playoffs or regular season.

"Respect is the first word anyone uses about Stew," said Eckersley. Catcher Terry Steinbach said "There's just a different feeling when he walks out to pitch. He makes everyone feel good about himself." Says coach Duncan, "David Stewart is a leader; he gives the other players so much confidence that they play better."

Stewart's one-time dominance could be based on complete games alone. He had 55 in his career, with 41 of those coming in his four dominant years. The leader in complete games is Clemens with 118, and if you take his four most dominant years

(1986, 1987, 1988, 2001), Clemens' complete game total is similar (42). It's a longshot that Dave is going to the Hall of Fame, but when he was at the top of his game, he was really at the top of major league baseball. And for that he deserves more attention than he's received.

Stewart served as pitching coach for three teams and Assistant General Manager for the Blue Jays, and was once regarded as a GM candidate. He did not get the job and instead started a national sports agency in San Diego called Sports Management Partners, and currently represents Eric Chavez, Matt Kemp, Chad Billingsley and others. The four-time 20-game winner instills confidence in his clients not only as a recent player, but also because he also served in front offices for both the A's and Jays.

Today, Stewart is quite active in his own San Diego community as well as his native Oakland. He recently teamed up with the Dodgers' Kemp to host a fundraiser benefiting autism research. Dave gives generously to multiple causes including public schools, the Oakland Boys Clubs, Just Say No, the MS Society, the Oakland Library and several other charitable and civic institutions. "There are hundreds of groups he helps that we don't know about," says Dave Perron, former Athletics director of community affairs. "They're run by people who come up to Stew on the street to ask for help, and he just can't say no to caring."

"I've never seen a man give as much in terms of his time, his money, and of himself," said former A's president Wally Haas. "He's one in a million."

Stewart and childhood friend Simpson, a UC Davis graduate, formed a nonprofit team called KidsCorps, which seeks corporate sponsorship for children's causes and for neighborhood revitalization. KidsCorps operates support programs for teenage mothers, drug education and learning-deficient children, and it sponsors four Little League teams, two softball teams, a track team, a dance group and a summer camp.

"In 1982, at Thanksgiving, I donated $500 to the Oakland Parents in Action, the group that started the national Just Say No program," said Stewart. "I found out that $500 could feed 1,000 people. Then Wornel told me he had ways to get us further involved, and that's how it started."

"I'm helped by the fact that the A's do more for their community than almost any other team," he continued. "The Haas family [former owner of the Athletics] is dedicated to giving. They rebuilt the fields where I used to play ball; they give more than $100,000 a year in tickets to the elderly and poor; they have days where kids get free tickets for donating books to the public schools; they give inner-city kids tickets for scholastic achievement. Everything I'm involved in, they're behind too. In these times that's important, because almost anytime you try to talk to corporations about funding, you get a two-word response: 'We're short.'"

Bob Howard, Stewart's old St. Elizabeth baseball coach, compares Dave's community mission to "a nonsecular ministry." But Stew sees it differently. "Most of what I do involves kids," he says. "And I think I get more out of it than the kids. All I really want is to be 11 or 12 years old for five hours a day every day for the rest of my life. Kids make me a kid again."

Stewart still visits the Victorian buildings in the old sections of Oakland. "This is the area we've been developing, with the city center, the restaurants, the shops, the hotels," he said. "It's going to be beautiful. The earthquake destruction and damage here is as great as it was in San Francisco, but Oakland never gets the media attention because we're not glamorous. But besides the highway collapse, the city's biggest department stores had to be closed, city hall may never reopen, and almost 1,000 poor people were homeless because a couple of old hotels collapsed. We were set back, badly. But we will endure. We will rebuild, and Oakland will be back on its climb."

Through 2004, only twelve African-American pitchers had won 20-games in a major league season. This dozen, under the direction of Mudcat Grant, called themselves the "12 Black Aces," and are an exclusive club: Don Newcombe, Sam Jones, Bob Gibson, Grant, Earl Wilson, Fergie Jenkins, Al Downing, Vida Blue, J.R. Richard, Mike Norris, Dwight Gooden and Dave Stewart.

In the 2000s, steroid use in baseball saddened Stewart as much as anyone but believes those who tainted the game should be regarded equally. "As a black man, looking at it through my eyes, you have to understand maybe race is the reason nobody wanted to look at Roger (Clemens) like they looked at Barry (Bonds)," Stewart said. "In years past, when all the speculation was on Barry, I said maybe you need to look at Roger as well. It's unjust people were looking only at Barry. They were exactly the same. The exact same creature."

Stewart has two children – son Adrian, 34, and daughter, Alyse, 29, who grew up near Los Angeles with his former wife, Vanessa. In 2009, Dave made the trip to Cooperstown, NY to help celebrate Henderson's enshrinement in the Hall of Fame.

In 2011 at the Coliseum, Stewart threw out the ceremonial first pitch prior to the opening day A's game against the Seattle Mariners.

Dave Stewart's mercurial big-league career lasted 15 seasons, but he is best known for his dominant four-year stretch with the Athletics from 1987 to 1990 in which he won 84 times and led the A's to three consecutive World Series appearances. His greatest season was 1989, when "Smoke" won 21 games, two more in the ALCS and two more in the World Series, winning the Series MVP award as the A's captured their fourth championship in Oakland. Glaring at batters from beneath the shadow of the bill of his cap, he will forever be known as one of the most intimidating and one of the best big-game pitchers in baseball history.

43

DENNIS ECKERSLEY

First he saved himself. Then he changed the game. Hall of Fame pitcher Dennis Eckersley is living proof that you can not only make a comeback… you can shine brighter than ever.

Dennis Lee Eckersley was born in Oakland on October 3, 1954, the second of Wallace and Bernice Eckersley's three children. Growing up in Fremont where he attended Washington High School, Dennis was a multi-sport athlete in baseball, basketball and football. He credits his parents and older brother with helping him build skill and confidence as a young athlete.

"My parents encouraged me and supported my passion for baseball every step of the way," remembers Eckersley. "My dad managed me, and he was a part-time groundskeeper at the same time. He came to every game, leaving work early to be there. Fathers didn't really do that back then. I had the chance to hone my pitching skills at a young age because I'd play with my older brother, Wally. He was two years older but he let me play with him and his friends. My mom used to work the snack bars in Little League games."

Baseball became his official profession when the 6-foot-2, 190 pound Eckersley was selected out of Washington High by the Cleveland Indians in the third round of the 1972 amateur draft, the 50th overall pick. He was 17 years old and three days out of high school. Dennis was another in a long list of 1970s Bay Area prep stars to play in the major leagues, including future teammates Rickey Henderson, Dave Stewart, and Carney Lansford.

"My passion for baseball was born as a little kid growing up in Fremont, California. Man, I'd listen to the Giants games late at night on a transistor radio. I could still hear the echo in my mind of Lon Simmons calling a home run call, *"And you can tell it goodbye."* I loved it," said Eckersley in his Hall of Fame induction speech. "Those were the days of Willie Mays and Juan Marichal. I wanted to pitch like Marichal and hit like Willie Mays. We didn't go to many Giant games, but when I did, I savored every moment. I couldn't take my eyes off Willie Mays. I was fascinated by that basket catch. I tried to emulate Marichal's high leg kick. And that's where the dream began."

The Indians in 1972 assigned Eckersley to their Reno affiliate, in the Class A California League. He appeared in only 12 games for the Silver Sox that year, going 5-5 with a 4.80 ERA due to control problems, a flaw he would work hard to improve. In 1973, he became one of Reno's top pitchers, posting a 12-8 record with a 3.65 ERA and earned a promotion to Class AA with San Antonio of the Texas League. Dennis turned in a stellar season for the Missions in 1974, winning 14 of 17 decisions with a 3.40 ERA, and reduced his walks per game to 3.2.

Barely 20 years old, Eckersley broke into the big leagues with Cleveland on April 12, 1975. He started his major league career where he would end it – in the bullpen. After pitching in relief for his first ten outings, Eckersley was given the unenviable task of starting against... who else? His hometown three-time World Champion Athletics. Oakland was ready for him in his first career start on May 25, 1975. Undaunted, calm, and cool, the young right-hander fired a complete-game, three-hit shutout. He would pitch an amazing 28 2/3 consecutive scoreless innings to start his career, a major league record.

"If it weren't for Frank Robinson taking a chance on a cocky 20-year-old, I wouldn't have gotten to the big leagues so soon," said Eckersley. "I'm indebted to Frank Robinson. I watched Frank closely, and I learned early on from one of the greatest ever. He was intensely competitive and his style rubbed off on me."

Eckersley slipped into a Cleveland rotation that was in a constant state of turnover. He really didn't "replace" anyone. He joined Fritz Peterson and Jim Perry as the only steady contributors on the starting staff. Dennis would finish the 1975 season at 13-7 with an outstanding 2.60 ERA, earning him *Sporting News* AL Rookie Pitcher of the Year honors. He finished runnerup in the AL Rookie of the Year voting to MVP and future teammate Fred Lynn. The young Eckersley overpowered hitters with a smoking fastball, a sinker, and a hard slider. Over time, he developed precise control. When the tall, thin hurler dropped down sidearm, he was nearly unhittable against right-handed batters.

Eckersley's time in Cleveland would feature other impressive achievements. In 1976 he struck out 200 batters. His career crown jewel – a 1-0 no-hitter versus the California Angels in Cleveland – occurred on May 30, 1977. He extended it to a dominating 21-inning hitless streak and was named to the AL All-Star team. Dennis would go 40-32 in his three seasons with the lowly Indians, later earning him a spot on the "100 Greatest Cleveland Indians Roster."

Cleveland traded Eckersley and catcher Fred Kendall to Boston before the 1978 season for pitchers Rick Wise and Mike Paxton, third baseman Ted Cox and catcher Bo Diaz. That same day, Eckersley's first wife Denise told him she wanted a divorce; she had become romantically involved with Eckersley's Cleveland teammate Rick Manning. The two later married.

"I never wanted to leave Cleveland, never. It was upsetting when I got traded to Boston," said Eckersley. "That first trade is the most painful, combined with the agony of a broken marriage. But little did I know that special times were to come."

Eckersley's first season in Boston was his best, compiling a 20-8 record, with a 2.99 ERA in 1978. The young flamethrower's unstyled hair and blinding fastball made him an instant favorite of Red Sox fans. Now part of a high-scoring team so unlike Cleveland, "Eck" became one of the AL's premier starters as the Red Sox battled rival New York in a heated pennant race. In his last four September starts, Dennis went 4-0 with three complete games and only three earned runs allowed while striking out 20.

Eckersley followed up his sparkling 1978 campaign with an equally impressive second season in Boston. Dennis finished 17-10 and matched his previous season's 2.99 ERA. He finished in the Top 10 in Cy Young balloting (7th), wins (5th), and ERA (3rd).

Dennis was now at the top of his game. Not yet 25 years old, he had already won 107 major league games and was living out his dream of being a major leaguer in a stadium like Fenway Park where capacity crowds were passionate about him and the Red Sox. His future was bright and limitless.

But then things turned really awful really fast. The 1980 season would usher in a long period of decline for the starting pitcher. Back and shoulder injuries began to nag him and over the next four seasons in Boston, Eckersley was a below-average 43-48. In addition, nightlife celebration and revelry were taking their toll. At 29, Eckersley was drinking his way out of big league baseball.

The Red Sox no longer saw Eckersley as a 20-game winner but as an average starter. Boston dealt him to the Chicago Cubs on May 25, 1984 with outfielder Mike Brumley for first baseman Bill Buckner, one of several mid-season deals that helped the Cubs to their first postseason appearance since 1945. Eckersley, however, pitched poorly in his start for the Cubs in the NL Championship Series against San Diego, who advanced to the World Series.

Eckersley's performance continued to deteriorate in 1986 when he posted a disappointing 6–11 record with a 4.57 ERA. After getting drunk at his sister-in-law's house in front of his daughter Mandy during the 1986 Christmas season, Dennis entered alcohol rehab in January, attending a 30-day treatment center in Newport, R.I. Eckersley explained years later that he accepted his problem after family members videotaped him and later played the tape for him.

Eckersley was traded again – this time for three minor leaguers – on April 3, 1987 to the Oakland A's where manager Tony LaRussa intended to use Eck as a setup man or long reliever. An injury to then-closer Jay Howell, however, opened the door for Dennis. A starter for 12 seasons, Eckersley's career was resurrected in the second half of the 1987 season as a closer. Considering where his career was headed just months before, saving games might have saved him.

"That off-season, after 1986, was probably one of the most difficult times in my life, both personally and professionally. This is when my life changed forever. My career hit a major downturn, and I was spiraling out of control personally. For the 12 years I pitched as a starter, I relied on raw talent and innate ability to get through. It worked most of the time, but times were changing. No one knew then, but I was fighting a major battle with alcohol and I knew I had come to the crossroads in my life. With the grace of God, I got sober, and I saved my life. I was a new man. I was a renewed man. It took a great deal of acceptance to come to terms with being an alcoholic, but the acceptance was key to my sobriety. If I had not gained acceptance at that time in my life, I would not be standing here today. My career would have not taken me this far."

Eckersley summed up his return from the brink this way: "There's good fear and bad fear. The bad fear is when you're feeling sick and almost paralyzed ... for me, it made me more aggressive. And the more aggressive I became, the better I was."

In Oakland, Dennis carved his place in baseball history over the next five seasons as one of the most unhittable relievers of all time. He defined baseball's new role of the one-inning closer while racking up four all-star appearances. A's starters were no longer expected to pitch into the last inning; there was another pitcher who was coming into the game in the ninth inning, no matter what. Eck saved 16 games in 1987 and then established himself as the most dominant closer of 1988 by recording a league-leading 45 saves.

"You never know when life is going to change forever. And in the spring of 1987, I was traded to the Oakland A's," said Eck. "I was happy about the trade, but I was even happier to be home again. My heart belongs in California."

Loaded with offensive talent, the A's won the AL West championship in 1988, the first of three consecutive titles. In the ALCS, Eckersley recorded four saves as the A's swept the Red Sox, the team who four years before had given up on him. His only regrettable moment of an otherwise spectacular season came in Game 1 of the World Series against the Los Angeles Dodgers. Attempting to save his fifth straight playoff game, Eckersley surrendered a walk followed by a game-winning walkoff home run to Kirk Gibson, one of the most dramatic moments in baseball history.

"I was hurt badly, and I sat in the trainer's room the whole game trying to rehabilitate as best I could, looking for an opportunity to help my team win," recalled Gibson. "I knew Dennis Eckersley was the best relief pitcher in baseball, and I kind of conditioned my mind to believe that if the opportunity arose, I could step up there and suck it up, and try to help my team out. We had a scouting report from [advance scout] Mel Didier that said Dennis Eckersley likes to throw a 3-2 backdoor slider to left-handed hitters. If you watch the film, when he went into a set position I called time and stepped out. I said to myself what Mel told me: 'Partner, as sure as I'm standing here breathing, you get Eckersley 3-2 in a big situation and you're going to see a backdoor slider.' Sure enough, there it was."

The Dodgers won Game 1 and the 1988 World Series Championship in five games. That stunning upset aside, Eckersley became one of the most dominant closers in the game at age 34. During the period 1987 to 1992, he saved 236 games for the A's.

"My success was mixed with some devastating losses. But (Oakland fans) always stood by me and I want to take this opportunity to tell you how much your affection and loyalty meant to me," he said in Cooperstown. "One moment I'll always remember was the ovation you gave me after returning home from that devastating loss to the Los Angeles Dodgers in 1988. I will never forget that moment."

Eckersley vowed to help the A's return to the championship in 1989 as he walked only three opponents in 57 2/3 innings. After three saves against Toronto in the ALCS, he redeemed himself in the World Series. He secured the victory in Game 2, and then saved Game 4 – the clincher – as the A's swept San Francisco 4-0.

"More important than personal awards is winning the World Series," said Eckersley. "That's the max that anyone could ask for. Let alone to have the ball in your glove for the final out of the World Series. That was the ultimate."

Eckersley's control became his trademark; he walked only 16 batters in 207 innings from 1989 through 1991. He allowed only five earned runs during the entire 1990 season, resulting in a microscopic 0.61 ERA, and walked only four in 73 1/3 innings. That season, Dennis became the only pitcher in baseball history to have more saves than baserunners allowed.

"He taught me something about fear," said LaRussa. "Eck tells me he spent the whole game being afraid. Fear makes some guys call in sick or be tentative. He uses fear to get him ready for every stinking time he pitches."

Once again on top, he earned more than $15 million during his Oakland years, a far cry from his $30,000 rookie contract in Cleveland. Colorful and at times controversial, Eckersley wore rock star hair and a moustache and his demonstrative gunslinger celebration after a strikeout often angered hitters. Blown saves were extremely rare, giving him another nickname: Mr. Automatic. Eckersley twice went 18 straight games without allowing a run. Fans began to feel part of something special – a feeling of knowing for sure that the A's would win if ahead after eight innings.

"We have a job to do here. We've worked hard to get where we are, and when we go on the field we expect to win," said Eckersley in the book *Oakland A's*. "You know you won't win all of the time, but you expect to, and when we don't, it's like, bummer. It really is. Others accept losing. We don't. We don't ever want to get a feeling for it."

Eckersley won the American League's Cy Young and MVP Awards in 1992 after posting 51 saves, a 7-1 record, a 1.91 ERA, and 93 strikeouts against only 11 walks in 80 innings. Only two relievers had previously accomplished the double feat: Rollie Fingers in 1981 and Willie Hernandez in 1984. No pitcher since has won both Cy Young and MVP in the same season, and no reliever after Dennis won the Cy Young until Dodger Eric Gagne did so in 2003.

"Dennis Eckersley was made in Oakland, firmed up in Fremont and raised to his glory in Oakland again," said Bay Area sportswriter Ray Ratto in *Baseball Digest*. "Nowhere else did he bring people to their feet simply by standing and removing his warm-up jacket, on nothing more than the promise of what was to come. Which was usually three and home."

Because of Eckersley, every MLB team wanted a reliever who could terminate a game after eight innings, save their pitching staff from overexerting themselves, and give fans something exciting to stay for. Today, practically all teams employ a dedicated closer who only appears in save situations. Complete games by a starter happen less often today than a save 40 or 50 years ago.

"They developed a platform for me to put up another 12 years, and that was my ticket to Cooperstown," he said of his years with the A's. "Those were the best years of my life. It was like magic."

His numbers slipped noticeably in 1993. Although Eckersley was still among the league leaders in saves, his ERA rose sharply, and his saves total never again eclipsed 36. He enjoyed marginal success from then until his retirement in 1998. Eckersley followed LaRussa from Oakland to St. Louis in 1996, and spent two seasons with the Cardinals before coming back to Boston to end his career as a setup man for Tom Gordon in 1998.

A six-time All-Star, Eckersley ended his 24-year major league career with a record of 197-171, 100 complete games, 2,401 strikeouts, 390 saves (fourth all-time) and a 3.50 ERA. His baseball career culminated in 2004 when he was elected to the National Baseball Hall of Fame in his first year of eligibility with 83% of the votes. Dennis earned induction into the Hall based on his success as both a starter and reliever. He was the first pitcher in Major League history to have both a 20-win season and a 50-save season and the only pitcher with both 100 saves and 100 complete games.

Dennis currently works as a studio analyst for the Red Sox on New England Sports Network. Unlike many other commentators, he is willing to point out unacceptable play by the home team. This has earned him the nickname "Honest Eck" among New England fans. Eckersley has been known to use the phrase "cheese" to refer to a pitcher's ability to throw in the mid- to upper-90s. He also calls the act of hitting a home run as "going bridge." Hair, be it on the head or the face, is "moss." He also spends time with kids Mandee, Jake and Allie and wife Jennifer. During the summer, Dennis lives in the upscale Turner Hill golf community in Ipswich, Massachusetts.

In 1999, Eckersley ranked Number 98 on *The Sporting News* list of The 100 Greatest Baseball Players and was nominated as a finalist for the Major League Baseball All-Century Team. On August 13, 2005, his No. 43 uniform was officially retired by the Oakland Athletics. The baseball field at his alma mater, Washington High School in Fremont, has been named in his honor. Dennis has also been named to the "Top 100 Players Ever" lists for Cleveland, Boston, Chicago, and Oakland.

In 2009, TBS television signed Eckersley to a multi-year contract to serve as an analyst for the network. Dennis provides his unique brand of analysis for MLB regular season, all-star and playoff games. "I'm thrilled to return to TBS for their MLB coverage," said Eckersley. "I thoroughly enjoyed my time with them this past season. The show is a great fit with my personality and I'm looking forward to the start of the season."

Dennis Eckersley blazed a unique path to Hall of Fame success. During his first 12 seasons, Eck won over 150 games as a starting pitcher, including a no-hitter. Over his final 12 years as a recovering alcoholic, he saved nearly 400 games, leading his hometown Oakland A's to three American League championships and a World Series crown. Five teams, 24 years, and one happy ending.

51

RANDY JOHNSON

Long before his 303 wins and five Cy Young awards, Randy Johnson had East Bay kids shaking in their shoes. The scowling Johnson stood 6-foot-9 by his senior year at Livermore High, a skinny yet menacing teenager with an awkward and downright wild delivery. From Granada Little League to pitching in the World Series at Yankee Stadium, Johnson's 22-year Hall of Fame career ranks among the greatest in pitching history.

Randall David Johnson was born September 10, 1963 in Walnut Creek to Carol Hannah Johnson and Rollen "Bud" Johnson. Randy grew up in nearby Livermore where Bud was a policeman and security guard while Carol performed volunteer work and odd jobs, but mostly stayed home to raise Randy and his five siblings.

As a young child, Randy enjoyed having fun with his friends and was an active participant in his elementary school classes. He was also an artful observer of his environment, which led to his lifelong interest in photography. Tall and gangly, Johnson stood out as a child, towering over his fellow classmates at school but still very agile and coordinated.

Not surprisingly, Randy excelled in sports. Although Johnson's height often caused him to feel somewhat awkward in social situations, it benefited him on the athletic field and enabled him to outplay other boys his age in several sports. He shined on the basketball court but baseball remained his first love. Randy was the only neighborhood kid who could make a ball hiss when he threw it and no one wanted to face him in pickup game because of his speed and wildness. Just standing in against him was a test of courage.

Bud, a former ski jumper and avid softball player in his native state of Minnesota, stood 6-6 himself and believed Randy could leverage his size to one day become a great pitcher. On summer evenings, after leaving his security job at Lawrence Livermore Labs, Bud would grab a glove, squat down on two creaky knees, and try to catch Randy's wild stuff. The Johnsons encouraged Randy to develop his pitching skills through Granada Little League. In 1972, the 8-year-old grabbed his glove and walked over to tryouts. When he got there, he saw more than 100 kids spread out over six fields. He did not recognize any friends or classmates and a lot of the boys looked older. He failed to bring the correct paperwork and ran home in tears. Carol walked Randy back to tryouts and got him signed up. With some coaching, he quickly became the best pitcher and hitter for his age group. Within a year, he was moved up two levels.

Throughout elementary school, Randy liked being one of the taller kids and by sixth grade he was pushing six feet. But when he sprouted seven more inches during middle school, he became painfully aware of the fact that people were staring at him. The once outgoing boy became shy and withdrawn as a teen. He spent less time with classmates and more time with his camera and photography.

Randy worked on his pitching in his driveway, throwing tennis balls at a strike zone he had taped on the garage door. He usually pretended he was Vida Blue, the Oakland A's lefthander who won MVP and Cy Young Awards in 1971. Randy threw so hard that he loosened the nails in the door and, after some of these practice sessions, Bud would hand Randy a hammer to drive them back in.

By the time he entered Livermore High School, Johnson was a star. Randy became the ace of both the Cowboy baseball and basketball teams. Now 6-foot-8, he led the led the entire East Bay Athletic League in basketball scoring in 1981 and 1982. On the baseball diamond under coach Eric Hoff, Randy's awkward motion and 90 mph fastball fired with a whiplike motion was virtually unhittable. And often uncontrollable. He began experimenting with a slider at this point, but it rarely found the plate. Fans sometimes laughed at how Randy's uniform fit him. His pants ended around his knees, and his jersey came untucked after each pitch. Opposing coaches, looking to rattle Randy, would demand that umpires make him tuck it in several times an inning.

The scouts who came to watch Johnson called him "Ichabod Crane." But when Randy had everything going, he was one of the best prep pitchers in the country. He routinely struck out 10 or more batters per game. And it wasn't purely about velocity. Johnson presented an imposing package, from his uncommon height and sometimes surly disposition to his rampant wildness.

"It always felt like the mound was a lot closer at Livermore than it was at other schools," said Dan Sweeney, who played for Amador Valley High School in Pleasanton in the early 1980s. "There weren't a lot of 6-9 guys living out here in suburbia." He described facing Johnson as "a harrowing experience."

Steve Gallagher, Johnson's catcher at Livermore High in 1982, became familiar with the sight of hitters backing away even before Johnson released the ball. One left-handed hitter from Dublin High essentially ignored the boundaries of the batter's box. He took his stance beyond the outer edge against Randy, far from home plate. Gallagher remembers saying, "Dude, you're going to have to get back in or we can't get started. Just close your eyes. It will be OK."

When Johnson pitched, the atmosphere was noticeably different than a typical high school game. A semi-circle of college and pro scouts formed behind the backstop at Livermore – a long row stretching from one dugout to the other, each scout equipped with a radar gun. As many as 27 scouts would attend a Cowboy game but when Johnson left the game in the late innings, the scouts – and fans – immediately departed.

"Nobody even threw close to that hard, but Randy's control just wasn't there," said former neighbor and opponent John Petlansky. "I had the chance to have a bunch of seams inscribed in my ribs and other places. ... The only way to get a hit off the guy was to bunt and run like hell."

Johnson didn't always dominate, given his control issues and trouble holding runners on base. It was not uncommon for Randy to strike out 15 batters but also walk nine or 10. Teams often ran like crazy against him, taking advantage of his slow delivery. Still, the intimidating aura and overwhelming power were hard to counter.

Mike Madden, son of Hall of Fame football coach and broadcaster John Madden, also batted against Johnson in high school. Mike was a left-handed hitting outfielder at Foothill High in Pleasanton. He was a "pretty good player," as John

Madden put it on his radio show, but Mike struggled against left-handed pitchers – even the ones who weren't 6-9 sidearmers that could reach 90 mph.

Johnson and Madden crossed paths twice during their junior year in a 1981 game at Livermore. Madden struck out, grounded out and decided on sticking to football and track as a senior. "I couldn't deal with a random, faceless lefty, let alone a guy that tall," said Madden. "He was tall and throwing serious gas. I was working with some fear issues and he had some control issues. Not a good combo."

As a senior in 1982, Johnson struck out 121 batters in 66 innings. In his final outing for Livermore, he pitched a perfect game against Dublin High. However, it was only the fourth win of the year for Randy as the Cowboys had a poor offense. When Johnson walked in a couple of runs, he often got hung with a loss.

After Johnson graduated from Livermore High, the Atlanta Braves selected him in the second round of the June draft. The team offered him a $50,000 signing bonus. Bud and Carol told Randy that beyond that first check, there were no guarantees in pro ball. Coach Hoff advised Randy to develop his skills in college. With scholarship offers on the table from several top schools, he decided to attend the University of Southern California, a powerhouse baseball program during the 1970s with a great reputation for sports and academics.

Johnson continued to play both basketball and baseball at USC. Under coach Rod Dedeaux, he worked on mastering pitches other than his fastball but still battled control problems. Randy thoroughly enjoyed his USC experience. He formed a wide circle of friends, and immersed himself into his declared major – Fine Arts. Randy wrote for the school newspaper and a local rock magazine, and also took advantage of the creative opportunities his classes offered. He pitched well for the Trojans, winning 10 games and saving five in his first two seasons.

As Johnson began his junior season in 1985, most experts believed he was ready for a breakout year. *Baseball America* ranked him as the fourth-best college pitcher in the United States. But the pressure got to 20-year-old Randy, and he did not manage adversity well. When umpires called balls or his fielders made errors behind him, he would lose his cool. Johnson did lead the nation in one category – walks with 104 in 118 innings. Baserunners often stole on him because of his complex delivery. Randy won just six times in 26 starts for the Trojans, and USC finished with their worst Pacific 10 record in school history. Randy was embarrassed and angry about his season and vowed to make up for it as a senior, but he never got that chance.

No one was more surprised than Johnson when the Montreal Expos selected him in the second round of the 1985 draft, the 34th overall pick. He was the second lefty taken, after Joe Magrane of Arizona was selected with the 18th pick by the St. Louis Cardinals. Randy was hardly ready for a pro career. He was concerned that he would have to battle his own body, now at its full length of 6-10. That gave him incentive to stay at USC and get his degree. Baseball was frustrating at this point anyway. But the Expos convinced him that if he could get a grip on his emotions, they could get a handle on his mechanics.

Johnson signed an Expos contract, deposited his bonus check, and headed off to his first professional assignment in Jamestown of the Class A New York-Penn League. He went winless in eight starts, but manager Ed Creech wasn't concerned. Randy's goal for his first minor league season was to find a pitching motion that he felt comfortable with, and then build on his confidence. The Expos felt strongly enough about Randy's potential to put him into a starting rotation in 1986. He pitched for West Palm Beach of the Class A Florida State League, under manager Felipe Alou. Some days Randy was dominant, and some days couldn't find the strike zone with a map. Alou and his staff worked on Randy's mechanics, trying to smooth the kinks in his delivery – no easy job for a guy who stood nearly seven feet tall. Randy made 26 starts with an 8-7 record. He led the league in walks, but his fastball – and a rapidly developing slider – were sharp enough to limit batters to a .211 average.

Randy spent the entire 1987 season with Jacksonville of the Class AA Southern League. He pitched deeper into games and went 11-8 with a league-high 168 strikeouts. His control was still a problem, but the team felt he was making progress. The only worrisome thing was how easily Randy lost his focus when things didn't go his way. Although such emotional breakdowns were not unusual in the minors, the Expos expected more from a USC senior.

In 1988, Johnson was promoted to Montreal's AAA team in Indianapolis. He also met his future wife Lisa at a charity golf event. She stood six feet tall and managed a photography shop. He had an impressive spring and claimed a spot in the Indians' rotation under coach Joe Kerrigan. Randy credits Kerrigan – a tall, lanky pitcher himself – with refining his delivery. During spring training, Johnson collided head-first with Expos outfielder Tim Raines, prompting his teammate to exclaim, "You're a big unit!" The nickname stuck.

The Expos were planning to promote Randy midway through 1988 when a batter lined a ball of his left wrist. Believing he had suffered a career-threatening break, Randy got so angry that he punched a bat rack on his way to the trainer's room.

When the x-rays came back, they revealed only a bruise on his left wrist – but his right hand was broken. Expos management, which had always questioned Randy's maturity, was furious and now considered him expendable. Johnson did make his major league debut that year, on September 15 after three seasons in the Montreal farm system. Randy made four brilliant starts for the Expos during the season's final month, compiling a record of 3-0 and an outstanding 2.42 ERA. He struck out 26 batters and walked only seven in just under 30 innings.

In 1989, Dennis Martinez, Bryn Smith, and Pascual Perez were all reliable veteran pitchers coming off good seasons. By throwing Randy and promising Kevin Gross in the mix, the Expos were hoping for an all-star rotation. Touted as a possible Rookie of the Year candidate, Johnson started off the 1989 campaign slowly for Montreal, going 0-4 with a 6.67 ERA in his six starts when the Expos finally pulled the plug. Locked a tight race in the NL East, Montreal had to make a move for a proven winner. On May 25, Randy and pitchers Brian Holman and Gene Harris were traded for Mark Langston of the Seattle Mariners. Coming off a great year for a horrible team, Langston was a pending free agent and the lowly Mariners gladly accepted three young pitching prospects.

Since breaking into the majors, Johnson quickly became one of the most feared pitchers in the game because of his lethal fastball, height, wild mullet hairstyle, and his angry, energetic demeanor on the mound. Part of his early intimidation factor still came from his lack of control. Once Randy arrived in Seattle, he finally started pitching the way everyone knew he could, though his statistics didn't yet reflect it. In 1990, Johnson led the American League in walks but he also threw a no-hitter against the Detroit Tigers and became the first left-hander to strike out Wade Boggs three times in one game.

Johnson showed glimpses of brilliance in his first four seasons in Seattle, averaging about a strikeout an inning and leading all AL pitchers with 241 strikeouts in 1992. The tall lefthander, however, had yet to master the mental game of pitching. Extremely emotional and volatile on the mound, Johnson showed little patience when his Mariner teammates made errors and he often expressed his disgust over his lack of run support. Johnson's great height also continued to affect his mechanics on the mound, making it difficult for him to maintain control of his pitches. As a result, he led all American League pitchers in walks in three of his first four years with the Mariners, while posting a combined record of only 46-44.

Mired in a losing streak, he sought the advice of some legendary flamethrowers, including Tom Seaver and Nolan Ryan. Johnson credits a session with Ryan late in

1992 that helped him take his career to the next level. In his next-to-last season with the Rangers, the 45-year-old Ryan said that he appreciated Johnson's talent and did not want to see him take as long to figure certain things out as he had taken. Because Randy would land on the heel of his foot after delivering a pitch, he usually landed offline from home plate. Ryan suggested that he land on the ball of his foot, which almost immediately improved his control. Texas pitching coach Tom House agreed with Ryan. This, they said, might be the key to the consistency that had eluded Randy.

Finding the strike zone more consistently almost as soon as he instituted the change, Johnson subsequently became one of baseball's most dominant pitchers. After tinkering for a couple of weeks, everything began falling into place. At one point, Randy hit 102 mph on the radar gun. With his fastball hitting spots and his curve and slider bending over the corners, Randy finished the year strong. Over his final 11 starts in 1992, he was 5-2 with a 2.65 ERA, giving up a mere 47 hits and averaging 10-plus strikeouts a game. His last start was an eight-inning performance against the Rangers in which he struck out 18. Randy finished 12-14 and led the AL with 241 strikeouts in 210 innings. He also led the league in walks for the third time with 144.

While Johnson was flying home to Livermore to visit his parents at Christmas, Bud suffered an aortic aneurysm. He died before Randy could get from the airport to the hospital. Randy laid his head on his father's chest and sobbed and even decided to quit baseball. Over the next few days, his mother Annie talked him out of it. The loss of his father eventually turned Randy to religion and he became more serious about Christianity. He drew a cross and his dad's name on his glove, and he's kept it for inspiration in tough spots. Johnson also decided to make his longtime relationship with Lisa official and married her in 1992.

Randy put it all together in 1993 and the Mariners started to improve under their fiery new manager, Lou Piniella. Randy's heater touched 100 mph on the gun a number of times and he perfected what was widely accepted as the game's best slider, which he dubbed "Mr. Snappy" for its tight, late break. The southpaw typically threw his signature pitch at a velocity that measured in the low 90s, prompting opposing batters to believe a fastball was coming. However, the ball broke down and in to right-handers just before it crossed home plate, causing them to swing at pitches that nearly hit them in the back foot. The combination of Johnson's height, velocity, and the movement on his breaking ball made the southpaw nearly impossible to hit. He was murder on left-handed hitters, holding them to a sub-.200 average and hitting more than a dozen of them during the year.

Johnson's breakout season included a 19–8 record, 3.24 ERA and the first of six 300-plus strikeout seasons (308). The key number was his walks total. He issued just 99 passes. In May 1993, Johnson again lost a no-hitter to a 9th-inning single and again the opponent was hometown Oakland. He also recorded his 1,000th career strikeout against the Minnesota Twins' Chuck Knoblauch. Randy led the AL in strikeouts and earned a spot on the All-Star Team for the first time. At the All-Star Game, Johnson threw a fastball over the head of Philadelphia Phillies first baseman John Kruk, who quickly surrendered. It is still replayed on highlights shows to this day. A similar incident would occur with Larry Walker in 1997.

The Mariners continued to improve as a team. They finished third in 1993 at 82-80 in a division where Oakland was now on the decline. Seattle had an exciting core of proven young veterans but injuries to Edgar and Tino Martinez and Dave Fleming put their chances of contention in 1994 in doubt. Some Mariner fans felt that by trading Johnson, the M's could fill every hole in their roster. Instead, Seattle traded shortstop Omar Vizquel to the Cleveland Indians for Felix Fermin and Reggie Jefferson. Fermin was a good all-around player who played steady shortstop until teenage prospect Alex Rodriguez was ready.

During the 1994 season, both Martinezes recovered from injuries and had productive years, as well as Fermin and Jay Buhner. Ken Griffey Jr. had a spectacular campaign and was leading the AL in homers with 40 when a strike ended the season after 112 games. Pitching became a major problem for Seattle but in the woeful AL West, a 49-63 record left them only two games shy of a playoff berth. Rapidly developing into the league's most intimidating pitcher, Johnson won 13 games and led the AL with 204 strikeouts, four shutouts and nine complete games. No other Mariner starter was effective, however, and new closer Bobby Ayala gave Piniella high anxiety despite saving 18 games. The Mariners were now just a couple of missing pieces away from being a pennant contender.

Randy was once again the subject of winter trade talks in 1995 and once again he was on the mound for Seattle on Opening Day. Although the starting rotation was erratic, the offense was in high gear with the two Martinezes, Buhner, Mike Blowers and new second baseman Joey Cora having career years. The only thing preventing the Mariners from moving ahead in the AL West standings was a broken wrist suffered by Griffey when he slammed into an outfield wall.

In early September, the division looked like a lock for the California Angels while the Mariners, Rangers and Yankees battled for the Wild Card. But an amazing stretch run by Seattle enabled the club to finish the year tied with the Angels. With New York eking out the Wild Card, it set up a one-game playoff between the Mariners and California. Johnson, a spectacular 17-2 at that point, three-hitted the Angels with 12 strikeouts to send Seattle to the playoffs for the first time in franchise history.

In the AL Division Series, The Mariners dropped two wild games in Yankee Stadium and found themselves in an 0-2 hole versus the budding New York dynasty. In Game 3, Johnson labored through seven innings and struck out 10 to earn a 7-4 victory, with mid-season pickup Norm Charlton sealing the win. Seattle also won Game 4 to even the series. In the deciding fifth game, the Mariners rallied from a 4-2 ninth-inning deficit to send the epic battle into extra innings. With the bullpen out of gas, Piniella looked to Randy on two day's rest to get the team to the AL Championship. Johnson's slow walk to the mound from the bullpen electrified the home crowd. Entering a 4–4 game, Johnson pitched the ninth, 10th, and 11th innings until he finally surrendered a run in the top of the 12th. But the Mariners scored twice on an Edgar Martinez double in their half of the inning to cap a dramatic ALDS victory.

Randy pitched well in two starts against the Indians in the 1995 ALCS, but Charlton was hammered in both games. Cleveland won the series in six games, denying Seattle its first trip to the World Series. Johnson won the Cy Young Award with an 18–2 record, 2.48 ERA and 294 strikeouts in just over 214 innings, then the best strikeout ratio in history. His .900 winning percentage was the second-highest in AL history behind Johnny Allen, who had gone 15–1 for Cleveland in 1937. Over the course of the season, lefties hit just .129 against him, while righties managed a .209 mark. Johnson remains the only Seattle pitcher to win a Cy Young.

The 1996 season was frustrating and painful for Johnson due to a back injury. After winning five games early in the year, he missed most of the season with a herniated disk. He returned to throw a few innings of middle relief but required surgery in September. The Mariners, fueled by 40-homer seasons from Griffey and Buhner plus a batting title from rookie shortstop Rodriguez, fell just short of the division title.

Johnson rebounded strongly in 1997 to post a stellar 20-4 record, an ERA of 2.28, and 291 strikeouts. Six times he struck out 14 or more in a game and twice he fanned 19. His ERA was under 2.00 most of the season and the only blemish on his season was a bruised middle finger suffered in August. Randy, however, finished second in a controversial Cy Young vote to Roger Clemens, who went 20-7 for the last-place Toronto Blue Jays. Johnson's dominant season left him with an overall record of 53-9 from May 1994 to October 1997, including a 16-game winning streak that fell one win short of the AL record. Seattle won the division as six Mariners cracked 20 or more homers, including Griffey's league-high 56. Behind Johnson, veterans Jamie Moyer and Jeff Fassero combined for 33 wins. In the ALDS, Randy was still bothered by his sore hand and went 0-2 as the Mariners were eliminated by the Baltimore Orioles.

Although Johnson was due to become a free agent at the end of the 1998 season, the Mariners' budget prevented them from making any serious contract extension offers. Seattle, quietly worried about his age and recent injury history, made little effort to keep him. When the team failed to contend in a weak division after four straight competitive seasons, Randy became frustrated and his record reflected it. He was 9-10 with a 4.33 ERA in July. On July 31, 1998, the Mariners traded Johnson at the deadline to the Houston Astros for Freddy García, Carlos Guillén, and a player to be named later.

The trade rejuvenated Randy. Suddenly in the thick of a pennant race, Johnson was the best pitcher in MLB over the last two months. He won 10 games and fired four straight shutouts in the Astrodome. In 11 starts, he went 10-1 with a microscopic 1.28 ERA, leading Houston to the playoffs. Despite only pitching for a third of a season in the National League, Randy finished 7th in NL Cy Young Award voting. He finished the year with a combined record of 19-11, an ERA of 3.28, and 329 strikeouts.

The Astros, winners of 102 games, started Johnson in the 1998 NLDS opener against San Diego. He pitched well enough to win, but Kevin Brown silenced the Houston bats in a 2-1 pitching duel. The teams split the next two games and Randy was again in a must-win situation. Once again, the high scoring Astro offense was limited to a run, this time by Sterling Hitchcock, and Houston was eliminated. Randy struck out 17 Padres in 14 innings of work with a 1.93 ERA, yet all he had to show for his efforts was a pair of losses.

With his outstanding August and September, Johnson priced himself out of the Houston budget and the Astros released him after the season. Randy signed for the 1999 season with the Arizona Diamondbacks, thanks to a four-year deal worth $52 million. Other suitors included the Rangers, Angels and Los Angeles Dodgers. The Jerry Colangelo-owned D-Backs were an expansion team created in 1998. Signing the 35-year-old Johnson turned out to be one of the best free agent coups in baseball history as Randy won the Cy Young Award in each of his four seasons. Free-spending Colangelo was quick to add talent to his new club as he signed Steve Finley, Tony Womack, Luis Gonzalez and Todd Stottlemyre to a roster that already featured veterans Matt Williams, Jay Bell and Andy Benes.

Under manager Buck Showalter, the Diamondbacks won 100 games and ran away with the NL West in 1999. Johnson led the team to the playoffs that year on the strength of a 17–9 record, a 2.48 ERA and 364 strikeouts. The numbers told only part of the story. The Arizona bullpen blew five leads, and in many of his defeats and no-decisions, the D-Backs failed to score more than two runs. Both Johnson and Pedro Martínez won 1999 Cy Young Awards, thus joining Gaylord Perry as the first pitchers to have won the award in both the American and National Leagues. Despite pitching more than 250 innings, Randy finished the season strong and erased all doubts about his age or durability. In the NLDS, the Wild Card Mets pecked away at him in the opening game and scored a shocking 8-4 triumph. New York won two of the next three, sending Arizona home.

The Diamondbacks failed to make the playoffs in 2000 despite the stretch-run addition of Curt Schilling from the Philadelphia Phillies and another awesome season from Randy. He went 19-7 with a 2.64 ERA and 347 strikeouts to claim his third Cy Young. He had been the clear favorite since April, when he won six times and gave up less than a run per game.

Arizona fired on all cylinders in 2001, when a full season of Schilling and Johnson gave the Diamondbacks baseball's most feared power pitching duo. The one-two purple punch combined for an amazing 90-24 record over the next two years, placing first and second in the NL in nearly every major pitching category. Johnson went 21-6 in 2001, with 250 innings pitched, a league-leading 2.49 ERA and 372 strikeouts. Again, he was an easy choice for the Cy Young, his fourth. The Diamondbacks also improved their offense, thanks to the additions of productive and popular veterans like Mark Grace and Reggie Sanders. Johnson struck out 20 batters in a game on May 8, 2001 against the Cincinnati Reds.

After winning the NL West title, the entire nation received its first opportunity to witness the shared brilliance of the two flamethrowers – a righty and a lefty – during the 2001 postseason. Schilling compiled a record of 3-0 with a 0.67 ERA and three complete games during the NL playoffs against the Cardinals and Braves. Meanwhile, Johnson went 2-1 including a 2-0 win over Atlanta, a three-hit shutout with 11 K's against Greg Maddux.

In only the fourth year of the franchise's existence, Johnson and Schilling carried Arizona to their first World Series appearance in 2001 against powerful New York. The Yankees were three-time defending MLB champions. Schilling threw smoke with a three-hitter win in Game 1, and Randy gave the D-Backs a two-game series advantage with a three-hit shutout in Game 2.

The Yankees, feeding off the emotions from New Yorkers after the 9/11 attacks, won all three games in the Bronx, each complete with late-inning drama. In two of the games, Arizona actually held the lead with two outs in the ninth. When the series returned to Arizona for Game 6, Johnson cruised to an easy 15-2 victory to force a Game 7. In the finale, Schilling was strong into the eighth, but left the game behind 2-1. Randy pitched a scoreless ninth and then watched from the dugout as the Diamondbacks did the impossible. They scored two runs against Mariano Rivera – the best closer in history – to win their first World Series championship.

Schilling went 1-0 in his three starts, compiling an ERA of 1.69 and striking out 26 batters in 21 innings of work, while allowing only 12 hits. Starting two games and entering another in relief, Johnson went 3-0 with a 1.04 ERA, while striking out 19 batters in 17 innings. He also allowed the Yankees just nine hits and tied a World Series record with three wins. The two aces were named co-winners of the World Series MVP Award. Schilling and Johnson also shared honors for the 2001 *Sports Illustrated* "Sportsmen of the Year."

In a freak accident during a 2002 spring training game against the Giants, Johnson threw a fastball that struck and killed a dove. The bird swooped across the infield just as Randy was releasing the ball. After being struck by the pitch, the bird landed dead amid a blanket of feathers. The official call was "no pitch."

The Diamondbacks defended their NL west title in 2002 with 98 wins. At age 38, Johnson had the best year of his brilliant career, capturing the Pitching Triple Crown. He led the league with 24 wins, 334 strikeouts, nine complete games, an .828 wining percentage and a 2.32 ERA. It was Johnson's fourth consecutive 300-strikeout season, also a record. He became the only pitcher in baseball history to post a 24–5 record. The numbers Johnson compiled 1999-2002 made him the most dominant left-handed pitcher in the game since Sandy Koufax.

Against the Cardinals in the '02 NLDS, the D-Backs seemed to lack focus. Randy was ambushed in Game 1, giving up five earned runs in six innings in a 12-2 blowout. When St. Louis topped Schilling 2-1 in Game 2, Arizona fans could feel the season slipping away. Two days later, Batista gave up four early runs and the Cardinals had swept Arizona out of the playoffs.

The large deals that Colangelo signed came back to bite the club in 2003, and the team started looking to cut expenses. The D-Backs were still competitive, winning 84 games but that wasn't nearly enough to catch the front-running Giants. The dominance displayed by the tandem of Johnson and Schilling came to an end in 2003 when Curt's arm problems limited him to 24 games. Randy underwent arthroscopic knee surgery in April and was not 100 percent until September, finishing just 6-8 and bringing to an end a spectacular six-year run of 120 wins and only 42 losses. Landing gently over his right knee, he was unable to snap his slider and lefties hit over .300 against him.

In 2004, Johnson went 16-14 for a punchless Arizona team. The D-Backs scored two or fewer runs in 17 of his 35 starts. Randy posted an ERA of 2.60 and a league-leading 290 strikeouts and, in the games where Arizona scored three or more runs, he was 13–2. As the D-Backs only won 51 games that year, he won 31.3 percent of his team's games – the highest for any starting pitcher since Steve Carlton's 45.8 percent in 1972.

On May 18, 2004, Johnson pitched the 17th perfect game in baseball history. At 40 years of age, he is the oldest perfect-game pitcher. Johnson struck out 13 on his way to a 2–0 win over Atlanta. The perfecto made him the fifth pitcher in MLB history to pitch a no-hitter in both leagues. On June 29, Randy struck out Jeff Cirillo of the Padres to become only the fourth MLB pitcher to reach 4,000 career strikeouts.

In 2005, New York sent pitchers Javier Vazquez and Brad Halsey, catcher Dioner Navarro and $9 million to Arizona for Johnson. He was 41, but 118-62 as a D-Back and one of the few who could match up with Boston's Schilling in a key game. Randy signed a $32 million, two-year deal.

Based in a big city for the first time in his career, Johnson faced new pressures and high expectations with the Yankees. His stay in New York got off to a rocky start after a street altercation with a photographer. "Get out of my face!" yelled an angry Johnson in a video clip broadcast nationwide. Randy later publicly apologized and then focused on baseball. He started on Opening Day for the Yankees in 2005, and the lefthander was a consistent winner (34-19) for New York over the next two seasons. He was 5–0 in '05 against the rival Red Sox and finished the season 17–8 with a 3.79 ERA and 211 strikeouts. In the '05 ALDS, Johnson had a disappointing outing in Game 3 against the Angels, allowing five runs in three innings. In Game

5, Johnson made an effective relief appearance but the Yankees were bounced from the playoffs.

In 2005, *The Sporting News* published a revised list of The 100 Greatest Baseball Players. Johnson did not make the original edition but with his career totals considerably higher and his 2001 World Series season taken into account, he was re-ranked at number 60.

Johnson won 17 games again in 2006 but suffered from back pain throughout the season. He was constantly "day to day" and his ERA of 5.00 was attributed to a herniated disk. In September, Randy started epidural anesthesia treatments to get ready for the playoffs. He started Game 3 of the ALDS against the surprising Detroit Tigers and allowed five runs. Kenny Rogers, meanwhile, shut out New York. Once again, Johnson did not deliver in the post-season for the Yankees and it was his last game in pinstripes.

The Yankees dealt Randy back to the Diamondbacks for the 2007 season for a package of five young players and prospects. He requested the trade after his brother passed away. The pressures of another year in New York, he felt, would be too much on top of this family tragedy. Johnson wanted to go home to his family in Phoenix. Unfortunately, he re-injured his back sliding in a June game. The pain had returned and this time, the herniated disk was removed entirely. His season was over. Suffering with injuries and lacking much of the velocity he once had on his fastball and slider, Johnson won a total of only 15 games for the Diamondbacks in 2007 and 2008. On June 3, 2008, Johnson struck out batter number 4,673, which surpassed Clemens for the number two spot on the all-time strikeout leaders list.

In December of 2008, Johnson signed a one-year deal with San Francisco for $8 million, with a possible $5 million in bonuses. On June 4, 2009, Randy became the 24th pitcher to reach 300 wins, beating the Washington Nationals (formerly the Montreal Expos) 5–1 in Washington, D.C. He became just the seventh left-hander to reach the 300 win milestone. On July 28, Johnson was placed on the disabled list with a torn rotator cuff, meaning he would not return until September, if at all. But on September 18, Johnson appeared against the Dodgers. At age 46, he was the second-oldest player in Major League Baseball, behind only Jamie Moyer of Philadelphia. He pitched in his last game October 4, 2009 against the Padres. On January 5, 2010, he announced his retirement from professional baseball.

Johnson finished his career second all-time in total strikeouts (4,875), 22nd in wins (303), and 57th in shutouts (37). He pitched two no-hitters, the second of which was a perfect game.

Over a 22-year career, Johnson played for six different teams. The 6-foot-10-inch power pitcher has been celebrated for having one of the most dominant fastballs in the game and was the second-tallest man ever to play in the major leagues. He regularly approached and occasionally exceeded 100 miles per hour during his prime. Randy's fastball, delivered from a tangle of arms and legs, is what struck fear into opposing hitters. It was "Mr. Snappy," that got them out. Johnson won the Cy Young Award five times, second only to Clemens' seven, and finished second in the balloting on three other occasions. The Big Unit led the league in strikeouts nine times, surpassing 300 six times. A 10-time all-star, he also had a league-best earned run average four times.

Throughout baseball history, the consensus among baseball experts has been that no pitcher taller than 6-4 or 6-5 could develop the necessary mechanics to be a consistent major league winner. Until age 30, Johnson's mediocre career supported that theory. For the rest of his career, he became the exception to the rule. In his later years, he became a control pitcher who just happens to have a 95-mph fastball. A slider, splitter and two-seamer developed in his late 30s gave him other weapons when he didn't have his best stuff. A gifted athlete whose intellect and competitiveness often conflicted, Randy got the most out of his ability and controlled his emotions enough to become the most dominant lefty since Koufax.

In 2010, Johnson threw out the ceremonial first pitch at the Mariners home opener at Safeco Field. Johnson and his wife Lisa have four children: Sammi (born 1994), Tanner (1996), Willow (1998), and Alexandria (1999). He also has a daughter from a previous relationship, Heather Renee Roszell (1989). The Johnsons are residents of Paradise Valley, Arizona.

Livermore children will get to grow up playing baseball on a diamond named after Johnson. A newly renovated field at May Nissen Park has been designated "Randy Johnson Junior Giants Field." Randy returned home for a dedication ceremony in 2009 at the field on Rincon Avenue and The Big Unit threw out the first pitch. The project held special meaning for Randy, as his legacy runs deep in his hometown. Johnson also helped fund the renovation of a 58-year-old field across from Marylin Avenue Elementary School – one of many schools suffering from budget cuts.

"When we signed Randy earlier this year, it was a natural connection. Wouldn't it be fantastic to do something in Livermore where you grew up? I know he is very excited about coming back," said Paul Giuliacci of the Giants Community Fund. The organization's flagship program is the Junior Giants, which sponsors baseball programs for underprivileged and under-served children.

Johnson guest-starred in a *Simpsons* episode aired in 2006. Randy appeared in the movie *Little Big League*, and also in a Right Guard commercial where he fired dodgeballs. Johnson appeared in several Nike commercials in 1998 and made commercial appearances for *MLB 2K9* with teammate Tim Lincecum, and for GEICO insurance. Johnson is co-owner of Alice Cooperstown, a restaurant in Phoenix. A 22-inch hot dog is available there called "The Big Unit." In 2001, Randy attended a U2 concert in Phoenix. Bono brought him onstage and Johnson circled the area with the recently captured World Series trophy.

One of the most intimidating pitchers to ever take the mound, Randy Johnson dominated opposing batters with an arsenal of pitches that included a blazing fastball and a wicked slider that fooled even elite hitters. One of only two pitchers to win five Cy Young Awards, Randy's 303 victories and 4,875 strikeouts have some experts ranking him in the Top 10 among baseball's all-time pitching greats. No pitcher in history struck out more batters per nine innings pitched (10.61) than Johnson. He defeated every major-league team at least once. Former Seattle manager Lou Piniella once proclaimed that "He is the number one dominating pitcher in baseball. I don't even know who number two is."

52

CC SABATHIA

Bankrupt and battered, the city of Vallejo certainly has its share of problems. A weak local economy and a recently slashed police force caused increases in unemployment, crime and downtown decay. But one of its native sons, a larger-than-life baseball pitcher headed for the Hall of Fame, has become one of its saviors. His name is CC Sabathia.

Carsten Charles Sabathia, Jr. was born on July 21, 1980 in Vallejo, the only child of Margie and Carsten Sabathia, Sr. His grandmother called him "CC," because his full name was too difficult to pronounce, and the nickname stuck. His mother Margie worked as an Air Force telephone operator. Carsten Sr., also known as "Corky," worked at Mare Island Naval Shipyard and was a big sports fan. His all-time hero was boxer Muhammad Ali. CC's father loved to describe Ali's championship matches in vivid detail for his toddler son.

CC's size and athletic skills were in his genes. A high school basketball and softball player herself, his mom Margie is six feet tall and her father was 6-feet-9. Sabathia men on both sides of the family were big, so there was little question that CC would one day outgrow his classmates. He was a talented neighborhood athlete and regularly competed in baseball, basketball and football. CC remembers first playing baseball around age four. He had an instant passion for the game which still burns bright. The kids Sabathia grew up with in the neighborhood played on the same youth teams with him all the way into high school.

Sabathia attended Loma Vista Elementary in North Vallejo and grew up rooting for the Oakland A's and the San Francisco Giants. When CC was in second grade, his teacher asked her students to name their dream job, excepting sports. CC still wrote *baseball player* and wouldn't consider anything else.

Carsten Sr. taught their only child how to catch and throw and hit, converted him from righty to lefty, coached his Little League teams and took him to pro games in the Bay Area including the Raiders, A's, Warriors, and Giants. His dad had a softer approach – every month or so he didn't show up for work at the shipyard or his other jobs and pulled CC from school so they could work out in the batting cages, just the two of them.

At an early age, Margie emphasized the importance of family and respect. With strong family support and confidence in himself, Sabathia knew he could accomplish great things. "Be confident" she always told him, "but be humble too." CC appreciated having a mother who understood sports and was able to help teach him both fundamentals and how to play with good sportsmanship. "She always made sure I was humble and appreciated the game."

Margie worked the night shift as a telephone switchboard operator at Travis Air Force Base so she could attend all of CC's daytime games. If he cussed or so much as slammed his helmet after popping up, she was on him quicker than any coach. "I'm a sports person," says Margie. "I was tough on CC but I was his strongest supporter, too. I was so young when I had him that he was like a best friend as well as a son."

"What Margie says, goes," says Robert Rigsby, who grew up attending church with her. "I love her to death, and I will never cross her in a million years." His wife is a judge. "I'm afraid of two people on this planet," Rigsby said. "My wife, who can put me in jail, followed by Margie Sabathia."

The family lived in a tough area of Vallejo known as "The Crest," a part of town made famous in the music world by native rappers Mac Dre and Mac Mall, who both referenced it in songs. Delinquents cruised up streets like Gateway Drive to buy drugs and homeless people were commonplace. Margie raised her son with a firm hand, knowing that he would avoid the trappings of growing up in a tough neighborhood. "I was pretty tough on CC," Margie says. "I knew I had to be."

When CC grew up in the late 1980s and early 1990s, the neighborhood was no paradise but the local economy had neighbors working and Mare Island was still going strong. The Crest was known more for a hardworking family town rather than the decaying crime-ridden area it has become. Fathers still coached baseball and were part of their sons' lives. "The Little League field where we went to play used to be full of fathers," said Dave Bernstine, a baseball coach at Vallejo High. "Now you see one or two."

Sabathia is a product of the Major League Baseball youth program called Rebuilding Baseball in Inner Cities (RBI). CC rooted for both the Giants and A's and his favorite players were Will Clark, Robby Thompson, Matt Williams, Jose Canseco, Mark McGwire, Dave Stewart, Dave Parker and Carney Lansford. When Barry Bonds came to town in 1993, 12-year-old CC embraced the slugger as his new hero, along with Ken Griffey Jr.

CC was the biggest kid in the North Vallejo Little League, a lefty pitcher so lethal he rarely gave up hits and fans called him "The Secret Weapon." Margie took a keen interest in her son's baseball career. She was so set on CC becoming a pitcher that she invested in catching gear for herself. But Sabathia had plenty to learn about sportsmanship back then, his mom told *Sports Illustrated*. One day, another 10-year-old about CC's size crushed a home run off Sabathia. He pulled the bill of his cap down over his eyes and started crying on the mound. Margie said she needed to take advantage of a teaching moment.

"I said, 'Are you crying? Are you serious, dude?'" Margie said in the SI article. Because he can't strike out every kid he faces? Because he gave up a hit or a run? No, Margie wasn't going to put up with that attitude. "Dude, please," she'd say to her son at inning's end. He would almost hear her thinking, Who do you think you are? You're that good? That untouchable? She didn't care if he got hit hard for six runs, so long as he didn't act as if he couldn't take the bad with the good. Dude, she'd say, there's always someone out there as good as you. You're going to get hit. Crying? Please!

"She came to the dugout and made me ride my bike home," CC remembered, smiling. "That was the end of the crying," Sabathia's mother said. "He wanted to win so bad, but I was always making sure he knew we were out there to have fun. And once he figured that out, he was fine. I tease him about that all the time now."

Margie would strap on the catcher's gear so her son could throw a few more pitches after practices were over. She always carried his birth certificate during tournaments because opposing coaches believed her son was too old to play. "My baby's been big his whole life," Margie said. "All of a sudden in kindergarten, he shot up. He constantly kept me buying shoes."

"We talk about everything," CC says. "She understands the game big-time. I've been able to talk about sports with her – all sports – since I was 12."

By age 12, CC was throwing gas; one of his fastballs shattered a kid's elbow. Margie, after a few fireballs caught her in the palm of her catcher's glove, said "Dude, I'm done. Mom's done. I cannot catch you anymore. You're past me." But then CC was just bigger and better than his peers, a lefthander ahead of all others.

Sabathia's parents divorced when he was 13. Sometimes couples break up and actually get along better. Margie and Corky, she says "became the best of friends once we split." Corky and CC didn't go to sporting events together anymore. But Corky moved in with Grandma Ethel, and since CC had been going to his grandmother's every morning his whole life, things seemed nearly normal. He had begun to grow in eighth grade and stood 6-3 as a freshman. He was throwing so hard and had grown so tall that pro scouts started hearing stories about a man-child breaking 90 mph.

Coaches in three sports at Vallejo High couldn't wait to get their hands on Sabathia in 1994. Vic Wallace, who ran the basketball team, turned him into one of the Bay Area's best power forwards. CC led the Apaches to within one win of the state championship. As a senior, CC had a great season for the Vallejo football squad, which made the state semifinals. He made All-Conference as a tight end and was heavily recruited by UCLA and the University of Hawaii. He signed a letter of intent to UH, but with an agreement that he might opt for baseball.

CC once got a D in history his sophomore year and Margie pulled him off the basketball team for the season. "He decided to try me and I pulled him," Margie says. "That's the one time he tested me. The coaches weren't happy with me but that's the way it was. I love sports, but my whole thing was school, school, school. I wanted CC to go to college."

CC even moved in with Grandma and his dad for a while in high school, at Margie's urging. But Corky had a new job at the nearby Concord Naval Weapons Station and something made him start to detach from the family. He showed up at fewer and fewer of CC's games and didn't drop by football practice like the other fathers. "They would tell my dad what I was doing," CC says, "but he wouldn't come see me. I didn't understand that."

By his junior year, CC was Vallejo's three-sport force. He was 6-foot-6 and 245 pounds, but always a gentle giant, and always ready to work hard. People were drawn to him by his sports exploits but stayed because of his humility. That junior year he met Amber Carter, a sophomore cheerleader. Supposedly, she went home and told her basketball player brother Joe, "CC's going to be your brother-in-law."

There's a huge, towering eucalyptus tree at VHS over a row of classroom buildings well beyond the right-field fence. The fence is 314 feet down the line, and the tree is another 150 feet beyond that. People who were at one game say that Sabathia once hit a ball that not only reached the tree but flew into the top of it somewhere, never to be seen again.

"Someone from Cleveland called and wanted to know what kind of kid he was," recalls Principal Saroyan. "I said, 'Maybe this sums it up best: if he was available, I'd take him as my son.' In every way I can think of, CC deserves everything he's getting. Even with all the money and everything, I can't ever see (him) getting a big head. If he did, even now his mom would pop him one."

During his senior season at Vallejo High, Sabathia posted a mark of 6–0 with a 0.77 ERA and 82 strikeouts in 46.2 innings. He threw 95 miles per hour. He also played first base and left field and hit .586, often as the cleanup hitter. Heading into the 1998 draft, CC was the top high school prospect in Northern California according to *Baseball America*.

The Apaches went 32-2 and lost in the state semifinals. Grandma Ethel – CC's "second mother" – had died in February, and he had spent most of the season depressed. But he didn't cry after the loss. Sabathia sat in a corner, smiling, and said, "Come on, guys, we had a great year. We did our best. This is the most fun I've ever had."

Cleveland Indians scout Paul Cogan followed Sabathia relentlessly, even attending some of his football and basketball games. There were times Cogan thought Sabathia might be even better as a first baseman and many in baseball figured he would sign with a National League team because of his slugging talent. Sabathia entered the 1998 MLB amateur draft after high school. His overwhelming size – 6-foot-7, 300 pounds – scared off some teams. A two-way player in high school, he was compared to Dave Parker as a hitter and to Vida Blue as a pitcher, but the

Indians felt his upside was highest as a starter. He already threw 95-98 MPH and snapped a good curve, but reports were mixed about his control and pitching aptitude.

Sabathia was selected by Indians with the 20th pick of the first round. The first overall pick was outfielder Pat Burrell of Bellarmine High. The Tribe had come within a couple of outs of winning the World Series the previous fall. Margie and CC had hired two relatively raw agents and negotiations crashed over the signing bonus. The agents told an anxious Sabathia to be patient. With nearly a month missed and CC desperate to pitch, Margie and CC sat on her bed and agreed on a plan. Margie phoned the Indians, bypassing the angry agents. When Cleveland general manager John Hart came to the phone and asked what it would take to get the deal done, Margie said $1.5 million. Hart responded with $1.3. Margie said, "We'll take it."

After signing his first pro contract, Sabathia's first minor-league stop was the Indians' rookie-league team in Burlington, North Carolina. The 17-year-old lefty pitched 18 innings, striking out 35. He made five starts for Burlington in the Appalachian League, posting a 4.50 ERA with 35 strikeouts and 20 hits allowed in 18 innings. He was a little disappointed, however, that the Indians didn't want to use him as a hitter.

"He's very down to earth and he really feels blessed to have the ability he has," said Burlington pitching coach Carl Willis. "He likes it to be fun and he enjoys his teammates. Even today, with his stature in the game as one of the best if not the best pitcher, there's not a huge ego that goes with that and that's why you see people gravitate to him."

In January 1999, CC picked his father up from a doctor's appointment and he told his son what Margie had known for two years: Carsten Sr. was HIV-positive. He needed CC to help take care of medical costs. "I never asked him how he got it," CC says. "I felt a lump in my throat, but I didn't cry then. I cried later on. I just prayed I could have him as long as possible."

In the minors, Sabathia possessed a mixture of great stuff, command problems and injury issues. He missed part of the 1999 season with an elbow injury. CC ended up pitching six games for Mahoning Valley in the New York-Penn League, posting a 1.83 ERA and 27 strikeouts in 20 innings. He appeared three times for Low-A Columbus with a 1.08 ERA and 20 K's in 17 innings. He pitched in seven games for High-A Kinston of the Carolina League (5.34, 29, 32). Sabathia's velocity hovered between 90 and 94 MPH but he had major command problems at Kinston. There were also complaints that he was too overweight and was destined to get hurt. CC was a combined 5–3 in 16 starts, with a 3.29 ERA and notched more than a strikeout per inning at each stop. Opponents managed just a .198 average against him. Mechanical refinements got his fastball back into the 94-98 MPH range, he continued to sharpen his curveball, and worked in an improved changeup. CC's personality blossomed as he gained a reputation as intelligent and very confident on the mound.

The following summer, the 20-year-old CC finished up his minor league apprenticeship with Class AA Akron. Corky drove out with Margie and helped their son get settled. CC spent the first half of 2000 with Kinston before moving up to Akron. He answered some doubts in 2000, posting a 3.54 ERA with 69 strikeouts in 56 innings for Kinston, then a 3.59 ERA with 90 Ks in 90 innings for Akron. CC had another solid season, pitching in the Futures Games in Atlanta and starting for the Indians in the exhibition Hall of Fame Game against the Arizona Diamondbacks. He was rated Cleveland's No. 1 prospect and the No. 2 prospect overall in the Eastern League.

In 2000, Sabathia was selected for the 28-man United States Olympic Team roster. He appeared in one pre-Olympic tournament game in Sydney, Australia, but was not on the official 24-man, gold medal-winning roster because he was called up by the Indians.

At the end of the 2000 season, CC went home to Vallejo and for the first time since he was 13, he and his father went to a Giants game. They didn't watch much. Instead, they walked the concourses checking out the new ballpark, the opposite of blustery Candlestick Park. "Seven years," Sabathia says. "We were just hanging out. It was pretty cool."

Sabathia entered spring training in 2001 with an outside shot at the major league rotation, but many people felt he needed AAA experience to sharpen his command. That didn't happen – he made the big team in spring training. Living up to the hype of his top-ranked prospect billing, CC exploded on the MLB scene in 2001. At the age of 20, he became the Tribe's most valuable starter, going 17–5 with 171 strikeouts. He joined Bartolo Colon and Dave Burba to give Cleveland a starting staff strong enough to win the AL Central Division.

In his first big league start, on April 8, 2001, Sabathia went 5 2/3 innings, allowed three runs and struck out three. He didn't get the win – that came April 13 at Detroit

– but the Indians beat Baltimore 4-3. His rookie command did wobble at times, but his stuff was so good that he was still effective. It didn't take long for Cleveland management to recognize what they had in their young lefty.

The youngest player in the majors, Sabathia led the AL in hits per nine innings (7.44), was third in win percentage (.773), fourth in strikeouts per nine innings (8.53), sixth in wins, and seventh in strikeouts (171). He finished second in the voting for AL Rookie of the Year, behind Ichiro Suzuki.

In the ALDS, CC started Game 3 against Seattle with the series tied 1-1. After walking in a run in the first inning, he dominated the rest of the way and the Tribe hitters torched the Mariners in a 17–2 victory. Unfortunately, the Indians scored just three more runs in the series and bowed out in five games. As soon as the series ended, GM Mark Shapiro locked up CC with a five-year deal. His success as a rookie was instrumental in helping the Indians reach the playoffs. There was no doubt at the end of the season that Sabathia was in the majors to stay. Over the next five seasons, CC consistently put up double-digit wins and strong strikeout totals.

An instant star rookie with the Indians in 2001, Sabathia's rewards started immediately: a big new contract, seats at a heavyweight title fight, and rumors linking him to tennis star Serena Williams. Amber, then a student at San Diego State, wanted to transfer and had been accepted to Cleveland State but when she heard CC's hesitant reaction, she knew what it meant. Young rich man, party time and feeling free. She stayed in San Diego and broke up with him. He was partying every night in Cleveland wearing flashy jewelry, something he had never done before. Margie visited him in May 2002, didn't like what she saw and sat him down just before she left. "Dude, I'm not feeling good," she said. "You're going out too much: You need to slow your roll."

A week later, after midnight on May 17, a phone call woke Margie out of a dead sleep. She picked it up, and there was CC's voice, trembling like a scared schoolboy. "Mom, there was a gun," he said repeatedly. "They put a gun to my head."

On May 17, 2002, Sabathia and a cousin were robbed at gunpoint in a downtown Cleveland hotel. CC lost more than $44,000 in cash and jewelry. He was shaken by the robbery, though others in his life later say he used it as a growing experience. "It was totally my fault," Sabathia told reporters the next day. "I put myself in this situation. There is no one to blame but me... I never had a gun pointed at me before. I put my life in their hands." CC started a day later, saying he wanted to use a few hours on the mound to clear his head, and allowed three hits and two runs in six innings against the Royals in a no-decision.

Earlier that night, Sabathia and his cousin Jomar Connors had gone to WISH, a nightclub in Cleveland's Warehouse District, for the birthday party of a local model. Also attending with them were former Cleveland State basketball stars Damon Stringer and Jamaal Harris. Sabathia was wearing $15,000 diamond earrings, a $26,000 necklace with a platinum cross and a $60,000 Rolex watch, plus he was carrying $3,200 in cash. Stringer left with Harris and retrieved a 9-mm pistol.

Sabathia and Connors left the party too, but in a hotel lobby CC noticed his watch was missing. Connors went back up to the room to search for it, when Stringer and Harris returned and showed Sabathia their gun. They forced him into the elevator and to the room, where they ordered CC and Connors to lie on the floor and picked them clean. Hotel security cameras captured Stringer and Harris leaving the building at 4:03 a.m. Both were arrested within days and pleaded guilty to aggravated robbery. Stringer would serve 25 months. Harris, who had CC's diamond in his ear when he was arrested, did 19 months.

The day after the robbery Sabathia publicly berated himself for having been in that situation, but by then he had already taken corrective measures. Just minutes after the incident, before he called his mother, he had dialed Amber and proposed. "If you were here, none of this would've happened," he said. "Let's just get married."

A week later, Amber packed up her things and headed for Cleveland. CC's mother and father had come in the day after the robbery, and CC hadn't let them out of his sight. Margie left after a week. Corky moved in and stayed for good. "That was it," Sabathia says. "He lived with me until the day he passed away." The robbery, CC believes, "was really a blessing in disguise. To have a gun to your head is scary, but it put everything in order. I had gotten the [baseball] contract and I was young, 21, and I felt like I was on top of the world. I had all this, and then I saw how quickly it could be taken away from me."

After his stunning rookie season, Sabathia faced high expectations in 2002. It wasn't until mid-season that he relaxed and began to meet them. With the exception of a near no-hitter in April, CC got pounded early in the year. He rediscovered the magic in his final 11 starts, winning seven times with an ERA below 3.00. His final numbers were unimpressive – 88 walks and a 4.37 ERA – but he won 13 times and fanned 149 in 210 innings. Cleveland struggled to score and sank to 74 wins.

CC continued his solid pitching into the 2003 season. He went five or more innings in all but one of his 30 starts and managed to notch 13 wins against only nine losses despite poor run support. His 141 strikeouts and 3.60 ERA ranked among the league's best. Sabathia threw the fastest fastball in the AL in 2003, averaging 93.9 miles per hour. He was also named to the AL All-Star team for the first time.

He and Amber were married in June 2003, and as CC was traveling to his first All-Star game, Margie called to say that Corky had been found to have terminal stomach cancer. Amber was pregnant and due in the fall. Corky lived through the summer and summoned the strength to fly to Cleveland in September, arriving exhausted. But he stood strong enough to stand outside the delivery-room door to hold the newborn boy, Carsten Charles Sabathia III. Then Corky flew back to Vallejo and, that December, died at age 47.

That winter, CC's weight rose well north of 300 pounds and he started thinking more seriously about his body. He drank two dozen cups of water each day. He hired a dietician and personal chef to guide him and began working with a strength coach. He dropped 15 pounds.

In 2004, CC's uncle Aaron Berhel died of a heart attack at 53. Then in June, Nathan, Aaron's 25-year-old son who had played ball with CC while growing up, severed an artery at a party in Vallejo and bled to death on the street. Sabathia viewed the body, pitched the next day and got the win. But for the rest of the 2004 season and into 2005, Sabathia carried images of his dearly departed with him to the mound. He wore a black rubber band on his wrist for his dad and had RIP NB stitched into his glove. He grew more disturbed by umpire calls. He screamed into his glove, overthrew—and got hit hard. "I'm going out there every single game," he says, "and pressing: I might throw a no-hitter today! I'm going to throw 100 mph! I'm doing this for Nathan, I'm doing this for my dad, I'm doing this for everybody. It was draining."

After five straight losses, Sabathia changed his mechanics. He began throwing a slider. And for the first time in a year, he gave himself permission to move on. "Something clicked, and I thought, I don't need to do this for them," CC said. "They're up there watching? Let them enjoy it. Have fun and do what you do. They wouldn't want me to pitch each game for them; that's not even how our relationships worked. My whole attitude—everything—changed."

The 2004 Indians retooled themselves around a group of young hitters including Travis Hafner, Victor Martinez, Grady Sizemore and Casey Blake. They won 89 games but fell short of a playoff berth. Sabathia had a disappointing season. After riding a 5–4 first-half record to an All-Star berth, he never really improved. He finished 11–10 with a 4.12 ERA. Fortunately, Cliff Lee and Jake Westbrook blossomed, giving the Tribe two more reliable starters. Though still young, CC was now in his pitching prime.

Amber and CC purchased a new home in nearby Fairfield in 2004. The property featured the Fireball Lounge, a home theater with multiple flat screens, recliners and state of the art sound. The covered cabana patio had a fireplace with ceiling fans and heat lamps. The pool featured a waterfall and a grotto with a hot tub. The project took about two years – just in time for MTV to film a segment of "Cribs."

In April 2005, Sabathia signed a two-year, $17.75 million deal with the Indians. He finished that season by going 10-1 with a 2.24 ERA over the last eight weeks. This marked his fifth straight season of 10 or more wins to start his career. He again threw the fastest heater in the AL in 2005, averaging 94.7 miles per hour. The Indians went 20–11 in his starts. Cleveland won 93 games but just missed the playoffs after a great September run.

Ready for the Indians to take the next step, Cleveland fans were disappointed in 2006. The club played inconsistently, sank below .500, and finished far out of the playoff race. Sabathia, 12–11 despite shoddy run support, had a breakthrough season in which he recorded a career low 3.22 ERA, third in the AL. Sabathia led the league in complete games, shutouts, and was eighth in strikeouts with 172. Most notably, he cut his walk totals by more than 20 from the previous year and by more than 50 from his rookie year. With fewer base runners, Sabathia was able to stay as aggressive as ever on the mound. With his excellent stuff, the majors took notice in 2006 that CC was now a complete pitcher.

When Sabathia took the mound in 2007, he pitched with a new confidence. He won with and without his best stuff and shrugged off the little mishaps that occur over the course of a long season. Focused completely on baseball, CC cruised to victories in his first five starts. After a poor outing against the hometown A's, he started another four-game win streak. His control was impeccable, and he was untouchable with two strikes. Sabathia was a workhorse, leading the league in starts and innings pitched and finishing the year with a career-high 19 wins, 3.21 ERA and 209 strikeouts. On May 21, CC recorded the 1,000th strikeout of his career, fanning Ichiro, the man who beat him out for the '01 Rookie of the Year award. Sabathia was the youngest lefty since Fernando Valenzuela and the youngest AL pitcher since Roger Clemens to reach the milestone.

The Indians won 96 games and captured the 2007 AL Central title as Grady Sizemore, Victor Martinez and Hafner had huge years at the plate. On September 28, Sabathia notched his 100th career win in his final start of the season. He became the youngest pitcher since Greg Maddux in 1993 to reach 100 wins. Only three 300-game winners were younger than Sabathia at the time of their 100th win - Maddux, Christy Mathewson and Walter Johnson.

The postseason began with a win for Sabathia, as he beat the Yankees in Game 1 of the AL Division Series, 12–3. He was not sharp, allowing a leadoff homer to Johnny Damon and laboring to throw strikes. With 114 pitches and six walks, he barely survived the required five innings to qualify for the win. The Indians wrapped up the series in four games. That gave CC had plenty of rest before Cleveland faced Boston in the AL Championship Series.

Sabathia and Josh Beckett hooked up in Game 1 of the '07 ALCS. The Tribe drew first blood on a Hafner home run, but by the fifth inning, CC was out of gas and out of the game, having yielded eight runs. Cleveland rebounded from the blowout loss and won the next three games. With a chance to close out Boston and send the Indians to the World Series for the first time since 1997, Sabathia again pitched poorly, allowing 10 hits and four runs in six innings in a 7-1 loss. Boston took the next two and went on to win the World Series title.

Sabathia won the AL Cy Young Award, the *Sporting News* Pitcher of the Year, the Warren Spahn Award, and the Players Choice Award for outstanding AL pitcher. CC became just the second Indian to win the Cy Young, following Gaylord Perry. Sabathia received 19-of-28 first-place votes to beat Boston's Beckett, the only major-leaguer to win 20 games during the season. Sabathia was also the first African-American pitcher to win the award since Dwight Gooden in 1985 and the first in the AL since Vida Blue in 1971. "Since that point?" said Shapiro, "He's been the most dominant pitcher in the big leagues."

With Sabathia and Lee leading the 2008 rotation plus an abundance of young talent on the roster, Cleveland fans had every reason to believe the Indians would rule the AL Central for a long time. But during another long, disappointing season, the Indians were unable to get anything going. They finished 81–81, a distant third in the division. CC began the 2008 season with a 6–8 record and a 3.83 ERA in 18 starts. He was leading the AL in strikeouts (123) while ranking second in innings (122.1) and tied for second in complete games (3). Despite the strong performances, the out of contention Indians could no longer afford to keep the All-Star lefty. With CC an impending free agent, the Indians sought to move him.

An in-season trade in July shifted the balance of power in the National League as Sabathia was traded to the Milwaukee Brewers for Matt LaPorta, Michael Brantley, Zach Jackson and Rob Bryson. During his press conference, Sabathia made it known to the assembled members of the media that he would prefer his name to be spelled "CC" rather than "C.C." On July 30, 2008, Sabathia took out a large $12,870 ad in the sports section of Cleveland's daily newspaper, *The Plain Dealer*. The ad, signed by Sabathia, his wife Amber, and his family read: "Thank you for 10 great years ... You've touched our lives with your kindness, love and generosity. We are forever grateful! It's been a privilege and an honor!"

The change of scenery did Sabathia a world of good. In Milwaukee, CC bolstered a pitching rotation which featured All-Star Ben Sheets, Jeff Suppan and Yovani Gollardo. Over the next three months, he posted an 11–2 mark and almost single-handedly pitched the Brewers into the playoffs. CC finished with a 17–10 record, 2.70 ERA and a career-best 251 strikeouts, trailing only the Giants' Tim Lincecum for the major league lead. Sabathia pitched three complete games in his first four starts with the Brewers, winning all four and leading Milwaukee to their first playoff appearance in 26 years.

CC's best performance came against the Pirates in August. Pittsburgh's only hit was a check-swing dribbler that CC bobbled when he attempted a bare-handed pickup. The play was ruled a hit, denying him a no-hitter. Sabathia also pitched a four-hitter against the Cubs to win 3–1 in the final game of the season, clinching a playoff spot for the Brewers. It was CC's 10th complete game of the year, the most by any pitcher in a single season since Randy Johnson threw 12 in 1999.

Before the 2008 postseason, Sabathia said he thought he'd be calmer in the playoffs this time. "Last year, I went into the playoffs thinking I had to throw no-hitters," he said. "That's why you saw me pressing a lot." The new outlook didn't help his results. Starting Game 2 for the Brewers in the NLDS against the Philadelphia Phillies, Sabathia didn't get out of the fourth inning, allowing five runs, six hits and four walks. His career postseason ERA ballooned to 7.92.

Although only in the National League for half a season, Sabathia finished sixth in the voting for the 2008 NL MVP award, behind Albert Pujols, Ryan Howard, Ryan Braun, Manny Ramirez, and Lance Berkman. CC had the most effective slider among major league starting pitchers. When batters swung at his pitches, they failed to make any contact 28 percent of the time, the highest percentage among '08 MLB starters.

During a Brewers series with the Cubs, Sabathia flew former high school coach Abe Hobbs into Chicago. He still considers Hobbs a second father and the man that "saved all of us" by showing boys in the Crest not just baseball but also to understand the work that excellence demands. Hobbs's oldest son Luke grew up around CC and is severely autistic. In Chicago, Abe and CC talked baseball and reminisced about a trip they'd made to Wrigley Field and Comiskey Park when CC was 14. Sabathia casually asked him about a treatment machine called a "hug box," effective in calming autistic patients. At $5,000, the cost was more than Hobbs could afford. "I got back from Chicago, and the machine was at my house," Hobbs said. "CC didn't mention it."

Following the 2008 season, Sabathia was the prime free agent in baseball. The Brewers, along with the Boston Red Sox and Anaheim Angels, tried valiantly to sign CC but all lost out to the New York Yankees, who signed Sabathia to one of the richest contracts in baseball history. Sabathia was 28 and had won 117 games, the most for any current pitcher his age. Yankees GM Brian Cashman had to have him. He offered seven years at $161 million, $60 million more than the Brewers or Angels. It was MLB's new standard for an offer you can't refuse. CC heard from Yankee fan LeBron James and Derek Jeter admitted he spoke to Sabathia about what it's like to play in New York. "He's asked questions about us," Jeter said. The two were friendly from playing against each other and meeting at All-Star games.

Now that the 2008 season proved that Sabathia played to win, he decided that a chance at winning a championship and the largest contract for a pitcher in MLB history was an unbeatable combination. CC said about his decision, "[The Yankees] got the best players, and they're committed; they always get what they need. If you really want to win, why wouldn't you come here? And once I couldn't answer that...."

In 2009, Sabathia made the move to the game's largest stage in New York. The Yankees also acquired A.J. Burnett and Mark Teixeira to fortify a roster that had failed to make the playoffs for the first time since the mid-1990s. Manager Joe Girardi announced that Sabathia would be the Opening Day starter and the starter for the home opener at brand new Yankee Stadium. In the season opener, Sabathia had a sub-par day against Baltimore. He was pulled after 4.1 innings, allowing eight hits, six runs, five walks, and zero strikeouts.

Sabathia found his groove as the season progressed. He won 19 games, becoming the ace that the Yankees so desperately needed. Another valuable CC contribution was his friendly, relaxed attitude in the clubhouse. Along with Burnett and newcomer Nick Swisher, he loosened things up during a year when the team was pressured to make it back to the postseason. Sabathia won the opening game of the ALDS against the Minnesota Twins, and New York went on to sweep the series. Next, CC notched two wins against the Angels in the ALCS, winning the series MVP award. He struck out seven in eight innings and allowed just one run in Game 1, a 4–1 victory. He returned to the mound in Game 4 and dominated on three days rest, as the Yanks won 10–1. They closed out the Angels in six games.

Sabathia started Game 1 against the Phillies in the 2009 World Series. He didn't have his best stuff, but managed to go seven innings and surrendered just two runs against the tough Philadelphia lineup. Both came on solo home runs by Chase Utley. Lee, CC's former teammate and good buddy, was the star, going the distance in a 6-1 Phillies win. Sabathia returned to the hill in Game 4, again on three days rest. He pitched into the seventh and left with the lead, only to see Joba Chamberlain taken deep by Pedro Feliz. The Yankees responded with three runs off closer Brad Lidge in the ninth for a 7-4 win and a 3-1 lead in the series. New York dropped Game 5 but jumped on Pedro Martinez early in Game 6, building a 7-3 lead. It ended, of course, with Rivera on the hill. CC celebrated his first World Series championship with the exuberance of a little leaguer.

Sabathia won his first championship ring with the Yankees, finishing 19–8 with a 3.37 ERA. He finished fourth in the AL Cy Young Award voting behind Zack Greinke, Felix Hernandez, and Justin Verlander. CC was third among AL hurlers with a 3.37 ERA while opposing batters hit .232 against him.

Sabathia's PitCCh In Foundation is a national nonprofit 501c3 organization started by CC and Amber in 2009 to enrich the lives of inner city youth through educational and athletic activities. Annually, PitCCh In conducts special events in Sabathia's hometown of Vallejo as well as the New York metropolitan area to encourage building of character and values CC was raised with. These include finding your own way as individuals by working hard, doing well in school, and taking advantage of learning opportunities, after-school programs, community sports and recreational programs.

In November 2009, Vallejo welcomed home Sabathia with an awards dinner and countless hugs. Sabathia returned the sentiment by delivering Thanksgiving turkeys to needy families, playing catch with local kids and helping raise money for programs the bankrupt city has slashed in recent months. Vallejo honored Sabathia at the annual Mayor's Image dinner today, a fundraiser for the local senior center and youth programs.

"Everybody here loves CC," said Tony Hodges, president of North Vallejo Little League, where Sabathia learned to play baseball. "His smile, his leadership – it's infectious. He can ride around here and he'll never get hassled."

Life in the Crest has steadily gotten worse since the government closed Mare Island in 1996. There's hardly money for rent—never mind sports fees—and few people care about youth baseball anymore. In 2009, thieves broke into the North Vallejo Little League office, stole 150 uniforms and the fund-raising food and candy, trashed the computers and trophies and tore down photos of alums like Sabathia. "It's not the same city," says CC. "A lot of closed businesses, a lot of my friends out of work. I feel like there's something I should do ... but I don't know what."

Facing a $16 million deficit, Vallejo in 2008 became the largest municipality in California to declare bankruptcy. Though Sabathia makes millions, there seems to be little resentment of his good fortune in Vallejo, because CC hasn't made the same mistakes as other pro athletes. He doesn't big-time his hometown with limos and fur coats. Each winter he's seen ducking into Vallejo High basketball games or working out with the school's baseball team. He walks in the annual Martin Luther King Day parade with his family.

Once he signed his Yankees contract in December, Sabathia stepped up his community involvement. He met with Vallejo High athletic director Tami Madson, football coach Mike Wilson, and school board member Hazel Wilson, and told them he wanted to supply the football, basketball and baseball teams with new uniforms — a cost Madson estimates at $100,000, more if footwear is included. Then Sabathia turned to Hazel and asked her to set up two "Charlie Hustle" college scholarships in memory of his cousin Nathan.

With Margie serving as his local point person, Sabathia also pledged more than 400 backpacks, each filled with supplies, to the kids at his elementary school, Loma Vista. "I also want to do a baseball academy, a Boys & Girls Club–type thing in north Vallejo, with indoor fields. Have a bus pick up kids from each elementary school, have them come do homework for 90 minutes, then the rest is baseball," he says.

Ten days into the 2010 season, Sabathia took a no-hitter into the eighth inning. With two out, former teammate Kelly Shoppach ripped a single to left field, ending the no-hit bid. On July 4, he earned his fourth All-Star selection, his first as a Yankee. On August 22, Sabathia recorded his 16th consecutive quality start, breaking a tie with Ron Guidry for the longest streak in franchise history.

Through the All-Star break in 2010, Sabathia did not let up. He closed the season with eight straight wins in eight consecutive starts to tie Tampa Bay's David Price for the AL lead in wins at 12. In September, Sabathia defeated the Orioles to become baseball's first 20-game winner, the first time he won 20 games in his career.

After allowing ten earned runs and 22 hits in 16 postseason innings, Sabathia was diagnosed in 2010 with a meniscus tear in his right knee, requiring arthroscopic surgery. CC began therapy immediately after the surgery and began his regular routine in preparation for spring training after three to six weeks. He lost 25 pounds during the offseason to prevent future problems with his knee.

As of 2011, Sabathia has slammed 25 hits in 101 plate appearances, making him one of the best-hitting MLB pitchers. On one occasion, he hit a 440-foot home run off Los Angeles Dodgers pitcher Chan Ho Park. He later said "I told everybody I was trying to hit homers today because I had two singles last year and everybody was all over me, saying I was a singles hitter. It was awesome." In his second game with the Brewers, Sabathia became the third pitcher in history to homer in both leagues in the same season and the first since Earl Wilson did it in 1970 with Detroit and San Diego.

Sabathia doesn't need to pitch with much trickery. He brings heat — fastball after fastball. He has a deceptively easy motion, and the ball at times seems to explode out of his body. CC's arm is a lethal weapon, keeping his velocity in the mid-90s with just enough movement to prevent hitters from digging in. His slider can be devastating. His sweeping curve and changeup are average, but they can be deadly working off his fastball. Once ahead in the count, he primarily uses his changeup to strike out right-handed batters, and his slider to strike out left-handers.

At 6-feet-7 and 309 pounds with his trademark hat cocked slightly to the side, CC's imposing presence on the mound becomes a gentle family man off it. His size 56 jersey, with three inches added to the sleeve and the length, may be the biggest ever worn by a Yankee. There is no record of any 310+ pound pitcher in major league history. Sabathia's bulk helps hide the ball in his delivery, and his height provides a steeper downward plane on his pitches. His reach allows him to release the ball a bit closer to the hitter.

By July 2011, Sabathia was on track to have the best season of his career. He was the AL All-Star starter and leading candidate for the Cy Young. CC's best performances came on July 9 against Tampa, as he pitched a four-hit, nine-strikeout complete game shutout and on July 27, a one-hitter vs. Seattle. The season featured a stretch where Sabathia won 11 of 12 decisions. As of September, he held a 19-8 record with a 3.01 ERA as the Yankees fought Boston for the AL East division title.

Sabathia married his wife and high school sweetheart Amber Williams in 2003, and has four children: CC III, Jaden, Cyia, and new baby Carter. Amber is a very upbeat mother and wife. At Yankee Stadium, she is often shown cheering on her husband, unconcerned about fans around her. Amber helps to keep CC happy, healthy and focused. Together they are the American Dream – Vallejo High School kids who remain happily married to this day despite nearly $200 million in baseball earnings. Amber shares in all his successes and helps him the through the highs and lows of the grind of a 162-game season. When Sabathia signed with the Yankees, the family moved from Fairfield to an 18,000 square-foot residence in Alpine, New Jersey and CC says they love life there, as well as being so close to Manhattan.

When Sabathia recently visited Thurmon Field – his recently-vandalized Little League field – it looked nothing like the ace remembered it, having fallen into extreme disrepair over the years. He looked out with dismay at the Vallejo field that was now overrun by weeds and unsuitable for baseball. Less than one year later, CC's foundation, PitCCh In, spent about $100,000 to help refurbish the field where the Yankee ace once pitched. The field on Whitney Avenue was re-done in an intense two-month construction project.

"We had a lot of help from some very dedicated people who are equally passionate as me about making sure kids get to play this great game of baseball," Sabathia said. "Thinking back to what was here in terms of weeds and old dugouts to what we have now; I'm as excited as the kids on the first day of the season."

The field was given new irrigation, infield dirt, bases, dugouts and an electronic scoreboard. The field was also re-seeded with 37,000 square feet of sod provided by West Coast Turf – the exact same turf as the Oakland Alameda County Coliseum, where Sabathia grew up cheering on the A's. In addition, the field was adjoined by a rebuilt snack bar with new electrical work plus the addition of a new water line, floor and roof. It turned out so well, Sabathia says he'd like to redo the fields at Vallejo High, his alma mater.

Thurmon Field's formal dedication featured Margie performing the ribbon cutting honors along with CC and Amber. It was timed to coincide with registration for the 2010 season, and Sabathia also pledged to cover the cost of the season fees for 100 Little Leaguers in North Vallejo this season. A baseball clinic was held on the field where CC was joined by Milton Bradley, Manny Parra and fellow Vallejo alum Joe Thurston to guide young players in drills.

"It has been such a pleasure to work with CC, Amber and Margie on this project," said Larry Harper, founder of The Good Tidings Foundation, which supervised and organized suppliers for the construction. "The three of them are truly committed and possess an unwavering amount of energy for the well-being of the deserving children in Vallejo."

In 2010, Sabathia again directed his PitCCh In Foundation to help first graders in Vallejo get a good start to the school year with new back-to-school backpacks. Each backpack contained folders, lined paper, rulers, erasers, pencil sharpener, crayons, a reading book, and a book marker along with an inspirational message from CC. But not just one school participated this year. CC made his backpack program available to all elementary schools in the district and their 1,500 first graders. The presentation of the backpacks and a video message from CC was introduced by Margie during a school assembly at Elsa Widenman School.

"I am a product of Vallejo schools – Loma Vista Elementary — and remember how important it was for me to feel prepared for that first day of school so that's why my mom, my wife Amber, and I feel so strongly about expanding this program," explained CC. "I wish I could be there myself to give each boy and girl a high-five as they get their backpack but I want them to know that I'll be thinking about them when I go out to pitch this week." CC and Amber also personally distribute back to school backpacks to children in the Bronx, New York.

Margie continues to be an active supporter and participant in the North Vallejo Little League and recently traveled to Williamsport, Pennsylvania where she was recognized as the National Little League Parent of the Year, an honor named for former President George and Barbara Bush and given to a parent of a major leaguer. Margie has long been involved in Little League and now runs the snack bar – "Margie's Place" – and helps oversee NVLL. While she serves up giant-sized "CC Dogs" drizzled with chili at the Little League snack bar, husband Al Lanier is the league's equipment manager. The kids in the league, she says, "keep her going," so much that when she saw them in the Opening Day parade this year, she hid in a corner of the concession stand and cried tears of joy.

Continentals of Omega Boys & Girls Club, a safe haven for Vallejo's youth for more than 40 years, has recently undergone a makeover thanks to support from Sabathia's PitCCh In Foundation. To reintroduce the Club's services, a Community

Outreach Day was held. The day-long community event was the culmination of a month-long project that included painting of the community center, landscaping, minor repairs, window replacement, new flooring inside the original gymnasium and a brand new outdoor basketball court.

"The Community Outreach Day is a wonderful opportunity to truly demonstrate to our Vallejo community how we are coming together to use these tremendous gifts. Not only are we refreshing the look of the facility, but we are giving people new hope through the variety of programs and resources provided by the Boys & Girls Club," said Sabathia.

Sabathia and Amber spent a recent Christmas back home in Vallejo, again pitching in to help the city where they grew up. Working with volunteers from their foundation, they renovated the Rosewood House, a shelter for homeless women trying to get off the streets. The entire building was landscaped, re-wired, re-painted and repaired to meet code requirements. Some of CC's old pals also helped out. CC also participates in Strikeouts for Troops, the charitable organization founded by Giants pitcher Barry Zito that assists wounded servicemen and servicewomen during their recovery. In 2010, Sabathia contributed $100 for every strikeout, raising $17,200.

Sabathia returned in 2011 to throw out the ceremonial first pitch as part of the North Vallejo Little League Spring Classic. Festivities prior to the game between the Yankees and the Cardinals of NVLL's Majors Division included a mini fanfest for all to enjoy. "This game represents the achievement of another major milestone in the 43-year history of North Vallejo Little League and our PitCCh In Foundation," explained Sabathia. "I certainly look forward to it and will enjoy the change of pace for me to be able to take in a night game in my home town in the middle of the Major League Baseball season and not be in uniform."

These days Margie Sabathia watches CC's games on television or from the stands, though she has another preferred location in mind: "Game day, if I am home, I don't even drive because I don't want to hurt anyone cause I'm nervous. Up until the eighth inning I'm nervous. My ideal seat would be in the dugout. I wouldn't bother anybody, just a little spot for the parents to sit in the dugout. Right there. I would love it."

Several starting pitchers in recent years have been crowned "the last 300-game winner." As starters throw fewer and fewer innings, wins have decreased while no decisions are common. With Randy Johnson the last to reach the lofty milestone, some say that there will never be another 300-game winner. At 176, Sabathia is the No. 1 contender to become the next one, having many factors in his favor. He began his career at a young age (20), is extremely durable (over 200 innings per season), strikes out hitters (7.6 per 9), and plays for a perennial winner with a great offense.

For this ace of the most storied franchise in baseball history, there's no reason not to believe that CC can continue to pile up the wins with one of the most feared lineups in baseball behind him. Though his contract contains an opt-out clause that could allow him to become a free agent, Sabathia said he has no intention of exercising it as he loves playing for the New York Yankees and his family loves life in New York.

Carsten Charles Sabathia Jr. has come a long way from North Vallejo in his 11-year MLB career. Standing as tall as the skyscrapers of New York City, CC is one of the game's most intimidating figures on the mound, but an introspective person off the field. The flame-throwing southpaw is a contender to win his second Cy Young Award, and perhaps his second World Series championship ring in the near future. Sabathia fans celebrate his pitching and CC's charities, generosity, leadership, and humbleness.

"The quality of the human being matches the talent," said Shapiro, who has known Sabathia since he was a teenager. "He's a great teammate, good father, and good husband. I've had the privilege of watching him grow to a man. He went through growing pains along the way, but he came out of it an impressive man in every good sense of the word. His mother is a great lady, a strong woman, and did a great job raising him."

Bay Area Legends

73

JOHNNY MILLER

Tall, lean and blonde, San Francisco native Johnny Miller was the PGA Tour's glamour boy of the 1970s — and also one of its elite players. He captured a U.S. Open championship in 1973 that featured an historic final round and he brought the British Open trophy home to California three years later. For a glorious three-year period, Miller piled up dozens of Top 10 finishes and ranked second in the world, behind only Jack Nicklaus.

John Laurence Miller was born on April 29, 1947 and he took up golf as a toddler under the watchful eye of his father Larry Miller and mother Ida Meldrum Miller. At seven years old, he was given to the pro at the San Francisco Golf Club, but some close to the Miller family say that Johnny's golf career originated from a tragic accident. His older brother drowned in a Pacific Ocean boating disaster when Johnny was 10. To help him deal with his loss, Johnny's father built a practice net in their garage and Johnny pounded golf balls on rainy afternoons while grieving and coming to terms with his brother's death.

"I was very lucky because my father was always positive and never pushed," said Miller. "He always called me Champ." Later, he was guided by teacher John Geertson, who shaped Miller's distinctive early wrist-cock takeaway.

Along with his sisters Sharon and Joan, Miller attended Lincoln High School in San Francisco where he received playing privileges and honed his skills on the majestic links of the Olympic Club. In 1963, he became a Junior Golf Section member at Olympic and quickly became the top player on its junior team. He won the San Francisco City Junior Championship in 1963 at age 16 and the following year won the 1964 U.S. Junior Amateur Championship at Eugene Country Club in Oregon.

"I'm very lucky to have had a creative father who comes from a background of artists and sculptors," Miller said. "He'd throw out so many things to me, swing-wise or course management-wise, that he'd bring me into new rooms of thought."

In 1965, Miller enrolled at Brigham Young University in Provo, Utah and continued to refine his swing. Johnny drew national media attention at the end of his freshman year when he won the low amateur at the 1966 U.S. Open at Olympic. Remarkably, the 19-year-old Miller had only gone to the event to caddy. He instead qualified for the event and went on to a highly impressive eighth-place finish against the best players in the world. Johnny's intimate knowledge of his home Olympic course helped him earn the first of his many Major Top 10s and earned him an invitation to the 1967 Masters.

"It was my first Open and I was running scared." said PGA golfer Lee Trevino regarding the 1966 U.S. Open. "But Johnny had some swagger, and he was already so good, it was like his forehead was stamped 'can't miss.'"

Future wife Linda met Johnny while they were co-eds at BYU, but Johnny's ties to the Mormon Church wasn't the only reason he selected Provo. "I think he chose it because the golf coach [Glen Tuckett] was a fast talker," said Linda, a non-Mormon who has since converted. After a year at an eastern school with an active social scene, Linda transferred to BYU, which turned out to be more consistent with her strict Philadelphia upbringing.

Miller, an All-American at BYU, graduated in 1969 at age 22 with a degree in physical education and qualified for the PGA Tour the same year. He moved to Silverado Country Club in the Napa Valley when he turned pro. He and Linda started their family in a house just a short cart ride from the clubhouse. Johnny earned only $8,364 in his rookie year and showed very little promise of the golf superstar that would one day emerge.

Johnny won his first PGA tournament – the Southern Open – in 1971, after nearly winning the '71 Masters. Miller finished at seven-under-par and tied for second place with Nicklaus, two strokes behind winner Charles Coody. Despite shooting 68 on Saturday and Sunday and holding a two-stroke lead with just four holes remaining, his Green Jacket dream slipped away.

Miller won his second tour event at the 1972 Sea Pines Heritage Classic. Later that season, he made a rare double eagle on the fifth hole at Muirfield during the 1972 British Open. His ball-striking skills, particularly with irons, were highly advanced but it was his streaky putter that often fell victim to the yips, forcing him to miss many easy putts.

By 1973, Miller had only two professional wins but had already experienced six U.S. Opens with Top 10 finishes in 1966, 1971, and 1972. The '73 venue was the challenging par-71 Oakmont layout near Pittsburgh, Pennsylvania. Miller was a 26-year-old who had yet to win that season, but by mid-June he had recorded eight Top 10 finishes in other PGA tournaments, which included a share of 6th place at the Masters.

With a USGA course rating of 77.5 and guarded by 200 bunkers, Oakmont was generally regarded in the golf community as one of the most difficult tracks in the United States. As if the challenge of Oakmont was not enough, Miller played the first two rounds with hometown fan favorite Arnold Palmer and his "Arnie's Army" gallery, at its largest in western Pennsylvania. Miller was two-under par (140) after the second round, but shot a five-over 76 on Saturday, inflating his tournament score to 216 and all but extinguishing any championship hopes.

On Sunday, June 17, 1973, Miller entered the final round in 12th place, six shots behind four co-leaders including Palmer. Starting at 1:36 pm, Johnny fired a record-breaking eight-under-par 63, in what is considered one of the greatest performances in U.S. Open and golf history. He outplayed the PGA Tour stars of the 1970s, including future Hall of Famers Nicklaus, Gary Player, Trevino, and Palmer, who was in the final pairing with John Schlee.

Miller got off to a blazing start by birdying the first four holes and hit all 18 greens in regulation with only 29 putts. His laser-like precision that afternoon bagged him five more birdies with only one bogey – a three-putt on the 244-yard par-3 eighth hole. Johnny finished five strokes under par (279) for the tournament, edging runner-up Schlee by a single stroke. With an original field of 150 players, only five players shot sub-par rounds at treacherous Oakmont in that final round, making his scintillating 63 even more amazing. Miller earned $35,000 for the victory.

Miller's 63 stands as a final round record for a major championship and also gave Johnny an enviable USGA double, as he had won the U.S. Junior Amateur crown in 1964. He became the only player to have won both the Junior and the Open. Although he had been a contender for several years, it wasn't until his astonishing 63 made golf history – and the endorsements rolled in. Miller followed the Oakmont triumph by placing second at the next major, the 1973 British Open Championship at Royal Troon. He finished three strokes behind winner Tom Weiskopf. Royal Troon was the first of Johnny's five consecutive Top 10 British Open finishes.

Miller further boosted his confidence by partnering with Nicklaus in the 1973 World Cup. "I played every day with Jack for a week, and I started to believe that at the time, I was actually better than him," Miller said. It seemed that a new golfing star was emerging and between the years of 1973 and 1976, Miller and Nicklaus were the dominant forces in golf. Miller went on to light up leaderboards in the mid-1970s with 14 tournament victories and was the PGA's Player of the Year in 1974. Miller won eight PGA Tour events that year, the most since Palmer scored eight wins in 1960 and a record that stood until Tiger Woods notched nine in 2000.

In the 1974 Tucson Open, Tom Watson played with Miller as he shot an incredible 61 in the final round to win by 14 strokes and said: "That was the best pure-striking round of golf I have ever seen." Miller answered the comment by saying that "For the past 12 months I've played better than anybody in the world" with his brutal honesty that has made him as many enemies as friends throughout his life.

Miller's PGA Tour money title in 1974 is the only one from 1971 to 1980 not won by Nicklaus or Watson. He was the leading money winner on the PGA Tour by far, amassing a then record $353,201, unseating Nicklaus as money leader for a season. By February 1, he had earned more in one month, $97,700, than many pros do in a season.

According to the World Golf Hall of Fame, "In golf's modern era, it's commonly understood that no player has ever achieved the brief but memorable brilliance of Johnny Miller. In 1974 and 1975 Miller hit the ball consistently closer to the flag than any player in history. At his best, Miller's game was marked by incredibly aggressive and equally accurate iron play."

"I've never played better in my life – my drives are longer and my putting much surer," Miller told *Sports Illustrated* in 1974. "I really want to win the Masters very,

very badly. I love the tradition – what it's meant to golf. If I don't win, I'll be as surprised as anyone."

Thousands of women followed Miller around the golf courses of America in the 1970s. He was their Robert Redford in Sears menswear and spikes. His square-jawed face, tan and lean, fit the role of golf pro as if cast by Hollywood. When he launched his long powerful swing and follow-through, Johnny was as electrifying as any athlete in the world. He won four more tournaments in 1975. "It was sort of golfing nirvana," Miller said later. "I'd say my average iron shot for three months in 1975 was within five feet of my line, and I had the means for controlling distance. I could feel the shot so well."

Miller began the 1975 season with three more victories before finishing second to Nicklaus at the Masters. Nicklaus eventually squashed Johnny's challenge to his throne by outdueling Weiskopf and Miller down the stretch. Johnny finished third at the British Open at Carnoustie, just a single stroke from a playoff. Miller was also a member of the victorious 1975 U.S. Ryder Cup team.

Miller captured his second major championship at the 1976 British Open. At Royal Birkdale, Johnny trailed 19-year-old Spaniard Seve Ballesteros by two going into the final round but rallied for a course record 66 to win by six shots over Ballesteros and Nicklaus. Miller earned £7,500 for the victory, about $14,000.

"Johnny was the best I ever saw at hitting pure golf shots," said fellow PGA pro Lanny Wadkins.

Johnny doubled his tour winnings in the early '70s by endorsing products ranging from men's clothing to Japanese tomato juice to Beautyrest mattresses. Many tournaments had competitions for a new car, and Miller seems to have driven off with more than his share. The driveway outside his condominium at Silverado Country Club came to look like a used-car lot. At one point in 1975, he owned a Thunderbird, a Porsche, a Ford station wagon, a couple of Dodges and a Ferrari.

All things that burn brightest usually end soonest. Miller's British Open win in 1976 marked the end of his reign at the top of the golf world as he didn't win another tournament until 1980. Johnny lacked the insatiable drive for success that drives elite athletes. Bored with golf, Miller spent a winter in Utah chopping down trees, which he says ruined his swing because his stronger body could not repeat his old swing. He changed clubmakers. The yips still showed up occasionally. Finally, Miller's priorities changed the moment he had the first of his six children in 1977.

After winning 24 PGA Tour events, he was burned out, plagued by injuries and just wanted to help Linda change diapers. "Golf wasn't enough for me," said Miller. "None of my competitors could understand that."

At the 1980 British Open, Miller holed a rare double eagle, otherwise known as an albatross. It was only the second time such a score was recorded in the British Open's long history. In 1981, he enjoyed one final spectacular season as he knuckled down for a reminder of the champ he once was. Johnny won twice and again became the world's leading money winner after a victory in the Million Dollar Challenge at Sun City, edging Ballesteros in a marathon nine-hole playoff.

During his playing days, Miller was sometimes called "The Desert Fox" because many of his wins came on the desert courses of Arizona and Southern California. As a committed Mormon with six children, he resented the constant travel of a Tour pro's life – he never enjoyed being on the road all the time.

"Now I'd like to be the player that everyone else wants to knock off, like Nicklaus," says Johnny. "But I don't think that can go on forever – my family means too much. Most of all I want to be a success as a father. "We're going to build a big house out in California. Don't be surprised if at some point down this road I unpack my bags, stay in the valley, play with my kids and drive my Porsche."

"I didn't value enough what it was to be a champion. I didn't buy into the majors as much as I should have," said Miller. "When I got to the mountaintop, I kind of looked at the scenery and wondered, 'Now what?' When Jack got there, he said, 'Where's the next mountain?'"

His last PGA victory – an upset even in his own mind – came at the 1994 AT&T Pebble Beach Pro-Am at age 46, where he posted a seven-under 281 to win by one shot. Playing on one of his favorite courses, Miller somehow kept making putts – at times while closing his eyes – and won by a stroke even after he had semi-retired in 1990 to take up broadcasting.

Miller finished his career with 25 PGA Tour wins and 105 Top 10 finishes. He played on two Ryder Cup teams, 1975 and 1981. In 1997, the National Golf Foundation honored the Miller family with that year's Jack Nicklaus Golf Family of the Year Award.

The World Golf Hall of Fame inducted Johnny in 1998. He was pleased that his peers also acknowledged his beliefs about the importance of the family. A video that featured Miller and Nick Faldo was shown during the induction ceremonies.

During a telephone interview with the Church News, Miller said: "What was interesting was that they emphasized the fact that family was more important than my golf. When they think of Johnny Miller, they think of family as well as golf. No other success can compensate for failure in the home."

Miller and his wife, Linda, have six grown children and their four sons have followed in their father's footsteps. John and Scott run the Johnny Miller Golf Academy and other Miller businesses and Andy is a member of the PGA Tour. During final round play at the 2002 U.S. Open at Bethpage, Andy sunk a hole-in-one – on Father's Day – 20 years after his father's hole-in-one at the 1982 U.S. Open at Pebble Beach. Youngest son Todd won the California high school golf championship and attended BYU. Their daughters are Kelly and Casi, both of whom attended the University of Utah.

Johnny and Linda are members of the Mormon Church of Latter Day Saints and have many grandchildren. Linda said Johnny has always been dedicated to the family and their marriage. "When he's home, he's Johnny Miller, daddy. He didn't bring the game home with him. He really enjoyed being with the children. He's very affectionate."

After retiring from the PGA Tour, Miller rarely played the Champions (Senior) Tour due in part to knee injuries and his fame as a golfer faded. Since retiring from regular competition, Miller has become a popular television commentator for NBC.

Miller was a breath of fresh air on golf telecasts, unafraid to call it as he saw it. As a commentator he became known for his straightforward and sometimes blunt remarks, which earned him the wrath of some players. One example came in 2008 during the broadcast of the U.S. Open's 18-hole playoff, when he referred to Rocco Mediate as "looking like the guy who cleans Tiger Woods' pool." Mediate, who has battled many physical problems throughout his career, nevertheless played superbly and later laughed off the remark.

He loves to talk about choking and even and says it is one of his favorite words. Miller has incurred the anger of many by discussing the phenomenon but he says he's a leading authority because he experienced it so often as a player. Many golf fans and professional golfers grew to love Miller's broadcasting but an equal number also disliked him intensely. For the first year-and-a-half, Miller took his lumps. Many of the members of the PGA Tour community verbally swung back. "I deserved the negative feedback from the players," he says. "They were thinking, 'What the heck is this guy doing to us?' I was a little raw."

At the 1991 Ryder Cup at Kiawah Island, South Carolina, Paul Azinger called him "the biggest moron." Azinger later tried to soften the blow by saying he meant to call Miller "the biggest Mormon." After the U.S. team beat the Europeans, Miller faxed his resignation to NBC Sports President Dick Ebersol, only to be talked out of it.

"NBC has a totally different style of covering golf," complained Azinger. "After a guy hits a bad shot, Johnny immediately questions: 'What happened there, Roger?' It's opinion. How the heck do they know?" In a not-so-subtle shot at Miller's departure from the Tour and hesitation to play on the Senior Tour because of struggles with putting, he said "Every time a guy misses a putt, it's not because of nerves. That's Johnny's frame of reference."

What is it inside Miller that moves him to speak so frankly? "I answer to the higher law, which is being true to yourself," he said. Being a Mormon is also a factor. "The secret in life is clear intention," said Miller. "If you want to do real well, you have a clear intention of what you want to accomplish, say it and make a commitment. I love teaching so much, I'm actually giving a lesson on TV. I will never just say, 'He hit that shot terrible, he's choking.' I might insinuate it, but I'll also tell how he corrects it. So I complete the circle."

"The joke at NBC is that it's not hard to make Johnny cry," says reporter Jimmy Roberts. "He's very easily touched." Many PGA pros might find that difficult to believe. In addition to being easily touched, Miller is honest, opinionated and about as subtle as a sledgehammer.

Golf has historically been broadcast in hushed, reverential commentary where players have grown up expecting to be discussed in glowing terms. But Miller continues to blaze his own trail. "That's the way I announce," he says. "It just is what it is. It doesn't matter if it's my wife or my kids. ... I don't like to say something unless it's unexpected. It bores me when somebody says it's a nice shot or a good putt. Watching golf that way is a good way to fall asleep."

"My goal in announcing is to speak just like I'm in the living room with you and we're having pizza and I'm just letting go. Whatever I think comes out. I'm going to do the best job with the most honesty inside me to say 'here's what I think just happened.' The announcing is a little bit like teaching. I address a player's mistakes and sort of give a lesson on TV. When I played, I didn't play down the middle and I don't announce down the middle. That would be boring."

"I respect him because he's been there," PGA pro Phil Mickelson said. "But sometimes I feel he goes over the line."

In the wake of Greg Norman's final-round collapse at the 1996 Masters, Miller said that "Greg can only play one way — aggressively. When he tries to play conservatively, his brain short-circuits. His wires get crossed, and sparks start flying. He could change, but it would take months of programming from a sports psychologist." Norman responded to Miller's comments by trying to organize the Tour players to ban the media from the locker room.

The 1999 U.S. Ryder Cup team turned against Miller after he said Leonard was playing so poorly he should go home and watch on TV. Using it as a rallying point to defeat the Europeans, one by one the U.S. players blasted Miller after they won. "I was pretty shocked," he said. "I did make a couple bogeys there, maybe a double bogey with the Justin Leonard thing. If you put me on the air for eight hours, I'm bound to screw up. I don't do this stuff on purpose. I'm not polished and professional like Bob Costas. I'm just Johnny Miller. I was that way before I was on television, saying the same things in my living room watching golf."

After 20 years at NBC Sports, Miller has developed into one of the most technically insightful, refreshingly outspoken and controversial commentators in sports. He wrote the well-received book *I Call The Shots*, a look at the PGA Tour's personalities during his peak years, current PGA stars, and broadcasting insights. Johnny has also written a column for *Golf Digest* for several years, offering advice into various aspects of golf. Miller has also made many TV and movie appearances including Kevin Costner's *Tin Cup*. In *The Associate* with Whoopi Goldberg, an aging billionaire is willing to trade all his assets in exchange for the opportunity to play a round of golf with Johnny.

Miller's partnership purchased Silverado Country Club on July 1, 2010. He also owns a golf design company and a golf academy, has made numerous golf instructional videos and designed the Thanksgiving Point Golf Course in Lehi, Utah, host of the Champion's Challenge. Johnny Miller Design was founded in 1984 and originally worked with Nicklaus and other designers. An urban golf legend holds that the golfer whose profile appears in the PGA Tour logo is Miller but according to the PGA Tour, the logo is not based on any one player.

In a *Sports Illustrated* fan survey, Miller was named Favorite Golf Analyst. In a 2002 survey, the readers of *Golf Digest* named Miller Best Analyst on Television for the third time. In the October 2003 issue of *Golf Digest*, Miller was named the most powerful person in television and 16th most powerful person in golf overall.

In 2002, Miller earned his fourth Emmy nomination for Outstanding Sports Analyst, a rarity for a golf commentator. "Johnny has an uncanny ability to predict what's going to happen," said NBC executive producer Tom Roy. "He doesn't second-guess, he first-guesses. He always goes out early in the morning and talks to players and caddies. He goes out on the course to examine the greens. At the Open he even steps off the fairways. He is so prepared when he goes on the air."

He recently formed the Johnny Miller Junior Golf Association, which opens the door for hundreds of young people who normally would not have the opportunity or the finances to learn the game of golf. "Sometimes I think that when we get up in heaven," said Miller. "God's going to let everyone be 28, and there's going to be this great tournament."

Hall of Famer Johnny Miller is best known today as an outspoken commentator and columnist whose golf insights have earned him critical acclaim, including multiple Emmy nominations. But for three years between 1973 and 1976, Miller played the game as well as anyone in the world. Even Jack Nicklaus was in awe of what Johnny could do. Two major championships are not nearly indicative of Miller's dominance, as his 25 PGA victories and his 105 Top 10 finishes attest. Forty years later, Miller's final round 63 at Oakmont for the U.S. Open title still remains one of golf's greatest and most unforgettable rounds.

88

LYNN SWANN

As his last name would suggest, Lynn Swann was one of the most graceful players ever showcased in the National Football League. His athleticism and sure hands made him one of the league's elite wide receivers and when given an opportunity to shine on the biggest stage in sports, he was nothing short of spectacular.

Lynn Curtis Swann was born on March 7, 1952 in Alcoa, Tennessee, just south of Knoxville. His father Willie was a maintenance worker in an aircraft plant and his mother Mildred worked as a dental hygienist. The youngest of three boys, Swann first demonstrated remarkable physical ability by walking at the age of seven months. When Lynn was two, his family moved out west to Foster City, California.

Disappointed at not having a daughter, Mildred encouraged Lynn to enroll in dance lessons, which he grasped quickly and excelled. He studied dance – including ballet, modern dance and tap – from the age of four until high school graduation. Swann has often said that his mother's insistence on dance training is what made him such a good athlete.

"When I was in grammar school," said Lynn, "I felt more comfortable on the dance floor than the football field. People think football and dancing are so different. They think it's contradictory for a boy to dance, but dancing is a sport." Those lessons would come in handy later in Swann's football career.

While it was his mother that introduced him to dance, it was his older brother Calvin that sparked Swann's passion for sports. Always willing to try whatever sport his older brother was playing, Lynn was usually one of the smallest players. "I was always smaller and younger than the other kids," he said. "My game had to be a mental one. I had to outsmart and out quick the other kids and take advantage of mistakes."

At Junipero Serra High School in San Mateo, Swann revealed a natural athleticism for sports, setting Padre track and field records, playing on the basketball team and excelling on the football team as a wide receiver for two seasons and a quarterback in his senior year. Lynn competed in both the pole vault and the long jump, in which he won the California High School State Championship with a jump of 25 feet, four inches. Swann was the first in a line of famous sports alumni from Serra, which also includes Barry Bonds, Gregg Jeffries, and Tom Brady.

"I want to thank my mother because when I was in junior high school, I received a scholarship to go to Serra High School in San Mateo, California and I did not want to go to this all-boys Catholic high school," said Swann in his Hall of Fame induction speech. "My mother made me go. She made me go on the foundation that education and what she instilled in my life have brought me here today."

While Swann had many good experiences in high school, not all were pleasant. As one of just nine African-Americans in a school of 900, he felt that some white classmates treated him differently off the basketball court or football field. At the same time, some of his black friends ostracized him for attending a white school and for taking on what they considered a white attitude. It was a perplexing situation for the good-natured Swann. "I learned very young the games people play," he said in a 1979 *Sports Illustrated* interview.

"Because I'm the youngest of three boys, whom my mother named Lynn because she wanted to have a girl," Swann recalled of his Serra days. "You would have thought that was tough. You try leaving football practice with a pair of tights named Lynn at an all-boys Catholic high school. You'll find yourself learning a few moves."

After earning high-school football All-American honors in 1969, Swann graduated from Serra in 1970 and was recruited by several colleges and universities. He even visited Notre Dame, where Coach Ara Parseghian discussed the possibility of making him a quarterback. His preference, however, was UCLA. When UCLA failed to extend an offer, Lynn accepted a scholarship to their cross-town rival, the University of Southern California.

Swann played in Los Angeles under legendary coach John McKay and competed in two Rose Bowls, helping the undefeated Trojans win the 1972 NCAA National Championship. In 1973, Swann's teammates elected him team captain and the team's Most Valuable Player. NCAA coaches unanimously named him to the All-America team.

He set the USC single-season record of 96 receptions, was second in receiving yardage with 1,562 yards and finished as the third-leading punt returner in Trojan history. He graduated from the USC School of Journalism with a Bachelor of Arts in Public Relations. One of Swann's USC roommates was baseball star Fred Lynn, who became the 1975 Rookie of the Year and MVP for the Boston Red Sox.

In the 1974 NFL draft, the Pittsburgh Steelers selected the 5-foot-11, 180-pound Swann with their first-round pick, the 21st player taken. Ed "Too Tall" Jones of Tennessee State was chosen first overall by the Dallas Cowboys. The Steelers also selected John Stallworth, Jack Lambert, and Mike Webster later in the same draft and launched its most spectacular winning streak in team history. Swann spent all nine of his NFL seasons in the Steel City, shattering numerous club records.

Already possessing one of the best defenses in NFL history, the Steelers began to dominate as Swann joined forces with fellow wide receiver Stallworth. With fresh talents Stallworth and Swann at wide receiver, quarterback Terry Bradshaw had a choice of targets and opponents could no longer isolate their defensive attention. During his rookie season, Swann led the league in punt returns with 577 yards on 41 returns, which was a Steeler record and fourth-best in NFL history. A backup at wide receiver, his touchdown catch in the AFC championship game against the Oakland Raiders clinched the victory for the Steelers.

"I'd like to say that we developed Lynn Swann," said Chuck Noll, Pittsburgh head coach. "But the truth is he was perfectly developed as a football player the first time he stepped on our practice field."

The 1975 season became the pinnacle of Swann's career. He caught 49 passes for 781 yards and an NFL-best 11 touchdowns. In an AFC championship game rematch against the Raiders, George Atkinson slammed Swann with a vicious hit. Carried off the field by teammate "Mean Joe" Greene, he suffered a severe concussion that hospitalized him for two days. Lynn surprised many by deciding to play against

Dallas in Super Bowl X. He responded with four spectacular catches for a Super Bowl record 161 yards and a touchdown, leading the Steelers to a 21–17 victory and becoming the first wide receiver in NFL history to earn Super Bowl MVP honors.

Super Bowl X had seen three lead changes entering the fourth quarter. With the Steelers leading by five points with 4:25 remaining, the game's drama intensified. From his own 36 yard line, Pittsburgh quarterback Terry Bradshaw dropped back and fired a shot to Swann who, in one of the most dramatic and unforgettable catches in NFL history, quickly converted the pass to a 64-yard gain. Stumbling over a defender, Swann was horizontal, parallel with the field in midair when he caught the ball. He juggled, tumbled and stretched out during the spectacular catch, still one of the Super Bowl's greatest plays.

"Lynn Swann was an idol. It would amaze me how he could fly through the air and make those catches," said 49ers wide receiver Jerry Rice, the NFL's all-time leading receiver. "I'll never forget the one versus Dallas. It was the greatest catch I've ever seen."

It was an opponent's intimidation tactic that angered and perhaps motivated Swann. Dallas defensive back Cliff Harris questioned Lynn's courage, and was surprised that the receiver made the decision to even play. Swann stated that such a challenge could not be ignored and, in fact, made him stronger throughout the game. "I read what Harris said," Swann told *First Down* magazine. "He was trying to intimidate me. He said I'd be afraid out there. He couldn't scare me."

Although fans remember the acrobatic 64-yard grab as Swann's greatest play, many believe it wasn't even his best catch of that *game*. Covered tightly by Cowboys cornerback Mark Washington late in the second quarter, Bradshaw threw high down the right sideline. The pass looked headed out of bounds as Swann leaped into the sky, snatched the pass, and twisted his body back in bounds with both feet in. The dramatic play covered 53 yards.

During the 1978 season, the Steelers made it back to the Super Bowl in a rematch against Dallas. Saving his best games for the playoffs, Lynn burned the Cowboys by catching seven passes for 124 yards and scored the final touchdown for a 35-31 Steeler win, their third championship in five years. The NFL named Swann, who had 11 touchdown grabs during the regular season, "Man of the Year."

The Steelers earned a trip to Super Bowl XIV in 1979 as Swann caught five passes for 79 yards and a touchdown in Pittsburgh's 31-19 win over the Los Angeles Rams. After winning his fourth Super Bowl ring, Lynn married Bernadette Robi, daughter of singer Paul Robi of The Platters, on June 10, 1979. The pair divorced in 1983, and Robi is currently married to boxing legend Sugar Ray Leonard. On June 23, 1991, Swann married psychologist Charena Shaffer and they have two sons – Braxton and Shafer. Shafer plays football for Pittsburgh's Central Catholic High School.

Swann, concerned about his concussions, retired from the NFL in 1982 after just nine seasons. He was only 30 years old. Lynn, who never called for a fair catch in his entire career, decided to take a vocal stand against unnecessary violence that existed in the game. His sometimes unpopular stance against unsportsmanlike and violent play eventually resulted in NFL rules changes.

At the time of his retirement, Swann's combined total of 364 receiving yards in four games ranked first in Super Bowl history. Today, Lynn is second all-time to Rice's 589 yards in four games. His total of three touchdowns is also second to Rice's eight. Besides his Super Bowl exploits, Swann's regular season totals of his short career included 336 receptions for 5,462 yards and 51 touchdowns (94th all-time). Additionally, he was named to the Pro Bowl and selected All-Pro in 1975, 1977, and 1978. Swann was named to the NFL's All-Decade Team of the 1970s, and to the Super Bowl Silver Anniversary Team.

"Lynn Swann didn't have the stats, but he sure as heck made an impact," former Steeler teammate Greene said. "No one made a bigger impact. It's like Gale Sayers. He didn't play a long time, but he made an impact. Lynn Swann had that impact. He played a lot of big games. I'm a great Lynn Swann fan."

Pittsburgh has been home to Swann and his family since he joined the Steelers in 1974. Today he remains as active off the field as he was on it. Recognized for his many achievements, Swann has received numerous honors for his work toward the continued growth and development of our nation's young people.

Armed with his professional athlete experience and a USC Journalism degree, Swann launched a "second career" – in sports broadcasting. He helped cover the 1984 summer Olympics in Los Angeles and the 1988 winter Olympics in Calgary. Since then, Lynn has spent 26 years as a sideline commentator for ABC Sports including *Monday Night Football* and *Wide World of Sports*. He has also landed bit roles in movies, and was chosen by President Bush as chairman of the President's Council on Physical Fitness from 2002 until 2005.

"There are those with great communication talents, the guys like John Madden, who have unique personalities that can be transmitted over the air," said Swann. "Then there are the athletes who trained and prepared for this work by spending time in broadcasting while they were active players."

When Lynn was inducted into the Pro Football Hall of Fame in 2001, he asked that Stallworth introduce him. To further assist Stallworth's bid for the Hall of Fame, Swann said in his acceptance speech: "I don't think I could be in the Hall of Fame unless there was a John Stallworth. The competition between John and me, the things that we made each other do in terms of working and getting ready, I knew I always had to be ready." Stallworth followed Swann into Canton the next year, in 2002.

Enormously popular in the Pittsburgh area, Swann entered the political arena. In 2006, he was the Republican nominee to run against the incumbent Ed Rendell for Pennsylvania Governor. Swann lost the election with 40% of the vote to Rendell's 60%. "If I didn't think Pennsylvania needed a change, I'd be content to stay at home, do the football thing, and play with my kids," Swann said during the campaign.

Swann has sat on the National Board of Directors for the Big Brother and Big Sisters of America since 1980. He is also a driving force behind a youth scholarship program for the Pittsburgh Ballet Theater School. Fifty percent of the proceeds from website sales of Swann's Hall of Fame memorabilia will go to those organizations. In August 2010, the *Pittsburgh Tribune-Review* reported that Lynn and two partners will be the ownership team for Pittsburgh's Arena Football League expansion franchise, the Pittsburgh Power. The Power went 9-9 in 2011, just missing the playoffs in their first season.

Lynn Swann accomplished nearly every goal a football player could possibly earn. High School All-American. NCAA National Champion. NCAA All-American. Super Bowl Champion. Pro Bowler. Super Bowl MVP. But it is the amazing grace and athleticism that fans will always be associate with him. He's been called the "Baryshnikov of the Gridiron." His style of receiving was not only spectacular, but was recognized as uniquely effective by teammates and coaches alike. Swann turned catching into a production. Like a ballet dancer, he could leap, hang in the air, twist, contort, and somehow come down with the ball. And his finest performances often came in the final act, when it meant the most.

BIBLIOGRAPHY

Joe DiMaggio

DiMaggio, Joe. Baseball for Everyone. New York: MacGraw Hill, 1949.

Lally, Richard. Bombers: An Oral History of the New York Yankees. New York: Crown Publishers, 2002.

Smith, Ron. Heros of the Hall. New York: Sporting News, 2002.

Athletes and Coaches of Summer. New York: MacMillan, 2000.

Notable Sports Figures. Farmington Hills MI: Thomson Gale, 2004.

Cramer, Richard Ben. Joe DiMaggio: The Hero's Life. New York: Simon & Schuster, 2004

Brinkley, Alan. The Unfinished Nation. New York: Knopf, 1993.

Goodman, Michael E. The History of the New York Yankees. New York: MacMillan, 2002.

Baseball Digest. Vol. 60, No. 3, 2001.

http://www.infoplease.com/ipa/A0775642.html#ixzz1HRHXecWH
http://www.joedimaggiobiography.com
http://www.netstate.com/states/peop/people/ca_jpd.htm
http://www.baseball-almanac.com/players/player.php?p=dimagjo01
http://www.handsonenglish.com/curr/March99.html

http://www.usatoday.com/sports/baseball/joed/joed09.htm

http://www.baseballinwartime.com/player_biographies/dimaggio_joe.htm

http://articles.sfgate.com/2009-05-17/sports/17203037_1_joe-dimaggio-s-san-francisco-dimaggio-family-dimaggio-boys/3

http://www.washingtonpost.com/wp-srv/sports/baseball/daily/march99/08/chrono08.htm

http://www.martinezgazette.com/news/story/i443/2009/08/24/hundreds-attend-joltin-joe-fundraiser

http://www.biography.com/articles/Joe-DiMaggio-9274899

http://www.pbs.org/wgbh/amex/dimaggio/peopleevents/pande03.html

http://www.helium.com/items/917111-biography-joe-dimaggio

http://www.helium.com/items/988447-joe-dimaggio-the-man-and-the-legend

http://www.helium.com/items/773681-joe-dimaggio-the-man-and-the-legend

http://thiscardiscool.blogspot.com/2011/02/joltin-joe-in-bay-area.html

http://espn.go.com/classic/000706joedimaggio.html

http://www.biography-and-biographies.com/Athletes/Joe-DiMaggio.htm

http://www.kosmix.com/topic/joe_dimaggio#ixzz1HRJdL6dy

http://en.wikipedia.org/wiki/Joe_DiMaggio

http://baseballhall.org/hof/dimaggio-joe

http://www.thd.org/semaphorearchives/157_The%20Semaphore_08-2001.pdf

http://baseballpastandpresent.com/2009/05/06/joe-dimaggios-boyhood-home/

http://www.baseball-almanac.com/quotes/quodimg.shtml

http://www.zetaboards.com/anthroscape/topic/1066753/

http://www.nydailynews.com/archives/sports/2006/09/17/2006-09-17_captain___the_clipper__jeter.htmlhttp://www.sfmuseum.org/hist10/dimaggio1.html

http://entertainment.howstuffworks.com/marilyn-monroe-later-career4.htm

Jason Kidd

Gray, Valerie. Jason Kidd Star Guard. Berkeley Heights, NJ: Enslow, 2000.

Thornley, Stew. Super Sports Star Jason Kidd. Berkeley Heights, NJ: Enslow, 2002.

Michael J. Goodman "Getting the point". Sporting News, The. FindArticles.com. 02 July, 2011. http://findarticles.com/p/articles/mi_m1208/is_n14_v218/ai_15773229/

http://www.ibtimes.com/articles/109758/20110207/top-5-best-passing-nba-point-guards-of-all-time.htm#page3
http://istreetball.com/profiles/blogs/the-mavs-are-the-worlds-team
http://www.secondshelters.com/2011/06/10/mavs-mavs-mavs-houses/
http://en.wikipedia.org/wiki/Jason_Kidd
http://www.jockbio.com/Bios/Kidd/Kidd_bio.html
http://articles.sfgate.com/2000-02-11/sports/28577498_1
http://www.slamonline.com/online/nba/2011/06/jason-kidd-has-his-ring-at-long-last/
http://www.clap.name/theleague/meandovine/?p=142

Bill Russell

Johnson, James W. <u>The Dandy Dons</u> Lincoln: University of Nebraska Press, 2009.

Hollander, Zander. <u>The Modern Encyclopedia of Basketball.</u> New York: Dolphin Books, 1979.

Russell, Bill. <u>The Russell Rules</u>. Minneapolis: Highbridge, 2002.

http://www.nba.com/history/players/russell_bio.html
http://www.nba.com/history/players/russell_summary.html
http://www.ibabuzz.com/prepcorner/2006/09/26/bill-russell-frank-robinson-mcclymonds/
http://www.highbeam.com/doc/1P2-17121357.html
http://sports.jrank.org/pages/4105/Russell-Bill-Growing-Up.html#ixzz16dT7jBDK
http://espn.go.com/sportscentury/features/00079684.html
http://www.contracostatimes.com/news/ci_16641891?source=rss&nclick_check=1
http://entertainment.howstuffworks.com/bill-russell-at.htm
http://www.nba.com/history/players/russell_bio.html
http://www.nndb.com/people/783/000023714/
http://en.wikipedia.org/wiki/Bill_Russell
http://www.brainyquote.com/quotes/authors/b/bill_russell.html#ixzz177GNIgcj
http://www.insidehoops.com/forum/showthread.php?t=189444

Willie Stargell

Stargell, Willie, and Tom Bird. <u>Willie Stargell.</u> New York: HarperCollins, 1984.

Okanes, Jonathan. "Willie Stargell." Knight Ridder/Tribune News Service Article: April 9, 2001.

http://pabook.libraries.psu.edu/palitmap/bios/Stargell__Willie.html
http://www.baseball-almanac.com/players/player.php?p=stargwi01
http://www.britannica.com/EBchecked/topic/761944/Willie-Stargell
http://www.associatedcontent.com/article/67908/willie_stargell_the_pirates_greatest_pg2.html?cat=14
http://www.answers.com/topic/wilver-dornel-stargell#ixzz1FqVlgr7T
http://www.helium.com/items/1552954-greatest-hitters-of-the-seventies
http://everything2.com/title/Willie+Stargell
www.buyhappier.com/willie-stargeil-autographed-baseball.html
http://www.highbeam.com/doc/1P2-1233490.html
http://www.encyclopedia.com/doc/1G2-2873100060.html
http://www.juggle.com/willie-stargell
http://en.wikipedia.org/wiki/Willie_Stargell
http://baseballhall.org/hof/stargell-willie
http://www.bronxbanterblog.com/2009/04/07/card-corner-willie-stargell/

Joe Morgan

Kirsch, George B. Encyclopedia of ethnicity and sports in the United States. Westport, CT: Greenwood, 2000.

Falkner, David, and Joe Morgan. Joe Morgan: A Life in Baseball. New York: W. W. Norton & Co., 1993.

Boston Globe, January 10, 1990, p. 25; January 11, 1990, p. 43.

New York Times, January 10, 1990, p. D25; January 11, 1990, p. B11; August 6, 1990, p. C4; August 7, 1990, p. B10.

Upscale, August, 1994, p. 116.

U.S. News & World Report, November 29, 1993, p. 18.

http://sports.espn.go.com/espn/otl/news/story?id=4546838
http://sportsillustrated.cnn.com/vault/article/magazine/MAG1121365/index.htm#ixzz1KOqltHQo

http://sportsillustrated.cnn.com/vault/article/magazine/MAG1159488/index.htm#ixzz1KOpL5sbn
http://sportsillustrated.cnn.com/vault/article/magazine/MAG1090957/1/index.htm#ixzz1KNoqTX79
http://www.mccoveychronicles.com/2009/10/15/1086467/another-open-letter-to-the-giants
http://digitalsportsdaily.com/mlb/4642-espn-fires-joe-morgan-and-jon-miller-.html
http://www.answers.com/topic/joe-morgan#ixzz1KNOxGM1a
http://www.answers.com/topic/joe-morgan#ixzz1KNOn2UdM
http://baseballhall.org/node/11138
http://baseball.wikia.com/wiki/Joe_Morgan
http://museumca.org/exhibit/exhi_bball_america.html
http://www.aeispeakers.com/speakerbio.php?SpeakerID=709
http://thebaseballpage.com/players/morgajo02.php
http://articles.sfgate.com/1998-01-16/news/17711250_1_east-oakland-public-forum-public-schools
http://www.oaklandmagazine.com/media/Oakland-Magazine/November-2007/Snapshots/index.php?gallery=461
http://sportsillustrated.cnn.com/vault/article/magazine/MAG1122224/index.htm#ixzz1KDR0BzVM
http://en.wikipedia.org/wiki/Joe_Morgan#Biography
http://sports.jrank.org/pages/3321/Morgan-Joe-Growing-Up.html#ixzz1KDPfZBI9
http://www.barrybonds.mlb.com/cin/hof/hof/directory.jsp?hof_id=119371
http://en.wikipedia.org/wiki/Joe_Morgan#Biography
http://www.baseball-almanac.com/players/player.php?p=morgajo02
http://pbspeakers.com/speakers/printSpeaker.asp?sID=12
http://www.helium.com/items/1933317-baseball-player-profiles-joe-morgan
http://entertainment.howstuffworks.com/joe-morgan-hof.htm

Lefty Gomez

http://www.pbs.org/wgbh/amex/dimaggio/filmmore/reference/interview/allen09.html
http://thebaseballpage.com/players/gomezle01.php
http://moregehrig.tripod.com/id1.html
http://www.mantecabulletin.com/news/archive/9599/
http://www.highbeam.com/doc/1G1-119340792.html
http://www.latinosportslegends.com/lgomez.htm
http://www.baseball-reference.com/players/gl.cgi?id=gomezle01&t=p&year=1934
http://www.baseball-almanac.com/quotes/quolgom.shtml
http://en.wikipedia.org/wiki/Lefty_Gomez

http://www.baseball-almanac.com/players/awards.php?p=gomezle01
http://www.fanbase.com/Lefty-Gomez
http://bleacherreport.com/articles/439366-the-bay-areas-100-greatest-athletes-of-all-time#/articles/439366-the-bay-areas-100-greatest-athletes-of-all-time/page/52
http://www.bashof.org/Hall_of_Fame_1981.html
http://web.userinstinct.com/5661781-lefty-gomez-recreation-center-ball-field.htm
http://www.findagrave.com/cgi-bin/fg.cgi?page=gr&GRid=3245
http://www.newworldencyclopedia.org/entry/Lefty_Gomez
Baseball Digest. Vol. 10, No. 4. 1951.
http://www.capecodbaseball.org/News/news2011/NewsCCBL_17Jan11.htm
http://web.minorleaguebaseball.com/news/article.jsp?ymd=20110410&content_id=17615010&vkey=news_t556&fext=.jsp&sid=t556
http://articles.sfgate.com/2007-07-09/sports/17253475_1_high-schools-jackie-robinson-joe-rudi/7
http://www.reference.com/browse/lefty+gomez
http://www.associatedcontent.com/article/73902/lefty_gomez_fast_pitcher_with_a_quick_pg2.html?cat=14

Norm Van Brocklin

http://www.pro-football-reference.com/blog/?p=7371
http://medlibrary.org/medwiki/Norman_Van_Brocklin
http://www.helmethut.com/College/Oregon/ORXXUO5051.html
http://en.wikipedia.org/wiki/Norm_Van_Brocklin
http://planetrams.5u.com/hall1.html
http://www.findagrave.com/cgi-bin/fg.cgi?page=gr&GRid=23959128
http://www.profootballresearchers.org/Coffin_Corner/23-02-888.pdf
http://reddevilsports.org/archive.html
http://www.profootballhof.com/history/decades/1950s/norm_van_brocklin.aspx
http://www.profootballhof.com/hof/member.aspx?PlayerId=221
http://www.bestbythenumbers.com/2007/12/nfl-athlete-number-11-norm-van-brocklin.html
http://www.sports-reference.com/cfb/players/norm-van-brocklin-1.html
http://www.footballsfuture.com/phpBB2/viewtopic.php?p=10884335

http://www.concretefield.info/forum/index.php?topic=20486.0
http://msn.foxsports.com/nfl/story/With-championship-memories-Van-Brocklins-daughter-returns-67120448

http://www.footballoutsiders.com/walkthrough/2007/every-stat-tells-story-hard-luck-hampton
http://www.collegefootball.org/famer_selected.php?id=40091

Tom Brady

http://www.georcoll.on.ca/tom-brady-college-career-.php
http://www.conservapedia.com/Tom_Brady
http://outofbounds.nbcsports.com/2009/11/18/the-amazing-true-story-of-tom-bradys-first-complete-pass/
http://sportsillustrated.cnn.com/multimedia/photo_gallery/1011/tom.brady.rare.photos/content.6.html#ixzz15nPxO0PF
http://sportsillustrated.cnn.com/multimedia/photo_gallery/1011/tom.brady.rare.photos/content.3.html#ixzz15nPbROH2
http://query.nytimes.com/gst/fullpage.html?res=9501E2DE1E3BF935A35751C0A9639C8B63&pagewanted=all
http://www.altiusdirectory.com/Society/2009/02/tom-brady-3rd-august-birthday.html
http://www.zimbio.com/Bridget+Moynahan/articles/38/HOT+TUESDAY+NEW+ENGLAND+PATRIOTS+QB+TOM+BRADY
http://www.maxpreps.com/news/85CGqLN9i0mLFr7AwfXqNA/starting-point--tom-brady-was-no-goody-two-shoes.htm
http://dailyitem.com/0200_sports/x691281840/In-San-Mateo-Calif-Tom-Brady-is-just-Tommy
http://www.kidzworld.com/article/5197-tom-brady-biography#ixzz15gDp5b9f
http://www.findri.com/football/brady/bio/index.php
http://www.pro-football-reference.com/players/B/BradTo00.htm
http://www.notablebiographies.com/news/A-Ca/Brady-Tom.html#ixzz16VmtFfQR
http://en.wikipedia.org/wiki/Super_Bowl_XXXVIII
http://www.patspulpit.com/2010/10/30/1783816/the-unfinished-story-of-why-tom-brady-is-better-than-peyton-manning

Dan Fouts

http://webcache.googleusercontent.com/search?q=cache:kzCGJ05ep1MJ:www.joinergolf.org/dan_fouts_bio.doc+%22dan+fouts%22+St.+Ignatius&cd=3&hl=en&ct=clnk&gl=us&client=firefox-a&source=www.google.com
http://entertainment.howstuffworks.com/dan-fouts-at.htm
http://www.californiasportshalloffame.org/inductees/2008/football/Dan-Fouts.php
http://www.glorifythepast.com/index.php/index.html/_/articles/classic/in-charge-in-san-diego-r85
http://www.freebasc.com/view/en/dan_fouts
http://www.fanbase.com/Dan-Fouts
http://www.siprep.org/video/tringali/tringali.cfm
http://bolttalk.com/chargers-fan-forum/20786-happy-birthday-dan-fouts.html
http://www.profootballhof.com/hof/member.aspx?PlayerId=71
http://www.bashof.org/Hall_of_Fame_1997.html
http://reference.findtarget.com/search/Dan%20Fouts/
http://people.famouswhy.com/dan_fouts/#ixzz1CSDv4KCT

Jim Plunkett

http://www.athletepromotions.com/athletes/Jim-Plunkett-appearance-booking-agent.php
http://docs.google.com/viewer?a=v&q=cache:wWhKGC3XuzoJ:www.a4t.org/Sermons/Brown/bethlehem_ephratah.pdf+%22jim+plunkett+was+born
http://losangelespublicrelations.com/jim-plunkett/02110
http://www.redroom.com/blog/steven-robert-travers/jim-plunkett-excerpt-the-good-bad-and-ugly-san-francisco-49ers
http://www.stanfordalumni.org/news/magazine/2010/novdec/features/plunkett.html
http://www.raidersonline.org/jim-plunkett.php
http://thebiglead.com/index.php/2010/09/16/comparing-jason-campbell-to-jim-plunkett/
http://www.ask.com/wiki/Jim_Plunkett
http://espn.go.com/classic/biography/s/Plunkett_Jim.html
http://sportsbettings.com/Jim-Plunketts-Biography_A1446.html
http://www.davidpietrusza.com/Plunkett.html
http://www.heisman.com/winners/j-plunkett70.php
http://www.articlecompilation.com/Article/Biography-of-1970-Heisman-Trophy-winner-Jim-Plunkett/1144595

http://blogs.mercurynews.com/buzz/2007/01/23/scenes-from-the-raiders-press-conference/
http://www.ibabuzz.com/oaklandraiders/2011/02/27/could-raiders-gamble-with-rfa-tenders/
http://sportscurmudgeon.com/blog/2008/01/
http://www.stanfordalumni.org/news/magazine/2010/novdec/dept/first.html
http://www.pro-football-reference.com/players/P/PlunJi00.htm

Frank Robinson

http://sports.jrank.org/pages/3970/Robinson-Frank.html#ixzz15JQ5kJNy
http://www.newworldencyclopedia.org/entry/Frank_Robinson
http://www.baseball-reference.com
http://www.baseballlibrary.com/ballplayers/player.php?name=frank_robinson_1935
http://www.ibabuzz.com/prepcorner/2006/09/26/bill-russell-frank-robinson-mcclymonds/
http://sports.jrank.org/pages/3962/Robinson-Frank-Early-Life.html#ixzz15J6WW5DC
http://sports.jrank.org/pages/3962/Robinson-Frank-Early-Life.html
http://unclemikesmusings.blogspot.com/2010/07/oaklands-all-time-baseball-team.html
http://www.examiner.com/unitarian-universalism-in-newark/george-powles-the-coach-who-saw-through-time?render=print
http://www.wsusa.org/index.php?option=com_content&task=view&id=58&Itemid=555
http://unclemikesmusings.blogspot.com/2010/07/oaklands-all-time-baseball-team.html
http://www.blackpast.org/?q=tree/Geography%3A+United+States/California
http://www.nndb.com/people/865/000023796/
http://www.biography.com/articles/Frank-Robinson-9460731
http://voices.washingtonpost.com/nationaljournal/2010/05/a_conversation_with_frank_robi.html
http://www.sportscity.com/MLB/500-Home-Run-Club#Frank%20Robinson

Gary Payton

Gray, Valerie. <u>Gary Payton Star Guard.</u> Berkeley Heights, NJ: Enslow, 2000.

Thornley, Stew. Super Sports Star Gary Payton. Berkeley Heights, NJ: Enslow, 2002.

http://bleacherreport.com/articles/17625-the-forefathers-of-oakland-basketball
http://www.nathanielturner.com/hookedthelegend.htm
http://www.hoopstarsonline.com/gary_payton/garypayton_biography.php
http://sportsillustrated.cnn.com/vault/article/magazine/MAG1137078/4/index.htm
http://www.oregonsportshall.org/gary_payton.html
http://community.seattletimes.nwsource.com/archive/?date=19901028&slug=1100844
http://oaklandnorth.net/2009/09/25/north-oakland-now-gary-payton-back-at-school/
http://www.oaklandseen.com/2010/11/23/contest-who-is-your-favorite-oakland-athlete/
http://bleacherreport.com/articles/550477-nba-power-rankings-the-50-best-point-guards-of-all-time#/articles/550477-nba-power-rankings-the-50-best-point-guards-of-all-time/page/43
http://bleacherreport.com/articles/245030-the-top-10-nba-point-guards-of-all-time#/articles/245030-the-top-10-nba-point-guards-of-all-time/page/3
http://www.nicekicks.com/gary-payton/
http://people.theiapolis.com/actor-6BG0/gary-payton/
http://archives.starbulletin.com/1998/02/16/sports/joe.html
http://www.slate.com/id/2086317/
http://www.athletepromotions.com/athletes/Gary-Payton-appearance-booking-agent.php
http://www.bookrags.com/biography/gary-payton-spo/
http://sports.yahoo.com/nba/news?slug=ycn-7776352

Rickey Henderson

Verducci, Tom, David Sabino. "Rickey Henderson" Sports Illustrated.com, 1993.

Roensch, Greg. Rickey Henderson (Baseball Superstars). Chelsea House, 2008.

Poole, Monte. "Rickey Henderson's early years" Oakland Tribune.com
Posted: 05/09/2009

http://www.encyclopedia.com/topic/Rickey_Henderson.aspx
http://signrickey.blogspot.com/
http://articles.sun-sentinel.com/1985-03-12/news/8501090638_1_rickey-henderson-henderson-won-t-long-johns
http://bats.blogs.nytimes.com/2008/06/11/random-thoughts-on-the-oakland-as/
http://oaklandfieldofdreams.org/?page_id=8
http://baseball.about.com/od/majorleaguehistory/tp/bestLFs.htm

http://www.usatoday.com/sports/baseball/hallfame/2009-07-21-rickey-henderson-hof_N.htm
http://fromtheheartofleo.blogspot.com/2009/07/rickey-henderson-and-jim-rice-enter.html
http://baseball.wikia.com/wiki/Rickey_Henderson
http://www.thebaseballpage.com/players/henderi01.php
http://www.baseball-almanac.com/players/player.php?p=henderi01
http://mlbmemories.com/2011/02/remembering-rickey-henderson-ruining-a-705-game-by-706/
http://www.thebaseballzealot.com/hall-of-fame/hof-09-rickey-henderson
http://rise.espn.go.com/baseball/articles/2010/09/02-rickey-henderson.aspx
http://en.wikipedia.org/wiki/Rickey_Henderson
http://www.pckprclothing.com/pckprblog/?tag=hall-of-fame-career
http://www.38thnotes.com/2009/02/keeping-as-baseball-in-oakland.html

Jeff Gordon

Gordon, Jeff. Racing Back to the Front - My Memoir. Dallas: Atria, 2003.

Wallner, Rosemary. Jeff Gordon. Edge Books, 2001.

http://sportsillustrated.cnn.com/vault/article/magazine/MAG1027993/6/index.htm#ixzz1EzrPYFPa
http://ezinearticles.com/?Jeff-Gordon---Everything-You-Need-To-Know&id=5284592
http://www.askmen.com/celebs/men/sports_60/83_jeff_gordon.html
http://jeffgordon.com/aboutjeff/
http://en.wikipedia.org/wiki/Jeff_Gordon
http://www.imdb.com/name/nm0330298/bio+"jeff+gordon
http://www.kidzworld.com/article/4180-jeff-gordon-biography#ixzz1EzixJytl
http://www.bookrags.com/biography/jeff-gordon-spo
http://www.jockbio.com/Bios/Gordon/Gordon
http://www.racewayreport.com/drivers/jgordon
http://www.nascar.com/2007/news/opinion/06/23/dcaraviello.jgordon.hometown/1.html
http://wiki.answers.com/

Barry Bonds

Savage, Jeff. Barry Bonds Minneapolis: Lerner, 2008.

Shatzkin, Mike. The Ballplayers. New York: Arbor House, 1989.

Athletes and Coaches of Summer. New York: MacMillan, 2000.

Notable Sports Figures. Farmington Hills MI: Thomson Gale, 2004.

Williams, Lance and Mark Fainaru-wada. Game of Shadows. New York: Gotham Books, 2007.

http://www.instantriverside.com/2011/04/riverside-native-barry-bonds-convicted-of-obstruction-of-justice/
http://www.celebritynetworth.com/richest-athletes/richest-baseball/barry-bonds-net-worth/
http://www.baseballlibrary.com/features/matchup.php?with=Barry_vs_Bobby
http://www.bookrags.com/biography/barry-bonds-spo/
http://www.biography.com/articles/Barry-Bonds-9542459?part=1
http://topics.nytimes.com/top/reference/timestopics/people/b/barry_bonds/index.html
http://thebaseballpage.com/content/barry-bonds
http://www.altiusdirectory.com/Society/2009/02/barry-bonds-24th-july-birthday_17.html
http://www.usatoday.com/sports/baseball/2003-08-24-mays-bonds_x.htm
http://www.slate.com/id/2139031/
http://www.baseball-almanac.com/quotes/barry_bonds_quotes.shtml

Helen Wills

http://www.newyorker.com/archive/1952/08/30/1952_08_30_031_TNY_CARDS_000235972#ixzz1LGBSOcGO

http://www.tennisforum.com/showthread.php?t=34200&page=14
http://freepages.genealogy.rootsweb.ancestry.com/~npmelton/women/whotxt/189-213.htm
http://blog.oregonlive.com/tennis/2011/01/helen_wills_and_the_great_berkeley_fire_of_1923.html
http://bleacherreport.com/articles/241404-helen-wills-moody-a-dominant-champion

http://www.history.com/this-day-in-history/helen-wills-moody-wins-final-wimbledon
http://www.californiagoldenblogs.com/2010/6/30/1546260/helen-wills-moody-cals-great
http://sportsthenandnow.com/2009/08/23/helen-wills-moody/#more-363
http://sportsthenandnow.com/2011/02/27/whos-no-1-16-women-in-tennis-who-held-the-top-spot-longest/#more-8401
http://www.nytimes.com/learning/general/onthisday/bday/1006.html
http://www.all-about-tennis.com/helen-wills-moody.html
http://www.newworldencyclopedia.org/entry/Helen_Wills_Moody
http://www.tennisfame.com/hall-of-famers/helen-wills-moody-roark
http://www.sports-reference.com/olympics/athletes/wi/helen-wills-1.html
http://sportsthenandnow.com/2009/10/28/queens-of-the-court-helen-wills-moody-shades-of-garbo/#more-1543
http://www.talkinbroadway.com/gwwm/1.html
http://www.berkeleyheritage.com/berkeley_landmarks/tennis_club.html
http://www.yelp.com/biz/berkeley-tennis-club-berkeley

O.J. Simpson

Simpson, O.J. with Pete Axthelm. The Education of a Rich Rookie. New York: MacMillan, 1970.

Simpson, O.J. I Want to Tell You. New York: Little, Brown, and Co., 1995. memoir)

Notable Sports Figures. Farmington Hills MI: Thomson Gale, 2004.

http://www.encyclopedia.com/topic/O.J._Simpson.aspx
http://www.usnews.com/usnews/news/articles/940627/archive_013057_5.htm
http://sports.jrank.org/pages/4446/Simpson-O-J-Early-Years.html#ixzz1OcJO8yUx
http://www.nndb.com/people/390/000022324/
http://en.wikipedia.org/wiki/Galileo_Academy_of_Science_and_Technology
http://ojsimpson.info/football.html
http://www.cnn.com/US/OJ/suspect/childhood.years/index.html
http://www.aaregistry.org/historic_events/view/oj-simpson-what-goes-must-come-down
http://espn.go.com/classic/biography/s/simpson_oj.html
http://community.seattletimes.nwsource.com/archive/?date=19940624&slug=1917206

http://books.google.com/books?id=ORy_m0oj_ioC&pg=PA140&lpg=PA140&dq=%22oj+simpson%22+%22potrero
http://www.cowboysplus.com/classic/halloffame/hof_rstaubach.html
http://www.biography.com/articles/Orenthal-James-Simpson-9484729?part=1
http://en.wikipedia.org/wiki/O._J._Simpson
http://www.rotten.com/library/
http://sportsillustrated.cnn.com/vault/article/magazine/MAG1088149/4/index.htm

Ollie Matson

http://news.google.com/newspapers?id=8PYaAAAAIBAJ&sjid=dU0EAAAAIBAJ&pg=4512,2677098&dq=ollie+matson&hl=en
http://cmgworldwide.com/news/?p=1341
http://en.wikipedia.org/wiki/Ollie_Matson
http://www.chron.com/channel/houstonbelief/commons/persona.html?newspaperUserId=bearfacts&plckPersonaPage=BlogViewPost
http://www.nytimes.com/2011/02/21/sports/football/21matson.html?_r=1
http://articles.sfgate.com/2011-02-20/sports/28613128_1_football-team-burl-toler-usf-team
http://www.profootballhof.com/hof/member.aspx?PLAYER_ID=143
http://www.profootballhof.com/hof/member.aspx?PlayerId=143&tab=Highlights
http://articles.latimes.com/2011/feb/20/local/la-me-ollie-matson-20110220
http://www.legacy.com/ns/obituary.aspx?n=ollie-matson&pid=148772388
http://www.thepilot.com/news/2011/feb/27/ollie-matson-back-remembered-one-best/
http://sports.espn.go.com/nfl/news/story?id=6139709
http://fifthdown.blogs.nytimes.com/2011/02/23/remembering-ollie-matson-hall-of-fame-running-back/
http://www.hickoksports.com/biograph/matsonollie.shtml
http://insightnews.com/sports/7365-actions-not-words

Max Baer

http://www.maltaboxing.net/component/content/article/35-boxers-of-yesteryear/405-boxers-of-yesteryear-max-baer
http://bleacherreport.com/articles/436252-the-25-greatest-jewish-athletes-of-all-time#page/7http://en.wikipedia.org/wiki/Max_Baer_%28boxer%29
http://www.jewishvirtuallibrary.org/jsource/biography/Max_Baer.html

http://www.topix.com/forum/city/livermore-ca/TF79AOUVUSFAMUUH0
http://boxrec.com/media/index.php/Max_Baer
http://www.newworldencyclopedia.org/entry/Max_Baer
http://www.maxbaer.org/
http://www.ibhof.com/pages/about/inductees/oldtimer/baer.html
http://en.wikipedia.org/wiki/James_J._Braddock

Dave Stewart

http://sportsillustrated.cnn.com/vault/article/magazine/MAG1069004/4/index.htm
http://www.hickoksports.com/biograph/stewartdave.shtml
http://www.upi.com/topic/Dave_Stewart/#ixzz1NOYwGLGr
http://www.washingtonpost.com/wp-dyn/content/discussion/2008/06/20/DI2008062002033.html
http://sportsillustrated.cnn.com/vault/article/magazine/MAG1066528/index.htm
http://bleacherreport.com/articles/214482-the-dave-stewart-story-on-and-off-the-field
http://baseballcardblog.blogspot.com/2006_09_01_archive.html
http://www.thebaseballpage.com/players/stewada01
http://articles.latimes.com/1990-10-16/sports/sp-2815_1_world-series
http://www.baseball-reference.com/bullpen/Dave_Stewart
http://weirdnews.about.com/od/othersports/ss/Baseball-World-Series-Mug-Shots_15.htm
http://www.baseballlibrary.com/ballplayers/player.php?name=Dave_Stewart_1957
http://www.nytimes.com/1994/08/23/sports/sports-of-the-times-stewart-still-in-there-pitching.html?src=pm
http://blackathlete.net/artman2/publish/Baseball_20/Former_Oakland_A_s_pitcher_Dave_Stewart_Turns_Agent_printer.shtml
http://www.ccsabathia52.com/2011/02/15/feb-15th-dave-stewart-a-salute-to-black-history-baseball-heroes/
http://www.baseball-almanac.com/players/player.php?p=stewada01
http://www.pbspeakers.com/speakers/speaker.asp?sID=123
http://www.life.com/gallery/23166/image/1397928#index/5
http://www.kosmix.com/topic/dave_stewart#ixzz1NQ1D6YuM

http://canadiansgirlsofsummer.com/2010/08/thursday-former-mlb-star-dave-stewart-arrives-at-the-nat/
http://www.wikipedia.org/wiki/Overstock.com_Coliseum+%22oakland+coliseum%22+wiki&cd=2&hl=en&ct=clnk&gl=us&source=www.google.com

Dennis Eckersley

http://www.baseballreference.com/players/e/eckerde01.shtml+%22Dennis+eckersley
http://en.wikipedia.org/wiki/Dennis_Eckersley
http://baseballhall.org/node/11306
http://www.baseball-almanac.com/players/player.php?p=eckerde01
http://www.brainyquote.com/quotes/authors/d/dennis_eckersley.html
http://top100redsox.blogspot.com/2007/03/100-greatest-red-sox-42-dennis.html
Dennis Eckersley — Infoplease.com
http://www.infoplease.com/ipsa/A0749941.html#ixzz1Dn9WjZDL
http://www.biographybase.com/biography/Eckersley_Dennis.html
http://www.fact-index.com/d/de/dennis_eckersley.html
http://bizofbaseball.com/index.php?option=com_content&view=article&id=2979:dennis-eckersley-signs-multi-year-extension-with-tbs&catid=57:television&Itemid=122
http://www.hickoksports.com/biograph/eckersleyd.shtml -
http://www.ericenders.com/kginterview.htm
http://www.123people.co.uk/ext/frm?ti=person%20finder&search_term=lee%2eckersley
http://www.thebaseballpage.com/players/eckerde01.php

Randy Johnson

http://epitching.com/page1
http://www.igomlb.com/2008/08/13/randy-johnson.html
http://www.jockbio.com/Bios/RJohnson/RJohnson_bio.html
http://en.wikipedia.org/wiki/Randy_Johnson
http://www.prosportsdaily.com/articles/livermore-to-welcome-randy-johnson-home-262271.html
http://www.baseball-reference.com/players/j/johnsra05.shtml?redir
http://articles.sfgate.com/2009-06-01/news/17208517_1_johnson-in-high-school-scouts-typical-high-school/3
http://mlb.mlb.com/news/press_releases/press_release.jsp?ymd=20090810&content_id=6354312&vkey=pr_sf&fext=.jsp&c_id=sf
http://thebaseballpage.com/content/randy-johnson-bio
http://bleacherreport.com/articles/131197-sf-giants-have-a-motivator-and-mentor-in-randy-johnson

CC Sabathia

http://www.minorleagueball.com/2011/2/21/2002265/career-profile-cc-sabathia-yankees
http://www.mlbexpertanalysis.com/blog/?p=336
http://www.nytimes.com/2009/04/06/sports/baseball/06yankees.html
http://www.pinstripealley.com/2008/12/26/702421/this-is-your-life-cc-sabat
http://www.mlb4all.com/player-profiles/cc-sabathia-pitcher-new-york-yankees.html
http://yankees.lhblogs.com/2010/09/21/cc-sabathia-on-real-sports-tonight/
http://baseball.dailyskew.com/2011/07/why-is-cc-sabathia-underrated-by-non-ny-fans.html
http://www.nydailynews.com/sports/baseball/yankees/2008/12/10/2008-12-10_the_real_cc_sabathia_new_yankee_an_ace_o.html#ixzz1Su8ff78O
http://www.nydailynews.com/sports/baseball/yankees/2008/12/13/2008-12-13_home_with_cc_newest_yankee_sabathias_roo.html#ixzz1Su8KNMBY
http://www.nydailynews.com/sports/baseball/yankees/2008/12/10/2008-12-10_through_the_years_newest_yankees_ace_cc_-2.html#ixzz1Su7rkanx
http://sportsillustrated.cnn.com/vault/article/magazine/MAG1153909/8/index.htm
http://www.mtv.com/news/articles/1643701/cc-sabathia-remembers-epic-paint-fight-on-when-i-was-17.jhtml
http://abclocal.go.com/kgo/story?section=news/local/north_bay&id=7861823
http://articles.nydailynews.com/2010-08-26/sports/27073676_1_snack-bar-teaching-moment-sportsmanship
http://www.pitcchinfoundation.org/cc-to-throw-out-first-pitch-at-spring-classic-2011/
http://articles.sfgate.com/2009-11-28/bay-area/17180901_1_cc-sabathia-vallejo-high-school-world-series
http://articles.sfgate.com/2007-07-04/home-and-garden/17252502_1_hot-tub-barber-beers
http://www.westernsod.com/little_league.php
http://www.kosmix.com/topic/cc_sabathia/Player-Profiles#ixzz1Su2RoxRW
http://www.ccsabathia52.com/bio/
http://www.chacha.com/topic/cc-sabathia
http://en.wikipedia.org/wiki/CC_Sabathia
http://www.jockbio.com/Bios/Sabathia/Sabathia_bio.html
http://bleacherreport.com/articles/284344-ranking-the-housewives-of-the-bronx#/articles/284344-ranking-the-housewives-of-the-bronx/page/6

Johnny Miller

http://www.ask.com/wiki/Johnny_Miller
http://www.espn.co.uk/onthisday/sport/story/135.html
http://www.mormonwiki.com/Johnny_Miller
http://pbspeakers.com/speakers/speaker.asp?sID=73
http://articles.sfgate.com/2010-07-02/business/21934842_1_golf-courses-silverado-johnny-miller
http://golf.about.com/od/golfersmen/p/johnny_miller.htm
http://www.worldgolfhalloffame.org/hof/member.php?member=1082
http://www.people.com/people/archive/article/0,,20063917,00.html
http://www.thegolfchannel.com/players/Johnny-Miller/
http://www.usatoday.com/sports/golf/usopen02/2002-06-13-miller-cover.htm
http://www.sporting-heroes.net/golf-heroes/displayhero.asp?HeroID=3450
http://www.eagleoaks.com/club/scripts/section/section.asp?grp=0&NS=JM
http://nbcsports.msnbc.com/id/23028887/ns/sports-golf/
http://www.insidesocal.com/tribpreps/2008/09/valley_powers_n.html
http://www.nicklaus.com/design/harborshores/Jack-Nicklaus-Johnny-Miller-Arnold-Palmer-and-Tom-Watson.php
http://thinkexist.com/quotation/nobody-ever-heard-jack-nicklaus-say-i-don-t-know/396611.html
http://articles.chicagotribune.com/2006-08-17/sports/0608170314_1_major-pga-winner-pga-championships/3
http://www.golfdigest.com/golf-courses/golf-travel/2011-03/long-drives-san-francisco#ixzz1GiSlL7TM
http://bleacherreport.com/articles/439366-the-bay-areas-100-greatest-athletes-of-all-time#page/3
http://people.famouswhy.com/johnny_miller/

Lynn Swann

Amerman, Don. "Swann, Lynn." <u>Notable Sports Figures</u>. 2004. Encyclopedia.com.

Worden, Amy. "Lynn Swann." The Philadelphia Inquirer, Philadelphia, October 29, 2006.

http://www.encyclopedia.com>.
http://www.answers.com/topic/lynn-swann
http://www.encyclopedia.com/topic/Lynn_Curtis_Swann.aspx

http://www.pro-football-reference.com/players/
http://pittsburgh.about.com/od/famous_locals/p/lynn_swann.htm
http://sports.jrank.org/pages/4728/Swann-Lynn-Born-in-Alcoa-Tennessee.html#ixzz17paYroPx
http://www.lynnswann.com/swann_docs/about/
http://www.profootballresearchers.org/Coffin_Corner/23-03-895.pdf
http://en.wikipedia.org/wiki/Lynn_Swann
http://www.mcmillenandwife.com/swann.html
http://wiki.answers.com/Q/What_cornerback_did_Lynn_Swann_make_an_unbelievable_falling_diving_catch_against_in_a_Super_Bowl#ixzz1B8BnLiqm
http://www.angelfire.com; http://www.stillers.com/stillfaith; the Time magazine website, http://www.time.com; the NFL Hall of Fame website, http://www.profootballhof.com; http://www.first-down.co.uk; the ESPN website, http://www.espn.go.com; and the NFL website, http://www.nfl.com.
Jet, July 30, 1984, pg. 49.
Sports Illustrated, January 16, 1984.

PHOTO CREDITS

From Top Row, Left to Right:

Barry Bonds - bongonews.com
Joe DiMaggio – nydailynews.com
Tom Brady - fashionindie.com
Joe Morgan – baseballcardnirvana.blogspot.com
Jeff Gordon – sportsbookgurus.com
Jim Plunkett – nndb.com
Willie Stargell – bleacherreport.com
Johnny Miller – golfnoise.com
Dave Stewart – playingfieldpromotions.com
Dan Fouts - chargertom.com
Bill Russell – bostonglobe.com
Norm Van Brocklin – sportsattic2.com
Frank Robinson - mvpgalleries.com
Helen Wills – brianfalati.wordpress.com
Rickey Henderson - ootpdevelopments.com
O.J. Simpson – wikipedia.org
Lefty Gomez - picasaweb.google.com
Lynn Swann – annoyatorium.com
CC Sabathia – mrissues.com
Randy Johnson – nndb.com
Gary Payton – thebreakdownshow.com
Dennis Eckersley – jpopp.com
Max Baer - allstarpics.net
Ollie Matson – hfboards.com
Jason Kidd – tucsoncitizen.com

ACKNOWLEDGEMENTS

Many thanks to the City of Vallejo, the City of Martinez, the Dublin Public Library, Robert Canavan, Kent Kelly, Lanse Shelton, Mark Skinner, Raul Orozco, Steven Feitlin, Edward Doering Jr., Sonny Ramirez, Andrew Meo, Peter Deutschman, and the citizens of San Mateo.

BAY AREA LEGENDS

ABOUT THE AUTHOR

Brian Michnowski, a Journalism & Media graduate of Rutgers University in New Jersey, has written sports articles for six U.S. newspapers, including the Los Angeles Times, the Orange County Register, and the Bergen (N.J.) Record. Mr. Michnowski has resided in and followed pro and college sports in California since 1987.

BAY AREA LEGENDS

CORRECTIONS & COMMENTS

Although every attempt of accuracy has been made, please submit any corrections or comments to brianmichnowski@yahoo.com All comments are welcome and will be answered individually.